This collection of essays by some of the most distinguished historians and literary scholars in the English-speaking world explores the overlap, interplay, and interaction between history and fiction in British imaginative and historical writing from the Tudor period to the Enlightenment. The historians discuss the questions of truth, fiction, and the contours of early modern historical culture, while the literary scholars consider some of the fictional aspects of history, and the historical aspects of fiction, in prose narratives of many sorts. The interests and inquiries of these learned, imaginative, and venturesome scholars cross at many points, casting significant new light on and offering numerous insights into the problematic and interdisciplinary areas where "history" and "story" meet, interact, and sometimes compete. Despite the theoretical questions posed, the discussions primarily focus on concrete works, including those of Thomas More, John Foxe, Thomas Hobbes, Adam Smith, and Edward Gibbon.

WOODROW WILSON CENTER SERIES

The historical imagination in early modern Britain

Other books in the series

Michael J. Lacey, editor, *Religion and Twentieth-Century American Intellectual Life*
Michael J. Lacey, editor, *The Truman Presidency*
Joseph Kruzel and Michael H. Haltzel, editors, *Between the Blocs: Problems and Prospects for Europe's Neutral and Nonaligned States*
William C. Brumfield, editor, *Reshaping Russian Architecture: Western Technology, Utopian Dreams*
Mark N. Katz, editor, *The USSR and Marxist Revolutions in the Third World*
Walter Reich, editor, *Origins of Terrorism: Psychologies, Ideologies, Theologies, States of Mind*
Mary O. Furner and Barry Supple, editors, *The State and Economic Knowledge: The American and British Experiences*
Michael J. Lacey and Knud Haakonssen, editors, *A Culture of Rights: The Bill of Rights in Philosophy, Politics, and Law – 1791 and 1991*
Robert J. Donovan and Ray Scherer, *Unsilent Revolution: Television News and American Public Life, 1948–1991*
Nelson Lichtenstein and Howell John Harris, editors, *Industrial Democracy in America: The Ambiguous Promise*
William Craft Brumfield and Blair A. Ruble, editors, *Russian Housing in the Modern Age: Design and Social History*
Michael J. Lacey and Mary O. Furner, editors, *The State and Social Investigation in Britain and the United States*
Hugh Ragsdale, editor and translator, *Imperial Russian Foreign Policy*
Dermot Keogh and Michael H. Haltzel, editors, *Northern Ireland and the Politics of Reconciliation*
Joseph Klaits and Michael H. Haltzel, editors, *The Global Ramifications of the French Revolution*
René Lemarchand, *Burundi: Ethnic Conflict and Genocide*
James R. Millar and Sharon L. Wolchik, editors, *The Social Legacy of Communism*
James M. Morris, editor, *On Mozart*
Theodore Taranovski, editor, *Reform in Modern Russian History: Progress or Cycle?*
Blair A. Ruble, *Money Sings: The Changing Politics of Urban Space in Post-Soviet Yaroslavl*

Continued on page following index

The historical imagination in early modern Britain

History, rhetoric, and fiction, 1500–1800

Edited by

DONALD R. KELLEY and DAVID HARRIS SACKS

WOODROW WILSON CENTER PRESS

AND

CAMBRIDGE
UNIVERSITY PRESS

PUBLISHED BY THE PRESS SYNDICATE OF THE UNIVERSITY OF CAMBRIDGE
The Pitt Building, Trumpington Street, Cambridge, CB2 1RP, United Kingdom

CAMBRIDGE UNIVERSITY PRESS
The Edinburgh Building, Cambridge CB2 2RU, United Kingdom
40 West 20th Street, New York, NY 10011-4211, USA
10 Stamford Road, Oakleigh, Melbourne 3166, Australia

First published 1997

Printed in the United States of America

Typeset in Sabon

Library of Congress Cataloging-in-Publication Data
The historical imagination in early modern Britain / edited by Donald
    R. Kelley, David Harris Sacks.
        p.   cm.
    ISBN 0-521-59069-8 (hc)
    1. Great Britain – History – Tudors, 1485–1603 – Historiography.
    2. English literature – Early modern, 1500–1700 – History and
    criticism.   3. Literature and history – Great Britain – History – 16th
    century.   4. Literature and history – Great Britain – History – 17th
    century.   5. Great Britain – History – Stuarts, 1603–1714 –
    Historiography.   6. Historiography – Great Britain – History – 17th
    century.   7. Historiography – Great Britain – History – 16th century.
    8. Great Britain – History – To 1485 – Historiography.   9. Imagination.
    I. Kelley, Donald R., 1931–   .   II. Sacks, David Harris, 1942–   .
    DA314.H57   1997
    941.05′072 – dc21   97-6160
                                                                                  CIP

A *catalog record for this book is available from*
the British Library

ISBN 0 521 59069 8 hardback

WOODROW WILSON INTERNATIONAL CENTER FOR SCHOLARS

The Center is the living memorial of the United States of America to the nation's twenty-eighth president, Woodrow Wilson. Congress established the Woodrow Wilson Center in 1968 as an international institute for advanced study, "symbolizing and strengthening the fruitful relationship between the world of learning and the world of public affairs." The Center opened in 1970 under its own board of trustees, which includes citizens appointed by the president of the United States, federal government officials who serve ex officio, and an additional representative named by the president from within the federal government.

In all its activities the Woodrow Wilson Center is a nonprofit, nonpartisan organization, supported financially by annual appropriations from Congress and by the contributions of foundations, corporations, and individuals.

WOODROW WILSON CENTER PRESS

The Woodrow Wilson Center Press publishes books written in substantial part at the Center or otherwise prepared under its sponsorship by fellows, guest scholars, staff members, and other program participants. Conclusions or opinions expressed in Center publications and programs are those of the authors and speakers and do not necessarily reflect the views of the Center staff, fellows, trustees, advisory groups, or any individuals or organizations that provide financial support to the Center.

Woodrow Wilson Center Press
Editorial Offices
370 L'Enfant Promenade, S.W., Suite 704
Washington, D.C. 20024-2518
telephone: (202) 287-3000, ext. 218

Contents

Preface

Imagination in its highest form is said to be the creative faculty of the mind, the department engaged in framing new images and conceptions, things and ideas hitherto unknown and previously nonexistent. As such, it has always been connected with the arts, verbal as well as visual. Imagination lives in the realm of fancy and of fiction, the antithesis of observable facts and empirically testable propositions. In a more general sense, however, the word "imagination" refers to the capacity of the mind to form images or concepts of what is not actually present to the senses and to evoke their relations with one another. As such, it can bring into view remote, absent, or previously occurring events as well as purely imaginary ones. In this meaning, it enjoys an intimate connection with the idea of memory, and has a close tie to the work of historians and to the purposes and practices of historical writing. History of necessity deals with the need to make present what has left only traces or remains by which it can be known. As a discipline concerned with recovering the past, history cannot but come to terms with the limits of representation this process entails; so despite its prosaic form, it has enjoyed an affinity, and sometimes an intense sibling rivalry, with poetry, its sister genre, and one of imagination's main fields of play.

This kinship was a subject of particular interest and concern in the early modern period, an era in which strenuous efforts were being made on many fronts – in the institutions of church and state as well as in the various arts and sciences and in popular culture – to recover and emulate the truths and traditions of the past and to command time-bound processes of change or overcome them. It is in this period, also, that recognizably modern forms of historical research and writing took shape in relation to, and often in passionate conflict with, the narrative arts and new genres such as the novel. Nowhere was this more true than in the British Isles. In recent years many of the same questions about the boundaries between and relations among the genres have once again become contested subjects in Europe and America, as historians have adapted or openly borrowed narrative techniques and representational practices from literature and as literary scholars have studied the role of history in shaping the artistic imagination and the role of the arts in upholding or confronting the institutions and structures of power in past time.

This collection of essays grew out of its editors' reflections on these contemporary discussions and the conviction we had that an examination of their early modern antecedents would be beneficial to present-day understanding, if only in demonstrating that our current questions and occasional doubts about the intellectual status of history and its relations with literature and the arts are not unprecedented. These thoughts took on more a concrete form during 1992–3 in numerous lunchtime conversations, when both of us were fellows of the Woodrow Wilson International Center for Scholars in Washington, D.C. In the course of them we formed the plan to bring together a group of distinguished students of historiography and of literary and cultural history to discuss and debate these questions, an idea that quickly received the enthusiastic support and vital assistance, financial as well as administrative, of James Morris, then director of the Division of Historical, Cultural, and Literary Studies at the Woodrow Wilson Center. He and Susan Nugent, his assistant, helped us organize the resulting conference, which was held at the Center in October 1993.

At the conference, seven of the following essays – those of Patrick Collinson, J. Paul Hunter, Joseph M. Levine, Annabel Patterson, Mark Salber Phillips, D. R. Woolf, and David Wootton – received a first hearing before a learned audience that included a number of eminent scholars especially invited for the occasion by the Center. The official commentators for the three main sessions were Fritz Levy, Linda Levy Peck, and J. G. A. Pocock. We owe them our profound thanks for their incisive remarks, which stimulated a wide-ranging and critical review of the central issues. At the close of our discussions the participants and guests encouraged us to publish a collection of essays on our theme and to recruit additional contributions to fill out the volume. A number of them expressed interest in contributing to it themselves. Once again Jim Morris and the Woodrow Wilson Center came to our aid with the necessary support, and within a short while the remaining contributors – Rebecca Bushnell, Patricia Craddock, Richard Helgerson, Fritz Levy, J. H. M. Salmon, and Patricia Springborg – had agreed to supply the essays you find here. Parts of Rebecca Bushnell's chapter have been excerpted from Rebecca Bushnell, *A Culture of Teaching: Early Modern Humanism in Theory and Practice,* copyrighted by Cornell University in 1996 and published by the Cornell University Press. They are used by permission of the publisher, Cornell University Press, for which we are grateful.

From the outset, the work of assembling this volume has been the joint effort of the two editors, who have shared the burdens throughout in making editorial decisions, in consulting with the contributors about revisions, and in negotiating with and responding to our publisher. Sacks took initial responsibility for drafting the preface, and Kelley for drafting the introduction, but the views expressed in each reflect our mutual understanding and result from our frequent discussions. In their finished form, both the preface and the introduction are products of what has always been a common enterprise.

In completing our editorial tasks, we are keenly aware of the debts we owe to all those who have aided us with this project. We have already mentioned Jim Morris. Without his commitment to our proposal, the funding he provided, and his administrative skills, we would have been unable to turn what initially existed only in our imaginations into the present reality. Similar gratitude is owed to Susan Nugent not only for her hard work in putting together the 1993 conference but for her sustained assistance in our communications with a very busy and peripatetic group of contributors and in assembly of the final version of the manuscript for the press. To Charles Blitzer, director of the Woodrow Wilson Center, and his gracious and very able staff, we also owe our deep thanks for making our stays as fellows of the Center so pleasurable and productive, and for always being ready to help as we proceeded with this volume. We are particularly grateful to Charles Blitzer for the encouragement he gave us. The same can be said regarding Joseph Brinley, director of the Woodrow Wilson Center Press, and his staff. Joe Brinley himself has taken a strong interest in our volume from its inception and has greatly helped us in bringing it through its various stages of production. The two readers he selected to review the manuscript, Anthony Grafton and John Pocock, also made invaluable contributions with their learned and exceedingly helpful comments and suggestions. Finally, we want to thank those scholars, not already mentioned, who attended our conference and advised and assisted us in getting this volume underway: Judith Anderson, Wyman H. Herendeen, the late J. H. Hexter, Lena Cowen Orlin, Lawrence Stone, and Perez Zagorin.

Donald R. Kelley
David Harris Sacks

WOODROW WILSON CENTER SERIES

The historical imagination in early modern Britain

1

Introduction

DONALD R. KELLEY AND DAVID HARRIS SACKS

There is a history in all men's lives,
Figuring the nature of the times deceas'd.
— *Henry IV, Part 2*, 1.1.80–81

. . . imagination bodies forth
The forms of things unknown. . . .
— *A Midsummer Night's Dream*, 5.1.14–15

"History" and "story" are derived from the same root, and they have converged again in modern times, especially through the recognition of their common dependence on imagination. Both history and literature are forms of cultural memory, and in this respect, too, they have a link with imagination. Historians pretend to recapture the past in all its fullness, but in fact they are bound by the limits and conventions of narrative prose. Nor can literary artists, even the most "classic" among them, remain free of the toils of history; for as Shelley admitted, "this is an influence which neither the meanest scribbler nor the sublimest genius of any era can escape."[1]

Since antiquity the *ars historica* and the *ars poetica* were sister genres, with overlapping issues and similar values. From the time of Cicero and Quintilian the art of history has made claims on truth, but like poetry, it has also aimed at beauty, or pleasure (*voluptas*), and goodness, or utility (*utilitas*).[2] In more recent times, too, the realization of such a common pedigree and such common purposes has reinforced the ties between historians and literary scholars and opened further what has been called

---

[1] Percy Bysshe Shelley, preface to *Prometheus Unbound*.
[2] See D. R. Kelley, "The Theory of History," in *Cambridge History of Renaissance Philosophy,* ed. Charles Schmitt and Quentin Skinner (Cambridge: Cambridge University Press, 1988), 746–62.

"the open boundary of history and fiction."[3] As historians have come to recognize the aesthetic dimension of their craft and the necessity to resort to imagination to fill in gaps in the narrative, so literary scholars are acknowledging the historicity of literature, its value as a reflection of bygone worlds not recoverable through conventional documents, and the use of literary criticism for the interpretation of such documentation.[4] Disciplinary frontiers cannot obscure the fact that historians and literary scholars are engaged in the common enterprise of finding human meaning in both "works" and "documents" (according to the distinction made by Martin Heidegger and popularized by Dominick La Capra).[5] Such, in any case, was the hope and the premise of the conference on which this volume is based.

In early modern England the distinction between history and literature was, at least technically, an anachronism. In fact "literature" encompassed history, since the term conventionally signified anything preserved in writing ("letters"), and so did the field already defined in the sixteenth century as the history of literature (*historia literaturae*) or literary history (*historia literaria*).[6] Within this literary field, however, there was a basic and generic division between the arts of history and of poetry; and as Michel de Certeau remarked, "This internecine struggle between history and story-telling is very old." It sets the truth of history into opposition not only to poetry but also to "genealogical story-telling, the myths and legends of collective memory, and the meanderings of the oral tradition."[7]

The struggle referred to by Certeau is indeed very old, appearing first in the practice of Herodotus and then in the theory of Cicero, whose "first law of history" (*prima lex historiae*) was to tell the truth and the whole truth.[8] According to this premise of the *ars historica,* it was for

---

[3] Suzanne Gearhart, *The Open Boundary of History and Fiction* (Princeton: Princeton University Press, 1984).

[4] See, e.g., A. D. Harvey, *Literature into History* (New York: St. Martins, 1988), and Lionel Gossman, *Between History and Literature* (Cambridge, Mass.: Harvard University Press, 1990).

[5] Dominick La Capra, *Rethinking Intellectual History: Texts, Contexts, Language* (Ithaca, N.Y.: Cornell University Press, 1983), 30.

[6] E.g., Christophe Milieu's *De Scribendis universitatis rerum historia* (Basel, 1551), bk. 5, "Historia literaturae," 244–305.

[7] Michel de Certeau, *Heterologies: Discourse on the Other,* trans. B. Marsumi and W. Godzich (Minneapolis: University of Minnesota Press, 1986), 199.

[8] Cicero *De oratore* 2.62.

poets, lawyers, orators, and other professional liars to violate this law. Philosophers agreed on the primacy of truth but, as usual, not on its nature. Plato famously banned poets from his republic (while drawing on their insights), whereas his student Aristotle contradicted him and elevated poetry, as the source of a high, more universal sort of "truth," to a place above history. For historians, however, the case was simpler: There is truth, and there is error. There is history, that is to say, and (in the words of Paul Verlaine) "all the rest is literature."

There is a deeper structure to this ancient debate, one tied to the Baconian (and Galenian) distribution of knowledge into the faculties of memory, imagination, and reason, which correspond to the genres of history, poetry, and philosophy.[9] According to this (again, as Francis Bacon admitted, "very old") scheme, the struggle between history and storytelling is reducible to the relationship between memory and imagination. For historians and scientists imagination has usually been seen as an obstacle to the faculties of memory and reason and has needed, as Bacon put it in his methodical way, "weights, not wings."[10] In literary tradition, on the other hand, imagination has appeared – like Hermes – as a divine messenger and poetry as a second theology or, in the humanist phrase, "another philosophy" *altera philosophia.*[11]

Which of the two, then, offered the best access to truth: History or Poetry ("imaginative," capital-L Literature in a modern sense)? Memory or imagination? Philosophy and psychology did not find the answer to this question at all easy, for Aristotle – still the reigning authority – had regarded imagination as very close to, if not an actual form of, memory, and certainly occupying the same part of the soul. Imagination in an Aristotelian sense was essential to the act of thinking and was prior to memory, which was in effect the subsequent recalling of images. If memory was the "mother of muses," imagination was their very act of procreation. Both faculties were ways of calling up representations of things absent but recoverable or thinkable – "So that," as Hobbes wrote, "*Imagination* and *memory,* are but one thing, which for divers considerations hath divers names."[12] This was also the view taken by Giambattista Vico, who helped

---

[9] Grazia Tonelli Olivieri, "Galen and Bacon: Faculties of the Soul and the Classification of Knowledge," in *Shapes of Knowledge from the Renaissance to the Enlightenment,* ed. Donald R. Kelley and Richard H. Popkin (Dordrecht, Netherlands: Kluwer, 1991), 61–82.

[10] Francis Bacon, *Novum Organum* 1.104.

[11] J. M. Cocking, *Imagination: A Study in the History of Ideas* (London: Routledge, 1991).

[12] Thomas Hobbes, *Leviathan,* ed. Richard Tuck (Cambridge: Cambridge University Press, 1996), p. 160.

restore the links between history and poetry by asserting the value of imagination against the primacy of reason argued for by Baconian and Cartesian philosophers.[13]

In many more concrete and practical ways this convergence must be apparent to all writers and readers. Essential to history writing, the question of truth haunts literary scholars as that of imagination haunts historians; and both, of course, look to their art as an access to the understanding of society, politics, and public life. History and literature are united, too, in questions of language, including the mutual dependence on metaphor and the "blurring of genres" that has occurred both in historiography and in literary forms such as drama and the novel.[14] In general, as literary artists, scholars, and critics have mined the treasures of history, so historians have exploited the resources of literary art; and it seems useful and opportune to encourage exchanges on this common ground extending across the disciplinary frontiers that constrict all of us.

But of course questions remain. Is this convergence of arts the maturing of history, as some historians like to think, or is it "the revenge of literature," as Linda Orr has called it?[15] Does it represent an advance toward a larger view of historical truth and a more critical understanding of literature, or does it defeat the purposes of both? Does a rapprochement between history and literary theory signal for the former a return to the sort of impressionism suggested by G. M. Trevelyan's famous "Clio, a Muse," which celebrated history as an art form? Does it mean for the latter the revenge of the "old historicism"? We hope not. In any case the answers to these questions will not come from discussions of methodology or philosophy but must lie in the quality of the projects undertaken in this interdisciplinary spirit; and this is the justification of the present volume.

The convergence of history and literature in the Elizabethan period has been an object of much scholarly comment. The later sixteenth century marked both an end to the "dead season of English poetry," according to George Saintsbury, and "the Period of Origins of modern English prose."[16] For F. Smith Fussner it also marked the beginning of the period

---

[13] Giambattista Vico, *On the Most Ancient Wisdom of the Italians,* trans. L. M. Palmer (Ithaca, N.Y.: Cornell University Press, 1988), 95, 161; and Vico, *New Science,* 699.

[14] See Clifford Geertz, *Local Knowledge: Further Essays in Interpretive Anthropology* (New York: Basic Books, 1983), 19–35.

[15] Linda Orr, "The Revenge of Literature," in *Studies in Historical Change,* ed. Ralph Cohen (Charlottesville: University of Virginia Press, 1992), 84–108.

[16] George Saintsbury, *History of Elizabethan Literature* (London: Macmillan, 1887), 1:28.

of "the historical revolution."[17] The common ground of these literary phenomena was, of course, language, which is perhaps the most concrete form of cultural memory, but which also, in an age of dawning historical awareness, maturing print culture, and self-conscious cultivation of "letters" becomes a more conscious and deliberate means of expressing this memory. In the contemporaneous works of Edmund Spenser and William Shakespeare, and of William Camden, Edward Coke, and Richard Hooker, Richard Helgerson has seen "what retrospectively looks like a concerted generational project";[18] and it was a project that continued into the period of what has been called "the Historical Renaissance,"[19] and indeed even into times of conflict and revolution. The papers in this volume continue and, we hope, extend and deepen discussions of this cultural and literary revival, which is founded on and informed by concerns with the forms, substance, methods, and truth-value of history and its relationship with imaginative writing.

The concept of history in early modern England appears, at first glance, to have been very conventional. History had begun its public life as a liberal art with an assured place in the humanist program of the liberal arts (*studia humanitatis*); and initially ancient topoi and concepts served to give definition to what remained essentially a literary genre.[20] J. H. M. Salmon examines one contribution to the *ars historica*, Degory Wheare's *Method and Order of Reading Histories* (first ed. 1623), which carries on from the similar works of Francesco Patrizzi (whose work was Englished by Thomas Blundeville), Jean Bodin, Bartholomäus Keckermann, Gerhard Vossius, and others. Rejecting myth, medieval credulity, and the extremism of both Catholics and Protestants, Wheare drew upon the work of modern historians like Phillipe de Commynes, Francesco Guicciardini, Jacques-Auguste De Thou, and Paolo Sarpi and philologists like

---

[17] F. Smith Fussner, *The Historical Revolution: English Historical Writing and Thought 1580–1640* (London: Routledge and Kegan Paul, 1962), on which see also Fritz Levy, *Tudor Historical Thought* (San Marino, Calif.: Huntington Library, 1967); Joseph Levine, *Humanism and History: Origins of Modern English Historiography* (Ithaca, N.Y.: Cornell University Press, 1987); and D. R. Woolf, *The Idea of History in Early Stuart England: Erudition, Ideology and the "Light of Truth" from the Accession of James I to the Civil War* (Toronto: University of Toronto Press, 1990).

[18] Richard Helgerson, *Forms of Nationhood: The Elizabethan Writing of England* (Chicago: University of Chicago Press, 1992), 1.

[19] Heather Dubrow and Richard Strier, eds., *The Historical Renaissance: New Essays on Tudor and Stuart Literature and Culture* (Chicago: University of Chicago Press, 1988).

[20] Especially Cicero *De oratore* 2.36: "History is truly the witness of times, the light of truth, the life of memory, the mistress of life, and the messenger of antiquity."

Joseph Justus Scaliger and Isaac Casaubon; and he turned to the ideas of the ancients – Polybius and Tacitus – in order to realize the political and civil potential that narrative history possessed. Like Bodin (and unlike Patrizzi), Wheare shifted emphasis from the writing to the reading, from the literary to the utilitarian aspects, of history.

The same sort of shift can be seen in sixteenth-century confessional debates, which likewise turned to history for aid and comfort. As Patrick Collinson remarks, John Foxe sought, in his martyrology, "a past both true and usable" – history both, in Cicero's words, as the "light of truth" and as the "mistress of life." There was no contradiction here since truth in Renaissance history was exemplary – offering "paradigms of moral and political behavior," as Herschel Baker put it.[21] Religious behavior, too, Collinson would add; and in any case, Foxe, writing in the tradition of sacred rather than profane history, pursued a truth higher than the small-minded factuality demanded of civil historians. Shaping his facts more with an eye to the self-fashioning of the self-described "godly community" of English Protestants than to the Ciceronian ideal, Foxe's *Acts and Monuments* appears to modern readers more as a myth than the mirror to which classical (and modern scientific) historians have aspired.

How has history, whose semantic fortunes have always intersected with those of "story," separated itself from such fictional impulses? This is the question asked by Joseph Levine, who takes Thomas More's *Utopia* as a test case. His conclusion is that this critical discrimination between imagined fiction and commemorated fact is a product of the scholarly attitudes of Renaissance humanism and that it is reflected specifically in *Utopia*, which displays More's consciousness of the disparity between human reality and ideals – of the lamentable fact that history does not provide the sort of utility that he sought in his social speculations – in conspicuous contrast to the beneficial way history operates in Utopia itself.[22] The historical sense displayed in *Utopia* is surely a function of the new science of philology to which More and his colleagues were drawn. Was it also a function of More's ironic self-awareness, literary role-playing, and inner tensions, which both connected him with and set him off from a society fallen so far from the religious ideals it professed?[23] How much was his perspective the product of his positioning as both

---

[21] Herschel Baker, *The Race of Time* (Toronto: University of Toronto Press, 1967), 16.

[22] See Alistair Fox, *Thomas More: History and Providence* (New Haven: Yale University Press, 1982), 69–71.

[23] Stephen Greenblatt, *Renaissance Self-Fashioning: From More to Shakespeare* (Chicago: University of Chicago Press, 1980), might be called as a witness in this connection.

insider and outsider? In More's work, history and literature are combined in ways that are still difficult to sort out.

In the barrage of Ciceronian commonplaces, history was also celebrated as the "messenger of antiquity," as both Wheare and Foxe, in their different ways, believed. This is the aspect of historical study examined more particularly by D. R. Woolf, who finds a new "historical sense" in more popular interests in the remains of bygone ages. Renaissance scholars had long since discovered antiquity in its material remains such as medals and coins.[24] By the seventeenth century such antiquarian curiosity was apparent in contexts not only of elite learning, such as the Society of Antiquaries, but also of popular culture, in which historical literacy was also making its appearance. Woolf illustrates this through an account of the finding of a treasure trove of antique coins in provincial England in the early seventeenth century. Here the history of things (in the words of George Kubler)[25] supplements the history of words to suggest the directions taken by historical curiosity, imagination, and interpretation in the effort to find present meaning in a dead and apparently irretrievable past.

The horizons of "history" in a modern sense were extended beyond politics, and literary and social boundaries were crossed, in a variety of ways. From a story of a "murder in Faversham" in Holinshed's chronicle, Richard Helgerson deduces a number of such new historiographical frontiers, including popular history, the history of crime and private life, women's history, local history, socioeconomic history, and anecdotal history.[26] Losing its aristocratic thrust and political edge, history broadened its popular appeal and added human richness and color as well.

This point is underlined by Annabel Patterson's study of what might be called the new anecdotalism of Tudor historical writing. In medieval exegesis, anecdotes, in the form of parables, were contrasted with historical and allegorical interpretation (teaching *parabolice* rather than *historice* or *allegorice*);[27] but these genres, too, became blurred. In a more

---

[24] See Roberto Weiss, *The Renaissance Discovery of Classical Antiquity* (Oxford: Oxford University Press, 1969), especially 167–79, on numismatics.

[25] George Kubler, *The Shape of Time: Remarks on the History of Things* (New Haven: Yale University Press, 1962).

[26] See also Annabel Patterson, *Reading Holinshed's Chronicles* (Chicago: University of Chicago Press, 1994), as well as Helgerson's own *Forms of Nationhood*.

[27] Ernst Robert Curtius, *European Literature and the Latin Middle Ages*, trans. Willard R. Trask (Princeton: Princeton University Press, 1953), 223.

secular form the historical anecdote not only enriched the content of historical writing but also suggested changes in the rules of evidence to accommodate the eccentric, the exceptional, and the secret as offering their own sort of – in a sense still symbolic or parabolic – illumination of the human condition.

Rebecca Bushnell opens up still another para-historical genre by showing the significance of gardening books in the fashioning and (in more than one sense) cultivation of the English countryside and the assimilation of nature itself, or at least a "second nature," to this literary and historiographical project. This underappreciated form of literature, which picks up and extends an old classical tradition and touches on the fields of natural history and chorography, is located at one of the intersections between agrarian life and Baconian science, between the particularity of the land and the growing generality of nationhood, between nature and art, and – like history itself – between experience and truth.

Three essays exploring the place of Thomas Hobbes in the historical culture of early modern England contribute to a portrait of a new Hobbes quite different from the conventional view held by philosophers and political theorists and more in line with the currently fashionable rhetorical approach, which emphasizes the humanistic, prescientific, practical dimensions of Hobbes's writings.[28] David Wootton looks not at the ahistorical Hobbes of *Leviathan* but rather at Hobbes the translator of Thucydides, qualified admirer of Machiavelli, and author of *Behemoth,* who – like Degory Wheare – searches history for intelligible causes, ways to understand the psychology of aggression, and a potential basis for political decision making.

In *Behemoth* Fritz Levy sees the traces of the early Thucydidean (rather than the later Euclidean) Hobbes and an illustration of the shift in Renaissance historical thought, in the context of war and constitutional conflict, from moral to political utility. Patricia Springborg, too, installs Hobbes in the older and gentler, or at least more prudent, humanist tradition with its concern for the imaginative recapturing of an immedi-

---

[28] *Perspectives on Thomas Hobbes,* ed. G. A. J. Rogers and Alan Ryan (Oxford: Oxford University Press, 1988); and cf. David Johnston, *The Rhetoric of Leviathan: Thomas Hobbes and the Politics of Cultural Transformation* (Princeton: Princeton University Press, 1986) and Quentin Skinner, *Reason and Rhetoric in the Philosophy of Hobbes* (Cambridge: Cambridge University Press, 1996).

ately usable past, which, while remote, is – through the "mirror of memory" – recoverable.

The literary sources of historiography are emphasized by J. Paul Hunter, who – through a reading of a sensationalist pamphlet of the 1660s, *The Second Spira* – examines the ambiguous attitudes toward truth in novelistic, protonovelistic, and journalistic forms of publishing and their expanding readerships.[29] In a period of Puritan inhibitions about fiction, prose fiction both before and even after "the novel" was tied to pretensions of historical truth, or at least expectations of veracity by the reading public, and only gradually declared its independence of historical memory and took its stand on literary imagination. Here readership joins authorship as an agent that shapes the forms, contents, and standards of fiction, nonfiction, and ambiguous areas in between.[30]

The expanding horizons, increasing depth, and growing complexity of history are the principal themes of Mark Phillips's essay on social and sentimental narratives in the eighteenth century. For Adam Smith history treated not only observable but also invisible events, such as the thoughts or even passions of historical agents; and such sentimentalism, rediscovered also in ancient authors such as Tacitus,[31] informed eighteenth-century narratives of the history of private life, epistolary history, and biography. The ethnographic turn of Scottish philosophy, illustrated by the work of Adam Smith, David Hume, Lord Kames, and Adam Ferguson, gave further impetus to these explorations of cultural history.

Patricia Craddock sees a parallel privatist and culturalist line of inquiry appearing tentatively in Edward Gibbon, who was drawn by literary and historiographical convention to heroic public figures but who also appreciated the achievements of men of science and letters, since it was the peaceful creators and benefactors rather than the public movers and shakers who contributed to the happiness of humanity, even though the latter tended to eclipse the former in terms of fame. Although not

---

[29] See also Hunter, *Before Novels: The Cultural Contexts of Eighteenth-Century English Fiction* (New York: Norton, 1990).

[30] On the narrative ambiguities of *res factae* and *res fictae* – and *Geschichte* and *historiae* – see Reinhard Koselleck, "History, Histories, and Formal Structures of Time," in *Futures Past,* trans. Keith Tribe (Cambridge, Mass.: Massachusetts Institute of Technology Press, 1985), 92–104; and further discussion by Hans Robert Jauss, *Question and Answer: Forms of Dialogic Understanding,* trans. Michael Hays (Minneapolis: University of Minnesota Press, 1989), 25 ff.

[31] On the experimental aspects of Tacitus see Arnaldo Momigliano, *The Classical Foundations of Modern Historiography* (Berkeley: University of California Press, 1990), 113 ff.

drawn as much as Hume to such intellectual "characters," Gibbon was moved to pay special biographical attention to two such civil heroes, Boethius and Petrarch.[32]

The stories about history told in this volume do not add up to a simple, Whiggish narrative of progress from myth to enlightenment, of "history" extricating itself from fictive "story," or even, on the literary side, of Literature and Imagination escaping the intellectual hegemony of History and Reason. Nor is there a "great tradition" in the dogmatic style of F. R. Leavis or a historiographical canon recognizable to older professional historians. Rather, the Baconian faculties and corresponding literary genres continued to intermingle in a striking variety of ways, reaching new social depths and cultural breadths precisely because of the conflict of faculties and the blurring of genres.

One thing may be clearer: What has become apparent in the past generation in the wake of the "new rhetoric" and renewed appreciation for the historical imagination was, four centuries and more earlier, reflected in the fictional and nonfictional writing of early modern England. We repeatedly see myth and other products of the imagination reflected in the stories that historians pretend are true – or see the truth emerging from the sleep of reason induced by modernity or in the creations of imaginations that, reversing Bacon's dictum, have been given wings, not weights. History is not over, the novel is not dead, imagination still flourishes, and there are always more stories to tell.

[32] See S. K. Wertz, "Hume and the Historiography of Science," *Journal of the History of Ideas* 54 (1993): 411–36.

2

Precept, example, and truth: Degory Wheare and the *ars historica*

J. H. M. SALMON

If they mention him at all, modern historians have not thought much of Degory Wheare, the first Camden Professor of History at Oxford. He assumed his post in 1623, the year in which William Camden died, and for the next twenty-four years lectured on Roman history from the text his patron had prescribed, the *Epitome* of Lucius Annaeus Florus. "The first incumbent," writes Joseph Levine, "took eight years to cover the first book [of Florus], drawing comparisons between ancient and modern events as he plodded along."[1] D. R. Woolf describes him as "a competent classicist and dull pedagogue . . . [who] continued to drone on through the civil war till his death in 1647, providing the history of academic tenure with an inauspicious beginning."[2] Even the work that earned Wheare a measure of fame, *The Method and Order of Reading Histories*, has been treated in patronizing fashion as "not entirely without merit as a compilation" and "repeating the commonplaces of the familiar Renaissance *ars historica*."[3] But *The Method and Order* was neither so dull nor so neglected in its time as its modern critics suggest. Between 1623 and 1710 at least six Latin and four English editions were published in England and two Latin ones in Germany, together with several variants and extensions in both countries.[4] It was the only widely known English

---

[1] Joseph M. Levine, *Humanism and History: Origins of Modern English Historiography* (Ithaca, N.Y.: Cornell University Press, 1987), 103.

[2] D. R. Woolf, *The Idea of History in Early Stuart England: Erudition, Ideology and the "Light of Truth" from the Accession of James I to the Civil War* (Toronto: University of Toronto Press, 1990), 329.

[3] H. Stuart Jones, "The Foundation and History of the Camden Chair," *Oxoniensa* 8–9 (1943–4): 178; Levine, *Humanism and History*, 103.

[4] As *De ratione et methodo legendi historias dissertatio* (Oxford, 1623, 1625; Cambridge, 1664); as *Relectiones hyemales de ratione et methodo legendi utrasque historias civiles et ecclesiasticas* (Oxford, 1637 and two 1637 variants; Oxford, 1662 and three 1662 vari-

example of the Renaissance *ars historica,* and the last of its type in Europe.[5] As such, it improved upon most of its precursors and showed awareness of the tensions within the genre. Its disparagement may be due to lack of sympathy on the part of modern historians for history seen as the source of moral lessons, and to failure to place the work within the context to which it belongs. This essay sketches the development of the *ars historica* in Europe and the climate of historical thought in England, and then considers the extent of Degory Wheare's achievement.

The first of many Renaissance works on the nature and purpose of history was the dialogue *Actius,* composed by the Neapolitan historian Giovanni Pontano at the end of the fifteenth century. The main sources for the *ars historica* came from the teaching of rhetoric in the late Roman republic and early empire, when the Stoics saw history as a vicarious means of acquiring prudence and applying it to both private and public life. Its catch phrases came from Cicero's *De oratore,* in which history was described as, among other things, the "guide to life" [magistra vitae] and the "light of truth" [lux veritatis].[6] The theme of what George Nadel has called "exemplar history" was encapsulated by the phrase of Dionysius of Halicarnassus in his treatise on the art of rhetoric: "History is philosophy teaching by examples."[7] Quintilian preferred practical Roman examples to abstract Greek precepts, and Seneca pronounced the celebrated dictum: "The journey is long by way of precepts but short and effective through examples" [longum iter est per praecepta, breve et efficax per exempla].[8] These tags maintain the superiority of history to moral philosophy, but

---

ants; Cambridge, 1684; Tübingen, 1700 and *Accessiones,* 1704, 1706, 1708); as *The Method and Order of Reading Both Civil and Ecclesiastical Histories,* trans. Edmund Bohun (London, 1685, 1694, 1698, 1710). Bohun himself reports two augmented Latin editions as *Relectiones hyemales* in 1635 and 1636. Some bibliographies mention a 1660 Latin Oxford edition and a 1664 Nuremberg Latin edition, but these have not been verified. Editions from 1662 carry the additions, or *Mantissa,* of Nicholas Horseman.

[5] On the *ars historica* see Eric Cochrane, *Historians and Historiography in the Italian Renaissance* (Chicago: University of Chicago Press, 1985), 479–87; Girolamo Cotroneo, *I trattatisti dell' "Ars historica"* (Naples: Giannini, 1971); George H. Nadel, "Philosophy of History before Historicism," in *Studies in the Philosophy of History,* ed. Nadel (New York: Harper Torch, 1965), 49–73; Beatrice Reynolds, "Shifting Currents in Historical Criticism," *Journal of the History of Ideas* 14 (1953): 471–92; Giorgio Spini, "Historiography: The Art of History in the Italian Counter Reformation," in *The Late Italian Renaissance,* ed. Eric Cochrane (New York: Harper Torch, 1970), 91–133; and Astrid Witschi-Bernz, *Bibliography of Works in the Philosophy of History, 1500–1800 (History and Theory,* Beiheft 12), (Middletown, Conn.: Wesleyan University Press, 1972).

[6] Cicero *De oratore* 2.9.36.

[7] Dionysius of Halicarnassus *De arte rhetorica* 11.2.19. This work is now generally attributed to an imitator of Dionysius.

[8] Cited in Nadel, "Philosophy of History," 55–6.

they do not suggest an inductive method whereby the reader defined moral principles by generalizing from historical facts. Indeed, the precepts had a logical priority over the examples and stood as self-evident moral ideals, although Cicero and the Stoics all too readily identified the good with the useful in terms of prudential morality. Here was one set of tensions perpetuated by the Renaissance practitioners of the *ars historica*.

According to the ancient rhetoricians, historical examples moved the reader to action more effectively than fiction or philosophy because they were true. Ascertaining truth involved setting critical standards of historical testimony, and these were not lacking. Cicero exemplified the principle of *lux veritatis* by requiring the historian to echew falsehood, to tell the whole truth, and to avoid prejudice. A century earlier, Polybius had established criteria of historical evidence known as the *normae Polybianae*, requiring eyewitness testimony and impartial interpretation. A century after Cicero, Tacitus defined true history as written with "neither anger nor affection" [sine ira et studio]. Yet perhaps the most authoritative critic of bias in history was Lucian of Samosata in the second century A.D., whose *De historia conscribenda* [How history should be written] inspired Pontano to launch the new genre of the *ars historica*. Lucian likened the independent historian to a man without a country, and offered the seemingly Rankean remark: "The historian's task is to tell the tale as it actually happened."[9] It seldom occurred to these classical authors that accurate representation of past reality was difficult to attain if the main purpose of the historian was to teach moral lessons. Didacticism, not idle curiosity, was to be the driving force of the *ars historica*, which thereby inherited tension between utilitarian and critical elements, between pragmatic education and undirected erudition.

The sixteenth-century authors of treatises on the nature and purpose of history not only referred to the standard classical epigrams, they also cited each other's opinions about them. Degory Wheare, who brought this practice to a climax, relied upon *Artis historicae penus,* a collection or "storehouse" of works on how to write or read history published by Johann Wolf at Basel in 1576 and 1579. In its second, two-volume version this collection reprinted sixteen modern *artes historicae*, dating from Pontano to Uberto Foglietta's *De ratione scribendae historiae* [On the method for writing history] and his *De similitudine normae Polybianae* [On imitation of the rule of Polybius], first published in 1574. He also

---

[9] Cited in Reynolds, "Shifting Currents," 477.

included Lucian of Samosata's *De conscribenda historia* and Dionysius of Halicarnassus's *De Thucydidis historia iudicium* [An appraisal of the history of Thucydides].[10] The 1576 one-volume version of the collection took its title from Jean Bodin's *Methodus ad facilem historiarum cognitionem* [Method for the easy comprehension of history, 1566], and described that work in the editor's preface as "the key to all histories." Bodin himself insisted upon his own originality. His desire to define the rules of a universal history that blended with comparative jurisprudence led him to investigate causal mechanisms. Like his colleague, François Baudouin, who expressed similar aims in *De institutione historiae universae et eius cum iurisprudentia coniunctione* [The Principles of universal history and its conjunction with jurisprudence, 1561], also reprinted in Wolf's collection, Bodin was indebted to that most method-conscious of the ancients, Polybius. However, this protoscientific approach to the history of institutions did not make Bodin any the less devoted to the didactic purpose of history:

[History] teaches us clearly not only the arts necessary for living, but also those objectives which at all costs must be sought, what things to avoid, what is base, what is honorable, which laws are most desirable, which state is the best, and the happiest kind of life.[11]

Others before Bodin had broken away from the rhetorical approach under the influence of Polybian reasoning. In *Della historia dieci dialoghi* [Ten dialogues about history, 1560] (also appearing in a Latin version in *Artis historicae penus*), Francesco Patrizzi even questioned the idea of history as *magistra vitae,* and asked what kind of exemplum a list of Babylonian kings constituted.[12] The aim of history, he argued, was the apprehension of truth (*la cognitione del vero*). Because he employed the dialogue form, Patrizzi frequently seemed to contradict himself, and hence his treatise illustrated the logical problems of the genre better than any other. For instance, after rejecting the exemplar approach, he went on to say that history could furnish useful lessons in politics. Polybius had insisted that one only learned from the historical experience of others if one investigated motives and causes. Establishing facts without showing causes provided no lesson. Patrizzi looked for a science of cause and effect, but in one passage called this philosophy rather than history.

---

[10] See Witschi-Bernz, *Bibliography,* 7–8, for details of authors and titles.

[11] Jean Bodin, *Method for the Easy Comprehension of History,* trans. Beatrice Reynolds (New York: W. W. Norton, 1969), 13–14.

[12] Spini, "Historiography," 102.

Moreover, in his fifth dialogue he questioned the Polybian criteria for historical evidence, and lapsed into a kind of Pyrrhonism where he allowed that exact truth about the past was impossible to attain.[13]

Not all the *artes historicae* cited by Degory Wheare were contained in Wolf's collection. For instance, he often referred to the comments on history offered by Juan Luis Vives in his book on the intellectual disciplines, *De disciplinis libri XX* (1531), which Wolf did not reprint. Others that Wheare quoted appeared after Wolf's volumes. Apart from Bodin's *Methodus,* the particular treatises on history to which he was most indebted included Bartholomäus Keckermann's *De natura et proprietatibus historiae commentarius* [Commentary on the nature and properties of history, 1610] and Gerhard Voss's *Ars historica* of 1623. These two scholars' debates on the relative importance of precept and example had a considerable effect on Wheare's own thinking. Polybius was central to Voss's approach to history,[14] whereas Keckermann favored Tacitus. In many ways European historiography in the late sixteenth and early seventeenth centuries was dominated by the rivalry between the ghost of the Greek historian of the heroic age of republican Rome in its struggle with Carthage and the spirit of the Roman analyst of tyranny and suspicion in the time of the principate. Degory Wheare steered a judicious course between the Polybian camp of Isaac Casaubon and the Tacitean following of Justus Lipsius – two modern scholars whose names, together with that of the equally erudite Joseph Scaliger, appear frequently in *The Method and Order.* If Polybius was a model for objective political explanation, Tacitus offered subtle insights into psychological motives and ways of conveying climates of opinion. Lipsius, who likened his own age to the wars and crises of the first century A.D., also used the sixth book of Polybius's *Histories* to write about the Roman army, as Patrizzi had done before him, but his greatest scholarly contributions were his editions of the works of Tacitus and Seneca, from whom he derived his own Neostoic moral philosophy. Casaubon produced his great edition of the surviving fragments of the writings of Polybius in 1609.[15]

---

[13] Julian H. Franklin, *Jean Bodin and the Sixteenth-Century Revolution in the Methodology of Law and History* (New York: Columbia University Press, 1963), 96–101.

[14] Arnaldo Momigliano, "Polybius' Reappearance in Western Europe," in *Essays in Ancient and Modern Historiography* (Middletown, Conn.: Wesleyan University Press, 1977), 93.

[15] On Lipsius see Mark Morford, *Stoics and Neostoics; Reubens and the Circle of Lipsius* (Princeton: Princeton University Press, 1991), 96–180; on Casaubon see the editor's introduction in *Isaac Casaubon, Polibio,* ed. Guerrino F. Brussich (Palermo: Sellerio, 1991), 19–43.

Plutarch had told the story that Marcus Junius Brutus spent the night before the battle of Pharsalus in Pompey's encampment copying out pieces from Polybius, and Casaubon credited the belief that these notes formed the basis of the *Excerpta antiqua*, a text of Polybian observations of Byzantine provenance known in Italy from the fifteenth century.[16] This text encouraged the late-sixteenth-century vogue for extracting precepts and examples from the works of classical authors into private commonplace books and published compilations. This offshoot of the exemplar approach sometimes included moderns such as Guicciardini on the Tacitean side and Machiavelli on the Polybian, but it was ancient historians such as Polybius, Sallust, and Tacitus who usually dominated the lists.[17] In this vein Lipsius produced his *Monita et exampla* [Admonitions and examples, 1605]; his disciple, Jean de Chokier, *Thesaurum aphorismorum politicorum* [A treasury of political aphorisms, 1611]; and the English writer Sir Robert Dallington *Aphorisms Civil and Military* (1613). Wheare, who devoted a long section of *The Method and Order* to "the manner of collecting the fruits of history," mentioned all these collections, and also made reference to the various pieces of advice by Vives, Bodin, and Keckermann on how to extract the best apothegms.[18]

There were virtually no English examples of the *ars historica* to compete with Wheare's work. In 1574 Thomas Blundeville, a client of the earl of Leicester, had adapted Patrizzi's dialogues and also a manuscript written by an Italian in Leicester's service, Giacomo Aconcio, to produce *The True Order and Method of Writing and Reading Histories*.[19] The work seems to have been little known. A more original *ars historica* was composed in Jacobean times by the Catholic Edmund Bolton, but remained in manuscript. Bolton was an acquaintance of those luminaries of English historical scholarship, William Camden, Sir Robert Cotton, and John Speed. His unpublished *Hypercritica, or a Rule of Judgment for Writing or Reading Our Histories*, was partly devoted to critical discussion of the fabulous aspects of British history invented by Geoffrey of Monmouth in

---

[16] Momigliano, "Polybius' Reappearance," 81.

[17] J. H. M. Salmon, "Stoicism and Roman Example: Seneca and Tacitus in Jacobean England," *Journal of the History of Ideas* 50 (1989): 216.

[18] Degory Wheare, *Method and Order of Reading Both Civil and Ecclesiastical Histories*, trans. Edmund Bohun (London, 1694), 319–62. All quotations from this work refer to this edition.

[19] This work is reproduced in *Huntington Library Quarterly* 2 (1939–40): 149–70. Spelling has been modernized in English titles and quotations throughout.

the twelfth century.[20] Bolton was an admirer of Tacitus, the author of *Nero Caesar* (1624), and the translator of the text used in Wheare's lectures, the *Epitome* of Florus (*The Roman Histories*, 1619).

At the end of Elizabeth's reign, when Degory Wheare was first seeking to establish himself at Oxford, a division existed between realist writers of "politick" history, who saw the past in terms of discontinuity and conflict, and those who sought to preserve the unchanging principles that gave Englishness its identity. The former were influenced by Polybius and Tacitus among the ancients and by Machiavelli and Guicciardini among the moderns. The latter were the votaries of the common law. There was also a divide between antiquarians, who felt the fascination of unrelated elements in the remote past, and those who stressed the need to provide coordinated narrative and to explain developments in the large. Of course, some crossed the boundaries between these categories. Among the most influential Taciteans of the time was Sir Henry Savile, who stood high in the favor of Queen Elizabeth, his former pupil, and retained the wardenship of Merton College after becoming provost of Eton in 1596. His association with the Oxford following of the rebellious Essex scarcely affected his reputation as a purveyor of prudent political advice and one of the greatest scholars of the age. He was not only a classicist who translated Tacitus and filled in the gaps in the latter's *Histories* with his own research, but also a much esteemed antiquarian who edited at least seven medieval English texts.[21] His most exacting work was a multivolume edition of the works of St. John Chrysostom. Bolton noted that Savile had lamented the lack of a general history of Britain to compare with classical models, and recorded that Savile, after attempting research in the records stored in the Tower, had turned in despair to the Christian fathers. Bolton's comment was not atypical of prevailing historical attitudes:

It is otherwise an affliction for those minds which have been conversant in the marvels and delights of Hebrew, Greek and Roman antiquities to turn over so many musty rolls, so many dry bloodless chronicles and so many dull and heavy paced histories as they must who will attain the crown and triumphal ensign of having composed a *Corpus Rerum Anglicarum*.[22]

---

[20] Edmund Bolton, *Hypercritica, or a Rule of Judgment for Writing or Reading Our Histories*, in J. E. Spingarn, *Critical Essays of the Seventeenth Century* (Bloomington: Indiana University Press, 1957), 1:82–115.

[21] May McKisack, *Medieval History in the Tudor Age* (Oxford: Clarendon Press, 1971), 64.

[22] Bolton, *Hypercritica*, 97.

Wheare also venerated Savile, whom he called "the great and eternally to be remembered ornament of our university."[23]

Bolton quoted an address to the reader, sometimes attributed to Essex himself, prefacing Savile's translation of Tacitus. This address not only commended Tacitus in the strongest terms but also provided the most uninhibited English version of the exemplar theory of history:

> There is no treasure so much enriches the mind of man as learning; there is no learning so proper for the direction of the life of man as history; there is no history (I speak only of the prophane) as well worth the reading as Tacitus. . . . For history, since we are easier taught by example than by precept, what study can profit us so much as that which gives patterns either to follow or to fly, or the best and worst men of all estates, countries and times that ever were? For Tacitus I may say without partiality that he hath written the most matter with best conceit in fewest words of any historiographer ancient or modern.[24]

This encomium was cast in doubt after Essex's rebellion. Although James I rehabilitated many of Essex's supporters and showed personal favor to Savile, Casaubon later persuaded the king of the dangers of Tacitean examples and of the superior qualities of Polybius.[25]

William Camden, an admirer of both Polybius and Tacitus, also crossed the boundary between antiquarianism and "politick" history, offering his *Britannia* to the former school and his *Annals of the . . . Princess Elizabeth* to the latter. Camden consulted Savile, who had recently created chairs of astronomy and geometry, about the terms of the Oxford professorship he wished to establish. When the delegates of the university required the lectures to be on ecclesiastical as well as secular history, Camden interceded at Wheare's request to ask that he should lecture only "on civil history, and therein make such observations as might be most useful and profitable to the younger students of the university, to direct and instruct them in the knowledge and use of history, antiquity and times past."[26] Camden's aims differed from those that had been expressed by Sir John Coke, the future secretary of state, several years earlier when Fulke Greville had begun to negotiate for a chair of history at Cambridge. Coke saw the lectureship as an opportunity to

---

[23] Wheare, *Method and Order*, 133.
[24] *The End of Nero and the Beginning of Galba. Four Books of the Histories of Cornelius Tacitus. The Life of Agricola*, 5th ed. (London, 1622 [1st ed. 1591]), unpaginated address to the reader. Cited in Bolton, *Hypercritica*, 97.
[25] Salmon, "Stoicism and Roman Example," 224.
[26] Jones, "The Camden Chair," 175. Wheare did in fact include a section on ecclesiastical history in *Method and Order*.

combat Puritan influence in church and state. "In my poor opinion," he wrote in 1615, "it is now as necessary to have diligent historians as learned divines, and that your historian be also a divine, able to join church and commonwealth together, which to separate is to betray. So shall your erection be a most fruitful and famous work, whereas if you plant but a critical antiquary instead of an historian, nothing can be more unthrifty or vain."[27] It took Greville twelve years to find a candidate. He failed to secure the services of Gerhard Voss, although the latter did visit England in this period. Eventually he appointed Isaac Dorislaus, who after the execution of Charles I became the new Commonwealth's envoy to the Hague and was assassinated by royalists. Dorislaus failed to fulfill Sir John Coke's ideals in any respect. When he began to lecture on Tacitus at Cambridge in 1628, his subject so scandalized the authorities that he was suspended. Degory Wheare's lectures on Florus, as well as his *Method and Order,* avoided such political quicksand. However, his friends and contacts might have suggested a measure of commitment to the very cause that Coke thought Greville's lecturer should combat.

Degory Wheare had Cornish connections. He became an intimate friend of the family of Sir Anthony Rous, a client of the third Earl of Bedford. Wheare entered Broadgates Hall (later Pembroke College) with Sir Anthony's son, Francis, in 1593, and a few years later acted as tutor to John Pym, whose mother had made a second marriage with the elder Rous. Wheare remained so close to Pym that in 1614 he acted as signatory to a deed placing Pym's estates in trust.[28] Pym's career in opposition to the policies of Charles I is too well known to require comment. Francis Rous made his name as a Puritan pamphleteer and critic of Arminianism, and sat in every parliament from 1625 to 1657. While his religious sentiments varied from Presbyterian to Independent, and at times reflected a mystic fervor, he was capable of hard-nosed secular politics. His tract *The Lawfulness of Obeying the Present Government* (1649) argued for allegiance to the Commonwealth by citing the irregular accession to power of some English kings and Roman emperors. He observed that St. Paul's celebrated injunction in Romans 13 ("Let every soul be in subjection to the higher powers") was probably written under Claudius or Nero,

---

[27] Coke to Greville, September 16, 1615, in Norman Farmer Jr., "Fulke Greville and Sir John Coke: An Exchange of Letters on a History Lecture and Certain Latin Verses on Sir Philip Sidney," *Huntington Library Quarterly* 33 (1969–70): 220–1.

[28] S. Reed Brett, *John Pym, 1583–1643: The Statesman of the Puritan Revolution* (London: John Murray, 1940), xxiv.

whose own elevation to the power said to be ordained of God was due to
the soldiery.[29] Degory Wheare kept in touch with Francis Rous and John
Pym for at least twenty years, but his letters to them, which he copied into
his letter book, are confined to personal and money matters.[30] It is possible, of course, that he wrote to them on other issues but kept no record.

Wheare was a fellow of Exeter College from 1602 to 1608. He then
left Oxford to join the household of Grey Brydges, fifth baron Chandos,
who had been imprisoned after Essex's attempted coup in 1601. Like
some others of Essex's following, Chandos became a favorite of James I.
Wheare accompanied the baron to the Netherlands in 1610, and on his
return lived at Sudeley Castle, where Chandos kept great state. On the
death of Chandos in 1621 Wheare took up residence at Gloucester Hall,
a former monastic establishment later to be incorporated into Worcester
College. He became principal there in 1626. Thomas Allen, the mathematician and collector of manuscripts, was also a member of Gloucester
Hall. It was he, together with Thomas Clayton, professor of medicine and
master of Pembroke, who brought Wheare to Camden's attention, and
pushed through his nomination with the university authorities.[31] Wheare
wrote several letters to Camden at the time he was taking up his new
duties. In one he showed his interest in Roman Britain, and told his
patron he was sending a manuscript of the *Antonine Itineraries*, providing Roman place-names in the second century A.D.[32] In another letter,
discussing his first lectures, he remarked how some in his audience had
asked for a written version of his address on method, which he had
delivered under the title *De ratione et methodo historias cum fructu
legendi* [On the understanding and method together with the profit of
reading histories].[33] This was the origin of his celebrated book. Wheare
sent copies of the second edition to Allen, Cotton, Godwin, Selden, and
Speed, among others, and carefully recorded the accompanying inscriptions in his letter book.[34] In a letter to Speed, which he also recorded,

---

[29] Francis Rous, *The Lawfulness of Obeying the Present Government* (London, 1649), 1–4.

[30] Bodleian MS Selden. Supra 81, items 96–9, 104, 105, 109, 154, 169, Bodleian Library,
Oxford.

[31] Bodleian MS Auct. F.2.21, pp. 2, 72. Wheare explains this in the dedication to Clayton of
the first two parts of the manuscript of his lectures on Florus.

[32] *Viri Clarissimi Gulielmi Camdeni et illustrium virorum ad G. Camdenum epistolae*
(London, 1691), 331. On the *Antonine Itineraries*, see Levine, *Humanism and History*,
82. It was discussed by Wheare's friend Thomas Godwin in his popular *Romanae
historiae anthologia, an English Exposition of the Roman Antiquities* (London, 1614).

[33] *Viri clarissimi Gulielmi Camdeni*, 341.

[34] Bodleian MS Selden. Supra 81, items 231–40.

Wheare remarked: "You are part of the family to which I attach myself as a kind of mentor."[35] Despite differences of opinion, a spirit of mission and fraternity pervaded the community of historians at this time.

Wheare maintained that the section of his lectures on Florus devoted to the Punic Wars was appropriate for his time because in both periods a contest for the mastery of the world was taking place.[36] Yet he drew few actual parallels with modern events. Occasionally he would refer to a modern ruler, such as the emperor Charles V, whom he compared with Scipio Aemilianus, the destroyer of Carthage, as someone who laid his plans with deliberation and executed them with celerity.[37] Few political opinions were apparent in the lectures. With reference to the earliest period of Roman history Wheare endorsed the necessity for powerful kings to enforce the loose union of shepherds and refugees who made up the Roman people after the foundation, and he then went on to explain how the retention of power proved incompatible with the people's growing desire for liberty.[38] In another lecture, this time on the Second Punic War, Wheare praised Hannibal for his foresight and prudence and his readiness to exchange the policy of war *à l'outrance* to negotiated settlement when circumstances demanded this course of action.[39] A prince, he said, must have the courage to hold to his objectives, and even greater courage to change them when necessary.

From the introductory or "divinatory" lecture (*oratio auspicalis*) and its first appearance in print in 1623, *The Method and Order* continued to be enlarged and rearranged in minor detail throughout the rest of the century. Ten years after the major edition of 1625 Wheare completed a new set of revisions, correcting such details as dates from creation, moving paragraphs from one section to another, and embodying some of the longer marginal notes in the text. This version, retitled *Relectiones hyemales* [Revised winter readings], was the one reedited in 1662 by Nicholas Horseman, who with false modesty added his *Mantissa* (a Tuscan word meaning "worthless addition") "concerning the historians of

---

[35] Ibid., item 202.
[36] Bodleian MS Auct. F.2.21, lectiones 154 and 162. The former lecture, delivered in October 1631, included a vigorous defense against the reproach that he had spent eight years covering the first of the four parts of Florus's *Epitome*.
[37] Ibid., folio 165 (individual lectures are not numbered in this part of the manuscript).
[38] Ibid., lectio 154. Wheare clearly believed in the rule of law. Discussing the nature of monarchy in *The Method and Order*, he wrote that God created this form of rule "so that men be governed by laws, justice and a good discipline" (38).
[39] Bodleian MS. Auct. F.2.21, lectio 193.

particular nations, as well ancient as modern."[40] This text was chosen for translation in 1685 by Edmund Bohun, who inserted a preface about the original author, and made many additions of his own describing later seventeenth-century historians and filling in the gaps left by Wheare in his account of medieval English chroniclers. In the 1694 and subsequent editions in English, Henry Dodwell's "Invitation to gentlemen to acquaint themselves with ancient history" was placed at the head of the volume. The Latin editions published in Tübingen in the early eighteenth century contained a great deal of further material to bring the whole thing up to date as a kind of encyclopedia of historiography.[41]

The 1635 version of *The Method and Order* began with a new prologue or *antelogium,* in which, after the customary references to Cicero and Quintilian, Wheare turned to Livy and restated the exemplar theory:

This is the most healthful and profitable attendant of the knowledge of history, that you may contemplate the instructions or variety of examples united in one illustrious monument, and from thence take out such things as are useful to thee, or to thy country, and that thou mayst wisely consider that what has an ill beginning will have an ill end, and so avoid it.[42]

Various types of history were then classified, beginning with Bodin's distinction among the divine, the natural, and the human. The last was subdivided into civil ("that which explains the rise or beginning, constitutions, increases, changes and affairs of empires, commonwealths and cities") and ecclesiastical ("that which principally describes the affairs of the church, though at the same time the transactions of monarchs and kingdoms are also inserted").[43] Other categories included world histories (such as Sir Walter Raleigh's), national histories, chronicles, biographies, and particular events such as Xenophon's *Anabasis* or Sallust's *Conspiracy of Catiline.* Wheare then launched into the main body of his text, which he divided into three parts, the first and largest of which listed major historians through the ages, provided commentaries from their critics, and suggested the order in which they should be read.

Like most *artes historicae,* Wheare's provided a chronology of the standard epochs since creation. If pagan chronology remained obscure for the earliest times, one could rely on the authors of the Old Testament, "those pen-men of the Holy Ghost," in Bohun's felicitous phrase.[44]

---

[40] Nicholas Horseman, *Mantissa,* in *Method and Order,* title page.
[41] For details of editions see n. 4, above.   [42] Wheare, *Method and Order,* 15–16.
[43] Ibid., 16.   [44] Ibid., 25.

Wheare made dutiful reference to the Protestant-oriented *Chronica* of Philip Melanchthon and Johann Carrion dating from the 1530s, but he also showed expert knowledge of the new calculations of Joseph Scaliger (*De emendatione temporum* [On the correction of dates, 1583], and *Thesaurus temporum isagogici canones* [A treasury of dates: introductory rules, 1606]). In particular, he noted Scaliger's exposure of the Chaldean annals of the Pseudo-Barosus, forged by Giovanni Annio of Viterbo in 1498, which had skewed sixteenth-century estimates of the second and third millenia B.C.[45] When discussing the time-worn concept of the four monarchies (Assyrian, Medo-Persian, Macedonian, and Roman), Wheare criticized Bodin, one of his most respected authorities, for attributing its invention to the Lutherans Melanchthon and Johann Sleidan.[46] Although chronology had been distorted by both Protestant and Roman Catholic polemic, Wheare, like Scaliger, remained dispassionate and used the most scholarly treatises, regardless of the religious allegiance of their authors. He cited the Huguenot scholar Jacques Cappel III (*Historia sacra et exotica ab Adamo usque ad Augustum* [Sacred and exotic history from Adam to Augustus, 1613]) beside the learned Jesuit Denis Petau (*Opus de doctrina temporum* [A work on chronology, 1627]; *Rationarium temporum in partes duas* [A table of dates in two parts, 1636]), and altered the dates he had used in earlier editions of *The Method and Order* to fit the revisions Petau had suggested.[47] When Bohun added a reference to Sir John Marsham's *Chronicus canon Aegyptiacus, Ebraicus, Graecus et disquisitiones* (1672), Wheare's careful adjustments became confused by Marsham's assumptions about Egyptian dynasties after the flood.[48]

The Method and Order passed over the supposititious pagan historians of remotest antiquity, whose credibility had been destroyed by Scaliger. Wheare noted that "Herodotus, the father of heathen history, begins where prophetic history ends,"[49] and then reviewed, in summary fashion, opinions about subsequent Greek historians, including Thucydides, Xenophon, and Diodorus Siculus, together with the biographers of Alexander, Arrian of Nicomedia, and Quintus Curtius. Dionysius of Halicarnassus

---

[45] Ibid., 45. See Anthony Grafton, "Joseph Scaliger and Historical Chronology: The Rise and Fall of a Discipline," *History and Theory* 14 (1975): 156–85.

[46] Wheare, *Method and Order*, 31. Cf. Bodin, *Method*, 291–302.

[47] Wheare, *Method and Order*, 34–6, 41.

[48] Ibid., 44. Grafton suggests that Marsham's errors originated with the theories expressed by Voss in *De theologia gentili et physiologia Christiana*, 1641. Grafton, "Joseph Scaliger and Historical Chronology," 177–8.

[49] Wheare, *Method and Order*, 50.

was sandwiched between later Roman historians. When Wheare turned to Polybius on Roman history his text became infused with a more vital spirit. He let Lipsius speak for him:

Oh great and glorious empire! And, I add, of long continuance! And therefore it is no wonder if it transcended, both in men and actions, that short and fleeting monarchy of the Grecians. The Grecians, said one, excel in precepts, the Romans in examples, both for peace and war.[50]

These words were adapted from Lipsius's *Tractatus ad historiam Romanam cognoscendam apprime utiles* [Particularly useful reflections on how to get to know Roman history, 1592], and repeated Quintilian's preference for example over precept. Wheare continued to depend upon Lipsius as he commented upon the better-known Roman historians. For instance, he cited Lipsius's praise of Sallust: "If it were left to me, I should in this catalogue not doubt to choose Salustius for president of the senate of historians."[51]

Sallust had lived through the collapse of the republic, and Tacitus, who for Lipsius was the Augustus of historians, had, as we have seen, chronicled the evils of the empire in the century that followed. Both had looked back to an earlier, more virtuous era. As Tacitus became the most read ancient historian in late-sixteenth-century Europe, surpassing even Livy in popularity, it became common to draw analogies between the Rome of Tiberius, Caligula, and Nero and the Europe of religious persecution, civil war, and absolutist government. No one did this more vividly than Lipsius:

Let everyone in him [Tacitus] consider the courts of princes, their private lives, counsels, commands, actions, and from the apparent similitude that is betwixt those times and ours, let them expect the like events. You shall find under tyranny, flattery and informers, evils too well known in our own times, nothing simple and sincere, and no true fidelity even among friends.[52]

It is not difficult to see why Casaubon was able to persuade James I of the superior virtues of Polybius. In citing this passage, Wheare seemed to be charting a dangerous course, but Savile's opinion could not be discounted, and Camden had admired both Tacitus and Polybius. He decided to hedge his bets. "The critics say," he wrote, "that he [Tacitus] had a new, concise and sententious way of writing, but as to the use and

---

[50] Ibid., 77.   [51] Ibid., 95.
[52] Ibid., 106–7. Cf. Salmon, "Stoicism and Roman Example," 200–1.

utility of his history they vary, or it may be rather fight each against other." Still, one could not ignore Lipsius, and Wheare quoted the latter's somewhat cryptic conclusion: "He is a wonderful writer, and does most seriously do what he seems not to make his business at all, for it is not only a history but a garden and seminary of precepts."[53] This opinion was reinforced with quotations from Christophor Coler, who had endorsed both Lipsius's favorable view of Tacitus and his doctrine of *similitudo temporum* in *De studio politico ordinando epistola* [A letter on how the study of politics should be organized, Strasbourg, 1621].

At this point Wheare decided to air the opposing view:

Isaac Casaubon, a person admired for his learning and virtue, here goes quite against the judgments of Lipsius and Colerus, for where he compares the other historians with his Polybius he affirms of Tacitus "that if his fortune had not deprived him a subject worthy of his faculties, he might have equalled any of the most excellent Greek or Latin historians, but such times, saith he, fell under his pen especially in his *Annals,* as if there were never any more polluted with vices, or more destitute of, or enraged against, all virtues.[54]

This was not so much to condemn Tacitus's talents as a historian as to indict those who in Wheare's own age found him a source of political counsel. According to Casaubon, those who did so were effectively calling modern rulers tyrants and instructing them in the techniques of oppression. Wheare ended his quotations from Casaubon with that scholar's restatement of the exemplar theory:

For, as good examples when they are frequently in sight, improve a man without his observation, so ill examples hurt us, for by little and little they sink into our minds, and have the effect of precepts being often read or heard.[55]

The debate was left undecided, but the reader was likely to give a small advantage to Tacitus.

The most obvious blind spot in Wheare's own versions of *The Method and Order* was his treatment of medieval historians and chroniclers. Under civil history he was content to suggest to readers who needed some framework of events that they should consult Flavio Biondo's *Decades* and Bartholomeo Platina's *Lives of the Popes*. Both these works were composed in the mid-fifteenth century, and could be augmented by Carlo Sigonio's *History of the Kingdom of Italy*. It is true that more attention was paid to actual medieval sources in the section on ecclesiastical his-

---

[53] Wheare, *Method and Order,* 107.　　[54] Ibid., 108.　　[55] Ibid., 108–9.

tory, but Wheare's predisposition toward the classics and his contempt for the miraculous aspects of Christian belief blinded him to the achievements of medieval learning. His heading for a chapter on the seventh century read: "Legends of saints. Oceans of miracles and wonders. The times of rodomontados and ignorance." This was topped off by a quote from Casaubon:

After these horrible inundations of the barbarous nations, the Roman Empire falling into ruins, and together with it all the knowledge of good learning fell also, and an amazing barbarity and ignorance poured in upon the western parts, and all the cultivation of the arts and wits withered away, as if they had been stricken with a pestilential vapour.[56]

This Renaissance denunciation of the early middle ages was succeeded by a lively account of the historians of early modern times. Wheare chose to give prominence to Cuspinianus (Johann Spieshaymer), who composed his humanist history of the German emperors at the court of Maximilian I, and to the two celebrated authors of histories of their own times, Paolo Giovio and Jacques-Auguste De Thou. Giovio began his narrative with the French invasion of Italy in 1494, De Thou with the first session of the Council of Trent in 1545. The latter was depicted as "the prince of historians of this age,"[57] whereas Giovio was unfairly criticized as an inventor of romance, an opinion Wheare borrowed from Bodin, who had stigmatized him as a poor imitator of Polybius when it came to writing current history.[58] Two other historians of this period received high praise. Philippe de Commines, the memorialist of Louis XI, was credited with discerning secret motives and concealed counsels, and, in the words of Lipsius, with delivering "salutary and rare precepts for our instruction, and that in a diffused way after the manner of Polybius."[59] Francesco Guicciardini, the statesman and historian of the Italian wars in the early sixteenth century, had been known from his *Ricordi* as a producer of apothegms and an admirer of Tacitus. Wheare cited the judgment of Lipsius, who called him "a wise and understanding writer who is able to make his readers such," and that of Bodin, who said that "he excelled all his equals in the judgment of great men, . . . and sprinkles grave sentences like salt."[60]

---

[56] Ibid., 260–1.   [57] Ibid., 128.
[58] Ibid., 127. Cf. Bodin, *Method*, 60–1. Eric Cochrane (*Historians and Historiography*, 369–77) praises Giovio for the care with which he collected his evidence, the skill with which he articulated it in terms of cause and effect, and the standards of objectivity he observed.
[59] Wheare, *Method and Order,* 130.   [60] Ibid., 128–9. Cf. Bodin, *Method*, 73.

The tone of *The Method and Order* changed again when the conflict-ing passions of Reformation and Counter-Reformation were at issue in the section on ecclesiastical history. Although he remained a secularist and a firm opponent of spiritual meddling in temporal affairs, Wheare was much more evenhanded than his earlier treatment of the saints and miracles of the early church might have suggested. He praised the history of the Reformation by Sleidan, but he admitted, as did Casaubon, that the Magdeburg Centuriators with whom Sleidan was associated had al-lowed their Protestant prejudices to lead them into error. He also ex-pressed admiration for Catholic scholars such as Sigonio and Mechior Cano, the Dominican counselor of Philip II of Spain. Cesare Baronio, who wrote his *Annales Ecclesiastici* to refute the Centuriators, was held in the highest esteem. Wheare called his *Annales* "a work which by the confession of the most learned men, and of Casaubon amongst them, is stupendious [*sic*] because that great person has in it digested the transac-tions of the whole Christian world."[61]

At the same time Wheare denounced ultramontane ideas that gave the pope authority over temporal rulers by "intoxicating readers with the pernicious doctrine of Hildebrand."[62] His model of antipapalist history was Paolo Sarpi's *History of the Council of Trent*, translated into English in 1620 by Savile's successor as warden of Merton, Sir Nicholas Brent. No other historical work was awarded such an accolade in *The Method and Order*. Wheare adapted the words of a second translator, Sir Adam Newton:

In the management of affairs, if you desire not only what was done or said discoursed, but also in what manner, and that when the event is told at the same time all the causes should be unfolded, and all the accidents which sprang from wisdom or folly, all these and a multitude of other such like things, which the great masters of history require in a good historian, he has performed so fully and exactly that in forming the history of one council, he hath represented all the perfections of history.[63]

Wheare's admiration for Sarpi and his selection of other unillusioned historians such as Commines, Guicciardini, and De Thou are as revealing as his respect for the sheer erudition of the greatest scholars of his day, Baronio, Casaubon, Lipsius, Scaliger, and Sigonio. He may at times have hidden his own opinions behind the views of others, but he always knew which critics to cite and which historians to choose for comment. Pruden-

---

[61] Wheare, *Method and Order*, 288–9. [62] Ibid., 292. [63] Ibid., 295.

tial lessons remained foremost in his thought, but they were usually linked, as in the case of Sarpi, with the importance of explaining cause and effect.

Wheare has been regarded as a classicist who had little time for English history. Even his translator, Edmund Bohun, wrote: "I am very much tempted to alter his title, and to call this piece *The History of Greek and Latin Historians.*"[64] This is unfair. Like Camden, Savile, and Selden, Wheare saw no inconsistency in combining his classical training with an interest in the English past. He devoted five chapters of *The Method and Order* to English history, although it is true they did not constitute the best informed part of his book. Moreover, he insisted that one should know one's own country first. At the start of the section on England he wrote, "In truth, to search out the great actions of other countries, and in the mean time despise our own, is a certain sign either of a most lazy inactivity or of a soft and unmanly delicacy."[65] He offered a similar sentiment when recommending John Speed's *Theatre of Great Britain* as essential reading for an English gentleman:

I do most earnestly exhort our young men, especially those who are of noble birth and intend to travel, that they would first peruse this beautiful *Theatre of Great Britain,* and run over all the parts of it before they travel into foreign countries or visit strange nations. . . . I think it preposterous, if not absurd to desire to see foreign and far distant things and in the mean time neglect what is nearer and at home. . . . Nor do I think there is any country under heaven which has so much reason to glory in the illustrious achievements of her children as ours hath.[66]

This passage also spoke of the unrivaled monuments and antiquities to be found in Britain – the only time when Wheare praised the antiquarian enterprise.

Degory Wheare had endorsed the skepticism of Scaliger toward the forgeries of Annio of Viterbo. He was equally dismissive of those myths of British antiquity that Selden called "intolerable anachronisms, incredible reports, and bardish impostures."[67] Thus he cited William of Newburgh, a near contemporary of Geoffrey of Monmouth in the twelfth century, who had discredited Geoffrey's tall stories about the Trojan Brutus and the sixty-eight kings who had supposedly ruled in the thousand years before Caesar's invasion. Wheare scorned "ridiculous inventions and fables of the ancient Britons," and deplored the practice of the

[64] Edmund Bohun, preface to *Method and Order* (unpaginated).
[65] Wheare, *Method and Order,* 132–3. [66] Ibid., 168–9.
[67] Cited in Levine, *Humanism and History,* 52.

chronicler who, "increasing them with his own additions and giving them the varnish of the Latin tongue, clothed them with the honourable name of an history." In the same passage he noted that John Twyne, the author of *De rebus Albionicis, Britannicis atque Anglicis* [Matters concerning Albion, Britain, and England, 1590], had called Geoffrey "the British Homer, the father of lies."[68] In fact, Wheare was rather like the early Tudor humanist, Polydore Vergil, who thought the Venerable Bede, William of Malmesbury, Matthew Paris, and Thomas Walsingham were the only reliable medieval writers.[69] At the same time, perhaps because Polydore Vergil was resented as a foreigner who had destroyed cherished English legends, Wheare called the Italian "a very faulty historian."[70] However, he was succinct and admiring on much Tudor historiography, such as Thomas More's *Richard III*, Francis Bacon's *Henry VII*, and Francis Godwin's *Annals of England under Henry VIII, Edward VI and Mary.* Camden's *Elizabeth*, of course, received special commendation.[71]

The two concluding parts of *The Method and Order* ("Concerning a Competent Reader" and "The Manner of Collecting the Fruits of History") reiterated the exemplar theme. History was "nothing but moral philosophy clothed in examples." The reader should have "an inclination and propensity of mind to follow what is good and shun what is evil, and turn all he meets with to his use and advantage, *for the principal end of history is practice, and not knowledge or contemplation.*"[72] Having said this, Wheare entered a controversy that forced him to reexamine the relationship among precept, example, and truth. The debate arose over an issue already mentioned, the question of exposing the unprepared reader to such evil actions as were manifest in histories like Tacitus's *Annals.*

The two texts that Wheare found most relevant to the assessment of "the competent reader" were the respective *artes historicae* of Keckermann and Voss. It has been noted that the former expressed a preference for Tacitus and the latter for Polybius, and yet, by some quirk of psychological inversion, the methods they advocated suggested the opposite. Keckermann believed that moral philosophy and politics were sciences with methodical rules like grammar, logic, and rhetoric. To expose the reader to historical examples without prior understanding of philosophical concepts and their relationship to each other was "a common and

---

[68] Wheare, *Method and Order*, 139–40.   [69] McKisack, *Medieval History*, 100.
[70] Wheare, *Method and Order*, 158.   [71] Ibid., 156–9.
[72] Ibid., 298–9. Italics in original.

very mischievous error and mistake for youth."[73] Voss, on the other hand, declared that "there is nothing of absurdity if one should choose to learn examples before precepts." Language could be learned without prior knowledge of grammatical rules. As Voss saw it, Keckermann should have distinguished between the writing and the reading of history, for only the former required prior understanding of "civil philosophy." A connected issue was the problem of historical explanation, and here each was more true to his preferred classical model. Voss, the follower of Polybius, maintained that there was a difference between a simple narrative of facts ("the naked and simple history of things") and "historical perfection which inquireth curiously into the circumstances and causes of events."[74] But Keckermann, the Tacitean, believed that the narration of actions should imply their explanation, and hence that both writer and reader must be trained in the art of inferring causative mechanisms.

Wheare sided with Keckermann. He did not think language could be properly learned without rules, and, in any case, the analogy between learning a language and political action was invalid. He asserted that "practical philosophy" was needed by both reader and writer of history, as some earlier authors of *artes historicae,* such as Uberto Foglietta, Sebastian Fox-Morcillo, and Giovanni Viperano, had stated.[75] Nor could a prudent reader ever be satified with a history that did not provide explicit causes, as Dionysius of Halicarnassus had shown among the ancients and Vives, and even Voss himself, had demonstrated among the moderns. Wheare also refuted a further argument from Voss invoking the opinion of Quintilian on the relative merits of Livy and Sallust. The whole debate about precept and example, and about the importance of explanation in history, seems to present the participants as anticipating some modern attitudes, but it has to be remembered that all who took part in these exchanges shared the desire to demonstrate the practical advantages history provided for life.

Mention has already been made of the manner in which the concluding part of *The Method and Order* cited the advice of Vives, Bodin, and Keckermann on how to extract aphorisms from history into a commonplace book, and of Wheare's allusions to existing collections of "the fruits of history" by Lipsius, Chokier, and Dallington. Wheare offered his own suggestions on how a reader might make useful observations on the

---

[73] Ibid., 300.   [74] Ibid., 301.
[75] Ibid., 304–5. These three were included in Wolf's collection.

Annals of Tacitus – not, interestingly enough, about the effects of corruption on public men, but about how to use stray remarks in the text to establish social status.[76] Another example of how to learn from history was taken from the story of Romulus and Remus as retold by Florus. Here the lesson concerned divine providence, but it gained sophistication by being compared with Herodotus's account of another foundation myth concerning a child exposed to die – this time that of Cyrus.[77]

An unexpected element in the final part of the book is Wheare's distinction between philology and philosophy. Philology was not confined to rhetorical niceties – nor even to the juridical interests of the legal humanists. It also applied to "ancient customs, all [the ancients'] rites, ceremonies and solemnities of what sort soever they are, and their sacred and civil places and actions, and the series of the monarchies and principal kingdoms of the world, the beginnings and migrations of families, the building of cities and the leading of colonies; all magnificent works, vast treasures, immense powers and stupendous prodigies."[78] This Foucault-like taxonomy had nothing to do with exemplar history; it was a list of curiosities, things worthy of remembrance for their own sake. If this antiquarian interest made a brief appearance at the end of *The Method and Order,* it was quickly counterbalanced by the definition of philosophy as generalizations or precepts about "polity and civil prudence." Such rules were intended as "monitors for the governing and regulating the lives of men in public and private, in peace and war."[79]

It remains to consider the fate of *The Method and Order* in the hands of its later editors. Nicholas Horseman, whose *Mantissa* was inserted in 1662 between the sections on civil and ecclesiastical history, was a Devonshire man, and a fellow of Corpus Christi at Oxford. His only other publication was *The Spiritual Bee,* in which he used a wide variety of historical and other anecdotes to illustrate particular morals. Lessons in humility, for example, were taught by the demagogue Agathocles, who after seizing power in Syracuse kept earthen pots on his table to remind him he had once been a potter, and by Queen Elizabeth, who heard a milkmaid singing while imprisoned during her sister's reign, and reflected that "peace and freedom of heart and contentment are more often to be found in a cottage than under a high and magnificent roof."[80] These

---

[76] Ibid., 337–8. [77] Ibid., 344. [78] Ibid., 322–3. [79] Ibid., 323.
[80] Nicholas Horseman, *The Spiritual Bee, or a miscellany of spiritual, historical, natural observations and occasional occurences applied in divine mediations* (London, 1662), 127, 124–5.

rather mawkish sentiments were quite unlike the opinions Horseman offered in his addition to *The Method and Order.*

Horseman provided detailed comment on the historians of the various peoples who had invaded the Roman Empire, and on the national kingdoms that grew from their settlements. Sometimes he duplicated material already covered by Wheare, but for the most part he added writers who had been overlooked. He had a preference for Renaissance historians, and said of Commines, Guicciardini, and Paolo Emilio, the humanist historian of France, that they were "so far from being inferior to Livy, Sallust and Tacitus that they might contest the precedence with them."[81] He had a quick eye for forgery, and noted that a history of the Franks from Troy to Clovis by a certain Hunibaldus was as spurious as "Berosus and the rest of those fabulous writers."[82] On the other hand he treated Huguenot polemics against Catherine de Medici as though they were objective history.

Horseman also discussed the historians of the Italian city-states. He found the histories of Florence by Leonardo Bruni and Poggio Bracciolini "mealy-mouthed in those things that relate to their intestine commotions, which is the reason Nicholas Machiavel assigns why he began his history from the foundation of the city, and not from the time the family of the Medicis obtained the sovereignty of that state."[83] He clearly had more than a sneaking respect for the realism of Machiavelli, whom Wheare had prudently omitted. However, he felt it necessary to offer a caution:

May I have leave here in passing to consider what may justly be thought of Machiavel. What he writes concerning princes and politics is so infectious that no man may approach this pest of mankind safely without the antidote of an *Antimachiavel,* or some other potent preservative. But then as to his *Florentine History,* he is not in that destitute of subtlety and an unusual prudence, and there are many things in it very rare and no less useful.[84]

Horseman's *Mantissa* broadened the scope of *The Method and Order* without betraying its intent. Such was also the general effect of the new passages added by the translator, Edmund Bohun, although his politics were not exactly in tune with those of the original author. Bohun was one of the most prominent Tory defenders of the policies of Charles II in the early 1680s.[85] He was widely known as an exponent of the rights of the

---

[81] Nicholas Horseman, *Mantissa,* in *Method and Order,* 182.   [82] Ibid., 203.
[83] Ibid., 222.   [84] Ibid.
[85] See Edmund Bohun, *An address to the free-man and free-holders of the nation* (London, 1682, 1683); and Bohun, *Reflections on a pamphlet styled a just and modest vindication*

Crown and an advocate of the doctrine of nonresistance, as exemplified in his *Defence of Sir Robert Filmer* (1684) and his edition of Filmer's *Patriarcha* (1685). It was, therefore, all the more surprising that his *History of the Desertion* (1689) should proclaim that William III had had just cause for war against James II, and that James had deserted the throne rather than abandon his plan to establish "absolutism and popery." Bohun reached this position because of his genuine fears for the Church of England, and chose to argue his case by a detailed history of events to demonstrate desertion, instead of directly undermining the principles he had earlier defended. There is an ironic parallel here with *The Lawfulness of Obeying the Present Government*, written forty years before by Wheare's friend, Francis Rous.

Bohun's version of *The Method and Order* was published in the same year as his edition of Filmer's *Patriarcha*. Inevitably there was a flavor of high-Tory sentiment in some of the additions Bohun made to Wheare's text. The historian of modern times that he most admired was the royalist Scot, Robert Johnston, author of *Historia Rerum Britannicarum, 1572–1628*, published in Amsterdam in 1655. In one of his additions where he quoted Johnston, Bohun described him as "a person in no way tainted with that Presbyterian leaven which then infected the Scottish nation almost generally, nor was he poisoned with the republican principles of the age."[86] Johnston had defended Mary Queen of Scots and denounced her execution. In similar vein, when describing histories of the civil war in an addition, Bohun launched into a diatribe against "the execrable murder of Charles the martyr."[87] This had not been the style of Degory Wheare, although Bohun seems nowhere to have distorted the sense of Wheare's Latin in his translation. Indeed, there were times when Bohun tried to catch the spirit of the original, as in one addition where Bohun cited the famous "sine ira et studio" passage from the *Annals* of Tacitus in a discussion of the distortion of truth under tyranny.[88]

Bohun kept up with the historical scholarship of his own day, and noted his reading in his personal diary.[89] He had some claim to being a historian in his own right. He composed a life of Bishop John Jewel to

---

of the proceedings of the two last parliaments (London, 1683). On Bohun see Mark Goldie, "Edmund Bohun and *Jus Gentium* in the Revolution Debate, 1689–1693," *Historical Journal* 20 (1977): 569–86.

[86] Bohun, in *Method and Order,* 164. A similar reference to Johnston occurs at pp. 177–8.
[87] Ibid., 165.   [88] Ibid., 176.
[89] *The Diary and Autobiography of Edmund Bohun Esq.,* ed. S. Wilton Rix (privately printed, 1853).

accompany his translation of Jewel's *Apologia pro ecclesia Anglicana* [Apology for the Church of England], and he wrote a continuation of Sleidan's *History of the Reformation,* which he also translated. Although it was avowedly derived from Robert Johnston, Bohun's best-known history was his *Character of Queen Elizabeth,* dedicated to Queen Mary in 1693. "History," he wrote in the preface, "is my beloved study. With it I would, if I had it in my power, grow old and die." He went on to remark, after the Tacitean manner: "Even princes themselves do borrow from history those counsels and assistances they shall hardly gain from courtiers and ministers."[90] Bohun was also the compiler of the highly successful *Geographical Dictionary,* which he claimed was indispensable for the understanding of ancient and modern history.

In the preface Bohun wrote for *The Method and Order* he compared it with the writings on history of Lipsius and Voss and declared it "the best in its kind that ever was yet published." The additions he made were intended to fill gaps in Wheare's list of historians of England, and especially to cover works published since the original author's death in 1647. He described a number of medieval chroniclers omitted in the Latin text, including Ingulph of Croyland, whose chronicle he failed to recognize as a forgery.[91] He also mentioned several recent antiquarians, such as Daniel Langhorne, who had produced a worthy study of Anglo-Saxon antiquities but still gave credence to the legends of Arthur, and Roger Sheringham, whose account of British origins still included the Trojans.[92] Another name to be added was that of Aylet Samme, the author of *Britannia antiqua illustrata* [Ancient Britain illustrated, 1676] and promoter of belief in Phoenician influence in pre-Roman Britain.[93] All this gave a stronger antiquarian slant to the section on English history, but this is scarcely surprising since Bohun was living through the great revival of English antiquarianism. To some extent this impression was offset by Bohun's inclusion of Jacobean "politick" historians and historians of the

[90] William Nicholson described it in *The English Historical Library* (London, 1714) as "a short system of her policies offered to our late sovereign and excellent Queen by the ingenious Edmund Bohun Esquire" (87).

[91] Bohun, preface to *Method and Order* (unpaginated); *Method and Order,* 149–55. On the exposure of Ingulph see David C. Douglas, *English Scholars* (London: Jonathan Cape, 1939), 219.

[92] Bohun, in *Method and Order,* 135. The relevant works are Langhorne, *Chronicon regum anglorum . . . ab Hengisto rege primo ad Heptarchiae finem* (London, 1679), and Sheringham, *De Anglorum gentis origine disceptatio* (London, 1670). See T. D. Kendrick, *British Antiquity* (London: Methuen, 1950), 161.

[93] Bohun, in *Method and Order,* 171. See Douglas, *English Scholars,* 68.

civil war.[94] He also listed Sir Richard Baker's *Chronicle of the Kings of England* (1643), which contained a catalogue of historians ranging from Gildas in the sixth century to Thomas Fuller, who had lived to see the restoration of Charles II.[95]

In the second, 1694 edition of the English *Method and Order,* Bohun inserted a reference to work on the chronology of the primitive church by Henry Dodwell,[96] whose "Invitation to gentlemen to acquaint themselves with ancient history" now served as a preface to Wheare's book. Dodwell had become Camden Professor in 1688, but was deprived three years later because his high-Anglican principles prevented his taking the oath of allegiance to William and Mary. Edward Gibbon was to testify to his "immense learning" when making a note in his journal on Dodwell's *Annales Quintilianaei.*[97] Dodwell's learning and reputation make it the more surprising to a modern mind that his "Invitation" was more crassly utilitarian than anything Wheare had written.

Like Bohun, Dodwell testified to the merits of *The Method and Order,* and pointed out that it had been intended merely to reinforce Wheare's lectures for students. His own "Invitation" was meant to show gentlemen the practical uses of historical example in politics and war. He thought that English farmers should read Vergil's *Georgics,* whereas architects should read Vitruvius. "And as other instances," he continued, "so particular this of history, it is much more fitted for the use of an active than a studious life, and therefore much more useful for gentlemen than scholars."[98] Dodwell went on to describe the ideals of the "practical Pythagoreans," whom he held responsible for the achievements of the Macedonian kings, and whose educational doctrines of discipline and control he likened to those of the Jesuits. In providing some modern examples of how to apply lessons from history, he compared the success of Lord Mountjoy, "a studious bookish man," in putting down Tyrone's Irish rebellion with the actions of other commanders, such as Essex and Sir John Norris. He

[94] Bohun, in *Method and Order,* 175–6.
[95] Ibid. See Sir R. Baker, *A Chronicle of the Kings of England from the Time of the Romans' Government unto the Reign of Our Sovereign Lord King Charles* (London, 1643), 1–93.
[96] Bohun, in *Method and Order,* 259.
[97] *The Miscellaneous Works of Edward Gibbon Esquire,* ed. John Lord Sheffield (London: B. Blake, 1837), 431. Gibbon's praise had, however, a sting in the tail, for he went on to write: "The worst of this author is his method and style; the one perplexed beyond imagination, the other negligent to a degree of barbarism."
[98] Dodwell, "Invitation to gentlemen to acquaint themselves with ancient history" (unpaginated), in *Method and Order.*

also suggested that if modern strategists followed the example of Aemilius Paulus, the Roman victor over Macedon at Pydna, they would bring the armies of Louis XIV in the Netherlands to open battle, rather than wasting their strength in siege warfare. This was practical advice indeed!

By the start of the eighteenth century *The Method and Order* was a much larger and more detailed work than Wheare had conceived when he first prepared it for his students. He himself had begun its expansion in 1635. Then Horseman had broadened its terms of reference, Bohun had brought it up to date, and Dodwell had reaffirmed and intensified its message "as philosophy teaching by example." From the first *The Method and Order* had reflected within the genre of the *ars historica* those tensions delineated by Patrizzi. The implications of Cicero's "lux veritatis" contended with those of his belief in history as the "magistra vitae," even though the practitioners of the art insisted that examples must be true in order to persuade. As against the advocates of the need to know philosophical precepts before grasping the sense of particular examples, the supporters of the innate force of historical example as a spur to action still held their ground. Particular truth in history had been complicated by the need to provide the whole truth encompassing motives and accidental or unforeseen forces, and hence cause and effect. The *ars historica* had entered a stage of transition when Bodin had proposed a Polybian method of comparative generalization, but the specter of Pyrrhonic doubt still lurked in the background. Degory Wheare had included all these elements in *The Method and Order*, and had even retained the flavor of classical rhetoric. It is true, of course, that exemplar history survived and reached a kind of culmination in Bolingbroke's *Letters on the Study and Use of History*, but this work was not in the tradition of the *ars historica*. Wheare could never have written: "Ancient history ... is quite unfit ... to answer the ends that every reasonable man should propose to himself." Nor could he have said: "To be learned about them [the ages before early modern times] is a ridiculous affectation in any man who means to be useful to the present age."[99] In combining, and trying to reconcile, the discordant elements of the *ars historica*, *The Method and Order* was the last of its kind.

[99] Lord Bolingbroke, *Letters on the Study and Use of History*, letters 4 and 6, in *Historical Writings*, ed. Isaac Kramnick (Chicago: University of Chicago Press, 1972), 49, 83.

3

Truth, lies, and fiction in sixteenth-century
Protestant historiography

PATRICK COLLINSON

I

John Foxe (and notwithstanding some glancing references to John Bale
and Miles Coverdale, Foxe will serve on this occasion as shorthand for
"sixteenth-century historiography") had a great deal to say on the subject of "truth." In a sense he wrote about nothing else. But he was
accused by his religious opponents of telling lies on an unprecedented
scale. And if he did not deliberately propagate fictions, in the sense of
inventing his stories, he wove his material into forms that were as fictive
as they were factual. Like his friend and mentor, Bale, he was a mythmaker, even, it has been said, "the prince of English historical myth-
makers,"[1] which is not to say that he was not also a great historian.
Jane Austen wondered why history was so dull, considering that so
much of it was made up. One could say that what makes Foxe's history
so arresting is that it is partly made up, or, given his models and materials, makes itself up.

In introducing a section of his *Acts and Monuments* that consists of
little more than a collection of original documents of the early German
and Swiss Reformations (presented with a minimum of commentary),
Foxe wrote that he was giving readers "a sight thereof," so that they
would not believe the "smooth talk or pretensed persuasions of men,"
especially in church matters, "unless they carry with them the simplicity

---

Among the many scholars who have helped me in my limited understanding of John Foxe
and the related matters discussed in this essay, I should like to single out Damian Nussbaum
and Alexandra Walsham.
[1] Leslie P. Fairfield, *John Bale, Mythmaker for the English Reformation* (West Lafayette,
Ind.: Purdue University Press, 1976), especially page 119; Glanmor Williams, *Reformation Views of Church History* (London, 1970), 62.

of plain truth."[2] That was to denigrate rhetoric and to equate "plain truth," like some sixteenth-century Ranke, with unadorned documents, to tell the story as it actually (or evidently) was. The anachronism is obvious and intentional. Foxe was not Ranke. So what did sixteenth-century historiography mean by the simple or plain truth?

In approaching the question of truth, and of different orders or kinds of truth, as well as the distinctions to be made between truth and falsehood, fact and fiction, it is as convenient as it is thoroughly unoriginal to begin with Sir Philip Sidney's *Apologie for Poetrie,* a text itself not noted for its originality and greatly indebted to the classic definitional statements of Aristotle and Cicero. Yet Sidney states the issues so neatly that even his intended or unintended misunderstandings and oversimplifications give us the best of all purchases on the subject.[3] According to Sidney, history claimed to stand for truth and the practical and ethical value of historical truth, what Foxe in one of his prefaces called "The Utility of This Story," a past both true and usable. Aristotle was primarily responsible for the distinction between history, an account of real events, and fiction, and Cicero wrote that according to the somewhat undeveloped capacities of Roman (rather than Greek) historiography, "it is enough that the man should not be a liar" [satis est, non esse mendacem]. "For who does not know history's first law to be that an author must not dare to tell anything but the truth? And its second that he must make bold to tell the whole truth?"[4] So William Camden, in the preface to his *Annales of Elizabeth,* which in its 1625 English edition would be called *The true and royall history of Elizabeth Queen of England,* wrote: "Which Truth to take from History, is nothing else but, as it were, to pluck out the Eyes of the beautifullest Creature in the world; and, in stead of wholesome Liquor, to offer a Draught of Poison to the Readers Minds" – while going on to explain that he was not constrained to tell the whole truth: "Things secret and abtruse I have not pried into."[5] Sidney was ironically impressed by Cicero's austere standard of factual

---

[2] *The Acts and Monuments of John Foxe,* ed. G. Townsend and S. R. Cattley (London: R. B. Seeley and W. Burnside, vol. 1, 1841, vols. 2–4, 1837, vols. 5–7, 1838, vol. 8, 1839), 4:295.

[3] Sir Philip Sidney, *An Apology for Poetry or the Defence of Poesy,* ed. G. Shepherd (London: Nelson, 1965), 105–12. For an excellent discussion of the issues traversed by Sidney, but more subtly by a number of other sixteenth-century authors, see William Nelson, *Fact or Fiction, the Dilemma of the Renaissance Storyteller* (Cambridge, Mass.: Harvard University Press, 1973), 49–55.

[4] Cicero *De oratore* 2.13.62.

[5] William Camden, *The History of the Most Renowned and Virtuous Princess Elizabeth Late Queen of England,* ed. and abr. Wallace T. MacCaffrey (Chicago: University of Chicago Press, 1970), 4–5.

accuracy. The lips of historiographers "sound of things done," Sidney wrote, and "verity" is "written in their foreheads." And Sidney was skeptical withal, for when all was said and done, the historian authorized himself for the most part on other historians (nothing changes!), "whose greatest authorities are built upon the notable foundation of hearsay."[6]

When Sidney questioned the usefulness of history, deflating the historian who claimed to be *testis temporum, vita memoriae, nuncia vetustatis*, he was of course repeating for the umpteenth but by no means the last time an old Ciceronian maxim. In 1599, the young John Hayward would introduce his *Life and Raigne of King Henrie IIII* with the familiar words: "Heereupon Cicero doeth rightly call history the witnesse of times, the light of truth, the life of memory, and the messenger of antiquity. . . . Neyther is that the least benefit of history, that it preserveth eternally both the glory of good men and shame of evill."[7] Thomas Blundeville, in his pioneering *The true order and methode of wrytinge and reading histories* (1574), did not know whether to deride or pity the folly of those who, "having consumed all theyre lyfe tyme in hystories," in the end knew nothing except trivial and useless dates, genealogies, "and such lyke stuff."[8]

But so far as Sidney was concerned, the historian could not but be useless, since he was the ineluctable prisoner of his facts, "tied, not to what should be, but to what is, the particular truth of things and not to the general reason of things." If it were only a matter of having a story told truly rather than falsely, one would of course choose the truth, as with the commissioning of a portrait. No one prefers a poor likeness. But if the question be one of use or learning, then fictions are "more doctrinable," for only fiction is free to favor virtue. The historian, "being captived to the truth of a foolish world, is many times a terror from well-doing, and an encouragement to unbridled wickedness."[9] Sidney might have been thinking of Sir Thomas More's *History of King Richard III*, and of the doubts about its ethically instructive value that may have inclined More to leave that annal of tyranny and unbridled wickedness incomplete.[10]

---

[6] Sidney, *Apology*, 97, 105.
[7] *The First and Second Parts of John Hayward's* The Life and Raigne of King Henrie IIII, ed. John J. Manning, Camden 4th ser. 42 (London, 1991), 63.
[8] Cited in D. R. Woolf, *The Idea of History in Early Stuart England: Erudition, Ideology and "The Light of Truth" from the Accession of James I to the Civil War* (Toronto: University of Toronto Press, 1990), 4–5.
[9] Sidney, *Apology*, 107, 109–11.
[10] See Professor Joseph Levine's essay elsewhere in this volume; and Alistair Foxe, "Thomas More and Tudor Historiography: *The History of King Richard III*," in *Politics*

Sidney knew full well, if only because Cicero had said it, that the bare distinction between historical fact and poetical fiction misrepresents what historians actually do. Even historiographers, he wrote, "have been glad to borrow both fashion and perchance weight of poets," especially since, as he suggested in a satirical passage that deliberately confused the distinct functions of antiquarians and historians, authorities and sources are often inadequate and uncertain. So it was that historians put speeches into the mouths of their characters "which it is certain they never pronounced." If Sidney had been widely read, more widely than he was, he would have known that the relation of the fictive and nonfictive in the classical discussion of such matters was more complex than his representation of them.[11] Cicero had taught that to tell the truth was indeed the foundation of history, but that the complete structure depended as much on the language of presentation as on material content: "Ipse autem exaedificatio posita est in rebus et verbis." This was said in a treatise whose subject was rhetoric, *De oratore,* where history was classified as none other than a branch of rhetoric. "Videstine, quantum munus sit oratoris historia?" [Do you not see to what an extent history is the business of the rhetorician?][12]

These commonplaces have a particular resonance with what will concern us in the bulk of this essay. But the conventions of Sidney's epideictic rhetoric prevented him from noticing how far these considerations, while serving his purpose to disparage history, simultaneously undermined his argument, which depended upon too rigid a distinction between history and fiction. Nevertheless, the two senses of truth with which Sidney dealt are fundamental to my argument. What is factually true, "the particular truth of things," may be at odds with what is true in another and perhaps higher sense, the sense that the Apostle Paul had in mind when he wrote in Philippians 4.8: "Whatsoever things are true . . . whatsoever things are of good report . . . think on these things."

Thomas Becon, a copious first-generation Protestant writer, defined truth as "Christ himself, the word of God," but added: "There is also a civil truth or verity . . . and that is when with that which is said the thing

---

and Literature in the Reigns of Henry VII and Henry VIII (Oxford: Basil Blackwell, 1989), 108–27.

[11] Sidney, *Apology,* 97. William Nelson comments on "two conflicting attitudes: on the one hand, the insistence of the Judaeo-Christian tradition on veritable reports, testified to as by witnesses in a courtroom; on the other, a sense that in tales of the past truth mattered little in comparison with edification or even entertainment." *Fact or Fiction,* 27.

[12] Cicero *De oratore* 2.14.62.

appeareth, and when we find words agreeing with the thing itself." Sidney professed to believe that there must be a conflict between these two senses of truth. John Foxe's huge enterprise in its entirety depended upon a denial of any such conflict.[13]

How do we account for Sidney's defensiveness? Was it more than a rhetorical pose? If we understand "poetry" in its modern sense, it may seem odd that Sidney should write of "this now scorned skill." But if he is understood to have written of fiction, then indeed the historian of literary genres, aware of the slow gestation of the English novel through the almost two centuries separating *Beware the Cat* from *Pamela,* may share with Sidney some sense of fiction's arrested development. If Sidney had chosen to consider the problem at the level of customer and readership mentalities, he would have found in his own age ample evidence of the satisfaction derived from stories that were either factual or purported to be factual, over against the unashamedly fictive. This preference may have a deep-seated and perennial quality to it. Ghost stories told in darkened school dormitories lose their point if they are not half believed as true stories; so too with magazines like *True Stories,* the improbable but always "true" stories I read in my youth in *Wide World Magazine,* and with newspaper columns like "Strange But True" or "Ripley's Believe It or Not." In Britain, the willingly gullible buy a paper (it claims to be a newspaper) with headlines like "World War II Bomber Found on Moon." Huge sums are spent on supposedly "authentic" works of antique art, and sometimes good money is thrown after bad in efforts to prove, or disprove, their authenticity, leading to reflections on "our obsession with originality and oldness." The pleasing fiction of a forgery, however cunningly contrived, has a limited value.[14]

One might make a similar point about the resurrection narratives in the New Testament, or about the Book of Mormon, prefaced as it is with the testimonies of witnesses who had seen and "hefted" with their

---

[13] The passage from Becon refers to *Prayers and Other Pieces of Thomas Becon,* ed. J. Ayre, Parker Society (Cambridge: Cambridge University Press, 1844), 604. Michael McKeon draws attention to a passage in Foxe in which "the two kinds of truth" are "suddenly severed": "To express every minute of matter in every story occurent, what story-writer in all the world is able to perform it?" Foxe insisted that he had better and higher things to do. *The Origins of the English Novel* (Baltimore and London: Johns Hopkins University Press, 1987), 93; citing *Acts and Monuments of Foxe.*

[14] Marion True et al., *The Getty Kouros Colloquium Athens, 25–27 May 1992* (Malibu, 1993); reviewed, *Times Literary Supplement,* 22 October 1993. On Sidney's defensive attitude toward "poor Poetry," see *Apology,* 95–6 and *passim;* and on its implications, see Nelson, *Fact or Fiction.*

hands the very gold plates from which Joseph Smith by mysterious means derived the text. There are sophisticated accounts of both Christianity and Mormonism that hold their doctrines and aspirations to be "true," more or less regardless of the literal truth of the historical events on which they are founded. However, neither Christianity nor Mormonism would be likely to survive the discrediting to universal satisfaction of its historical-factual credentials, for all that Sidney suggests that the New Testament might well be more "doctrinable" if it were fiction than if it consisted of an accurate, unadorned account of certain historical facts.

The case as it concerns sixteenth-century literary and subliterary tastes and genres can be illustrated at random from the titles of relatively ephemeral products of the Elizabethan and early Stuart press, in which reports, however improbable and unreliable, are presented to the gullible reader as "true" and fully attested;[15] and, said Ben Jonson (in *The Staple of News*) "no syllable of truth in them." The subject may be wonders and monsters, as with *The true description of two monsterous chyldren born at Herne in Kent,* a ballad of 1565; or remarkable "providences," such as *A true relation of two most strange accidents lately happening at Chagford* (1618); murders – *A true report of the murther committed in the house of Sir J. Bowes* (1607), *The lamentable and true tragedie of M. Arden of Faversham* (1592); foreign wars – *A brief and true rehersall of the victory which the protestantes of Holland had against the duke of Alba* (1573); voyages and discoveries – *A true discourse of the late voyage of discoverie: for finding a passage to Cathaya* (1578), *A briefe and true relation of the discoverie of the north Part of Virginia* (1602); even romantic fiction – *The true history of the tragick loves of Hipolito and Isabella, Neapolitans, Englished* (1628). Groups of men in the alehouse who greeted new arrivals from London with "what news?" also validated their own reports with "if what I say be not true." This was called for, given the notorious unreliability of "news." Joseph Mede of Cambridge, who received and passed on the news on a regular basis, could write of "the newes of the day among our Speculatives in Paules" (i.e., the nave or "walk" of St. Paul's Cathedral) and frequently reported that such news as the death of Spinola or the duke of Buckingham's departure for the Ile de

---

[15] The "epistemological stance" of ballad texts, in which "strange but true" almost becomes "strange, therefore true," is discussed in McKeon, *Origins,* 46–8. See also Lennard J. Davis, *Factual Fictions: The Origins of the English Novel* (New York: Columbia University Press, 1983), 47–56.

Rhé had proved false. But the fear of false rumor implied the high premium placed on accuracy. Preachers who used the "if what I say be not true" formula in the pulpit were being indecorous and could find themselves reported in jest books, like the "very ridiculous" minister of Halstead in Essex, William Glibery, who used to say "if what I say be not true ye may hang me for the veriest knave in Halstead." For Scripture was self-authenticating, requiring no such warranties as to its truth. One implication of the utterly authentic scriptural norm was a process of self-censorship that tended to inhibit any publication that, far from being "true," was unashamedly fictional.[16]

In this broad sense, all histories published in the sixteenth century claimed to be true, even while the distinction between "history" and "story" was still blurred, the tales of Arthur being presented as history, even by those who admitted that if not entirely false they contained substantial elements of the mythical.[17] One might suppose that when it was reported, in the early-seventeenth-century, that men read Foxe's *Book of Martyrs* (as *Acts and Monuments* was popularly called) as "a book of credit, next to the book of God," that was to accord to Foxe a special, near-scriptural status. But secular chronicles, too, were "credited" in the same way, Holinshed's *Chronicles* calling itself, and in princi-

---

16 Joseph Mede's news letters are in British Library, MSS Harleian 389, 390, the remark about "our Speculatives" occurring on fol. 277r of Harl. 390. John Rastell's *A. C Mery Talys* (1526) includes (sigs. Dii–Diiv) the story of the Warwickshire preacher who told his auditory: "Yf you beleue me not, then for a more suerte & suffycyent auctoryte, go your way to Coventre, and there ye shall se them all played in Corpus Cristi playe." Preaching in Cambridge in 1627, Thomas Edwards, the future author of *Gangraena*, affirmed: "If all this be not true, then this book (clapping his hand upon the holy Bible) is full of falshoods, and God himself is a lyar, and Christ himselfe a deceiver"; *Cambridge University Transactions During the Puritan Controversies of the 15th and 17th Centuries*, ed. J. Heywood and T. Wright (London, 1854), 2:362. Both preachers were in breach of pulpit decorum. For Glibery's preaching, see Public Record Office, S.P. 12/159/27. He is called "a verie ridiculous preacher" in the Puritan survey of the ministry in Essex, *The Seconde Parte of a Register,* ed. Albert Peel (Cambridge: Cambridge University Press, 1915), 2.163. Glibery finished up in the pages of Martin Marprelate and may have given us our word "glib." See my essay, "Ecclesiastical Vitriol: Satire and the Construction of Puritanism," in *The Reign of Elizabeth I,* ed. John Guy (Cambridge: Cambridge University Press, 1995), 150–70. On the Bible as "the touchstone by which all other tales of the past must be tested," see Nelson, *Fact or Fiction,* 20–1.

17 See, for example, Christopher Middleton, *The Famous Historie of Chinon of England, with his strange adventures for the love of Celestina daughter to Lewis King of Fraunce* (1597), ed. W. E. Mead, Early English Text Society, o.s. 165 (1925). Michael McKeon points out that as late as the late seventeenth century, not even in the catalogs of the book trade was any clear distinction drawn between (on our terms) "history" and fiction, "another sort of Historyes which are called *Romances*." However, in this state of "generic chaos," typical of Renaissance literary culture, the distinction was perfectly accessible and just as often made. McKeon, *Origins,* 26–8.

ple all chronicles, books of "credit."[18] Claims to be credited were built
into virtually every publication asserting historical status. Thus, George
Cavendish, in his *Thomas Wolsey, late Cardinall. his lyffe and deathe,*
refers in his preface to the "malycious ontrowthe of others," and offers to
replace untruth with truth. "Therfore I commyt the treuthe to hym that
knowyth all trouthe." The opening words of the text that follows are:
"Trewthe it ys." That Cavendish ends his life of Wolsey with the story of
how he, the author, lied to the king and the council about the cardinal's
last words following the advice of an experienced courtier – "if ye tell
them the treuthe . . . you should undo yorself" – is a complicating and
enriching circumstance, for it suggests that truth is a thing of onionlike
layers.[19]

Was Cavendish telling the truth about his lie? It was unusual to admit
to a falsehood. In the first Elizabethan edition of Foxe's *Acts and Monuments* (1563), the Marian martyr John Careless would not admit to his
judges that there were any serious doctrinal differences among the heretics confined in the various London prisons. Asked whether he knew the
notorious antipredestinarian free-willer Henry Hart, he denied it. "But
yet I lied falsely, for I knew him indeed and his qualities too well." In all
subsequent editions, Careless's frank admission was suppressed, presumably as incompatible with the truth that the martyrs were supposed to
have expressed in all their speeches and actions. And that too was a kind
of lie.[20] Whether it could ever be lawful to tell a lie in a good cause had
been debated by St. Augustine and St. Jerome, and the issue was never far
away from the religious controversies of the sixteenth century, as Perez
Zagorin has shown.[21] Sometimes only a lie could preserve the truth.

How much did truth matter? Daniel Woolf suggests that what was

---

[18] "Next unto the holie scripture, chronicles do carry credit." Raphael Holinshed, *The
firste volume of the Chronicles of England, Scotlande, and Irelande* (London, 1577),
766.

[19] *The Life and Death of Cardinal Wolsey by George Cavendish,* ed. R. S. Sylvester, Early
English Text Society, 243 (1959), 4, 183–6. Judith H. Anderson comments: "The meaning of *truth* alters and evolves in this biography." *Biographical Truth: The Representation of Historical Persons in Tudor-Stuart Writing* (New Haven: Yale University Press,
1984), 27–39.

[20] *Acts and Monuments of Foxe,* 8:164–6. See also Patrick Collinson, "Truth and Legend:
The Veracity of Foxe's *Book of Martyrs,*" in *Clio's Mirror: Historiography in Britain
and the Netherlands* 8, ed. A. C. Duke and C. A. Tamse (Zutphen, Netherlands: De
Walburg Pers, 1985), 44; reprinted in Patrick Collinson, *Elizabethan Essays* (London:
Hambeldon Press, 1994), 169.

[21] Perez Zagorin, *Ways of Lying: Dissimulation, Persecution and Conformity in Early
Modern Europe* (Cambridge, Mass.: Harvard University Press, 1990).

lacking in Tudor and early Stuart historiography was "a reason for divergent points of view," since "historical narrative had yet to be firmly tied to the wagon of ideological and political conflict."[22] That undervalues the passions aroused throughout the sixteenth century by conflicting accounts of national origins, and in particular by the question of the British History. This version of the island's story had been immortalized and to a great extent fabricated in the twelfth century by Geoffrey of Monmouth's *Historia regum Britanniae,* an excellent example, with all its prolific Arthurian progeny and many afterlives, of the difficulty of defining a history as distinct from a romance in anything like modern terms. We cannot even be certain that Geoffrey was not having his joke at the expense of the past, intentionally but covertly writing a kind of fiction. The later Middle Ages and Renaissance would witness many such sportive literary exercises, one of them called *Utopia.* Polydore Vergil said some caustic things about Geoffrey and conjured up the ghost of Gildas to exorcise him. John Leland was duly angry with Polydore, as was the Welsh antiquary Humphrey Llwyd, who also attacked the rival account of Scottish origins purveyed by Hector Boece and later by George Buchanan. But it is true that many of the authors who ventured into this minefield wrote within the polite convention of referring judgment in the matter to the reader and declining to adopt a rigid position in a case so uncertain. Even Camden wrote that he would be the last to stand in the way of anyone who might want to believe in the story of Brutus and his Trojans: "For mine owne parte, let Brutus be taken for the father, and founder of the British nation. I will not be of a contrarie minde," adding later, "I refer the matter full and whole to the Senate of Antiquaries, for to be decided."[23]

In the extensive learned apparatus that he contributed to Michael Drayton's prodigious chorographical and hydrological poem, *Poly-Olbion,* John Selden gently reprehended the credence that the poet still attached to the British History, although he knew full well that part of Drayton's motive was to be as tactful as possible to the Welsh, those "Cambro-Britons" who certainly had to be allowed to believe such things, whether true or not.[24]

---

[22] Woolf, *The Idea of History,* 35.
[23] William Camden, *Britain* (London, 1610), 6–8.
[24] Michael Drayton, *Poly-Olbion: Or a chorographical description of Great Britain . . . digested in a poem* (London, 1613–22).

II

Only very occasionally was John Foxe willing in this fashion to defer to
the indifferent judgment of his readers. A rare example of his use of this
trope concerns the ecclesiastical miracles recorded by the early church
historian Eusebius, "wherof let every reader use his own judgement."[25] It
was fundamental to Foxe's essentially polemical purpose on no account
to condescend to historical ignorance or condone false notions about the
past. In a preface addressed to the queen, he explained that he wrote in
English for the sake of the common reader who was wrapped in blind-
ness, all "for wanting the light of history." In another preface he wrote:

For, first, to see the simple flock of Christ, especially the unlearned sort, so
miserably abused, and all for ignorance of history, not knowing the course of
times and true descent of the church, it pitied me that this part of diligence had so
long been unsupplied in this my-country church of England.[26]

So, relatively speaking, Woolf is not wrong to suggest that the arena of
ecclesiastical history represents an exceptional case in sixteenth- and
early-seventeenth-century historiography, exceptional that is for involving extreme ideological conflict over competing versions of truth. For in
this arena, the question of truth had an urgent life-and-death quality.
Indeed, on the distinction between truth and error lay matters beyond life
and death and of transcendent importance. So Bishop Latimer spoke of
"peace" as a "goodly word," and "unity" as a "fair thing." "[But] peace
ought not to be redeemed . . . with the loss of the truth; that we should
seek peace so much, that we should lose the truth of God's word." The
Elizabethan Catholic controversialist Thomas Stapleton was no less willing to pay the price of truth: "Truth purchaseth hatred." "Therefore,"
Latimer went on,

whereas ye pray for agreement both in the truth and in uttering of the truth, when
shall that be, as long as we will not hear the truth, but disquiet with crafty
countenance the preachers of the truth, because they reprove our evilness with the
truth. And to say the truth, better it were to have a deformity in preaching, so that
some would preach the truth of God.[27]

[25] *Acts and Monuments of Foxe,* 1:272; cited in John R. Knott, *Discourses of Martyrdom
in English Literature, 1563–1694* (Cambridge: Cambridge University Press, 1993), 42.
[26] *Acts and Monuments of Foxe,* 1:504, 514.
[27] Both passages from Latimer refer to *Sermons of Hugh Latimer,* ed. G. E. Corrie, Parker
Society (Cambridge: Cambridge University Press, 1844), 487. Stapleton's remark appears in the epistle introducing his translation of *The History of the Church of England
Compiled by the Venerable Bede* (Antwerp, 1565). Cited hereafter as Stapleton, epistle.

Here were seven "truth's" in seventy words!

Ecclestiastical historiography during this period saw fierce conflicts. There were fierce conflicts over truth, not only between parties but within parties and their minds and consciences. Bishop Jewel observed that truth and falsehood were near neighbors: "The utter porch of the one is like the porch of the other; yet their way is contrary; the one leadeth to life; the other leadeth to death; they differ little to the shew. . . . Thereby it happeneth that men be deceived; they call evil good, falsehood truth."[28]

Thomas Harding, the Elizabethan Catholic apologist with whom Jewel had a great controversy, and who attacked Foxe, had begun, like Jewel, as the Protestant disciple of Peter Martyr. Archbishop Cranmer was forever invoking truth. Henry VIII told him, "For suerlie I reckon that you will tell me the truth." But in the last hours of his life, Cranmer first recanted the beliefs of his religious maturity as heresies, prefacing his recantation with "now is time and place to say truth"; he then renounced his recantations, with remorse for having acted "contrary to my conscience and the truthe."[29] Foxe wrote to make the distinction between truth and error objective and unmistakable, in the tribunal of history.

The "plain" or "simple" truth to which Protestants were attached had a different appearance from the truth professed by Catholic controversialists. It belonged to a set of values that identified purity with simplicity and plainness and rejected what were peceived as Catholicism's elaborate, man-made ritual and theatrical excess. Protestants, as John King has observed, rejected any substitution of artifice for truth.[30] The truth that was simplicity itself was biblical truth, which was held to be literal and self-evident, and which was best articulated in the plain style of Tyndale's biblical mode and Latimer's pulpit voice, as well as in the plain shepherd's tongue that Spenser appropriated from the fourteenth century. Of course the so-called plain style was never artless. *Artis celare artem.* Nicholas Udall wrote of the English version of Erasmus's New Testament *Paraphrases:* "For divinitie, lyke as it loveth no cloking, but loveth to be simple and playn, so doth it not refuse eloquence, if the same come without injurie or violacion of the truth." Erasmus's translators had

---

[28] *The Works of John Jewel,* ed. J. Ayre 4, Parker Society (Cambridge, 1850), 1167.

[29] See also Patrick Collinson, "Thomas Cranmer," in *The English Religious Tradition and the Genius of Anglicanism,* ed. G. Rowell (Wantage: Icon Press, 1992), 79–103.

[30] John N. King, *English Reformation Literature: The Tudor Origins of the Protestant Tradition* (Princeton: Princeton University Press, 1982), 138–60, and passim.

eschewed elegance of speech for "a plain style," so that "rude and unlettred people" should not be deprived of a true understanding.[31]

In Foxe, style and language are inseparable from the populist strategy that aimed the book at the more or less common people who to such a conspicuous extent throng the pages, both as martyrs and spectators of martyrdom. Hence all those extremely vivid illustrations, no less than 160 of them in the 1570 edition. Yet there is a tension between this almost "tabloid" presentation and the extreme bulk, and expense, of the text illustrated, for how many of the "rude and unlettred" had access to a book costing half a year's wages? The word "strategy," then, is used advisedly, and to indicate another of Foxe's rhetorical tropes. Whether the English Reformation really enjoyed the popular basis that the trope regularly invokes is a question that has divided recent historians of those events, the so-called revisionists and their allegedly Whiggish opponents. If the revisionists are right in their denial that the Reformation was a demotic affair, then the blame may be laid on Foxe, who, the revisionists say, their opponents follow all too faithfully.[32]

Foxe did not claim inerrancy for his book in every detail (many modern historians have been less modest about their accomplishments), but he did regard the version of ecclesiastical history that it presented as in all essential respects true. His purpose was "to open the plain truth of times lying long hid in obscure darkness of antiquity." Foxe's own question, however – "But what is in this world so ... true that it will not be contraried?" – anticipated his critics. For Foxe's Catholic detractors, his book was not some curate's egg, good and bad in parts. It was all bad, consisting entirely of lies, "as full of lies as lines." The Jesuit Robert Parsons claimed to have discovered more than 120 lies in less than three pages. "As though," Foxe told the queen, "neither any word in all that story were true, nor any other story false in all the world besides." Five years earlier, Thomas Stapleton, professing "zeale to the truth," had

---

[31] Cited ibid., 141.

[32] On the use to which some of Foxe's illustrations were put, as well as cheaper products that were a spin-off from Foxe, see Tessa Watt, *Cheap Print and Popular Piety, 1550–1640* (Cambridge: Cambridge University Press, 1991), 90–1, 94, 147, 158–9, 223–4. The revisionists' opponents referred to include A. G. Dickens, *The English Reformation* rev. ed. (London: Batsford, 1989); the revisionists themselves, Eamon Duffy, *The Stripping of the Altars: Traditional Religion in England, 1400–1580* (New Haven: Yale University Press, 1992); and Christopher Haigh, *English Reformations: Religion, Politics, and Society under the Tudors* (Oxford: Oxford University Press, 1993).

assured Elizabeth that the faith of the English Church for nine hundred years had been "the true and right Christianitie."[33]

Foxe's claim to embody *testis temporum, lux veritatis* was rooted in his method, a plain but advanced historical method that placed a premium on the testimony of original sources and that pointed forward to the essentially Protestant professionalism of nineteenth-century historical positivists. To quote the title of the 1563 edition in some of its fullness: These were *Acts and monuments . . . gathered and collected according to the true copies and wrytinges certificatorie, as wel of the parties themselves that suffered, as also out of the Bishops Registers which were the doers therof.* It has been said that not least among Foxe's merits was that he discovered the Public Record Office.[34] The effect is best described as deceptively authentic, since while some of the sources had the ineluctable objectivity of official court records, others were highly subjective first-person accounts of trials recorded by the martyrs themselves, together with their letters and other remains, carefully edited.

Nevertheless, nobody any longer accuses Foxe of gross manipulation, still less of the fraudulent forging of his evidence of which he stood accused by his nineteenth-century critics. There is no need to spend time defending his basically sound practice as a transcriber and editor of documents. Historians can say that he was one of us. That is not to say that Foxe felt bound to publish all the evidence available to him, nor to deny that he often disregarded history's second law, according to Cicero, to make bold to tell the whole truth. We have already seen that embarrassing evidence, for example John Careless's holy lying, could be suppressed between one edition and the next. Faced with further scandalous details of theological dissension and of prevarication in the letters of the martyr John Philpot, which included a letter to Careless about the free-willers, Foxe and his editorial assistant Henry Bull discussed what to include, what to suppress. Stripped of the merely mundane, the letters of the martyrs appeared all the more sublime in their single-minded scriptural exultation.[35]

Yet Foxe's appetite for historical information "for its own sake" some-

---

[33] *Acts and Monuments of Foxe,* 1: 502–3; Collinson, "Truth and Legend," 31; and Stapleton, epistle.
[34] I am not sure whether Professor A. G. Dickens ever committed that statement to print, but I have heard him make it verbally more than once.
[35] See Susan Wabuda, "Henry Bull, Miles Coverdale, and the Making of Foxe's *Book of Martyrs,*" in *Martyrs and Martyrologies: Studies in Church History,* vol. 30, ed. Diana Wood (Oxford: Basil Blackwell, 1993), 256–7.

times took over. Among his papers in the Harleian manuscripts, there are nearly one hundred closely written folios, detailing the scandals, corruptions, and law suits that in the reign of Edward VI tore the Welsh diocese of St. David's apart and damaged the reputation of its first Protestant bishop, Robert Ferrar.[36] Ferrar suffered martyrdom under Mary, and his ordeal was hailed (from the safety of exile) by a fellow bishop: "O most happy Ferrar, more strong than yron!"[37] A correspondent later begged Foxe not to meddle with the St. David's case in the "augmentyng" of his history. "The controversye was for prophane matters and therfore unmeet for your hystorye. We must be cyrcumspect in owr doyngs that we geev the papysts no occasyon to accuse us for persecutors whych we lay so much to their charge."[38] Foxe ignored this advice and printed all fifty-six articles indicting Ferrar of worldly-mindedness and gross pastoral neglect. For example, his enemies alleged that the bishop had spent all his time and labor in discovering mines, and that all his conversation had been about such worldly matters as "baking, brewing, enclosing, ploughing, mining, of mill-stones."[39]

Foxe's excuse for printing this unsavory stuff was that it would give other bishops warning "to be more circumspect, whom they should trust and have about them." He may very well have had in mind the early Elizabethan bishop of Norwich, John Parkhurst, whose lack of worldly wisdom opened up his diocese to sharks and con men.[40] Foxe called Ferrar "twice a martyr" and printed his replies to the articles of accusation, defending his reputation and, as he moved on to the scene at the stake, freely calling him "godly Bishop Ferrar." Ferrar told a sympathizer that "if he saw him once to stir in the pains of his burning, he should then give no credit to his doctrine." Foxe added: "And as he said, so he right well performed the same."[41] But it is perhaps signifi-

[36] BL, MS Harl. 420, no. 12, fols. 80–178.
[37] *An epistle wrytten by John Scory the late bishop of Chichester . . . unto all the faythfull that be in pryson in Englande* ("Southwark," *recte* Emden, 1555), sig. A3.
[38] Richard Prat to John Foxe, 20 January 1560, BL, MS Harl. 416, fol. 176.
[39] *Acts and Monuments of Foxe,* 7:4–9.
[40] For Foxe's excuse, see ibid., 21. For Parkhurst's incompetence and its consequences, see *The Letter Book of John Parkhurst Bishop of Norwich Compiled During the Years 1571–5,* ed. R. A. Houlbrooke, Norfolk Record Society, 42 (Norwich, 1975); Diarmaid MacCulloch, *Suffolk and the Tudors: Politics and Religion in an English County 1500–1600* (Oxford: Oxford University Press, 1986), 184–7; and Felicity Heal, *Of Prelates and Princes: A Study of the Economic and Social Position of the Tudor Episcopate* (Cambridge: Cambridge University Press, 1980), 251–2. Foxe's East Anglian connections, especially in the 1560s, make it likely that he had Parkhurst in mind.
[41] *Acts and Monuments of Foxe,* 7:26.

cant that Foxe placed in immediate juxtaposition to Ferrar's story a much fuller account of the only other Welsh martyr he records, the obscure and elderly Cardiff fisherman Rawlins White, who, as it happens, was burned in the same month as the bishop.[42] The circumstantial details include White's urging the smith to make sure that he was chained fast to the stake, "for it may be that the flesh would strive mightily" (almost the same words attributed to Bishop Ridley in the same circumstances);[43] his arranging the straw around him to make a little shelf on which to lean to give "good ear and attention" to the sermon preached over him; and his appearing "altogether angelical" – a Polycarpian touch – with the white hairs sticking out from under his kerchief.[44] As with Holinshed's *Chronicles,* Foxe's material was not necessarily so haphazardly arranged as it may appear.

There is some rather more damaging evidence to which I among others have drawn attention, that in his efforts to approximate all heretics whatsoever to a model of "godly" and acceptable Protestant orthodoxy, Foxe deliberately suppressed or glossed over opinions that were beyond the pale as much in Protestant as in Catholic perception. Faced with confessions of gross errors in the doctrine of the Trinity by some of his Kentish martyrs, Foxe merely commented: "To these articles what their answers were likewise needeth here no great rehearsal. . . ." Some of this material survives in Foxe's papers not in the form of transcripts but in the very pages roughly torn from the original trial register of Archdeacon Nicholas Harpsfield, effectively removing them from the public domain. Since the foliation is not continuous, it is just possible that other pages, more incriminating still, were actually destroyed, a capital offense for any historian to have committed.[45] We look forward to the shedding of further light on such matters in the critical edition of Foxe that Professor David Loades now has in hand, 150 years after that great Victorian editor, J. G. Nichols, first called for it.[46]

---

[42] Ibid., 28–33.   [43] Ibid., 550.   [44] Ibid., 33.

[45] Ibid., 8:326, 300. See also 254. See Collinson, *"Truth and Legend,"* 41–4.

[46] Nichols drew attention to the need for a scholarly edition of Foxe in editing *Narratives of the Days of the Reformation, Chiefly from the Manuscripts of John Foxe the Martyrologist,* Camden Series, o.s. 77 (London, 1859). The British Academy is currently funding a "Foxe's *Book of Martyrs* Project" under the guidance of Professor Loades. In an appendix to his *John Foxe* (Boston: Twayne Publishers, 1983), 117–19, Warren W. Wooden compares the accounts of a particular episode in the 1563, 1583, and Victorian editions of *Acts and Monuments,* illustrating both the need for such an enterprise and the difficulty that it will inevitably entail.

III

With the literary studies made by Helen White and William Haller in the 1960s, and more recently by Warren Wooden and John Knott, interest has shifted from the scrutiny of Foxe's accuracy and reliability as a historian, on the narrow terms of the English empirical tradition, to appreciation of the rhetorical and literary accomplishments of *Acts and Monuments,* or to what Wooden calls Foxe's artistry.[47] The year 1963 was a landmark, for it witnessed the publication both of Helen White's *Tudor Books of Saints and Martyrs* and Haller's famous study, *Foxe's* Book of Martyrs *and the Elect Nation* (published in the United States as *The Elect Nation*).[48]

For Haller, the question was not whether Foxe told the truth as we would have it told, but what he took the truth to be and induced so many of his countrymen at such a critical moment to accept as such: "Whether the facts and the meaning of the facts were in every respect what he made them out to be, we need not inquire."[49] Following Haller, and the important corrections in his reading of the text and understanding of its reception by Katherine Firth, Richard Bauckham, and V. Norskov Olsen, much attention has been concentrated on the apocalyptical and chronological framework of *Acts and Monuments,* together with cognate questions of ethnocentricity. Was it either Foxe's intention or the inadvertent effect of the book to create in what Foxe called "this my-country church of England" a Miltonic sense of manifest and unique destiny, of England as not only *an* elect nation but *the* elect nation of God?[50] That grand subject lies beyond the scope of this modest essay, with its more limited concern with truth, lies, and fiction.

By now we should be thoroughly sensitized to Foxe's literary strategy of validating the Protestant Church and its "true" faith in the patient yet triumphant witness of the martyrs. We now know that these martyrs of the Reformation were represented as not only successors but replications

---

[47] Wooden, *John Foxe,* 76.
[48] Helen C. White, *Tudor Books of Saints and Martyrs* (Madison: University of Wisconsin Press, 1963); William Haller, *Foxe's* Book of Martyrs *and the Elect Nation* (London: Jonathan Cape, 1963); and *The Elect Nation: The Meaning and Relevance of Foxe's* Book of Martyrs (New York, 1963).
[49] Haller, *Foxe's* Book of Martyrs, 15, 187.
[50] Richard Bauckham, *Tudor Apocalypse* (Appleford, Abingdon: Sutton Courteney Press, 1978); Katharine R. Firth, *The Apocalyptic Tradition in Reformation Britain 1530–1645* (Oxford: Oxford University Press, 1979); and V. Norskov Olsen, *John Foxe and the Elizabethan Church* (Berkeley and Los Angeles: University of California Press, 1973).

of the early Christian martyrs; that Latimer's ever memorable words to Ridley at the stake, "be of good comfort . . . and play the man," were an echo of the heavenly words uttered to St. Polycarp as he entered the arena; that the martyred Bishop Hooper was modeled on that same Polycarp in many respects. That spirited, not to say alienated, gentlewoman Anne Askew, victim of a late Henrician episode of persecution, was presented (by John Bale in the first instance) as a kind of protomartyr of this latest age, the counterpart of Blandina, the second-century slave girl martyred in Lyon: a remarkable case not only of Reformation fashioning but of self-fashioning, since Askew herself prepared most of the materials out of which her legend was composed.[51] Foxe himself was, as it were, a reincarnation of the martyrologist and inventor of ecclesiastical history, Eusebius of Caesarea.

The Eusebian quality of Foxe is particularly evident in the preface called "The Utility of This Story," where the martyrologist contrasts the themes of secular historiography, "the roar of foughten fields, the sacking of cities, the hurlyburlies of realms and people," with "the lives, acts, and doings, not of bloody warriors, but of mild and constant martyrs of Christ." These martyrs, Foxe wrote "declare to the world what true Christian fortitude is, and what is the right way to conquer," adding, "With this valiantness did that most mild Lamb, and invincible Lion of the tribe of Judah first of all go before us."[52] Eusebius must have been well known to Foxe before the publication of his first English edition in 1563. But in 1579 he was introduced to a wider audience in Meredith Hanmer's translation. Hanmer was an obscure and by no means respectable individual who can have been little more than a functionary in an enterprise guided by Foxe. The printer was the Huguenot Vautrollier, with whom Foxe and a small team of translators were working in the late seventies to produce a little library of works by Martin Luther in English.[53] Headed by Luther's lectures on Galatians, these books presented

---

[51] *Acts and Monuments of Foxe*, 7:550. See Collinson, *Elizabethan Essays*, 99–101; and John N. King, *Tudor Royal Iconography: Literature and Art in an Age of Religious Crisis* (Princeton: Princeton University Press, 1989), 207–11.

[52] *Acts and Monuments of Foxe*, 1:521–3.

[53] The Hanmer translation is *The auncient ecclesiasticall histories wrytten by Eusebius, Socrates, and Euagrius* (London, 1577, 1577, entered with the Stationers, 1579). For Meredith Hanmer's distinctly spotty reputation, see *Dictionary of National Biography*. The Vautrollier Luther translations (original editions) are *Short-Title Catalogue* nos. 16965, 16975, 16989, and 16993. See G. R. Elton, "Luther in England," in *Studies in Tudor and Stuart Politics and Government* (Cambridge: Cambridge University Press, 1992), 4:230–45.

Luther at his most "comfortable," and were perhaps intended as a pro-
phylactic against the pastoral damage thought to be caused by Calvinism,
of which Foxe, as a spiritual physician, had first-hand experience.[54] These
were the only translations of Luther available to the English-speaking
Protestant world for three hundred years to come.

There is no need to restate at any length the many valuable contributions made to our appreciation of Foxe's text by his modern literary
critics, though it is worth mentioning John Knott's convincing argument
that what distinguishes the Foxeian narrative from those of the early
church martyrologists is the combative, contentious behavior of the Protestant martyrs as they confront their accusers and judges, contrasted with
the more passive disposition of the primitive martyrs. Knott's explanation
is contextual and circumstantial. Eusebius wrote in the secure enjoyment
of the peace of the church, recording martyr victories that had achieved
their earthly as well as heavenly vindication. Although there were parallels between the Constantinian peace and the Elizabethan settlement,
which Foxe made something of, if only for courtesy's sake, the struggle
between Protestantism and Catholicism, which Bale and Foxe constructed apocalyptically and cosmically as the war of the two churches,
Christ and Antichrist, was still being fiercely fought, even as Foxe wrote.
Even the English persecution was very recent, and some of the persecutors
were still alive. So Askew was frankly presented as a resourceful debater
and even a scold, not at all like Blandina, except that Blandina as depicted
by Bale and Foxe was not a little like Askew.[55] Knott has shown how Foxe
edited the account that the protomartyr John Rogers wrote of his own
trial to heighten its polemical effect. If Rogers himself recorded not only
what he said but what he would have liked to say, Foxe converted his
words into what Foxe would have liked him to say, writing some of his
lines for him.[56] Although these resourceful, aggressive courtroom performances were succeeded by the constrained passivity of the executions,
Foxe's critics were given grounds on which to complain that his so-called
martyrs were not in the least martyrlike in their behavior. Where was that
humility that adorned the true martyr?

---

[54] Thomas Fuller in his *Worthies of England* told the story of the Kentish matriarch Mrs.
Mary Honywood who suffered from a chronic religious melancholy of the kind for
which Calvinism has often been blamed. She told Foxe that she was as sure to be damned
as the glass that she hurled to the floor was to be broken. But then there happened a
wonder. The glass rebounded entire. Fuller, *The Worthies of England*, ed. J. Freeman
(London, 1952), 273–4.
[55] Knott, *Discourses of Martyrdom*, 57–8.   [56] Ibid., 11–32.

In what is left of my space, I shall first pick a couple of bones with literary scholarship and then consider some of the wider implications of what may be called the textualization of Foxe. We have hardly begun to come to terms with the great generic diversity of this huge, sprawling text, in Wooden's phrase "a medley of literary forms," embracing comedic and romantic as well as annalistic elements, not to mention the Protestant recension of the medieval literary tradition of the *ars moriendi,* which is such a large part of its rationale, together with copious controversial polemic. Much work remains to be done. In Wooden's words, "modern critics have taken only the first harvest."[57]

Both of my bones concern miracles, matters of truth and fiction. An argument of Helen White, reinforced by John Knott, runs like this: When Foxe disavowed, as he did, the name of martyrologist, he was distancing himself from the hagiographical tradition enshrined in *The Golden Legend,* which had been published in English as recently as 1527. When he called himself a mere storyteller, he meant that he did not deal in legends. Helen White remarks that Foxe's book "is full of the contempt of the sixteenth-century Reformers for the miracle and the miracle-monger." The miracles of Thomas Becket were "lying miracles," "monkish miracles and gross fables." Knott suggests that Foxe "minimizes the intrusion of the supernatural," making his martyrs not saints but "models of Christian heroism," manifesting the invincibility of true faith. They were "more closely connected to a sustaining human community, and more fully human" than the martyrs and saints of Catholicism.[58]

This is helpful, but it undervalues the marvelous tokens and signs that Foxe occasionally reported, as it were in spite of himself, and that may well have held a more prominent place in popular Protestant memory and imagination than Foxe himself allowed. White acknowledges this: "Old habits die hard." Wooden emphasizes that the final "tokens" of the truth and efficacy of the martyrs' faith, which abound in his set-piece scenes, were "a palpable substitute" for the fantastic and discredited miracles of *The Golden Legend.*[59] When Thomas Stapleton translated and published *Bede's History of the Churche of Englande* (1565), he defended the miraculous in the pages of Bede and asked why, if "straunge and uncredible miracles and visions" were inadmissible, there was so much material of

---

[57] Wooden, *John Foxe,* 115.
[58] White, *Tudor Books of Saints and Martyrs,* 164–7; Knott, *Discourses of Martyrdom,* 33–46.
[59] White, *Tudor Books of Saints and Martyrs,* 164; Wooden, *John Foxe,* 45–6.

this kind in Foxe. "Ar there not also in that donghell heaped a number of miserable miracles to sette forth the glory of their stinking martyrs?" "Iff the Crosse of saint Oswalde seme a superstitious tale, how much more fonde and fabulous is the tale of one that suffred at Bramford, with a greate white crosse, appearing in his brest?"[60]

But there are miracles, and miracles. In his *A fortresse of the faith* (1565), Stapleton conceded that "as for the miracles of Fox in his Actes and monuments, his owne felowes esteme them but as civill thinges, and such as may happen by course of reason. And in dede they are no other, such of them as are true."[61] White and Knott rightly insist that the ability to withstand an excruciatingly painful and prolonged death was the real miracle, repeatedly witnessed in Foxe's pages. Were these "civil" things, subject to rational explanation and medical and psychological description, miracles only in the debased and commonplace sense in which we use the word today? Was the courage of the martyrs no more than a simple function of their humanity, albeit a redeemed and elevated humanity, of which any Christian was in principle capable?

We must be careful not to impose our modern way of seeing things on a writer of Foxe's generation. To represent the heroic endurance of his martyrs as a merely human achievement, with "no sense of being transformed by the presence of Christ," secularizes and modernizes to excess. Although the miraculous in the perception of Protestants is no simple matter, it may be cautiously defined as occurrences within and not outside the course of nature (no talking heads or bleeding statues), but according to a causation not, on our terms, natural, "nature" being not the efficient, or sufficient, cause. When Foxe wrote of the preservation of the Princess Elizabeth during her sister's reign as "a singular miracle of God," he meant just that. In the 1570 edition, the providential presentation of this story was accentuated by suitable marginal notes and running headlines, perhaps with the intention of admonishing both queen and reader. It was not Elizabeth's strength of character that had preserved her but God.[62] Foxe's classical humanism may have disposed him to represent the deaths of his heroes as, at one level, human achievements. But

[60] Stapleton, epistle, fols. 8v–9r.
[61] Thomas Stapleton, *A fortresse of the faith* (Antwerp, 1565), fol. 99v.
[62] I am indebted to the study of this text made by Damian Nussbaum as a bibliographical exercise for the M.Phil. degree in medieval and Renaissance literature at Cambridge University, and to discussions with Mr. Nussbaum. See also his M.Phil. dissertation, "Foxe's *Acts and Monuments*: Development and Influence. Dramatising Contests and Contesting Dramas: The Ritual and Representation of Tudor Heresy Executions," 1993.

they were achievements inconceivable without the power of a transcendent yet intrusive God, all of whose workings were marvelous.

To say so much and no more is to sell Foxe and his Protestant readers and their age short. After the account of Elizabeth's travails, Foxe entered what Annabel Patterson might want to call his anecdotage, as *Acts and Monuments* peters out in a catalogue of such particular providences as the loathsome, shameful deaths of the persecutors, in the manner of the *De mortibus persecutorum* of Lactantius, paired with the equally remarkable escapes and preservations of many of the godly. It would be hard indeed to exaggerate how all-pervasive is this kind of providentialism in the early modern mentality, not only before the Reformation but after it. To the modern mind, this may appear the ultimate and most comprehensive of superstitions.

Foxe's appendix of cautionary tales was not the end of a lingering and outmoded tradition, but rather the harbinger of a new wave of morally correct credulity, which for more than a century to come would be fostered by sensational broadsheets and pamphlets, and by such substantial and ambitious albums as Thomas Beard's *Theatre of Gods Judgements* (editions in 1597, 1612, 1631) and Samuel Clarke's *Mirrour or looking-glasse both for saints, and sinners, held forth in some thousands of examples* (1657). This material was so traditional in form, content, and moral values that it would not be appropriate to call it a literary genre peculiar or even proper to Protestantism. But it was manifestly compatible with a Protestant worldview, or theodicy. In Beard's stories (some of them centuries old), the earth opens up to swallow its blaspheming victims, Sabbath-breaking hunters father children with dogs' heads, and punishments fit the crime in bizarre ways that manipulate where they do not defy nature. Such tall stories claimed, of course, to be "true," but in what sense or degree is a nice question.[63] Foxe is by comparison so restrained that the White-Knott argument threatens to reenter through the back door.

We return from the providential fantasies of God's violent theme park to Foxe's generally more believable stories. Did these things happen very much as Foxe describes them? This is my second bone to pick. Referring

---

[63] These suggestions draw freely on Alexandra Walsham's Cambridge Ph.D. thesis, "Aspects of Providentialism in Early Modern England" (1995) and especially on her chapter on Thomas Beard. See also Peter Lake, "Deeds against Nature: Cheap Print, Protestantism, and Murder in Early Seventeenth-Century England," in *Culture and Politics in Early Stuart England,* ed. Kevin Sharpe and Peter Lake (Basingstoke and London: Macmillan, 1994), 257–83.

less to such improbable tales as the bull of Chipping Sodbury, which was the instrument of divine providence in goring to death a bishop's chancellor, and more to the edifying and apparently authentic scenes of the martyrdom of Rogers, Hooper, Ridley, Latimer, and quaint old Rawlins White: Were these narratives true? A no-nonsense historical positivist like Sir Geoffrey Elton had no doubt that they were. Foxe did not have to invent the persecutions.[64] (But something depends upon what one means by "invent.") Curiously enough, modern literary scholarship, with which Elton tended to have no truck, seems to agree, perhaps because even so-called new historicists are ultimately indifferent to what actually happened in history. So Knott only once touches on the reliability of Foxe's narratives in this crucial respect. Commenting on the "apparent serenity" of John Rogers as he broke the ice, washing his hands in the flames "as one feeling no smart," Knott remarks: "At least, this is Foxe's interpretation of the scene, one likely to have been shared by the committed Protestants in the crowd."[65]

But are we really to believe in such scenes as Foxe describes? It stretches our credulity and sensibility that such agonies could have been so stoically borne. The master of "sheer horror"[66] spares us none of the gory details: Ridley leaping about in a badly laid fire, shouting "I cannot burn"; Hooper reviving a poor fire with the fat dropping out of his fingers' ends; the young Dartford linen draper Christopher Wade holding out his extended arms as a sign, until he was "altogether roasted."[67] If it really was so, then we may have to invoke something like Seymour Byman's rather shaky historical psychology, fitness training, as it were, in the disciplines of sustained asceticism (another paradox, for these were essentially Catholic disciplines).[68]

On the whole, it may be safe to accept Foxe's word for it that these deaths were martyrlike. It is significant that when the Dutch Anabaptists were burned in Smithfield by the Elizabethan government (in spite of

---

[64] G. R. Elton, *Reform and Reformation: England 1509–1558* (London: Edward Arnold, 1977), 386.

[65] Knott, *Discourses of Martyrdom*, 12.

[66] White, *Tudor Books of Saints and Martyrs*, 160–2.

[67] *Acts and Monuments of Foxe*, 7:551 (Ridley), 6:658 (Hooper), 7:319–21 (Wade).

[68] Seymour Byman, "Ritualistic Acts and Compulsive Behaviour: The Pattern of Tudor Martyrdom," *American Historical Review* 83 (1978): 625–43; and Byman, "Suicide and Alienation: Martyrdom in Tudor England," *Psychoanalytical Review* 61 (1974): 355–73. Warren Wooden is another student of Foxe who has drawn attention to the painful physical tests to which the martyrs subjected themselves, experimenting with their capacity to bear the pain. *John Foxe*, 44–5.

Foxe's pleas and protests), their deaths were observed to be not martyrlike. They died "in great horror with roaring and crieng."[69] (But the
recorded observations are hostile, and we do not know how an Ana-
baptist source might have represented these deaths.) Many in the crowds
who attended the Marian burnings came expressly to observe the manner
of the victims' deaths. For example, the seven thousand present at Bishop
Hooper's execution, perhaps 15 percent of the population of Glouces-
tershire (it was market day, and the boughs of a great elm tree were
"replenished with people"), were there "to see his behaviour towards
death."[70] The Catholic controversialist Miles Huggarde,[71] as vivid a
writer as Foxe himself, quoted against the incinerated Latimer Latimer's
own words from an Edwardian sermon in which he had dismissed the
suggestion that certain Anabaptists were true martyrs because they had
gone to their deaths "intrepid." Intrepid let them go. Augustine had
taught: "Martyrum non facit poena, sed causa." Just so, said Huggarde.
He scorned the "brainsick" fools who scrambled for bones and ashes to
use as relics and miracle cures (were these the same people as Foxe's
godly and restrained spectators?). But he never once suggested that the
martyrs themselves were not "intrepid," which surely he would have
done if the testimony of thousands of still living observers had allowed
him to.[72] Only a tincture of doubt persists. In the early Elizabethan
interlude *New Custom,* the vice character Cruelty exults with nostalgic
glee as he remembers the burnings over which he had presided. In the fire,

[69] John Stow, *The Annales of England* (London, 1592), 1162. Walter Strickland reported to
Edward Bacon that they "died stubernly and nether patiently nor martir like." Folger
Shakespeare Library, MS L.d.568. In the next century, the Leveler Richard Overton
would ask: "Who writ the Histories of the Anabaptists but their Enemies?" Cited in
McKeon, *Origins,* 77. However, note also the manner of the death of the radical Arian
heretic Francis Kett, who was burned at Norwich on 14 January 1589. The Norwich
minister William Burton reported that "he went leaping and dancing: being in the fire,
above twenty times together, clapping his hands, he cried nothing but blessed be God . . .
and so continued untill the fire had consumed all his neather partes, and untill he was
stifled with the smoke." Cited in *Dictionary of National Biography,* s.v. Kett. The future
Bishop Joseph Hall wrote to a Norfolk recusant about the joyful death of a priest, Robert
Drewrie, executed at Tyburn on 26 February 1607: "How many malefactors have we
known that have laughed upon their executioners, and jested away their last wind! You
might know. It is not long since our Norfolk Arian leaped at his stake." Cited in F. L.
Huntley, *Bishop Joseph Hall, 1574–1656: A Biographical and Critical Study* (Cambridge, England: D. S. Brewer, 1979), 66.

[70] *Acts and Monuments of Foxe,* 6:650.

[71] See Joseph Martin, "Miles Hogarde: Artisan and Aspiring Author in Sixteenth-Century
England," in *Religious Radicals in Tudor England* (London: Hambeldon Press, 1989),
83–105.

[72] Miles Huggarde, *The Displaying of the Protestants* (London, 1556), fols. 36–7, 41.

the victims had made a noise like a pack of hounds.[73] So we lily-livered moderns would be inclined to expect. Foxe supplies details of only a fraction of around three hundred burnings. Were some of the others deficient in martyrlike edification?

To conclude, in spite of that elusive fragment, that Foxe told it the way it was, is emphatically not to deny that the power of his narrative depended upon the manner in which he told it, upon style and artistry. On the contrary, in spite of Wooden's and Knott's valuable studies, we have only begun to explore the riches of the fictive constituents of *Acts and Monuments.* I can do little more than sketch out some of the lines of enquiry that merit more extensive investigation, such as recent studies, the new critical edition, and even these modest suggestions, may stimulate.

The point from which all such investigations must embark is the consideration that Sidney's distinction between the factual and the fictional, however useful for his rhetorical–polemical purpose, is unhelpful and even false, as Sidney himself admitted when he noted that historians had been glad to borrow both fashion and weight of poets. Judith Anderson, in her study of the representations of historical persons in Tudor literature, *Biographical Truth,* is struck by the convergence rather than the divorce of fiction and history in the texts she treats, fiction being defined not as pure nonfactual invention but as "the deliberate and creative shaping of fact." Anderson quotes Hayden White's *Tropics of Discourse:* "Novelists might be dealing only with imaginary events whereas historians are dealing with real ones, but the process of fusing events, whether imaginary or real, into the comprehensible totality ... is a poetic process." "In every historical account of the world," White continues, it matters little "whether the world is conceived to be real or only imagined; the manner of making sense of it is the same."[74] Wooden comments on

---

[73] The passage, from *A new enterlude No lesse wittie: then plesant, entituled new Custome* (London, 1573), is worth quoting in full:

Crueltie: By the masse there is one thing makes me laugh hartely ha, ha, ha
Avarice: I pray thee what is that?
Crueltie: What? ha, ha, ha, I can not tel for laughing
I would never better pastime desier
Then to here a dosen of them howling together in the fier
Whose noyse as my thinketh I could be compare:
To a crie of houndes folowing after the Hare.
Or a rablement of Bandogges barking at a Bear,
ha, ha, ha.

The copy in the Huntington Library bears the (spurious?) signature of "Wm Shakespeare."

[74] Hayden White, *Tropics of Discourse: Essays in Cultural Criticism* (Baltimore: Johns Hopkins University Press, 1978), 97–8, and chapter 3, "The Historical Text as Literary

Foxe's consciously artistic preference for the descriptive over the hortatory mode, which crowds his narratives with closely observed circumstantial detail. That such minute particulars were caught, that they actually existed, is trivial in comparison with the use to which they were put. Even where they held no emblematic significance (and often they did) circumstantial details lent the appearance of verisimilitude.[75]

Some historians may by now be cross with me for making such large concessions to the textuality of both historical sources and historical compositions, as they would be downright angry with Roland Barthes for describing historical narratives as "verbal fictions whose fictionality has been forgotten."[76] Having elsewhere attacked Natalie Davis's *Fiction in the Archives* (with some willful misunderstanding of her intentions), John Bossy writes in the preface to his enthralling *Giordano Bruno and the Embassy Affair* that it reads like a novel, but with this difference: that the events happened. He is a historian and historians tell true stories about the past.[77] For historians it must matter very much whether Foxe, who is our principal and often only source for much of what we know about the English Reformation, wrote true stories or not. If documents, many of them, have a certain textuality, historians need to know they can put their trust in texts as documents.

That being the case, Foxeian studies ought to address a formal question. Do all Foxe's stories enjoy, or even lay claim to, an equal status? Are they all meant to attract the same amount of credence? I would suggest not. In the main body of the text, consisting of great slabs of cumulative, chronological narrative, rolled along on their supporting documentation, Foxe expects and for the most part deserves to be believed. He is not inventing his material in the sense of making it up. But the tail end of the book consists of a kind of delta of wandering, inconsequential, anecdotal

Artifact," passim; Anderson, *Biographical Truth*, 1–5. Anderson excludes *Acts and Monuments* from her *Biographical Truth* on the surprising and hardly necessary ground that Foxe's lives are "formulaic and repetitive." "Foxe's book is not about men but about martyrs." In a sense, the subject is not mankind but the Holy Spirit. Anderson, *Biographical Truth*, 2, 3.

75 Wooden, *John Foxe,* 71–75.
76 Roland Barthes, "Historical Discourse," in *Structuralism: A Reader*, ed. Michael Lane (London: Penguin Books, 1970), cited in Keith Thomas, *History and Literature: The Ernest Hughes Memorial Lecture 1988* (Swansea: University College of Swansea, 1988), 23.
77 John Bossy, *Giordano Bruno and the Embassy Affair* (New Haven: Yale University Press, 1991), 1–2. Bossy's attack on Natalie Zemon Davis's *Fiction in the Archives: Pardon Tales and Their Telling in Sixteenth-Century France* (Princeton: Princeton University Press, 1988) appeared in the *Times Literary Supplement*, 7 April 1989.

streams. These stories of divine judgment and mercy may be largely
fictional and may have been so understood by both Foxe and his readers.
The story of the bishop's chancellor and the bull was too good a story to
omit for the trivial reason that in reality the chancellor lived on for many
more years.[78] Other anecdotes, like the dreadful fate recorded of the
twelve-year-old girl, a foolish maiden, who said that God was "an old
doting fool," were told as warning examples and exactly resemble the
fabulous contents of Beard's *Theatre,* or the repertory of tales from medieval pulpits and *florilegia* that Beard appropriated.[79] It is not clear that
John Myrc's congregations or Thomas Beard's readers believed or were
expected to believe all these stories, or that they needed to in order to
benefit from them. Wooden's comment that Foxe was "surely unwise" to
accept some of the more dubious of his tall stories may underestimate his
literary sophistication. Foxe could make use of a story of "incredible
strangeness," but only in what he calls "some out-corner of the book,"
not in "the body of these Acts and Monuments."[80]

In Foxe's extended, fifteen-thousand word narrative of the miraculous
preservation of Queen Elizabeth in her sister's reign,[81] it is certain that
some episodes were invented, or willfully falsified. For example, Foxe
must have known that when Elizabeth was arrested at her house at
Ashridge and taken to London and eventually to the Tower, she was first
allowed to recuperate from an illness, and was not summarily removed
"alive or dead," as his account suggests. This freestanding piece is evidently not history in the same sense that the main body of the *Book of
Martyrs* is history. What should we call it? I do not suppose that I shall be
allowed to call it an early version of the novel.

Foxe's account of Princess Elizabeth's ordeal was the source for
Thomas Heywood's *If You Know Not Me You Know Nobody* and for
other plays. And Shakespeare depended upon Foxe for a whole scene of
his *Henry VIII.* So another fruitful line of enquiry will concern the question of theatricality, a question extending well beyond the use of theatrical metaphors, which are as common in *Acts and Monuments* as in Sir

---

[78] J. F. Mozley, *John Foxe and His Book* (London: SPCK, 1940), 164.
[79] According to Foxe, these stories tell of "The severe punishment of God upon the persecutors of his people and enemies to his word, with such, also, as have been blasphemers,
contemners, and mockers of his religion." *Acts and Monuments of Foxe* (London, 1839),
8:628. The lamentable story of the twelve-year-old "wench," Denis Benfield of Wal-
thamstow, supplied to Foxe by William Maldon and his wife, occurs at 8:640.
[80] Wooden, *John Foxe,* 23; McKeon, *Origins,* 92.
[81] *Acts and Monuments of Foxe,* 8:600–25.

Thomas More.[82] Foxe was himself a dramatist, author of an academic comedy, *Titus et Gesippus,* an ambitious apocalyptic drama, *Christus Triumphans,* and of other Latin plays no longer extant. Like his friend and mentor, John Bale, he believed in attacking popery with the full repertoire of the three Ps, which included not only preachers and printers, but players.[83]

The trials and executions of heretics were carefully stage-managed affairs, a literally dramatic and richly ritualized demonstration of orthodoxy, which martyrs and martyrologists appropriated and inverted for their own equally dramatic and didactic purpose.[84] And if Foxe's conscious theatricality reflected the inherent theatricality of his material, the production of the text enhanced its dramatic status. Investigations of *The Book of Martyrs* as theater should not neglect those bibliographical insights that Don Mackenzie has characterized as "the sociology of texts,"[85] including the typographical layout of the page, and what may be inferred from the typography about the ways in which the text may have been read. We know that *The Book of Martyrs* was read "thoroughly," which is to say, systematically, and that it was presumably read aloud, especially in godly Protestant houses. But that by no means exhausts the questions that may be asked about the manner of the reading. The nineteenth-century edition is useless when addressing this question. G. Townsend and S. R. Cattley do not tell us, for example, that in the 1570 edition, the speeches given to Queen Mary and Princess Elizabeth in the encounter marking the climax of Foxe's account of Elizabeth's preservation are for the first time broken up into short paragraphs, one for each interlocutor, so presenting the visual representation of a play text.[86]

The two-way traffic between Foxe's enormous tome and some of the more popular and ephemeral literature of the day, a somewhat incongruous relationship of elephant and gnat, deserves more attention than it has

---

[82] Nussbaum, "Dramatising Contests and Contesting Dramas."

[83] Patrick Collinson, *From Iconoclasm to Iconophobia: The Cultural Impact of the Second English Reformation* (Reading, England: Reading University, 1986), 15; Collinson, *The Birthpangs of Protestant England: Religious and Cultural Change in the Sixteenth and Seventeenth Centuries* (Basingstoke and London: Macmillan, 1988), 103, 114. See also Paul Whitfield White, *Theatre and Reformation: Protestantism, Patronage and Playing in Tudor England* (Cambridge: Cambridge University Press, 1993), passim.

[84] See David Nicholls, "The Theatre of Martyrdom in the French Reformation," *Past and Present* 121 (1988): 49–73; and Nussbaum, "Dramatising Contests and Contesting Dramas."

[85] D. F. McKenzie, *Bibliography and the Sociology of Texts: The Panizzi Lectures 1986* (London: British Library, 1986).

[86] I owe this information to Damian Nussbaum.

yet received. On the one hand, *Acts and Monuments* incorporates the texts of broadside ballads, such as "The Fantasie of Idolatry," a song of fifty stanzas on the folly of going on pilgrimage (preserved by Foxe from oblivion), and the very popular "The Exhortacion of Robert Smith unto his Children," a Marian prison ballad known by its composer as "Rogers Will."[87] On the other, it includes a number of essentially Protestant and improving ballads derived from Foxe or from similar texts, such as Bale's account of Anne Askew or Coverdale's *Letters of the Martyrs*. These included *The godly and virtuous song and ballad of John Careless*, sung to the tune of "Greensleeves," but also to a melody of its own called "The tune of John Carelesse," evidently popular since in its turn it was appropriated for other purposes. In a little book published in 1577, "Rogers Will" was accompanied by ballads attributed to other Marian martyrs, including Bradford and Hooper, making what has been called by Tessa Watt "a miniature book of martyrs," one both affordable and portable. "The most rare and excellent history of the Dutchesse of Suffolks calamity," adapted from Foxe by Thomas Delony and set to the tune of "Queen Dido" (1602), was still in print in 1754.[88] The evidence of this material ought to be prescribed study for those historians who believe that Protestantism and popular culture were incompatible in 1754.

To appreciate Foxe as a living text that recorded performances and invited performance, and that fed on a popular Protestant culture and nourished it in return, is to point to yet another helpful approach, and one suggested both by Knott and by Richard Helgerson in his *Forms of Nationhood*.[89] *Acts and Monuments* was both the product and the possession of a godly community, one of those "imagined communities" which, according to Benedict Anderson, include modern nations.[90] The "invisible church" of Foxe and other apocalyptic writers is just such an imagined community. Its members are readers who imagine themselves in invisible fellowship with thousands of other readers and, one may add,

---

[87] Collinson, *Birthpangs*, 106; John Foxe, *Acts and Monuments* (London, 1563), sigs. 3U2–3U2v.

[88] Collinson, *From Iconoclasm to Iconophobia*, 17, 17 n. 67, 35; Tessa Watt, "Piety in the Pedlar's Pack: Continuity and Change, 1578 to 1630," in *The World of Rural Dissenters, 1520–1725*, ed. Margaret Spufford (Cambridge: Cambridge University Press, 1995); Watt, *Cheap Print and Popular Piety*, 100–1, 95, 317–18; 91–4.

[89] Knott, "The Holy Community," chap. 3 in *Discourses of Martyrdom*; Richard Helgerson, *Forms of Nationhood: The Elizabethan Writing of England* (Chicago: University of Chicago Press, 1992), 265–6.

[90] Helgerson, *Forms of Nationhood*, refers to Benedict Anderson, *Imagined Communities: Reflections on the Origin and Spread of Nationalism* (London: Verso, 1983).

with generations of Christians no longer living. Foxe was, as it were, but the amanuensis of this godly community, which both constructed his book and was constructed by it. More materially, Foxe was, at least initially, but one member of a Protestant network actively committed to recovering and recording the history of the Marian persecution and the monuments of its martyrs, a collective that included Edmund Grindal, Miles Coverdale, Latimer's servant Augustine Bernher, and the neglected Henry Bull, Foxe's Magdalen contemporary, whose contribution to the preservation and editing of the all-important "Letters of the Martyrs" preserved, since the sixteenth century, in Emmanuel College, Cambridge, was very considerable.[91] And we should include in the joint authorship of *The Book of Martyrs* not only its star performers, the highly self-conscious writers of all those letters and examination transcripts – Rogers, Bradford, Careless, and Philpot – but the cast of thousands, that "godly multitude" in Smithfield and elsewhere that made the imagined myth of the godly community credible.

Foxe's pages are peopled by, on the one hand, large, undifferentiated, uniformly godly crowds, and on the other by remarkable and exemplary individuals, good and bad, called by Wooden "tent-post figures," and the subject of extended biographical treatment.[92] These elements are made to interact almost cinematically at the scenes of martyrdom. Thus Foxe sets the stage for the last of the Smithfield burnings: "It was appointed before of the godly there standing together, which was a great multitude, that so soon as the prisoners should be brought, they should go to embrace them and to comfort them; and so they did," with "the godly multitude and congregation" making "a general sway toward the prisoners, meeting and embracing, and kissing them."[93] As for the "tent-posts," in spite of Judith Anderson's reservations about the formulaic and repetitive limitations of Foxe as biographer, it is precisely the conventions controlling his fashioning of the lives, personalities, and conduct in extremis of his martyrs that deserve scrutiny. Whether or not they really cracked jokes on their way to the fire, or fetched great leaps, or clapped their hands in the flames for sheer joy, it was necessary to include such details as manifestations of that *apatheia* which, in the Aristotelian ethical scheme, is true courage, a mean between cowardice and rash self-destruction.[94]

[91] See Wabuda, "Henry Bull." Coverdale's *Certain most godly letters* (London, 1564) was more properly the work of Bull.
[92] Wooden, *John Foxe*, 51–2.
[93] *Acts and Monuments of Foxe*, 8:559.   [94] See Collinson, "Truth and Legend," 48.

Plutarch depended upon Aristotle, and Foxe was the Plutarch of the sixteenth century. Why has no one commented on the Plutarchan device of the double biography as deployed by Foxe in the most celebrated of all his scenes, the martyrdom of the two bishops, Ridley and Latimer? The point of the device is to employ contrast to illuminate the admirable qualities of two dissimilar individuals (or, in other circumstances and for other purposes, to prefer one to the other). Erasmus used it in his double portrait of John Colet and Jacques Vitrier.[95] So we are shown Ridley, in his handsome fur-trimmed gown and tippet, "such as he was wont to wear being bishop," a man still physically and intellectually fit, his pockets full of valuable trifles to give away as keepsakes, his watch, his napkin, some nutmegs. And then we catch sight of Latimer, struggling along behind in his poor frieze coat all worn and his comical headgear, "which at first sight stirred men's hearts to rue upon them, beholding on the one side, the honour they sometimes had, and on the other, the calamity whereunto they were fallen." And yet Latimer, who while still clothed appeared "a withered and crooked silly old man," stripped to his shroud "stood bolt upright, as comely a father as one might lightly behold."[96] We do not necessarily have to doubt the nutmegs or any other of these circumstantial details. Foxe's informant was probably Latimer's faithful servant Augustine Bernher,[97] who was certainly present and who lived on into the reign of Elizabeth to assist both Foxe and Coverdale with their martyrological labors.

It remains relevant that Foxe, in his carefully balanced presentation of this material, proves himself to be every bit as much a humanist, a product of the Renaissance, as he was a Protestant and a creator of the English Protestant tradition. More attention could well be paid to his Stoicism, which, more than any distinctly Christian ethic, may have sustained that unusual aversion to violence, which, Foxe wrote, made it hard for him to pass by the very slaughter yards without a sense of revulsion and pity for the poor beasts.[98] It may even have been Stoicism that made Foxe a martyrologist.

---

[95] Erasmus to Jodocus Jonas, 13 June 1521, *Opus Epistolarum Des. Erasmi Roterodami,* ed. P. S. and H. M. Allen (Oxford: Clarendon Press, 1906–58), no. 1211, 4:502–27. An English translation is in *Desiderius Erasmus: Christian Humanism and the Reformation: Selected Writings,* ed. John C. Olin (New York: Harper and Row, 1965), 164–91. See Jessica Martin, "Izaak Walton and his Precursors: A Literary Study of the Emergence of the Ecclesiastical Life," Cambridge Ph.D. thesis, 1993, 78–85; and Dr. Martin's forthcoming monograph on the same subject.

[96] *Acts and Monuments of Foxe,* 7:547–9.

[97] I owe this suggestion to Dr. Susan Wabuda.   [98] Mozley, *John Foxe and His Book,* 86–7.

It mattered that Latimer should be presented as upright and comely, a wholesome old man. In one of his providential anecdotes, Foxe told of a man in a pub in Abingdon who boasted that he had seen "that ill favoured knave Latimer when he was burnt," and that he had teeth like a horse. In that very hour, the man's son hanged himself, not far away.[99] Disgusting and shameful deaths, gross physical deformities, were reserved for the persecutors, and mainly for the clergy. (The lay officers in Foxe's perception were often only doing their job.) I do not think that we need to believe that Bishop Stephen Gardiner had toenails like claws, any more than that King Richard III was grossly deformed from birth.

All this fashioning, which was indeed a self-fashioning by and of the Protestant community through Foxe, was achieved by means of language. How the English Protestant community contrived within a very few years to invent its own demotic, a language of heightened emotion, warmth, fervent exhortation, and, above all, biblical resonance, is a question not only still to be answered but almost never put, except in a German work of the 1920s, Levin Schücking's *The Puritan Family*.[100] It is Foxe's rhetorical style that above all deserves the serious evaluative study it has never received, and that an earlier generation, C. S. Lewis to particularize, disparaged. In a chapter of his *English Literature in the Sixteenth Century* called "Drab and Transitional Prose," Lewis said of Foxe: "His English style has no high merits. The sentences have not the energy to support their great length." Foxe was "an honest man" (as Cicero had written, "it is enough that the man should not be a liar"), but not "a great historian."[101] Warren Wooden helpfully adjudicates. Examples of the lumbering, tottering sentences Lewis describes are not hard to find in a work whose style is plastic rather than uniform. But neither is it difficult to discover sentences that are "spare, compact, and distinguished by highly functional syntax," the work of "an impressive prose craftsman."[102]

Finally, we return to the matter of truth. Insofar as Foxe is to be charged with falsifying on a large and general scale, then it was his language that did the falsifying, and altogether insidiously. Language turned into sweet societies of faithful favorers – into innocent lambs of Christ, decorous and dignified, loving and meek – men and women who

[99] *Acts and Monuments of Foxe*, 7:547–9.
[100] Levin L. Schücking, *The Puritan Family: A Social Study from Literary Sources*, trans. Brian Battershaw (London: Routledge and Kegan Paul, 1969).
[101] C. S. Lewis, *English Literature in the Sixteenth Century Excluding Drama* (Oxford: Oxford University Press, 1954), 299–301.
[102] Wooden, *John Foxe*, 62–4, 76.

in reality were creatures of passion as well as of flesh and blood, whose street language, when Foxe happened to catch the *ipsissima verba,* was robust and abrasive.[103] And yet what a fictive triumph it amounts to! Lewis's judgment can no longer be sustained. We cannot better the verdict of Helen White: "Foxe proves himself a storyteller of quite remarkable power, one of the greatest of a great age."[104]

[103] Collinson, "Truth and Legend," 48–50.
[104] White, *Tudor Books of Saints and Martyrs,* 160.

4

Thomas More and the English Renaissance: History and fiction in *Utopia*

JOSEPH M. LEVINE

I

One of the more elusive questions in charting the history of the modern historical consciousness is to ask when and how history tried to separate itself from fiction. Perhaps the trouble arises because the distinction between the two is so fundamental and yet so problematical, so full of difficulty, that there are some in our own contemporary culture who would deny it altogether. Indeed, for the modern skeptic there are many arguments to collapse the discrepancy between knowing and inventing the past, between discovering what actually happened and making it up, and it has recently become harder to defend the traditional distinctions between objective and subjective description, fact and value, truth and poetry. Doubt has spread even among historians.[1] The one thing that seems reasonably clear is that there was once a time during the Middle Ages when no one seemed much concerned about the problem, and that it was only later, beginning with the Renaissance, that it began to arise. I have written elsewhere about the peculiar role that humanism seems to have played in generating the early modern conceptions of history and fiction;[2] here I should like to return to the subject by having another look at that most fascinating of all texts in the early English Renaissance: Thomas More's *Utopia*. Whatever else More may have meant to do in that controversial work, he was certainly preoccupied there with the

---

[1] I have made a few observations about this matter in "Objectivity in History: Peter Novick and R. J. Collingwood," *Clio* 21 (1992): 109–27.

[2] See Joseph M. Levine, "Caxton's Histories: Fact and Fiction at the Close of the Middle Ages," in *Humanism and History: Origins of Modern English Historiography* (Ithaca, N.Y.: Cornell University Press, 1987), 19–53. The one general book on the subject remains the suggestive little volume by William Nelson, *Fact or Fiction: The Dilemma of the Renaissance Storyteller* (Cambridge, Mass.: Harvard University Press, 1973).

relationship between the real and the ideal in human life, and thus, inescapably, with the distinction between history and fiction. In reexamining his work, I hope therefore to throw some more light on the general problem of the early modern historical consciousness, as well perhaps as on that equally intractable problem of how to read Thomas More. And I would like to suggest further that such a reading may be useful in putting some life back into the old idea that there really was some sort of "renaissance" in England, and that it began in More's generation.

Perhaps one should tread carefully when even the joint editors of the Yale *Utopia* cannot agree about how to interpret it.[3] Yet despite the immense controversy that has always beset this troublesome text, it seems possible to reduce the chief interpretative question to a single problematical point. The quarrel, I think, has never really been about what *Utopia* says, but rather about what it means. More's description of the ideal state is plain enough; but its purpose remains obscure. Whether we view it as medieval or modern, Christian or secular, communist or bourgeois, serious or frivolous, it seems to me that much will depend on what we think were Thomas More's intentions in writing his work. And so we must make some effort to recover More's situation in order to infer his aim in writing and publishing the *Utopia*. Can we discover what he meant his readers to get out of his work?

The difficulty arises, of course, in the relatively neglected first book, the so-called dialogue on council. It will not do to dismiss this introduction too casually, or treat it separately on the ground that it was composed after the main body of the text. More chose to publish his finished work as a whole and with deliberate calculation by posing a problem. He sets Utopia in a quarrel, ambiguously, but one must suppose intentionally. If it is true that ambiguity "does not enhance the value of social comment," we must not therefore beg the question.[4] To assume that *Utopia* is the kind of social comment where clarity prevails is to assume the author's intention and not to prove it. Of two things only may we be reasonably sure: *Utopia* is ambiguous in the form we have it (as the quarrels of the critics have shown) and *Utopia* is purposefully composed. Why may not More have intended ambiguity?

---

[3] Thomas More, *Utopia*, ed. Edward Surtz and J. H. Hexter, vol. 4 of *The Complete Works of Thomas More* (New Haven: Yale University Press, 1965). Page references in the text will be to this edition, but I shall quote occasionally from the sixteenth-century translation by Ralph Robinson.

[4] J. H. Hexter, *More's Utopia: The Biography of an Idea* (Princeton: Princeton University Press, 1952), 11. See also Hexter, "The Composition of Utopia," in *Utopia,* xv–xxiii.

To what end? Before we attempt an answer we should be as clear as we can about the nature of the ambiguity. Insofar as it is formal, it results from More's choice of dialogue, a dialogue in which he sets himself (and his friend Peter Giles) in a realistic setting, at odds against his own chief spokesman, the obviously fictional Raphael Hythloday.[5] Insofar as it is substantive, it results from the unresolved dispute within the dialogue over the value of social comment. In the first instance, More has chosen an old literary device by which he can present two different viewpoints, but he has deliberately concealed his own opinion. The Hythloday of the dialogue is clearly as much More's invention and mouthpiece as the More and Giles of the dialogue. That the one is a complete fiction and the other two are founded on historical reality might well incline us to identify with the latter. But Hythloday so dominates the dialogue – not to say the rest of the book – that we are left uncertain. How can we be sure that the More in the dialogue is identical with the More who has composed the dialogue? Hythloday has the fullest say; More has the last word. The very form of the invention leaves us puzzled.

But the argument between More and Hythloday is even more puzzling. It begins when Giles and More urge Hythloday to go into public service. They have been moved by the obvious wisdom of this extraordinary traveler who has seen so much of the new world and whose head is stocked with the examples of so many foreign peoples. His wisdom is the wisdom of political experience as it was usually attributed to the student of history[6] – but all Hythloday's knowledge is of the contemporary world. Hythloday declines public service, at first on the ground that there is nothing in it for him who is already satisfied with his lot; then (in answer to their argument that he owes it to the public) on the ground that his knowledge would be unwelcome. Here Hythloday interpolates a long reminiscence in which he recalls an argument at the table of Cardinal Morton

---

[5] This formal ambiguity is reinforced by More's style, particularly his insistent use of litotes, the rhetorical figure in which something is affirmed by using a double negative, and which has often been overlooked by his translators; see Elizabeth McCutcheon, "Denying the Contrary: More's Use of Litotes in the *Utopia*," in *Essential Articles for the Study of Thomas More*, ed. Richard Sylvester and G. P. Marc'hadour (Hamden, Conn.: Archon Books, 1977), 263–74.

[6] *Utopia*, 52–4. Typically, Thomas Elyot praises history as a fund of worldly experience (echoing Cicero's popular *De officiis*) in *The Boke Named the Governour* (1531), ed. H. H. S. Croft (London: C. Kegan Paul, 1883), vol. 1, chaps. 10–11, esp. pp. 82, 90–1. Besides Cicero, a locus classicus was Diodorus Siculus in the preface to the *Historical Library*; see for example the contemporary translation by John Skelton, ed. F. M. Salter and H. L. R. Edwards, Early English Text Society, no. 233 (London, 1956), 5–12.

about crimes and punishments in order to show that advisors are typically sycophantic and self-serving.[7] That done, he resumes his objections to service by offering two hypothetical examples to show how unwelcome his advice would be. In the first, he suggests how he would try to persuade a prince not to go to war to enlarge his kingdom; in the second, he suggests how he would try to persuade him not to raise taxes to enhance his own wealth and glory, but sacrifice his own interest for the general good. Significantly, More does not dissent from any of this but agrees that such advice would indeed be unwelcome and ineffectual. Apparently, Hythloday and his new friends share exactly the same perception of reality; they have no illusions about princes or their advisors, and their pessimistic views about this might have come right out of Machiavelli.

The difference between them occurs when More insists on Hythloday's serving the government anyway. The kind of advice that Hythloday has been suggesting is of no use; one needs something more subtle and indirect, something more devious, a practical and not an academic philosophy. More agrees with Hythloday that "School philosophy is not unpleasant among friends in familiar communication; but in the counsels of kings, where great matters be debated and reasoned with great authority, these things have no place."[8] Fortunately, there is another philosophy, "more civil," that suits the occasion. Politics is like a play and requires that words be spoken appropriate to the situation. A realistic councillor must play his part accordingly, "with comeliness, uttering nothing out of dew order and fashion." The successful politician requires rhetoric, not philosophy. There is no point intruding into the drama "other stuffe that nothing pertaineth to the matter . . . though the stuff you bring be much better" – you will only spoil the play. If you would succeed, therefore, in giving counsel and influencing events, you must renounce your haughty principles, and "with a crafty wile and a subtle train study and endeavor yourself, as much as in you lieth, to handle the matter wittily and handsomely for the purpose." Not that this will bring perfection; the best that one may hope for is to modify things slightly, or to put off the worst, "For it is not possible for all things to be well, unless all men were good, which I think will not be possible this good many years!" Still, one does not desert a ship in a storm simply because one cannot tame the winds.

---

[7] Hythloday explains the reason for telling his tale at its conclusion. *Utopia*, 85.

[8] I here follow Ralph Robinson's English translation (1551; 2d ed. 1556), modernized from the version given by J. H. Lupton (Oxford: Clarendon Press, 1895), 97–104; cited hereafter as *Utopia* (Lupton). Cf. *Utopia*, 98–102.

Hythloday is unmoved (98–9). To follow More's prescription is to compromise and endanger one's ideals. Plato was right to see that philosophers want to avoid meddling in politics. What good can it do to wink at naughty counsels and pestilent decrees! That is what the church has done in making Christ's teaching acceptable to the people![9] This time More listens silently and does not respond; neither side is allowed to win the argument.

The first book closes when Hythloday offers the specific advice he would wish to give a king: that private property be eliminated (100–9). Earlier, he had paved the way for that radical remedy by recounting his argument in Morton's household. There he had inveighed against the injustices in English economic and social life, against punishing criminals unfairly and imprudently for crimes that they were in some cases being forced to commit because of the rapacity of the landowners. Hythloday's picture of the sharp practices of the wealthy – of rack-renting, enclosing, and so on – and of the evils of war and its economic dislocation, is justly famous for its realistic description. There is no ambiguity here, despite the fact that it occurs in a fictional dialogue. Hythloday proposes several possible remedies drawn from his observations abroad. One might simply alter or enforce the existing laws that restrain the wealthy; or one might make the punishments more equitable to suit the crime and reimburse the victim. When even these half-measures are rejected by the company, it is clear that a more radical solution, indeed any true solution to the problem would have been out of place.[10]

Eventually, however, at the end of the first book, Hythloday offers what must be read as his own "school philosophy" (that is to say, still a conversation among friends) (98–9). He claims to have been to a country where crime and all basic social problems have been completely eliminated by drastically removing all the possible motives for them. In Utopia there is no private property, hence no reason to steal, nor any possibility of greed, ostentation, and the rest. Nor is there any need to change human nature, which presumably remains constant. The result is a kind

---

[9] "But preachers, sly and wily men, following your counsel (as I suppose), because they saw evil men willing to frame their manners to Christ's rule, they have wrested and wried his doctine, and like a rule of lead have applied it to men's manners, that by some means at the least way they might agree together. Whereby I cannot see what good they have done, but that men may more sickerly be evil." *Utopia* (Lupton), 102; cf. *Utopia*, 100–1.

[10] Laws might lighten and mitigate the evils, "but that they may be perfectly cured and brought to a good and upright state, it is not to be hoped for, whiles every man is master of his own to himself." *Utopia* (Lupton), 109; cf. *Utopia*, 104–6.

of perfection, although one that has somehow been imposed and continues by restraint. Utopia has been constructed carefully to show just how the elimination of private property – and hence every sinful occasion – can be accomplished, right down to the smallest detail. Hythloday tries to meet every practical objection, but he does not fool anyone, least of all the Thomas More in the dialogue who has been patiently listening.

More remains unconvinced there. Even before Hythloday begins to describe his utopia, he registers a doubt. Hythloday's notion, he argues, could not possibly work, because without the rewards of private property there would be no incentive to produce anything.[11] Hythloday's answer is to describe the utopia he has actually seen: the ideal society that by its very name means nowhere. He attempts to meet every practical objection. But when Hythloday has finished his description at the end of Book 2, More repeats, though only to himself, some doubts about the utopian solution. Once again his skepticism is entirely practical. Utopia will not work because no one will want it to; the common opinion, he is sure, is that all those things that are denied in Hythloday's ideal state – wealth, glory, power, ostentation, etc. – are truly desirable and should not be eliminated.[12] We are back to where we started: The perfect solution to social and political problems, however we imagine it, is not possible in this life, since men are sinful and will not allow it. The only possibility is to retreat and save one's own soul (as Hythloday), or engage for very small, though perhaps still worthy, gains (as More in the dialogue). In short, both sides – and thus the author – agree about what the realistic *and* the idealistic alternatives are; we are left only with the problem of which to choose. It is not surprising to discover that just at this time the author was himself considering the real possibility of entering royal service.[13]

---

[11] Cicero had vigorously objected to the elimination of private property; for some anticipations of More's argument in scholastic philosophy, see *Utopia,* 382 n.

[12] Common property, More reflects, means the end of all nobility, magnificence, splendor, and majesty (*nobilitas, magnificentia, splendor,* and *maiestas*), "which are in the estimation of the common people, the true glories and ornaments of the commonwealth" [*vera ut publica est opinio decora atque ornamenta Republicae*]. *Utopia,* 244. Quentin Skinner sees correctly that "common opinion" is not necessarily the opinion of the common people, but more aptly that of the public, including many of the humanists. Skinner, "Sir Thomas More's *Utopia* and the Language of Renaissance Humanism," in *The Languages of Political Theory in Early Modern Europe,* ed. Anthony Pagden (Cambridge: Cambridge University Press, 1987), 153 n.

[13] Hexter imagines More thinking to himself, "Should a man like me, Thomas More, enter the council of my King, Henry VIII of England?" J. H. Hexter, "Thomas More and the Problem of Council," in *Quincentennial Essays on St. Thomas More,* ed. Michael Moore (Boone, N.C.: Appalachian State University, 1978), 61. Hexter has meticulously reconstituted More's situation on the eve of *Utopia,* first in his *More's Utopia* and again in his

Now it seems to me that More's originality of thought lies just in this radical disjunction between the real life that he perceived and his political ideals – more perhaps than it does in his actual description of Utopia. In this he has at least one contemporary parallel: the Italian, Niccolò Machiavelli. It is interesting to see in this regard that both men refer contemptuously to the many works of political advice that had already been offered by others – all of which are futile because they propose idealistic remedies to corrupt princes.[14] Both agree on the wickedness of their situations and the essential depravity of human nature; and both see the hopelessness of simply prescribing morality. But More, unlike Machiavelli, was still unwilling to submit and give in to the practical requirements of the moment. He was still too good a Christian, too much an idealist, for that.[15]

The principal ingredients in More's recipe for perfection, he insists, lie easily accessible in reason and Scripture, more particularly in the classical philosophers, especially Plato, and in the Gospels. The Utopians have both: reason at first unaided, but then bolstered by the appearance of Greek books fresh from the Venetian presses; then the Bible that they also receive from their European visitors, who bring news of Christ along with the classical authors. Both are swiftly and easily assimilated to their own culture.

More's Christian humanism is thus easily established. And it is just in

introduction to the Yale edition. For More's actual involvement in politics and law, see Geoffrey Elton, "Thomas More, Councillor," and "Sir Thomas More and the Opposition to Henry VIII," in *Studies in Tudor and Stuart Politics and Government* 1 (Cambridge: Cambridge University Press, 1974) 129–72; and his more recent essay "Thomas More," in ibid., III (1983), 344–72, and review of the *Works of Sir Thomas More*, 444–60; Margaret Hastings, "Sir Thomas More: Maker of English Law?" in *Essential Articles*, ed. Sylvester and Marc'hadour, 104–18; and J. A. Guy, *The Public Career of Thomas More* (New Haven: Yale University Press, 1980).

[14] Philosophers had already given much counsel to kings in published books, Hythloday remarks, but kings had not been willing to take their advice. *Utopia*, 87. More has Plato in mind and his bad experience with King Dionysius, but he may also have been thinking of Erasmus's *Institution of a Christian Prince*, which was published (with two other classical precedents by Isocrates and Plutarch) just before *Utopia* in 1516. For Machiavelli's disparagement of previously imagined polities and his own desire to write about things as they really exist, see *The Prince*, chap. 15. For the traditional literature, see A. H. Gilbert, *Machiavelli's Prince and its Forerunners* (Durham: Duke University Press, 1938); and Felix Gilbert, "The Humanist Conception of the Prince and *The Prince* of Machiavelli," *Journal of Modern History* 11 (1939): 449–83.

[15] Though "parts of *Utopia* read like a commentary on parts of *The Prince*," *The Prince* had not yet been published. R. W. Chambers, *Thomas More* (New York: Harcourt, Brace, 1935), 132. For Machiavelli's pagan posture against modern attempts to rehabilitate him, see Mark Hulliung, *Citizen Machiavelli* (Princeton: Princeton University Press, 1983).

these years that he went to bat for the new learning, the Greeks against the modern "Trojans," in a series of public and private letters where he vigorously defended the utility of classical learning.[16] Yet it is characteristic that even on this point he allows at least one ambiguity. In Utopia there are two orders of friars who are particularly virtuous and voluntarily do the dirty work of society. However, one lives according to ascetic rules and refuses to marry or eat meat, while the other participates freely in Utopian life. The first, we are told, is considered the more holy by the people, the second the wiser. Utopian wisdom, we have learned earlier, is the wisdom of Greek moral philosophy, where happiness is the object and pleasure the instrument.[17] But More refuses here to choose between the two Utopian alternatives, and his biographers tell us that he himself vacillated between them throughout his own life, drawn almost equally to the monastic life and the life of public employment.[18] The fit between medieval Christianity and Renaissance humanism, like the fit between More's own active and contemplative allegiances, was not, apparently, quite perfect.[19] The *Utopia,* it seems, is first of all a dialogue of the author

[16] See the letters to Dorp (1515), to Oxford (1518), to Lee (1519), and to a monk (1519), all collected in *In Defense of Humanism,* ed. Daniel Kinney, vol. 15 of *Works* (1986). In general, see Paul O. Kristeller, "Thomas More as a Renaissance Humanist," *Moreana* 65–6 (1980): 5–22.

[17] "This is their view of virtue and pleasure. They believe that human reason can attain to no truer view, *unless a heaven-sent religion inspire man with something more holy.* Whether in this stand they are right or wrong, time does not permit me to examine – nor is it necessary." *Utopia,* 178. In *A Treatise on the Passion,* ed. Garry E. Haupt, vol. 13 of *Works* (1976), 37, 43, More seems to echo this passage; he specifically allows the pagans to win salvation by natural reason. Utopian philosophy, according to his Yale editors, is a modified form of Epicurianism, *Utopia,* 441–3, 446–7, 451–3. But see also George M. Logan, *The Meaning of Utopia* (Princeton: Princeton University Press, 1983), 145–78.

[18] The young lawyer chose to live "religiously" in the Charterhouse without taking vows; the Lord Chancellor never gave up wearing a hair-shirt and other austerities. See William Roper, *The Lyfe of Sir Thomas Moore Knighte,* ed. Elsie Vaughan Hitchcock, Early English Text Society, o.s. 197 (London, 1935), 6, 48–9; and Nicholas Harpsfield, *The Life and Death of Sir Thomas Moore, Knighte,* ed. Elsie Vaughan Hitchcock, Early English Text Society, o.s. 186 (London, 1932), 17, 64–6. According to Roper, More's hardest moment was to close the garden gate behind him, leaving his family for his fate; *Lyfe,* 72–3.

[19] According to Germain Marc'haudour, "this startling passage has not received enough attention." However, Father Marc'hadour does not notice much tension here. "*Utopia* and Martyrdom," in *Interpreting Thomas More's* Utopia, ed. John C. Olin (New York: Fordham University Press, 1989), 63–5. Among other things, More also leaves the sacrament of ordination an open question in Utopia; according to Hythloday, when last seen, the Utopians were still disputing the matter. *Utopia,* 218. See Edward L. Surtz's puzzlement, *The Praise of Wisdom* (Chicago: Loyola University Press, 1957), 151–2. For other discrepancies between Utopian reason and Christian religion, see Logan, *Meaning,* 219–20.

with himself, self-conscious to a supreme degree, but not always completely resolved.[20]

Among the ancients, it is Plato who most obviously inspired More; *The Republic* is evidently his literary and philosophical model. It too is a dialogue that turns into a monologue; it too begins with the problem of justice and becomes an effort to describe the ideal state. It too considers the elimination of private property, though only for the guardian class. And it too ends somewhat ambiguously about the prospect of realizing true justice in this life. (The republic, admittedly, is to be found "nowhere on earth.")[21] More read Plato with attention but did not forget that the ancient Greek had failed in his own attempt to bring philosophy to a real king.[22] For More, who had read Plato and (better still) the Bible, and who had the benefit of both reason and revelation, the problem was not so much how to define justice as to see whether it could be realized in the state. Perhaps that is what the quatrain in the Utopian tongue at the beginning of the book means when it announces that "Alone of all lands, without the aid of abstract philosophy, I have represented for mortals the philosophical city." And it may be what the humanist Beatus Rhenanus had in mind when he wrote that "the Utopia contains principles of such a sort as it is not possible to find in Plato. . . . Its lessons are less philosophical . . . but more Christian."[23] To More the problem seems less of knowing than of doing the good; he was, we know, as much attracted to St. Augustine as he was to Plato.[24] But if More faltered for a moment between the choice of an ascetic life or a worldly one, he did not doubt for a moment that the good life was measured by the deeds done in it. (Both

---

[20] It is "a dialogue of More's mind with itself." David Bevington, "The Dialogue in Utopia," *Studies in Philology* 58 (1961): 496–509; cf. Robert C. Elliott, "The Shape of *Utopia*," *English Literary History* 30 (1963): 317–44. For More's choice of the active over the contemplative life, see Harpsfield, *Life*, 18.

[21] *Republic* 592B. This passage may have been the inspiration for More's title; see Logan, *Meaning*, 131 n. The prevailing contemporary view was that Plato's republic was impractical; see the passages from Erasmus and Thomas Starkey's *Dialogue* included by Surtz in *Utopia*, 375 n.

[22] More reminds Hythloday that his "favorite author," Plato, had said that there would never be a perfect commonwealth unless philosophers became kings, or kings philosophers. Hythloday replies, "But, doubtless, Plato was right in foreseeing that if kings themselves did not turn to philosophy, they would never approve of real philosophers . . . [as] he found from his own experience with Dionysius." *Utopia*, 87. The story is told in Plato's own epistles, esp. 7 and 8, as well as elsewhere, and the Platonic advice was endlessly quoted; see *Utopia*, 349–50 n.

[23] Rhenanus to Willibald Pirckheimer, 23 February 1518, in *Utopia*, 253.

[24] More lectured on *The City of God* as a young man; see Roper, *Lyfe*, 6; Harpsfield, *Life* 13–14.

kinds of friars, and all the citizens of Utopia, find justification in good works.[25]) In this admittedly ambiguous preference for the life of action over the life of contemplation, public service over philosophical retreat, More remained at one with most of his fellow humanists.

II

It was More's realism, along with his humanism, that was new in England. His allegiance to Greece and Rome he shared with his friends, Erasmus, John Colet, and the rest. His realism was more his own, a result perhaps of his actual experience in public life, as well as the new political setting.[26] J. H. Hexter puts it well: "More achieves a clarity of vision about the world he lives in unsurpassed by any contemporary but Machiavelli and perhaps Guicciardini."[27] More had been trained as a lawyer, unlike most of his friends, who were in the church or the university. It is true that his political career had been barely launched, but he had served the City of London in various positions, and was destined for royal favor. He was neither a cleric nor an aristocrat, and so quite outside the dominant culture of his time: the culture of chivalry and the church. *Utopia* is expressly critical of each, and overtly hostile to the pretensions of both the church and the aristocracy to rule. There is some truth to the charge that *Utopia* is a bourgeois book, though More's attention was on the past, not the future.[28] Its originality derives first of

---

[25] See the passage (with the marginal gloss, *vita activa*) in *Utopia,* 224. Later, More's biographer seems to have felt it necessary to apologize for More's choice of the active life. Harpsfield, *Life,* 18.

[26] I shall restrict the term largely to the ethical and political domain. Ethical realism, Johan Huizinga says, "can spring from a need to see and depict life, man and the world as they really are, and no better, stripped of all trappings of an ideal or conventional form, without illusions." "Renaissance and Realism," in *Men and Ideas,* trans. James S. Holmes and Hans van Marle (New York: Meridian, 1959), 290–1. However, Huizinga specifically denies the association of realism with the Renaissance or any other period. Nor was he much interested in drawing the distinction between history and fiction that I am trying to make.

[27] J. H. Hexter, "*Utopia* and its Historical Milieu," in *Utopia,* ci. For a further comparison, see Hexter's *Vision of Politics on the Eve of the Reformation: More, Machiavelli, Seysell* (New York: Basic Books, 1973), esp. 179–203.

[28] For an exaggerated view, see Russell Ames, *Citizen Thomas More and his Utopia* (Princeton: Princeton University Press, 1949). Hexter is justly hard on Ames but understates the undeniably bourgeois element in More's personal background: the City of London, its commerce and legal profession. More may not have been their spokesman in *Utopia;* nevertheless he was their employee in real life. See Hexter, "*Utopia* and its Historical Milieu," in *Utopia,* liv–lvii. More's most recent biographer, Richard Marius, emphasizes More's City connections in *Thomas More: A Biography* (New York: Knopf, 1985). For More's legal and political career, see Hastings, "Sir Thomas More," 104–18; and J. A.

all from its social and intellectual setting, to which it was unreservedly opposed.

I shall not dwell here on the failing culture of chivalry, except to say that by More's day it had lost almost all real connection with practical life.[29] When More was young he could have read in the only English books of his time, the publications of England's first printer, William Caxton, a complete description and hearty endorsement of the traditional culture of the aristocracy. It is true that Caxton, who was as thorough a bourgeois as More, laments the decline of chivalry in his day, but he can think of no alternative and urges its revival on the king as though it were still perfectly usable.[30] He seems to feel no discrepancy between the military ideals of a class in disarray and the actual situation of his readers. The "veil of illusion," to use Jacob Burckhardt's old phrase, was still in place. However, the tension between the real world of politics – the world of "bastard feudalism" – and the idealized fictions of the later Middle Ages was now becoming acute, and the humanists who first spotted it suddenly found an English audience in their growing awareness of that discrepancy.[31] In Italy the humanists had long ago discovered an alternative to chivalry in the political culture of antiquity and sold it to their Italian masters. They had ventured a new style and a new training for public life in which the rhetoric of antiquity was given preeminence as a practical preparation for their new situation. They saw in classical culture a set of political ideals to be imitated, and they found the ancients more contemporary than their immediate forbears. In a word, they preferred the forum of Cicero to the court of King Arthur, the *De officiis* to the *Morte d'Arthur*. And so they transformed their education and culture accordingly.

Guy, *Public Career*. For the restriction of the power of priests in Utopia, see Surtz, *Praise of Wisdom*, 160.

[29] See Arthur B. Ferguson, *The Indian Summer of English Chivalry: Studies in the Decline and Transformation of Chivalric Idealism* (Durham: Duke University Press, 1960). I prefer this view and the older literature to the recent effort by Maurice Keen to rescue chivalry for politics, since even he recognizes that changes in the technology of warfare and the practical functions of knighthood had altered profoundly by the end of the fifteenth century. See Maurice Keen, "Huizinga, Kilgour and the Decline of Chivalry," *Medievalia et Humanistica*, n.s. 8 (1977): 1–20; and Keen, *Chivalry* (New Haven: Yale University Press, 1984).

[30] See Caxton's translation of Ramón Lull's *The Book of the Ordre of Chyvalry*, ed. Alfred T. P. Byles, Early English Text Society, o.s. 168 (London, 1926), 121–5; and Levine, "Caxton's Histories," 47–9.

[31] I return to Burckhardt and the "veil" at the end of the essay. See Huizinga, *The Waning of the Middle Ages*, trans. F. Hopman (London: E. Arnold and Co., 1924), chaps. 4–7; K. B. McFarlane, "bastard feudalism," *Bulletin of the Institute of Historical Research*, 20 (London, 1945), 161–80.

Of course, Englishmen had for a long time been in contact with Italy, but for the most part they were content to ignore all this. However, as the tension grew between the real conditions of practical life and the old ideal of aristocratic rule, which had been invented in very different circumstances, Italian humanism came suddenly alive in Renaissance England.[32] It was More's generation that first perceived the value of this cultural alternative and began to propagate it successfully among the political classes in England. And it may have been More who understood its implications best, better even than the humanist friends with whom he shared so much. Of course, there was still too much continuity with the Middle Ages – in society and politics and culture – for this emancipation to be complete; even contemporary Italy was making an accommodation with the aristocratic court. More himself remained caught between two worlds, and something of the ambiguity in his work lies there. His supreme merit is in his self-consciousness about the alternatives.

More read Plato then, not as a philosopher, but as a humanist rhetorician. More's wisdom derives from experience in the world, not retreat into contemplation. Hythloday is not Socrates, nor even Erasmus, although he takes a little from each. More's practical political skills were tied to his real experience and to his humanist eloquence, to the need to persuade the wealthy and powerful of their political obligations. Just so was he to make his own career in parliament and the King's council.[33] *Utopia* is not, therefore, a philosophical tract, but a rhetorical one meant to persuade by its literary skill.

For the humanist rhetorician, it was poetry and history along with oratory that furnished the models for expression and the fund of examples that constituted political wisdom.[34] Through poetry and history, the

[32] This is not to deny the anticipations sketched by Roberto Weiss, *Humanism in England during the Fifteenth Century,* 2d ed. (Oxford: Blackwell, 1957). But no fifteenth-century Englishman (except perhaps for one or two who remained abroad) assimilated classical culture and put it to use like the generation that came to maturity in the 1490s: William Grocyn, Thomas Linacre, Colet, Erasmus, and More. See Denys Hay, "The Early Renaissance in England," and "England and the Humanities in the Fifteenth Century," in *Renaissance Essays* (London: Ronceverte, 1988), 151–231.

[33] See William Nelson, "Thomas More, Grammarian and Orator," in *Essential Articles,* ed. Sylvester and Marc'hadour, 104–18.

[34] Students, More writes in his contemporary letter to Oxford (1518), must learn prudence in human affairs, "and I doubt that any study contributes as readily to this practical skill as the study of the poets, orators and historians." *In Defense of Humanism,* ed. Daniel Kinney, vol. 15 of *Works* (1986), 139. This, of course, is the ancient sophistic, so vigorously opposed by Socrates in *The Republic,* and dismissed by the rest of classical and medieval philosophy.

individual could come to extend his own limited personal experience of the world. And this is just what Hythloday is purported to have done. He has traveled to a new world and seen for himself how things work elsewhere; he is ready on every occasion to support his arguments with an appropriate example. The only difference is that instead of finding his examples in the classical books, he has made them all up!

Hythloday's examples, including the utopia itself, are therefore, like himself, all deliberate fictions, although they are presented as histories. More has gone out of his way to give the traveler's story all the trappings of verisimilitude. Erasmus had already suggested that if an entirely fictional narrative was to be used to make a point, "we must make it as much like the real thing as possible."[35] So More provides a map of Utopia and an alphabet for the language. He furnishes introductory letters of friends to attest to its historicity. He supplies a detailed and realistic setting for the scene of the dialogue and the description of Utopia. Nevertheless, the whole discussion in the prefatory epistles and Book 1 has alerted us to the likelihood that this is a fiction, and many of the persons and places are deliberately given names that declare their fictional character.[36] As far as I can see, no reader was ever taken in, and More was both attacked and admired for the "fictions" he had invented.[37] It became

---

[35] *De Copia*, ed. Craig R. Thompson, trans. Betty Knott and Brian McGregor, in *The Collected Works of Erasmus* (Toronto: University of Toronto Press, 1978), 24:634. See Logan, *Meaning*, 29–30.

[36] "We forgot to ask, and he forgot to say," writes More to Giles in the preface, "in what part of the world Utopia lies. I am sorry that point was omitted. . . ." *Utopia*, 42. See also Walter R. Davis, "Thomas More's *Utopia* as Fiction," *Centennial Review* 24 (1980): 249–68; and Richard Sylvester, "*Si Hythlodaeus Credimus*: Vision and Revision in *Utopia*," in *Essential Articles*, ed. Sylvester and Marc'hadour, 290–301. As for the names, the old view of Sir James Mackintosh, that "All the names which he invented for men and places were intimations of their being unreal," remains standard. See R. J. Schoeck, "Levels of Word-Play and Figurative Significations in More's *Utopia*," *Notes and Queries*, n.s. 1 (1954): 512; J. D. Simmonds, "More's Use of Names in Book II of *Utopia*," *Der Neuren Sprachen*, N.F. 10 (1961): 282–4; and Surtz, "*Utopia* as a Work of Literary Art," *Utopia*, cxlvii. Thus the Polylerites, whom Hythloday pretends to have visited, are "People of Much Nonsense"; the Achorians who live near Utopia are "without place, region, district," etc. *Utopia*, 343 n., 358 n. And of course More refers to his work as *Nusquama* (nowhere) when he sends it to Erasmus in 1516 and in subsequent letters; see Erasmus, *Opus epistolarum Des. Erasmi Roterodami*, ed. P. S. and H. M. Allen (Oxford: Clarendon Press, 1906–58), 2:339, 346, 354, 359, 372.

[37] So William Tyndale accused More of "feigning" matters in *Utopia*. Tyndale, *An Answer to Sir Thomas More's Dialogue* (1530), ed. Henry Walter, Parker Society, 44 (Cambridge, 1850), 193. On the other hand, Thomas Wilson praised him for his "feined Narrations and wittie invented matters (as though they were true in deede)." Wilson, *Arte of Rhetorique* (1553); quoted with many other examples in Jackson Campbell Boswell, *Sir Thomas More in the English Renaissance: An Annotated Catalogue*, Medieval and Renaissance Texts and Studies, 83 (Binghamton, N.Y., 1992), 336–7 and

customary to couple the *Utopia* with Plato's *Republic,* and sometimes
with Cicero's *De oratore,* Xenophon's *Cyropaedia,* and Castiglione's
Courtier, as fictional ideals, all "faire shadows in the aire," "too good to
be true."[38] When Thomas Smith, a generation later, elected to describe the
English commonwealth as he believed it was, he deliberately set his subject apart from the fictional commonwealths of More and Plato, "such as
never were nor shall ever be, vaine imaginations, phantasies of philosophers to occupie their time and to exercise their wittes." Even More's
biographer, Nicholas Harpsfield, described *Utopia* as "an inventive drift
of Sir Thomas More's owne imagination and head," rather than "a very
sure knowen story."[39]

In 1517, a second edition of *Utopia* appeared at Paris under the aegis
of the young English humanist Thomas Lupset. Among its variations, the
most important was a new letter from More to Peter Giles, appended to
the text. In it, More carries his game further. He pretends to answer a
critic who had objected that if the work was true it was absurd; if a
fiction, then it was lacking in judgment. More replies that if he had dared
to introduce any fiction, it would have been only as embellishment, and
he would anyway have tipped off the learned reader to his design by using
fictional names, suggesting (for example) that the island was nowhere,
the city a phantom, the river without water, and the ruler without a
people.[40] If after that any reader still wanted to doubt the history, More
adds, let him seek out the others who were present at the conversation, or
indeed Hythloday himself, who was still alive and well – now off somewhere in Portugal![41] They would soon find that More, at least, had been a
faithful historian in reporting his conversation with Hythloday, though

---

passim. More's early Italian readers had no trouble discerning the fiction and (among the
friends of Machiavelli anyway) complaining about its impracticality; see Francesco
Vettori, *Sommario della istoria d'Italia* (1527), in *Scritti storici e politici,* ed. Enrico
Niccolini (Bari, Italy: Laterza, 1972), 145; and (from a more sympathetic point of view)
N. L. Tomeo to Pole (1524) in Surtz, *Praise of Wisdom,* 6.

[38] James Cleland, *Institution of the Young Nobleman* (1607); Samuel Purchas, *Purchas his
Pilgrimage* (1613). Cited in Boswell, *Sir Thomas More,* 64–5, 252. For other examples,
see ibid., 9, 86, 90, 103, 121, 158–9.

[39] Sir Thomas Smith, *De Republica Anglorum,* ed. L. Alston (Cambridge: Cambridge
University Press, 1906), 142. Harpsfield, *Life,* 104.

[40] See also Arthur E. Barker, "*Clavis Moreana*: The Yale Edition of Thomas More," in
Essential Articles, ed. Sylvester and Marc'hadour, 227; and Peter R. Allen, *Utopia* and
European Humanism: The Function of the Prefatory Letters and Verses," *Studies in the
Renaissance* 10 (1963): 100–1.

[41] In an earlier prefatory epistle, Giles writes to Busleyden confirming More's recollection
that they had forgotten to ask where Utopia was, and he repeats some speculation that
Hythloday was either dead or that he had returned to Utopia. *Utopia,* 24.

whether Hythloday had been equally reliable in his account of Utopia was another matter. More could not vouch for that. "I am responsible for my own work alone and not also for the credit of another." The joke was a bit much, and it is not surprising that it was suppressed in the next edition (1518) and afterward. It was hardly necessary to make plain what every sophisticated reader surely knew already: that More had invented and labeled both his fictions, the conversation with Hythloday (nonsense) and the description of Utopia (nowhere).[42]

Now if there is anything unusual about all this, it is, I believe, in the self-consciousness of the author, which he willingly shares with his readers. Throughout the Middle Ages authors had invented fictions and passed them off as histories, or written histories into which they intruded fictions, almost without criticism.[43] The most notorious of these may have been that twelfth-century monk Geoffrey of Monmouth, who seems to have invented (or borrowed) an entire fictional history for early Britain, culminating in the legendary Celtic King Arthur. His work was immediately employed by both poets and chroniclers, who embellished it vastly and took it for true, right down to Thomas More's day. Caxton received the story from Sir Thomas Malory and in one of his noblest publications insisted on publishing it as genuine.[44] It would be nice to know what More thought about it; his father owned a copy and even recorded More's birth in it. All we know is that he once made a joke about one of the sillier stories in the legend.[45] Perhaps his silence is suggestive. More's acquaintance, Polydore Vergil, was just then questioning its veracity, while More's friends and fellow humanists, Erasmus and Vives, were equally appalled by the immorality and improbability of the stories that were based on it. It was not long before English humanists were ready to discard the whole thing pretty completely on both grounds.[46] What Geof-

---

[42] On this point see the letter of Beatus Rhenanus (1518) in *Utopia*, 253. For the name Hythloday, meaning "expert in trifles" or "well-learned in nonsense," see *Utopia*, 301; for Utopia as "nowhere," see n. 36, above.

[43] "Readers coming to medieval historians for the first time may be perplexed to find patent fictions presented as part of a true account; readers of medieval fictions may wonder why invented stories are offered as 'true.'" Ruth Morse, *Truth and Convention in the Middle Ages: Rhetoric, Representation, and Reality* (Cambridge: Cambridge University Press, 1991), 4.

[44] Levine, "Caxton's Histories," 40–5.

[45] Richard Pace tells the story, *De fructu qui ex doctrina percipitur*, ed. and trans. Frank Manley and Richard Sylvester (New York: Ungar, 1967), 105–7.

[46] Erasmus dismissed the Arthurian romances in the same year as *Utopia* in his *Institutio principis Christiani*. See *The Education of a Christian Prince*, trans. Lester K. Born (New York: Columbia University Press, 1968), 200. Polydore Vergil criticized the story in the

frey thought he was doing is now beyond retrieval, but it is clear that no medieval author was willing to declare his purpose by making a bold distinction between fiction and history. When they told a fiction they pretended it was history; when they recounted a history, they included fiction; and neither authors nor audience seemed much to care.[47]

What was missing, apparently, was the early modern idea of history, in which it was thought that something like a true and literal description of the past could be winnowed out and distinguished from fiction. Medieval historiography worked largely by accretion, rarely ever by subtraction; a story once told gained authority by mere reiteration and the passage of time. In this context the humanist cry *ad fontes* was revolutionary. But equally important, there was lacking an idea of fiction independent of received tradition, fiction as something with a value all its own that could be deliberately and purposefully *invented,* as opposed to a "history" that had to be *discovered* in a contemporary authority. What may have been required was a jolt of recognition, a shock to the English consciousness, perhaps like that delivered by Giangaliozzo Visconti to the Florentines at the beginning of the Italian Renaissance, which (according to Hans Baron) shook them from their medieval illusions about their own past and created a new critical history.[48] The English were not so lucky; and

Anglica Historica, which More may have seen. See Denys Hay, *Polydore Vergil* (Oxford: Clarendon Press, 1952), 109–11. See also Robert P. Adams, "Bold Bawdy and Open Manslaughter: The English New Humanist Attack on Medieval Romance," *Huntington Library Quarterly* 23 (1959): 33–44; Nelson, *Fact or Fiction,* 98–105; and Levine, "Caxton's Histories," 48–9, 231.

47 C. S. Lewis for one doubted that any English author, including Chaucer, believed he was writing fiction; according to Lewis, all proceeded as though they were composing histories. Lewis, "The English Prose *Morte,*" in *Essays on Malory,* ed. J. A. W. Bennett (Oxford: Clarendon Press, 1963), 22. For other authorities on this matter, see Levine, "Caxton's Histories," 216 n. 3, 219 n. 20.

48 See Hans Baron, *The Crisis of the Early Italian Renaissance,* 2d ed. (Princeton: Princeton University Press, 1966); and Baron, *In Search of Florentine Civic Humanism* (Princeton: Princeton University Press, 1988), esp. 1:254–5, 2:6–12; 67, where Baron makes some suggestions about how his thesis might be applied to the English Renaissance. There are appreciations of Baron by Denys Hay and August Buck and a bibliography of his writings in *Renaissance Studies in Honor of Hans Baron* (Florence: G. C. Sansoni, 1971). The fullest effort to apply the civic argument to English culture remains Arthur B. Ferguson, *The Articulate Citizen of the English Renaissance* (Durham: Duke University Press, 1965). Whether the Milanese wars were required to liberate Florentine civic humanism has been much debated and is not relevant to our argument. What is required is an appropriate social-political context. See most recently Donald Kelley, *Renaissance Humanism* (Boston: Iwayne, 1991), 14–28. For civic humanism generally, see the works of Eugenio Garin, esp. *Italian Humanism: Philosophy and Civic Life in the Renaissance,* trans. Peter Munz (New York: Harper and Row, 1965); and William J. Bouwsma, *Venice and the Defense of Republican Liberty* (Berkeley: University of California Press, 1968). It is worth emphasizing that Utopia is a republic.

the Middle Ages receded only imperceptibly before the gradual alteration of English political and social life. However, More was especially well situated in his London setting to understand these changes, and they are wonderfully well illustrated in Hythloday's description of the realities of English life in Book 1, where all chivalric considerations are banished and the aristocracy portrayed merely as rapacious landlords and courtly sycophants. It certainly looks as though More understood that there was a fundamental difference between the facts of life and their contemporary representation, between history and fiction, and one that mattered. One has only to compare his account of chivalry with that of his contemporary, Stephen Hawes's *Pastime of Pleasure,* or any of Caxton's many publications.[49] But *Utopia* is very different from these works and Geoffrey of Monmouth in another way; unlike them, it was *meant* to be read and understood as a deliberate fiction. While there were many then who continued to believe in Geoffrey's "old Welsh book" (and a few today who have not yet given up the search), it does not appear that anyone ever sought out Raphael Hythloday.

As often happens, theory followed afterward, and it was only later that another Englishman, Sir Philip Sidney, remembering (among other things) More's "feigned image of poetry," discovered a justification for poetic invention; his defense of poetry is apparently among the first to do so in England.[50] But by then, the time of Queen Elizabeth, the distinction between history and fiction, which had been earlier elaborated on the continent by such as Giraldo Cinthio and Ludovico Castelvetro, had become almost commonplace.[51] On the one side, the historians were busy

---

[49] Hawes "looked with regretful longing upon the Middle Ages," writes a modern editor, and "upon the vanishing glory of chivalry, with its fantastic conception of honour and courtesy," and he hoped somehow to renew it. Both the form and content of the poem depend on an early-fifteenth-century predecessor, John Lydgate. William Edward Mead, introduction to *The Pastime of Pleasure,* by Stephen Hawes, ed. Mead, Early English Text Society, o.s. 173 (London, 1928), xli. There were four editions of the work, 1509, 1517, 1554, and 1555.

[50] *The Defence of Poesie,* in *The Prose Works of Sir Philip Sidney,* ed. Albert Feuillerat (Cambridge: Cambridge University Press, 1963), 3:15. "The defense of poetry . . . is a defense not of poetry as against prose but of fiction against fact. . . . What is in question is not man's right to sing but his right to feign, to 'make things up' . . . that debate, properly viewed, is simply the difficult process by which Europe became conscious of fiction as an activity different from history on the one hand and from lying on the other." C. S. Lewis, cited in Harry Berger, "The Renaissance Imagination: Second World and Green World," *Centennial Review* 9 (1965): 39.

[51] See Giraldo Cinthio, *On Romances,* trans. Henry L. Snuggs (Lexington, Ky.: University of Kentucky Press, 1968), 51, 167; Ludovico Castelvetro, *On the Art of Poetry,* trans. Andrew Bongiorno (Binghamton, N.Y.: State University of New York Press, 1984), 3ff, 92ff. In general, see Baxter Hathaway, *The Age of Criticism: The Late Renaissance in*

defending their practices against the feigning of romance; on the other side, the poets were only too pleased to announce their freedom from the facts.[52]

III

It was, therefore, out of a realization that there was a disjunction between the real features of English public life and the idealized versions of medieval fiction that I think the modern separation of history from fiction was first conceived.[53] Chivalry had been invented as a set of fictional ideals to meet the needs of medieval feudalism; Renaissance England badly required a new set of fictional ideals to replace the old ones, which no longer seemed to matter. *Utopia* can thus be understood as an attempt to create one, but it differs fundamentally from chivalric romance by *openly pretending* that it is history: in other words, by *displaying* its fictional character. The ancients had long ago defended the idea of poetry as suited to the purpose of teaching morality, and Aristotle (in the humanist *Poetics* that the Middle Ages generally ignored) had declared its superiority to history in that respect. When finally Philip Sidney came to reconsider the subject in a work that was indebted both to Aristotle and to his humanistic predecessors, he argued vigorously for the superiority of poetry over history in exemplifying the highest ideals, precisely because the poet could shape his work freely and without the constraints of a recalcitrant reality. "If the poet do his part aright, he will show you . . . nothing that is not to be shunned. . . . Where[as] the historian, bound to tell things as

---

Italy (Ithaca, N.Y.: Cornell University Press, 1962), and the works cited in Levine, "Caxton's Histories," 232 nn. 133–5.

52 For the *artes historicae,* see the collection in Johann Wolfius, *Artis historicae penus* (Basel, 1579), several of which were known in England. Thomas Blundeville's *True Order and Methode of Wryting and Reading Hystories* (1574) was adapted from the works of Patrizzi and Acontius; see the version edited by Hugh G. Dick in *Huntington Library Quarterly* 3 (1940): 149–70. In "Caxton's Histories" (51, 51 n.), I have quoted from William Shakespeare, John Marston, Thomas Dekker, George Chapman, and Ben Jonson to show the new confidence in the independence of fiction.

53 This could be extended to More's view of the religious life also, although that is a large matter that deserves separate treatment. More certainly shared with Erasmus a disdain for popular hagiography, which he complained had interpolated many pious frauds into ecclesiastical history; see his defense of Lucian's *Philopseudes* in the dedicatory letter to Thomas Ruthall that was prefixed to his translation. *The Translations of Lucian,* ed. Craig R. Thompson, vol. 3 of *Works* (1974), 5–7. A contrast between the real lives of monks and friars and the idealized orders in Utopia is set up in the first book of *Utopia,* when at Morton's dinner table they are criticized for idleness, and again later when Hythloday points out how the church had deliberately corrupted Christ's teaching by making it agreeable to everyone.

things were, cannot be liberal, without he be poetical of a perfect pattern."[54] His contemporary, George Puttenham, also singling out the *Utopia*, made exactly the same point.[55]

I think that More must have understood this already. He saw that his fictional utopia could be more perfectly shaped to his ideal than any real polity in the past, not excluding Greece and Rome,[56] and so he drew up his ideal state in the shape of an imaginary example. The more acutely he observed the realities of contemporary life, without any of the illusions of late medieval chivalry, the freer he became to invent remedies.[57] It seems to have been his direct experience with contemporary affairs along with his Christian dissatisfaction with human nature that told him that history *could* not furnish him with a perfect example. And so he found himself, perhaps for the first time in England, suddenly emancipated from the necessity of concealing his views in a history. Admittedly, he pretends that his account is historical, and so doffs a satirical cap to an old convention, but he clearly wants everyone to know that it is a pretense.[58] Having separated the real and the ideal in his own mind, he was ready to separate fiction from history.

---

[54] Sidney, *Defence*, 3:16. Both poetry and history have the advantage over philosophy that they teach concretely by example, and thus move the reader to action.

[55] The first poets were historians, Puttenham says, and did not worry about using "feined matter or [matter] altogether fabulous," because poetry could teach by invented examples at least as well as by true ones. "The poet hath the handling of them to fashion at his pleasure, but not so th'other which go according to their veritie and none otherwise without the writers great blame." *The Republic* and *Utopia* are his best illustrations. Both the authorship and the date of composition of this work remain problematical. See George Puttenham, *The Arte of English Poesie*, ed. Gladys Willcock and Alice Walker (Cambridge: Cambridge University Press, 1936), 40–1.

[56] "It far surpasses and leaves a long way behind the many celebrated and much lauded commonwealths of the Spartans, Athenians and Romans." Jerome Busleyden to More (1516), in *Utopia*, 34. More was widely read in classical history; see the poem of Robert Whittington to More (1519), *Huntington Library Quarterly* 26 (1963): 147–54; Erasmus to Guillaume Bude, *Opus Epistolarum*, 4:577; and Hexter, "Composition," in *Utopia*, lxxxi–xcv.

[57] "The presentation of a defective contemporary world is meaningful only when seen against the contrasting ideal world. Vice-versa, the ideality of that realm finds its meaning only in its vis-à-vis position to reality. And that means its clear and distinct demarcation as irreality." Hubertus S. Herbruggen, "More's *Utopia* as Paradigm," in *Essential Articles*, ed. Sylvester and Marc'hadour, 262. See also Kevin Corrigan, "The Function of the Ideal in Plato's *Republic* and Sir Thomas More's *Utopia*," *Moreana* 27 (1990): 42. It seems to me that Thomas Nashe is saying something like this when he characterizes *Utopia* in the *Unfortunate Traveller* (1594). See Jackson Boswell, "The Reception of Erasmus's *Moriae* in England through 1640," *Erasmus of Rotterdam Society Yearbook*, 7 (Oxon Hill, Md., 1987), 80.

[58] Here too there was classical inspiration in the satires of Lucian, which More and Erasmus had earlier read and translated; see More, *Translations of Lucian*.

Still, it will not do to hurry this separation too far when the idea was yet so new and imperfect. More may well have grasped the idea that a writer was free to invent a fiction, and that fiction might even be preferable to history in the description of an ideal. But the corollary, still implicit, was that to describe reality, history might be preferable to fiction. It is not surprising, therefore, that More set to work on a history at this very time, and that its subject was that wicked and realistic prince Richard III, who (according to Shakespeare) "set the murderous Machiavel to school."[59] The contrast between the ideally good rule of Utopia and the brutally bad rule of More's contemporary prince could hardly be more stark – and in its way instructive. But More's problem remained unresolved: It was more than ever difficult for him to see what the relationship was between the ideal of his imagination and the reality of life. And it was just here that More paused – he completed neither the English nor the Latin version of his history. The sticking point seems to have been his perception of the intractability of real politics. For if it was hard for him to see how the ideal of Utopia could be applied to real life, it must have been equally difficult for him to see how the grim realities of history could be made to serve the good life. Certainly, More had no illusions about an easy assimilation of the two. We have seen that in *Utopia* neither More nor Hythloday ever argues for the immediate application of high principle to real life; and both agree that the obstacle is human nature and desire. How far then could a realistic portrayal of the wicked life be helpful? "History," Sidney was to point out later, "being captivated to the truth of a foolish world, is many times a terror from well-doing, and an encouragement to unbridled wickedness." Not all tyrants got their due.[60] Of course, Richard did; but what about the successful and unprincipled Henry VII?[61] With something like that in mind, More may well have hesitated.

It is possible, then, that More's commitment to a realistic history was inhibited by his perception of political reality in much the same way that his idealism was hampered by his sense of what was practical. To be sure, there were some advantages to this dichotomy. *Utopia* gains in plausibil-

[59] *Henry VI, Part 3* 3.2.

[60] Sidney, *Defence*, 3:18. So too Richard Sylvester "The History of King Richard III," vol. 2 of *Works* (1963), ciii.

[61] More fell afoul of Henry VII toward the end of his reign and may well have hesitated before celebrating him as a moral agent. Roper tells the story of More's unpleasant encounter with the king in *Lyfe*, 7–8. When Henry died, More wrote a Latin poem rejoicing at the end of slavery. See Richard Marius, *Thomas More: A Biography*, 51–2.

ity from its close attention to the details of ordinary life, even while we suspect its practicality. *The History of Richard III* earns its moral stature, despite its close attention to the details of the king's wicked politics, by forecasting a just end. More's history is not impressive for its fidelity, but it is startlingly original in its lifelike descriptions, lengthy speeches, and splendid dialogues, few of which could have been authorized by the sources. In truth, *The History of Richard III* is almost as much fiction as it is history, though it is a fiction imagined as though it had happened that way.[62] Here again More was helped by classical precedent, for in ancient times historians had employed classical rhetoric for similar purposes and without embarrassment – thereby deliberately fudging the distinction between poetry and history.[63] Sidney repeats the received tradition when he points out that "a feigned example hath as much force to teach as a true example (for as to move, it is clear, since the feigned may be tuned to the highest key of passion)."[64]

Indeed, it looks as though More understood that the rumor and hearsay that he reports were not from eyewitnesses, and that the speeches and descriptions that fill his work were therefore not the literal truth.[65] But the moral value of his story, the dissuasive effect of a bad example, seems (for the moment anyway) to have overcome whatever scruples he might have had, and his history is more like Hythloday's Utopia than he dared to admit. Had he wished to use his history for a more practical purpose, as a guide to success in actual politics – as did Machiavelli, or his later English disciple, Francis Bacon – he would have to have written it differently, more realistically. More knew the world well enough and without illusions, but he had no desire to submit to it. If he did not finish writing

---

[62] "It is questionable whether More regarded himself as writing history; his story is more like a drama . . . for which fidelity to historical fact is scarcely relevant." A. R. Myers, *History Today* (1955), 4: 515. See also A. F. Pollard, "The Making of Sir Thomas More's *Richard III,*" in *Essential Articles*, ed. Sylvester and Marc'hadour, 421–35; L. F. Dean, "Literary Problems in More's *Richard III,*" in ibid., 315–25; and Alison Hanham, *Richard III and the Historians* (Oxford: Clarendon Press, 1975), 163, 166–8.

[63] Critical historiography did not develop by imitating the ancients, but by recovering them through the invention of the methods of philology and archaeology. Here it is Erasmus who might have taught More. More seems to have been particularly influenced by the recent recovery and publication of Tacitus's powerful portrait of the tyrant Tiberius, a dark and uncertain history that might well have caused alarm, even as it served him as a model. Sylvester, "The History of King Richard III, in *Works* (1963), xc–xcvii.

[64] Sidney, *Defence*, 3:17; cf. Thomas Wilson, *The Arte of Rhetorique* (London, 1553), 101v, 104.

[65] See Alistair Fox, *Politics and Literature in the Reigns of Henry VII and Henry VIII* (Oxford: Blackwell, 1989), 125–6.

his history, it may have been the result of immediate circumstances;[66] but he may also have found it unsatisfactory for his purpose. (He was eventually to disavow *Utopia* also, when it seemed unsuitable.) By 1516, the radical disjunction between his moral ideals and his perceptions of the real world had begun to oppress him, and he preferred to take flight in fancy, not history, knowing full well that it made a difference, and asking his readers to share that difference with him. As long as he remained in such a humor, realistic history, with its emphasis on the wickedness of human behavior, could hardly be expected to provide much solace. In this respect at least, fiction clearly had all the advantage.

IV

Burckhardt is no longer in fashion today and the "problem of the Renaissance" has largely been dismissed from the textbooks, having long ago outlived its usefulness.[67] Among other things, aggrieved medievalists have properly restored the manifold achievements of the ten lost centuries after antiquity that Burckhardt seemed to deny, as well as the many anticipations of what had once seemed so original to the Renaissance.[68] It was, in any case, never easy to see how Burckhardt could have relevance to an English scene that was so thoroughly different in setting from Italy, so much further removed from antiquity, and so much more obviously continuous with everything medieval. Yet there is a sense in which Thomas More can be seen as a perfect Burckhardtian prototype, as startling and unprecedented in his setting as any in the great gallery of Italian Renaissance originals.

No part of Burckhardt's work has caused so much distress as that passage at the beginning of the second part of his book where he gives the fullest description of what he takes to be the essential character of the Renaissance. He has already described the new political situation in

---

[66] *Richard III* ends in the English version with Morton encouraging Henry, Duke of Buckingham, to rebellion against Richard III. In 1514, the son, Edward, Duke of Buckingham, became Henry VIII's heir; by 1521, he was accused of treason and executed. The parallel may well have occurred to More and given him pause. See Hexter, in *Utopia*, lxix; and Hanham, *Richard III*, 188–9.

[67] For a history of the problem, see Wallace Ferguson, *The Renaissance in Historical Thought: Five Centuries of Interpretation* (Boston: Houghton Mifflin, 1948); and, more recently, William Kerrigan and Gordon Braden, *The Idea of the Renaissance* (Baltimore: Johns Hopkins University Press, 1989), 11–13.

[68] The result can be a long Middle Ages that purports to last at least until 1789; see Jacques Le Goff, *Time, Work, and Culture in the Middle Ages,* trans. Arthur Goldhammer (Chicago: University of Chicago Press, 1980), ix–xi.

Italy that generated the mentality that (for the first time since antiquity) saw the state as a "work of art," that is, as an object of reflection and calculation. Now he says that during the Middle Ages, "both sides of the human consciousness – that which was turned within as that which was turned without – lay dreaming or half awake beneath a common veil." It was in Italy during the Renaissance that this veil was first lifted and "an *objective* treatment and consideration of the state and of all things in the world became possible," while at the same time a *subjective* understanding of the individual also developed.[69] The proposition is so ambitious and so general (so Hegelian despite Burckhardt's disclaimers) that it has even troubled some of his admirers.[70] Yet it makes sudden sense when applied to the Thomas More of *Utopia*, not only in the obvious way that his work displays an objective treatment of the state, but in the open subjectivity of the author who is accessible to us as no previous Englishman. More's dialogue with himself is as unprecedented in English literature as is his deliberate "self-fashioning."[71] And this is attested to by his son-in-law's remarkable biography, the portraits by Holbein, and by other contemporary sources, which manage somehow to describe and display the interiority of More's life as though under the influence of his public introspection.[72] His self-deprecating sense of hu-

---

[69] Jacob Burckhardt, *The Civilization of the Renaissance in Italy,* trans. S. G. C. Middlemore (London: Phaidon, 1965), 2, 81.

[70] See Sir Ernst Gombrich, "In Search of Cultural History," in *Ideals and Idols* (Oxford: Phaidon, 1979), 43; and Hans Baron, "The Limits of the Notion of Renaissance Individualism: Burckhardt after a Century," *In Search of Florentine Civic Humanism,* 2:155–81.

[71] I refer, of course, to Stephen Greenblatt, *Renaissance Self-Fashioning from More to Shakespeare* (Chicago: University of Chicago Press, 1980). Greenblatt defines the term as "an increased self-consciousness about the fashioning of human identity as a manipulable, artful process" (2); he indicates his own debt to Burckhardt on his first page and again on pp. 161–2. Greenblatt see More's *Utopia* as "the perfect expression of his self-conscious role-playing and an intense meditation upon its limits" (33). So far, at least, we agree, though I am not sure that Greenblatt or any of the new historicists would be very comfortable with my distinction between history and fiction.

[72] Even Utopian music reflects this new inwardness. According to E. E. Lowinsky, "one of the basic tenets of the Renaissance [was] that the true function of music is to express in tones the inner world of man. And while this ideal originated in vocal music, it was an Englishman who, at the beginning of the century, foresaw its application to instrumental music." Lowinsky, "English Organ Music of the Renaissance," *Musical Quarterly* 39 (1953): 542. More, *Utopia,* 236 and 236 n. Huizinga had already noticed this example in "Realism," 300. For More's meticulous observation of living things, see Erasmus's portrait in his letter to Ulrich von Hutten, 23 July 1519, *Opus Epistolarum,* 4:12–23. For Holbein's remarkable portraits of More and his family, see David Piper, "Hans Holbein the Younger in England," *Journal of the Royal Society of Arts* 111 (1963): 736–55; and Stanley Morison, *The Likenesses of Thomas More* (London: Burns and Oates, 1963).

mor may be unique in its time and has lost nothing through the passage
of the centuries. Next to him, his predecessors and most of his contemporaries remain two-dimensional.

What I am suggesting, then, is that More's originality, his modernity,
rests on his self-consciousness; and that his self-consciousness allowed
him to separate himself from his world and view it objectively, even while
he remained self-absorbed within his own soul. He was probably the first
person in England to explore the tension between the real and the ideal,
and thus between history and fiction, in a way that is still interesting to
us. He is, in Burckhardt's terms, the first English Renaissance individual.
But as the first of his kind he lived apart from other men, cut off from his
contemporaries and thoroughly uncomfortable in his time. We can read
him as a harbinger of things to come but we should not exaggerate his
modernity. It is only when the social and cultural scene shifted sufficiently
to turn everything medieval into anachronism that More's precocious
self-consciousness will become general and everyone will think of keeping
a diary and writing an autobiography. But by then, paradoxically, *Utopia*
will have turned itself into a classic and appear to have values that are
timeless, even though its own argument can probably best be understood
and appreciated by retrieving the peculiar circumstances of its original
composition.

5

Little Crosby and the horizons of early modern
historical culture

D. R. WOOLF

The importance of antiquarianism in the creation of modern attitudes to
the past, and of modern historical method, has long been acknowledged.
Building on the work of classicists and Europeanists such as Arnaldo
Momigliano, students of English historiography in particular have pointed
out the ways in which confrontation with the archaeological and documentary remains of ancient and modern times reoriented history away from a
recitation of events toward an appreciation of cultural change, institutional development, and social evolution. Works by Thomas Kendrick,
David C. Douglas, Stuart Piggott, F. J. Levy, J. G. A. Pocock, Arthur B.
Ferguson, Joseph M. Levine, and Stan A. E. Mendyk demonstrate how the
antiquarian methods developed by John Leland, William Camden, Henry
Spelman, and others, growing out of the powerful tradition of Renaissance
scholarship that included Flavio Biondo, Poggio Bracciolini, Lorenzo
Valla, Guillaume Budé, and Joseph Scaliger, provided the foundations for
the great achievements of eighteenth- and nineteenth-century historians
like Edward Gibbon, while gradually diminishing belief in legendary personalities such as Albion, Samothes, and Brutus the Trojan.[1]

I am indebted for their comments and criticism to the participants (and especially to Linda
Levy Peck, Annabel Patterson, Richard Helgerson, and John Pocock), and members of the
audience at the 1993 Woodrow Wilson Center conference at which a very different version of
the present essay was read. Helpful criticisms have been offered by David Harris Sacks,
Donald R. Kelley, Mark Kishlansky, Jack Crowley, and Paul Fideler. I wish also to thank my
past and present graduate students, Kathryn Brammall, Greg Bak, Krista Kesselring, and
Ruth McClelland-Nugent for discussions of the material and themes covered herein. The ar-
chivist and staff of the Lancashire Record Office have been unfailingly helpful during and
since my research there in 1992 and 1995. Above all, I am grateful to Brian Whitlock Blundell
for his keen interest in and assistance to my pursuit of his family's past. The research for this
chapter was funded by the Social Sciences and Humanities Research Council of Canada.
[1] A. D. Momigliano, "Ancient History and the Antiquarian," in *Studies in Historiography*
(London: Weidenfeld and Nicolson, 1966), 1–39; T. D. Kendrick, *British Antiquity* (Lon-

My task is not to dispute this "high" account of the origins of history. Rather, I wish to broaden it beyond its usual concerns – matters of evidence, literary craftsmanship, and philological technique – into a consideration of the social and cultural grounds in the early modern period that gave rise to the very methodological advances that are usually accredited wholly to intellectual stimuli such as "humanism." The present essay touches on traditional historiographical issues but plumbs more deeply for some of the defining characteristics of early modern English historical culture between the early sixteenth and early eighteenth centuries to speculate on that culture's relation to the profoundly historical popular mindset of the modern West. The term "historical culture" is nothing more than a convenient shorthand for the perceptual and cognitive matrix of relations among past, present, and future, a matrix that gives rise to, nurtures, and is in turn influenced by the formal historical writing of that era, but that also manifests itself in other ways, including many that look decidedly suspicious from the point of view of modern historical method.[2] A historical culture consists of habits of thought, languages and media of communication, and patterns of social convention that embrace elite and popular, narrative and nonnarrative modes of discourse. It is expressed both in texts and in commonplace forms of behavior, for instance in the keeping of time, in the celebration of anniversaries and birthdays, and in the resolution of conflicts through reference to a widely accepted historical standard such as "antiquity." The defining characteristics of a historical culture are subject to material, social, and circumstantial forces that, as much as the traditionally studied intellectual influences, condition the way in which the mind thinks, reads, writes, and speaks of the past.

don: Methuen, 1950); David C. Douglas, *English Scholars 1660–1730*, rev. ed. (London: Eyre and Spottiswoode, 1951); Stuart Piggott, *Ruins in a Landscape: Essays in Antiquarianism* (Edinburgh: University Press, 1976), and *Ancient Britons and the Antiquarian Imagination: Ideas from the Renaissance to the Regency* (London: Thames and Hudson, 1989); F. J. Levy, *Tudor Historical Thought* (San Marino, Calif.: Huntington Library, 1967); J. G. A. Pocock, *The Ancient Constitution and the Feudal Law: A Study of English Historical Thought in the Seventeenth Century. A Reissue with a Retrospect* (Cambridge: Cambridge University Press, 1987); Arthur B. Ferguson, *Clio Unbound: Perception of the Social and Cultural Past in Renaissance England* (Durham: Duke University Press, 1979); Joseph M. Levine, *Humanism and History: Origins of Modern English Historiography* (Ithaca, NY: Cornell University Press, 1987); Stan A. E. Mendyk, *"Speculum Britanniae": Regional Study, Antiquarianism and Science in Britain to 1700* (Toronto: University of Toronto Press, 1989).
[2] My usage of this expression derives not from Sande Cohen's semiological investigation of the modes of current academic historical signification in his *Historical Culture: On the Recoding of an Academic Discipline* (Berkeley, Los Angeles, and London: University of California Press, 1986), but from Bernard Guenée's important study, *Histoire et culture historique dans l'Occident médiéval* (Paris: Aubier, 1980).

This essay will address some of these issues concretely by examining a relatively obscure incident at the beginning of the seventeenth century. Unraveling this single event and placing it within a number of cultural contexts (contexts that can be further illustrated by reference to other contemporary sources lying further afield) may provide an agenda for future research into early modern historical thought and writing. Such research will link formal historiography to issues that were of basic importance in defining the mentality of contemporaries: the applicability of the past to daily life; nostalgia; reverence for and capitalization on family ancestry; the relationship between time and space; and the circulation of historical knowledge in both textual and nontextual forms.

THE PATH TO THE HARKIRKE, AND WHAT MR. BLUNDELL FOUND THERE

The story that now concerns us indirectly involves the usual historiographical questions of scholarship and the interpretation of evidence, but it takes place off the beaten track rather than at the centers of learning, London, Oxford, and Cambridge. It occurs, instead, at the geographic and social margins, in the northwest of England, on the manor of a struggling minor gentleman who was both regionally (he lived in rural Lancashire) and religiously (he was a firm recusant) outside the mainstream. It begins not with any epoch-making date in political history, nor with the publication of a landmark historical text such as Camden's *Britannia* (though that book has its place in the narrative), but on an ordinary day when those involved had anything but historical research on their minds.

On the morning of Monday, 8 April 1611, it was particularly wet and muddy at Little Crosby, a village of about forty households within the parish of Sefton in the West Derby Hundred of Lancashire, a few miles north of Liverpool. Thomas Ryse (the fourteen-year-old son of John Ryse, a local tenant farmer), was taking the cattle of his father's landlord, William Blundell (1560–1638), from the hall to graze in a nearby field. His path took him directly across a ditch that marked one end of a section of demesne land known locally as the Harkirke (fig. 1), where a day earlier an old man from the village – a Roman Catholic like Thomas Ryse and many of the other tenants and neighbors – had been buried. What caught young Thomas's eye on this morning was the glint of something unusual, a number of silver coins like no others that the lad had seen, lying on the sandy soil at the edge of the ditch.

Figure 1. Tombstones at the Harkirke. *Photo by John Daley, Crosby Herald. Courtesy of Brian Whitlock Blundell*

Perplexed at his find, the boy picked up a coin and took it back to the hall, where he showed it to the other servants. One or two were able to read, such as Edward Denton, Blundell's secretary, but none could explain the strange letters on the coin.[3] Nevertheless, there was much discussion. No doubt someone even wondered aloud what the piece would be worth, though it would now have to be given up to the lord of Little Crosby; turned up on his property, it could not be sold, as such objects often were, to a traveler with antiquarian interests. Eventually the servants were joined by their master, William Blundell, who had overheard

---

[3] Denton is the author of many of the rentals in Lancashire Record Office (hereafter Lancs RO), DDBl (Blundell of Little Crosby). See especially DDBl Acc. 6121, fol. 97. Denton would survive to serve, in the 1630s, William's grandson, William "the Cavalier," who in 1663 enjoined his heirs to take due account of the "long and faithful service of . . . Edward Denton, performed to my grandfather and myself," and show kindness to Denton's nephew and his family "according as he regardeth or ought to regard his ancient tenants." *Crosby Records: A Cavalier's Note Book,* ed. T. E. Gibson (London: Longmans, Green, 1880), 250. (Hereafter cited as *Cavalier's Note Book.*) Denton died on 7 May 1656 according to the Cavalier's notes in "Great Hodge Podge," fol. 185r. This volume, together with a distinct volume entitled "Hodge Podge the third," is part of the uncatalogued series (which includes the "account" described below) in Lancs RO DDBl Acc. 6121.

the discussions. "I comminge into the kitchen amongst them whoe were lookinge and musing at them," he tells us, "I presentlie tooke the coine and laide it uppe." Blundell was an educated man, apparently with a variety of books on history and antiquities in his personal library, or available from nearby acquaintances; he had even consulted, if he did not actually own, as heretical a tome as John Foxe's fervently anti-Catholic *Acts and Monuments*.[4] He was passingly familiar with old coinage from reading Camden, and he even knew some old English from reading Asser's *Life of Alfred* and Bede's *Ecclesiastical History*. He knew intuitively that the prized object was a very old coin indeed, probably – though this would require some research on his part to confirm – dating from the Saxon period.

Blundell's discovery was the unexpected reward for an act of charity that he had performed for "suche Catholiques either of myne owne howse or of the neighbourhoode." According to the reminiscences of Blundell's own grandson and namesake (William, known as "the Cavalier" [1620–98], who inherited both his grandfather's property and his antiquarian tastes), Little Crosby was an almost entirely Catholic manor lying within a formally Protestant parish.[5] The younger William commented in the 1640s that it had known no beggars, alehouses, or Protestants within living memory, and the recusant roll of 1641 bears him

---

[4] Evidence of his knowledge of Foxe is in Lancs RO DDBl Acc. 6121, unfoliated notebook, which is also the source of this account of the find. The works referred to specifically by Blundell are in this version of his narrative, together with the verbal descriptions of coins, but are absent from the roll version from which it was apparently copied, Lancs RO DDBl 24/12. Both versions were drafted by Blundell himself. No specific list of Blundell's personal books survives, and a search by the present author of the library at Crosby Hall in February 1995 failed to turn up any books that were owned by him rather than by later descendants, with the conspicuous exception of his Douai Bible, discussed below. Nevertheless, it is plain that he indeed owned a number of books because the probate inventory of his goods (Lancs RO DDBl 24/13, compiled 6 July 1638) lists him as worth £665 19s. 11d. and includes the tantalizingly vague "item in boockes, 5 £." An attempt to follow up these unnamed books through the inventories of surviving family members such as his daughter-in-law Jane (mother of William the Cavalier), who died in 1640 and whose goods included one pound's worth of unnamed books, and the Cavalier himself, for whom no inventory survives, failed to provide further clues as to the older William Blundell's reading.

[5] Lancs RO DDBl 24/10 inquisition after the death of William Blundell (deceased 2 July 1638); this incidentally lists the younger William as being eighteen years, twelve weeks, and six days old on 16 October 1638; consequently underage, he fell under the jurisdiction of the Court of Wards (PRO WARD 7 91/184) as well as of the Duchy of Lancaster (PRO DL 7 28/154). The younger William Blundell was the author of *A History of the Isle of Man*, edited by William Harrison for the Manx Society (vols. 25, 27 [1876, 1877]), wherein several of the books quoted by his grandfather are also used.

out.[6] It was a community of close, neighborly ties between coreligionists that cut across and overlaid the division of social status that distinguished the landlord from his tenants and servants. The apparent solidarity of the Blundells with their social inferiors over religious matters, stretching to William Blundell's passive support for the riot recounted below, must be read in the context of the normal legal and social disputes to which Little Crosby, judging by its court rolls, was far from immune.[7] But as far as loyalty to the old church was concerned, the senior Blundell and most of his tenants were of the same mind.

Blundell himself was the scion of a family that had held the manor since the mid-fourteenth century (fig. 2).[8] He was no stranger to the persecution of Catholics during what he hoped would be a passing "tyme of these troubles" under established Protestantism, and had been sent in his youth to study at the English College in Douai. His father, Richard, was imprisoned in Lancaster Castle in 1590, charged with harboring a seminary priest; he died there in 1591.[9] William, then in his early thirties, was imprisoned at the same time; after his release, he was quickly rearrested and spent two years in prison in London.[10] A search of the hall

[6] Recusant role of 1641 cited in W. Farrer and J. Brownhill, ed., *The Victoria History of the County of Lancaster* (Folkstone, England: Dawson, for the University of London Institute of Historical Research, 1990), hereafter cited as *VCH, Lancaster,* 1:259; T. Gibson, ed., *Crosby Records: A Chapter of Lancashire Recusancy,* Chetham Society, n.s. 12 (1887), contains a transcription of the notebook version of William I's account of the coin hoard together with the burial register of the Harkirke from 1611–1753. References to the account will be principally to the notebook version, which is unfoliated; I have therefore provided the equivalent reference in Gibson's printed version, which is largely but not entirely accurate.

[7] See Lancs RO DDBl 48/1, 2, 3, 4 Little Crosby court rolls 1557–1637. Thomas Ryse (the cowherd) would be in trouble as late as 1637 for having "sheared grasse . . . contrary to an former order," for which he was fined 3d; judging by 48/3 (courts baron of 2 April 1628 and 21 October 1634) there were considerable instances of illegal building, threshing, and water diversion requiring the squire's direct intervention.

[8] For the Blundell coat of arms and lineage, see John Burke, *A Genealogical and Heraldic History of the Commoners of Great Britain and Ireland* (London: Colburn, 1834–8), 2:527–30. The earliest record of the family in the manor dates from 1199. By 31 Hen. 8, James Blundell, Esq., held Little Crosby of Sir William Molyneux by knight's service, as well as lands and messuages and tenements in Much Crosby of the king as duke of Lancaster, in socage by fealty. Burke erroneously reports Richard Blundell, William's father, as dying in 1567.

[9] Lancs RO DDBl 30/1, indictment of William Blundell for harboring Robert Woodrooffe alias Witheroope of Burnley, seminary priest 24 August 1590, and writ of outlawry against Blundell, 26 March 1599.

[10] Lancs RO DDBl 30/4, enrolment of recusancy fines in Little Crosby 1595–1656; M. M. C. Calthrop, ed., *Recusant Roll no. I, 1592–3: Exchequer Lord Treasurer's Remembrancer Pipe Office Series,* Catholic Record Society 18 (Wigan, England, 1916), 185, 189 (Michaelmas 1592); H. Bowler, ed., *Recusant Roll No. II, 1593–94,* Catholic Record Society 57 (1965), 78; H. Bowler, ed., *Recusant Roll No. III, 1594–95,* Catholic Record Society

Richard Blundell (d. 1591)=Anne

William Blundell I the Recusant (1560–1638)=Amelia or Emilia Norris

Nicholas Blundell I (d. 1631)=Jane Bradshaw   Margaret Blundell

William II the Cavalier (1620–1698)=Anne Haggerston

William III (1645–1702)=Mary Eyre

Nicholas II the Diarist (1669–1737)=Lady Frances Langdale

Frances Blundell (1706–1773)=Henry Peppard (1692–1771)

Nicholas Peppard (1741–1795; assumed name Blundell in 1772)

Figure 2. Simplified Genealogy of the Blundells, 1560–1772. This chart shows only the direct line of succession and siblings mentioned in this study.

late in the 1590s forced William to flee; his wife, Emilia, was also committed to prison and released only on the intercession of friends at court.[11] Both Blundells received pardons at the accession of James, but this did not mitigate the persecutions by Protestant neighbors and shrieval officials, who conducted frequent raids on his cattle and searches of the hall through the next three decades, culminating in the sequestration of the estate during the civil war.[12] Toward the close of 1610, a young woman

61 (1970), 169, for a forty-pound fine levied on Emilia Blundell, William's wife. Both Richard and William Blundell appear in J. R. Dasent, ed., *Acts of the Privy Council of England 1598–99* (London: HMSO, 1905), 118, 220, for contributions required by recusants; William is also listed as a recusant in a 1601 signet bill. W. P. W. Phillimore, ed., *An Index to Bills of Privy Signet* (London: British Record Society/Index Library, 1890), 49.

[11] Lancs RO DDBl 30/2, orders relative to imprisonment of Emilia, his wife, 31 May and 8 July 1599.

[12] PRO E 179/131/318, schedule of recusants liable to poll tax, 1626, listing Emilia Blundell; E 179/132/340, subsidy assessment 17 Car. 1 (1641), assessing the younger William Blundell for £7 28s. (i.e., £8 8s.) and an additional twenty-eight shillings "for his lands beeing a convicte & Recusante"; VCH *Lancashire*, 1:259; J. Gillow, *A Literary and Biographical History, or Bibliographical Dictionary, of the English Catholics* (1885–1902; reprint, New York: Burt Franklin, 1968), 1:248–50, for entries on both William Blundells; and Blundell's own account in *Crosby Records*, 22 ff., 32. For the general context of Catholic persecution and confessional relations in this period see the following: Patrick McGrath, *Papists and Puritans under Elizabeth I* (London: Blandford Press, 1967); John Bossy, *The English Catholic Community 1570–1850* (London: Darton, Longman and Todd, 1975), esp. chap. 6, "Types of Religious Behaviour"; J. C. H.

had been refused burial in the parish by John Nutter, the vehemently anti-Catholic parson of Sefton, because of her recusancy. Miserably, her family had planted the corpse at the side of the main road, but it soon rained, and several horsemen, drays, and carriages trundled across the site, disturbing the body, parts of which were later found on the road; when "swyne beganne to wroote her bodie uppe" and eat it, her family "layd a great number of paving stones uppon the grave" as a temporary but hardly adequate solution.[13]

Out of both piety and paternalism, Blundell resolved to set aside a small corner of his demesne land as a Catholic burial site to serve Little Crosby and adjoining manors like Ince Blundell and Much or Great Crosby. He chose a location at some remove from the manor house, "a place called of ould tyme (as it is nowe also) the Harkirke." He had two of his tenants, John Ryse (father of our observant cowherd) and Thomas Marrall (or Marrowe),[14] dig a ditch on two sides of the Harkirke, the two others being already fenced. This separated the cemetery from the path to the common field, marking it off as informally sacred ground. (A year or so later Blundell would build a wall, so pleased was he with his coins, an "unexpected gyfte from Heaven."[15]) Although the ditching was completed shortly before Christmas of 1610, the makeshift graveyard was not needed until the following spring, when at noon on 7 April the corpse of William Mathewson, having similarly been denied burial in the Sefton churchyard, was transported to the Harkirke, "carried and attended or accompanied" by the old man's neighbors, and interred while Blundell, whose own neighborliness knew some limits, sat home at dinner. It was this second disturbance of the soil, coupled with the wet weather, that had caused the earth to disgorge its numismatic treasures.

Aveling, *The Handle and the Axe: The Catholic Recusants in England from Reformation to Emancipation* (London: Blond and Briggs, 1976), chaps. 2, 6. At the time this essay was completed I had not yet seen J. A. Hilton, *Catholic Lancashire: From Reformation to Renewal 1559–1991* (Chichester, England: Phillimore, 1994), and I thank Dr. Michael Mullett for pointing it out to me.

[13] Lancs RO DDBl 24/11, "A note of what was done to the baliffes the 26 of October last," fol. 1; cf. the account of Blundell's grandson, William Blundell the Cavalier, in a letter to James Scarisbrick of 29 April 1655. "Great Hodge Podge," DDBl Acc. 6121, fol. 85v (reprinted in *Crosby Records*, 42).

[14] The Marralls had been tenants of the Blundells for some time; Blundell's grandson, William the Cavalier, observed in the 1660s that several villagers had famous, if earthy-sounding, names; Marrall ("marrow") being perhaps related to Sir William Marrow, a fifteenth-century mayor of London. *Cavalier's Note Book*, 183–4.

[15] William Blundell the Cavalier to Rev. Thomas Blundell, SJ, 29 December 1686, *Crosby Records*, 44.

Blundell had the boy Thomas lead him to the precise spot where he had found the mysterious money, a corner of the Harkirke beside a "gap" that had not been enclosed. With them went the servant Denton and Blundell's son Nicholas (future father of the Cavalier), then a young man.[16] They were joined at the site a few minutes later by Richard Blundell the younger, William's brother, a priest who had been a longtime chaplain to the Houghtons, a Catholic family of nearby Lea Hall. Before very long, they had found several more coins but, the hour being late, the party returned to the hall for dinner, only to come back to the cemetery in the mid-afternoon. Perhaps eager to gather as many of the coins as he could, Blundell now took most of his family along, including his wife and his widowed mother, Anne, whom it "pleased" to visit the site of the discovery. They were to be rather disappointed, finding only a few more coins. Nevertheless, at the end of the day, Blundell had in his hands a minor hoard of "about 4 score, none bigger than a groat or smaller than 2 pence," and several more unidentifiable fragments.

It was as well that Blundell found the coins when he did. In 1624, when just under seventy Catholics from Sefton and nearby parishes had been buried, the Harkirke was set upon by agents of his inveterate foe, Sir Ralph Assheton, then sheriff of Lancashire. Thirty men knocked down the walls and scattered the stone markers that Blundell and his people had used instead of crosses in a fruitless bid to keep their funerary activities secretive. Blundell's tenants put up some show of resistance, in part because their cattle were being seized, and the result was a riot. Blundell was eventually fined £2000 by Star Chamber, in the Easter term of 1629, not only for the riot but, according to Blundell's own account, "for suffering a place of buriall in my Demaine."[17] It is clear from the voluminous Star Chamber documents in the case that the graveyard was in fact of secondary interest to the sheriff, and it does not feature, unlike the riot, in all the interrogatories. It is also plain that Blundell and several of his servants, especially Denton, attempted to feign innocence of direct encouragement of the riot and, in Denton's case, of the deliberate erection of the graveyard; the secretary would testify that the Harkirke was no more

---

[16] Nicholas would predecease his father in 1631, leaving his son, the younger William, then aged eleven, as the older William's heir.

[17] PRO E 159/469, entries of estreats into Exchequer; *Crosby Records*, 34–40. Blundell's brother-in-law, Sir William Norris, was also fined for an altercation with John More, a local JP, arising from Norris's protests about More's persecution of his family. Ibid, xxiii.

than a place for letting the cattle cross to pasture.[18] Although the penalty was subsequently reduced,[19] this was not the last such invasion of his land or his hall. Such persecutions took and continued to take their toll on his family, but also strengthened their adherence to Rome. In 1615 Blundell's twenty-three-year-old daughter, Margaret (d. 1647), would abandon England to become a nun at the English Augustinian house of St. Monica's in Louvain, where she took the name of the Anglo-Saxon saint Winifred.[20] Her kin at home obstinately stuck to both their faith and their land, and a century later William's great-great-grandson, another Nicholas (1669–1737), would pen an informative diary of life in the area.[21] Nor did the destruction of the markers spell the end of the graveyard, which continued to receive the remains of family members, Sefton and neighboring Lancashire Catholics, and the occasional priest until 1753.[22]

Blundell immediately set himself the task of trying to identify his coins, which he did with reference to books that will be discussed in the final section of this essay. The hoard is now known to have been deposited by the Danes within a few years of their retreat to Northumbria in A.D. 910,

---

[18] PRO STAC 9/1/2; Denton's answer is at fol. 304v, and he was supported in this denial by William Norreys, one of those charged in the riot (fol. 305). Blundell's own answer and admission of how he came to set up the burial ground is at fol. 553. The case itself has been thoroughly studied, though not from this perspective, in Frank Tyrer, "A Star Chamber Case: Assheton v. Blundell 1624–31," *Transactions of the Historic Society of Lancashire and Cheshire* 118 (1966 [1967]): 19–37.

[19] Lancs RO DDBl 30/6, copy of letters close: Charles I to Lord Treasurer Richard Weston, recommending reduction of the fine from £2000 to £250, 19 May 1631; the verso refers specifically to the £2000 having been levied for both the riot and rescue as well as for "mainteyninge a church yard for the buriall of seminarie priests & popish recusants." That Blundell's income was grossly insufficient to cover such a fine is clear from valuations of the estate at various points before and after the civil war: in 1660 his grandson would be assessed at 8s. 8d. for his fifteenth while the twenty tenements and properties, such as Thomas Marrall's, were liable to rates as low as 3d. "A true particular of ye fifteene wch every Person is to pay within Little Crosby," 1660, Acc. 6121, "Great Hodge Podge," fol. 72v.

[20] William the Cavalier's children would continue this tradition. Lawrence Stone, *The Family, Sex, and Marriage in England, 1500–1800* (London: Weidenfeld and Nicolson, 1977), 24, 111–13. It is Sister Winifred Blundell who is the source of much of the information on the cemetery's creation and destruction, having related the story to the sister conventicant who penned *The Chronicle of the English Augustinian Canonesses Regular of the Lateran, at St Monica's in Louvain,* ed. Dom A. Hamilton (Edinburgh and London: Sands and Co., 1904–6), 1:153.

[21] *The Great Diurnal of Nicholas Blundell of Little Crosby, Lancashire,* ed. Frank Tyrer and J. J. Bagley, 3 vols. (Record Society of Lancashire and Cheshire, 1968–72).

[22] Gillow, 1:247; VCH, *Lancashire,* III, 89; and *Great Diurnal of Nicholas Blundell,* 1:138, 146, 296. Nicholas refers, for instance (ibid., 1:309), to the burial of his spinster great-aunt, Frances (youngest sister of William II, the Cavalier), in December 1711 at the age of eighty-one. The complete burial records are printed in *Crosby Records,* 69–85.

and numismatists have identified in it the coinage of kings Alfred the Great, Edward the Elder, and Cnut of Northumbria. In many cases, Blundell's assessment of the individual pieces was not far off. He even recognized varieties of the ecclesiastical coinage of York and East Anglia, though he and most local inhabitants mistakenly called these "the money of Sainte Peter," thinking them coins especially minted for Peter's pence. He was more thoroughly stumped by some foreign coins that bore "strange and to me unknowen inscriptions." Blundell set down at least two accounts of his find, each of which contains his pen and ink drawings of thirty-five of them. The first of these is a lengthy two-membrane roll of the sort that often contained deeds, surveys, and family pedigrees.[23] A surviving copperplate of the coins, probably derived from this, dates from as early as 1613. The second of Blundell's accounts is a small duodecimo paper notebook of twenty-seven leaves, bound in a medieval missal, in which he tells his story of the establishment of the cemetery and the circumstances of the initial coin find and subsequent treasure hunt. This version features one less coin than the roll, but it includes something that the roll lacks, detailed verbal descriptions of the coins together with references to several medieval and modern historical works.[24] Both versions are headed by a quotation from the apocryphal book of Tobit, given in Latin and English, that speaks to the recusant's placing of God before monarch: "To hyde the secret of a kinge is goode; but to reveale and confesse the woorke of God is an honorable thinge."[25]

In fact, Blundell had not hidden but "revealed" the secret of a king in uncovering and deciphering these artifacts, buried long ago on the site of

---

[23] Lancs RO DDBl 24/12; *Crosby Records*, 42, 63.

[24] Lancs RO DDBl Acc. 6121 includes the copperplate, which was sent by William's great-great-grandson, Nicholas II (the diarist), to London through a Liverpool printer named John Aldridge, who had several prints made "of the money found in the Harkerk." *Great Diurnal of Nicholas Blundell*, 1:86 (12 June 1705). William Blundell the Cavalier had already printed up to two hundred copies in 1676. Gibson, preface to *Crosby Records*, xv. Images of the coins were obtained from a manuscript in Corpus Christi College, Oxford, by the publishers of Sir John Spelman's *Aelfredi Magni Anglorum Regis invictissimi vita tribus libris comprehensa* (Oxford: at Sheldonian Theatre, 1678), sig. c2r-v and table 3: "Nummi in hac tabula descripti reperti sunt Aprilis 8. anno 1611. in loco *Harkirke* [in black letter] dicto in paroecia Sephtoniae Comitatu Lancastriae; & habentur tum manu descripti in Bibliotheca C.C.C. Oxon. tum aere incisi & excusi." The manuscript referred to by Spelman is CCC Oxon MS 255, fols. 82–3, and is an inferior copy made by a later draughtsman, in the judgment of R. H. M. Dolley, "A Further Note on the Harkirke Find," *Numismatic Chronicle*, 6th series, 15 (1955): 189–93, for which reference I am grateful to Mr. Brian Whitlock Blundell.

[25] Lancs RO DDBl 24/12 and DDBl Acc. 6121. Blundell himself marks the epigraph, on both roll and notebook, as "Tob. 12 vs. 7," but this has been misleadingly transcribed by Gibson as "Iob" [i.e., Job] in *Crosby Records*, 45.

a church. In having them printed and circulating their images (arranged in the shape of a cross) so that, as his grandson put it, "ye copyes flew abroad in ye country," he had also revealed the miraculous work of God in preserving these vestiges of remote antiquity over the centuries, within formerly hallowed territory, and restoring them to view as a sign of divine pleasure at Blundell's charity and the people's adherence to Catholic burial rites.[26] And by turning his account into a family record, Blundell was also asserting a proprietary claim to objects recovered on his demesne – a claim that flew in the face of the English law of treasure trove and brought him once again into potential conflict with authority.

Although inconsistently enforced by the Crown over the centuries, the law of treasure trove was reasonably clear by the early seventeenth century.[27] Its earliest expressions come from the various *laga*, or laws, of the Anglo-Saxon and Anglo-Norman kings. Blundell certainly knew of these laws, since, as we shall see, his admiration of certain Saxon monarchs (especially Alfred and Edward the Confessor) was based on a belief that the interests of spirituality and temporality, church and crown, had been balanced and harmonized in the England converted by "Austin" (Augustine of Canterbury), through the beneficent acts of "Catholic Saxon kings" well disposed to Holy Church and conscious of their duty to Rome.[28] Although William Lambarde's *Archaionomia* (1568), a standard

---

[26] The Cavalier reported in 1655 that his grandfather had in fact caused copies of his drafting of the coins to be printed, "ye brazen cuts wherof are now extant with me." *Crosby Records*, 42. The younger William Blundell believed his grandfather had published "because he knew well yt *to reveile ye works of God was an honorable thing*. Ibid., emphasis in original. British Library, Harleian MS 1437, art. 8 (loose paper near end) is a surviving copy from Blundell's original copperplate (though perhaps not from his initial printing) of the coins. Their arrangement in the form of a cross in this print (they are not so arranged in either the roll or the notebook) evidently vexed Humfrey Wanley, who identified thirty-two of the coins as Saxon and three as foreign. An antiquary of a later age and different interests, Wanley commented in his account of the manuscript in the Harleian *Catalogue* that its author had "more superstition than learning." *A Catalogue of the Harleian Manuscripts in the British Museum*, 4 vols. (London: HMSO, 1808), 2:51–2.

[27] The definitive work is George Hill, *Treasure Trove in Law and Practice from the Earliest Time to the Present Day* (Oxford: Clarendon Press, 1936), 185–255. The Crown had at various times since the twelfth century granted by patent limited rights to search for and take treasure, and in 5 Ed. 1 (1276–7) Sir Robert Blundell de Crosby made over to his son Nicholas all his lands in Annosdale (now Ainsdale) but saved to himself "Shipwreck" in that and other estates. Burke, *Commoners*, 2:528; and *Cavalier: Letters of William Blundell to his Friends, 1620–1698*, ed. M. Blundell (London, New York, and Toronto: Longmans, Green and Co., 1933), 1.

[28] The phrase is William the Cavalier's, who claimed, in a letter to his son Thomas Blundell, SJ (29 December 1686), that he had sent several of the coins into Wales "for better security in ye tyme of War," together with family muniments, and that many of these too were lost. *Crosby Records*, 44; and B. J. N. Edwards, "The Vikings in North-West

source for the early law codes, is not among the works that Blundell cites specifically, the evidence suggests that he was familiar with these laws, for they are alluded to in the bogus chronicle known as Ingulph of Croyland and in other works that Blundell had certainly read and cites.

So far as Blundell's hoard is concerned, the critical aspects of treasure law are twofold. First, any silver, bullion, or coin found *hidden* in the earth (as opposed to merely lying abandoned on the surface) was treasure trove owed in entirety to the Crown. The *Leges Henrici primi*, compiled in the early twelfth century, give exclusive claim on such treasure to the king. Second – and here the matter of where the coins were discovered is crucial – the somewhat later law code known as the Laws of Edward the Confessor (which in the seventeenth century was erroneously held to be of eleventh-century, pre-Norman, origins) bestows gold and silver on the king *unless* it be found in a church or cemetery. In such case the gold still belongs to the Crown, and half the silver, but the remaining silver must be given to the church.[29]

These laws, and the law of treasure generally, have been neglected in earlier accounts of Blundell's find, yet they provide an important piece of the puzzle. They help to explain, for instance, some of Blundell's apparently odd behavior, such as using his family (including household servants) rather than having tenants or laborers gather the coins, since other laws of trove, contained in Henry de Bracton, expressly prohibit the hiring of men to dig for treasure while permitting purely fortuitous discoveries made by landowners and their immediate families.[30] The laws also explain the careful language of the notebook and roll accounts, in which Blundell cautiously asserts a claim to the coins while scrupulously documenting that they were found accidentally and *lying on the surface* (albeit disturbed by his tenants' illicit funerary activities) and had not been deliberately dug for. He thereby provided himself the basis for a case that the coins were not, in fact, true treasure trove. Finally, all this helps to sort out the confusion regarding the eventual fate of the coins, some of

England: The Physical Evidence," in *Viking Treasure from the North West: The Cuerdale Hoard in its Context,* ed. James Graham-Campbell (Liverpool: National Museums and Galleries on Merseyside, 1992), 58–60. I am indebted to Mr. Edwards for having shown me a copy of this article before its publication.

29 See Edward the Confessor's laws, no. 14, "De thesauris," in William Lambarde, *Archaionomia,* 2d ed. (Cambridge, 1643), separately paginated and appended to Abraham Wheloc's edition of Bede's *Ecclesiastical History* (Cambridge, 1643): "Thesauri de terra domini Regis sunt, nisi in Ecclesia vel in coemeterio inveniantur: Et licet ibi inveniantur, aurum regis est, & medietas argenti, & medietas Ecclesiae ubi inventum fuerit, quaecunque ipsa fuerit vel dives, vel pauper."

30 Hill, *Treasure Trove,* 193.

which were sent for safekeeping by William the Cavalier into Wales
(probably to his kinsmen the Banisters at Wrexham) in 1642, at the start
of the civil war, and were subsequently lost. It is clear from the first
William's account of the discovery that he found many more coins than
he actually drew and described, though probably not the "three hundred" that his grandson fancifully recalled in the 1680s.[31] Those selected
by Blundell in 1611 or 1612 for drawing, engraving, and publication
were almost certainly the coins that the Cavalier, who inherited them,
would send to Wrexham thirty years later.

As to the others, they were turned by the first William Blundell into a
pyx and chalice that remained in later centuries at Little Crosby's Catholic
church. The chalice was stolen in the nineteenth century; the pyx (fig. 3)
remains in the sacristy of Little Crosby Church, bearing the inscription
"This was made of silver found in the burial place / W. Bl."[32] Blundell
himself had kept the thirty-five most interesting coins, those that appear in
the two extant accounts, and then given up the rest as a pious offering. In
doing so, he was paying heed to the law of Edward the Confessor, a pious
king whom he knew had regularly paid Peter's pence, and returning half of
this discovered silver to the church. Yet more was at stake than obedience
to an obscure treasure law. In returning the coins into historical time, and
giving them back to the church, Blundell was also reversing a painful
episode of more recent history, the spoliation of church plate and property
that had begun during the reign of Henry VIII, when, as Blundell put it,
new religions had been "coined" each day, out of monastic and chantry
property, in sharp contrast to the harmonious coexistence of church and
crown that Blundell believed (however naively) had marked the Anglo-
Saxon era.

SPACE, TIME, AND TRADITION

A conventional historiographical analysis would see the Little Crosby
episode as simply one more example, and a minor one at that, of the
development of antiquarian interests in the seventeenth century – hardly
worth more than a footnote in an account of early modern historical

---

[31] *Crosby Records*, 43.
[32] Edwards, "Vikings in North-West England," reports the pyx as having been stolen, like
the chalice, but this is incorrect. The present author is grateful to Mr. Brian Whitlock
Blundell and Canon Roger Daley for showing him the pyx, now at Little Crosby Church
(and for providing photographs); a spectrographic analysis of the pyx in the 1970s
demonstrated that it was made of silver consistent with the age of the coins.

Figure 3. William Blundell's pyx, Little Crosby Church. *Photo by John Daley, Crosby Herald. Courtesy of Brian Whitlock Blundell*

thought. But Blundell's detailed narrative of his servants' discovery and of his own historical detective work opens a window onto a number of different cultural transactions and intellectual assumptions. The story raises questions concerning the significance of objects from the past for their elite collectors and for the humble folk who found them, and the mental world of the rural Catholic squire attempting to make some sense of his find. What did Blundell, and the numerous other like-minded gentry around the English countryside, imagine such objects as coins, urns, "giant" bones, and the like to be? For that matter, what did the Thomas Ryses of the time, unfamiliar with much of national history, make of such trinkets that they turned up while ploughing, digging, or building? And can the negotiations between servants and masters, vulgar and learned, over the residue of the past tell us something about the workings of the historical imagination in early modern England?

The best point of departure lies at the place of discovery. The make-shift graveyard was itself an intersection of historical inheritance, community ritual, and sustained religious disobedience, for all that it yielded those classic symbols of royal authority, coins of the realm. Its creation was the act of a community marginalized by recent political circumstances, and of a religion whose practitioners throughout the land were much given to wishful recollections of the past.[33] Blundell had himself authored, while in prison, a "dittie" lamenting the persecution of "Those whom they suspect or knowe / Ancient truthe affectinge, new fond faithes rejecting" and protesting "What in Sefton we endure / For no strange opinion, but that ould Religion / Austin planted here most sure." Much of this verse is suffused with nostalgia, and with a firm conviction that time and the weight of history are on the side of Catholicism, here identified with social justice and an older, preinflationary coinage:

The tyme hath been wee hadd one faith,
And strode aright one ancient path,
The thym is now that each man may
See newe Religons coynd each day.

. . . .

The tyme hath beene the prelate's dore
Was seldome shotte against the pore,
The tyme is now, so wives goe fine,
They take not thought the kyne.[34]

---

[33] On Catholic nostalgia see K. Thomas, *The Perception of the Past in Early Modern England* (London: Creighton Trust Lecture, 1983), passim. Another Lancashire example of a Catholic intensely interested in the past is provided by Christopher Towneley (1604–74), an antiquary and the uncle of Richard Towneley, the natural philosopher (1629–1707). See Chetham's Library, Manchester, MSS C.6.1–2 for two volumes of notes for the history of Lancashire, part of a proposed history by Richard Kuerden (1623–90?) and Christopher Towneley; MSS D.3.1–13 contain several books of further material (mainly copies of family evidences, but some inscriptions and genealogies) compiled by the older Towneley for the proposed history. For their activities see C. Webster, "Richard Towneley (1629–1707), the Towneley Group and Seventeenth-Century Science," *Transactions of the Historic Society of Lancashire and Cheshire* 118 (1966[1967]): 51–76.

[34] *Crosby Records*, 24–9; Lancs RO DDBl Acct. 6121, "Great Hodge Podge," fol. 132r, Latin verses on "An expostulation or chyding of Jesus with man perishinge throughe his

Blundell was, in short, a defender of walking in "antient pathes."[35] A further indication of his views is provided by the annotations that he made in his copy of the Douai Bible (with selected apocryphal books), which was published in two volumes in 1609–10, and which he may already have owned at the time of the incident of the coins. Rather like some Protestant readers, but with obviously different aspirations, Blundell read the Scripture as a prophetic text, paying close attention to such episodes as the successive captivities of the children of Israel: Thus Exodus 40, which records the Israelites as dwelling in Egypt for "some foure hundred thirty yeares" was glossed by Blundell "430 years," as if anticipating a similar period of trials for English Catholicism. A later manuscript note in the printed gloss on the Apocrypha has Blundell writing, "They adored God & then the king." And on the conflict of Israelites and Philistines at 1 Kings 13.19 we find him commenting, "how great was ye subjection of the Isralites to ye Philistines."[36]

"Harkirke," the name of the spot at which the coins were found, is an Old English word, derived from the Anglo-Saxon All hāra Cyrice, and handed down by tradition from a time when a "grey and hoary" church, long vanished, had stood on the spot; it appears in local records from as early as 1275.[37] Blundell's tenants and neighbors used the term, inherited from generations of local inhabitants, without paying much attention to it, but all across England some of the most commonplace signs of rudimentary historical thinking came from people's creative explanations for such place-names. And Blundell himself had certainly fathomed the significance of the spot in choosing it for his burial ground.[38]

In modern historical thinking, time must precede space, the moment of an occurrence go before its location. Events happen *at* a particular time, or *from* one time *to* another, and we must fix them chronologically before

---

owne fawlte; translated out of Latin verse into Englishe as foloweth by Wil. Bl."; ibid., 135v–136r ff. for more ditties and music written by William.

[35] The phrase, from Jeremiah 6.16, appears in Lancs RO DDBl Acc. 6121; *Crosby Records*, 63.

[36] Crosby Hall, Little Crosby, Liverpool, *The Holie Bible faithfully translated into English, out of the authentical Latin*, (2 vols., Douai: Lawrence Kellam, 1609–10). Blundell's note on the gloss on the Apocrypha appears at 2:1115; his comment on the Israelites and Philistines is at 1:59. I am extremely grateful to Mr. Brian Whitlock Blundell and Mr. Mark Whitlock Blundell for making the family library and deposited papers available to me.

[37] Lancs RO DDBl 50/16; Edwards, "Vikings in North-West England," 58.

[38] For early modern burial practices and another religious minority, the Familists, at almost exactly the same date, see Christopher Marsh, *The Family of Love in English Society, 1550–1630* (Cambridge: Cambridge University Press, 1994), 218–31.

we can do much else with them. When always precedes modern historians' where, to say nothing of their how and why. This was true for Renaissance narrative historians as well (for whom chronology was the first and geography the second, and subordinate, "eye" of history), but not for the antiquaries of the late sixteenth century, who began with locations, rather than events; this was one reason that many of them protested that their "chorographies" and "surveys" were not, according to long-accepted rhetorical conventions, "histories" at all.[39] Such fine generic distinctions are often belied by actual contents, in this case by the inevitable inclusion of historical episodes in most antiquarian texts. A more significant difference emerges from the manner in which local communities constituted and defined the boundaries of the historical. They put place first, ahead of time. For the locals of Little Crosby, remembered images of the vanished "hoary church" preceded and transcended the importance of any date, any precise temporal pigeonhole. A modern historian or even a casual visitor would instinctively want to know when the place was given such a name, in what period, and in whose reign.

The primacy of space over time on the mental horizons of the local community does not mean that there can be found in such settings no sense of their relation. On the contrary, it is worth recalling that the coins were found precisely because the landlord, in responding to the needs of his tenants and coreligionists, had decided to mark an artificial sacred zone. The new burial ground was consecrated by neither law nor established church, but purely by the manorial community's sense of the importance of the customary rite of passage, and by its belief in the religious significance of this particular place. The phantom Saxon church helped to soften the ad hoc character of the arrangement. This kind of practice was not the exclusive preserve of Catholicism. Every Protestant parish in England, in consecrating particular spaces to sepultural and sacramental purposes, demonstrated some such understanding of the burden of the past. So did the Ascensiontide ritual of beating the bounds, which established and annually proclaimed to the contiguous world the frontiers of a parish, for economic as well as symbolic reasons.[40] The perambulation

---

[39] D. R. Woolf, "Erudition and the Idea of History in Renaissance England," *Renaissance Quarterly* 40 (1987): 11–48.

[40] The link between antiquarianism and a strong sense of local space is not coincidental: the earliest county chorography, by William Lambarde, was entitled *The Perambulation of Kent.* Elizabethan and early Stuart contributions to the genre were invariably called either descriptions or, more commonly, "surveys," the works of John Norden in the 1590s, for instance, being the work of a professional surveyor. Only in the mid-seventeenth century, with massive tomes like Dugdale's *Antiquities of Warwickshire*

asserted parochial control over those things that lay within, and defended parishioners against incurring, in the absence of precise surveys, responsibility for foreign paupers, or for the repair of buildings, roads, and bridges that had not traditionally lain in their charge. Since it conserved the boundaries of a space that had been defined time out of mind, it was also a repetitive rite of communication among the young, the aged, and the dead, between the present and the past, paying heed to the biblical injunction (Proverbs 22.28) "Do not move the ancient boundary-stone which your forefathers set up." That the seventeenth century produced local maps and estate surveys in greater numbers than previous eras was similarly a consequence of a need to ensure the accurate memory of familial and parochial boundaries beyond a living generation, a need all the more pressing in the face of a volatile land market and of cataclysmic events like the civil war, which caused the destruction of many traditional landmarks. Such, for instance, was the explanation for one rector's codification of his Essex parish's boundaries at the end of the century. "In the time of the long Rebellion the landmarcks of our parish were cut downe, and it would be difficult for posterity to find out the proper precincts which our parish are incompassed withal," wrote Robert Poole of Belchamp Otten, who was himself adding a perambulation to the parochial accounts in his keeping "that this may be a memorial to posterity" and thereby prevent future litigation.[41]

THE ANCESTRAL AND THE ANTIQUARIAN

Blundell's sense of obligation to his coreligionists was complemented by a fervent understanding of his duty to his ancestors and descendants. The latter he served in various ways, by keeping elaborate estate records, by keeping up the fabric of village properties, and by tending to the improvement of his land. When still a relatively young man, he had added what his descendants would still call, forty years later, a "new" orchard. An oak that he planted as a sapling during Elizabeth's reign would grow over the decades and come to symbolize for both him and his grandson the long-standing connection between the family and its land. In about 1629, when young William, his grandson, was nine, old William showed him

(1656), did the close connection of the genre with its roots in local documents, and in ceremonies of spatial definition, become less prominent. The previous usage continued, however, in the "natural history" genre of authors like Robert Plot and Charles Leigh.

[41] Essex RO D/DU 441/96, pp. 22–3, Belchamp Otten parish accounts, 1700–1701.

the tree and made the boy encircle it with his arms, whereupon the child found that "my finger ends did overreach each other some little, less than an inch I take it." By way of demonstration, the older man told him "that he did plant that tree when it was like a small twig which he showed me (less than ordinary riding rod)." Years later, when William II was 43, and still reveling in the return of the monarchy – of which the oak was a traditional emblem – he made a point of encompassing the tree once more, "clipping it in my arms as high as I could well reach, standing on the west side, and I found it to be 9 inches (within less than one straw's breadth) more than I could fathom." He was struck by the longevity of this minor landmark, a living connection between him and his children and the generation of his grandfather, who, as he recorded there for his children's benefit, "was born [in] 1560."[42]

The measurement of the tree was a rare and incidental ritual for both William Blundells, albeit one that quietly proclaimed the family's past and future ties to its property, suggesting both permanence and growth in the face of disturbances from a hostile world beyond the village. A more frequent occurrence was the funeral, which testified to transience and decay. The burial ceremony, in Little Crosby as elsewhere, was a rite of both communion and separation between the living and the dead, including the recently deceased as well as speechless generations of ancestors, lords, tenants, and laborers.[43] But in a Catholic enclave such as Little Crosby, the ritual was both confessionally exclusionary, widening the parochial religious divide, and, within the manor, socially integrative. Where Protestant burials were tied to an official body of the church and to salvation through Christ alone, Catholic funerary rituals instead linked the deceased and survivors to a vanished religious community of the past.[44] In

---

[42] *Cavalier's Note Book*, 214. For a similar example from the later seventeenth century involving trees and grandfather-grandson inheritances, see the "Book of William Storr." Samuel Storr was a Yorkshire Quaker who at the age of eighty-four wanted to be buried in his own father's former land at Holderness, and had "got a man to proune for me graftes from my fathers mulberry tree in holderness for my grandsoneses gardens," thereby transplanting the family tree from Holderness to Wislow, then occupied by his grandson, William (principal author of this manuscript), Samuel Storr's two sons having predeceased their father in the 1690s. Borthwick Inst., York, MD 112, p. 129 for William Storr's perspective on the ancestral trees. At p. 273 is a mulberry leaf allegedly from the same tree, pressed into the volume in 1919.

[43] For further evidence of these relations in another part of England, see Richard Gough's well-known account of his parish and its spatial and hierarchical arrangements, *The History of Myddle*, ed. D. Hey (Harmondsworth, England: Penguin, 1981).

[44] On traditional Catholic versus Protestant attitudes toward death, see Eamon Duffy, *The Stripping of the Altars: Traditional Religion in England, 1400–1580* (New Haven: Yale University Press, 1992), 301–76.

marking off the Harkirke as a quasi-sacred spot (all the more suitable, because of its name, for the interment of human remains), and then in actually carrying out the burial of Mathewson's and later cadavers, Blundell and his tenants were honoring through reenactment a practice inherited from their forebears; and they were doing so in quiet defiance of the sheriff and of what, to them, seemed a relatively recently and precariously established Protestant Church. In scraping over the wet sand for antique groats they were indirectly doing the same thing, gathering nostalgic reminders of their remote progenitors, as another northwesterner, Charles Leigh, would recognize a century later in justifying local antiquarianism. "To know what our ancestors were, cannot be more lively delineated to us, than by the ruines we discover of those days, hence it is that by penetrating the bowels of the earth, we can trace the footsteps of our forefathers, and imprint upon our minds some ideas of their times."[45]

Early modern England was a society immensely conscious of ancestry, even though a degree of social mobility ensured that long lineage mattered relatively little, in comparison with much of the rest of Europe, in defining the essentials of status. There was no ancestor worship of the sort practiced in some Far Eastern countries then and now, no totemic icons of grandparents alongside images of saints and the virgin in Catholic dwellings; and the Protestant majority was even louder in its disapproval of anything approaching reverence to the long-departed. Ancestors in early modern England were not cohabitants of the household, any more than were living grandparents commonly to be found under the same roof as grandchildren (gentry exceptions like the Blundells being in a minority); and they did not provide semideistic links between the present generation and the eternal by making the dead perpetually present.[46]

Nevertheless, the dead and departed had a passive role to play. Commemorated in funeral monuments and honored in the maintenance of public and familial rituals, immediate and remote ancestors provided the gentry and peerage with a significant means of self-identification and social distinction. The tendency to wrap up familial status in the clothing of ancestry was more a characteristic of the landed, who had written evidences of their long-term location within the realm, than of their social

---

[45] Charles Leigh, *The Natural History of Lancashire, Cheshire, and the Peak, in Derbyshire*, 2d ed. (Oxford, 1720), b. 3, p. 1; copy in Lancs RO.

[46] For a different attitude toward ancestors from that in early modern England, see F. L. K. Hsu, *Under the Ancestors' Shadow: Chinese Culture and Personality* (New York: Columbia University Press, 1948), esp. 154–65; and F. W. Kent, *Household and Lineage in Renaissance Florence* (Princeton: Princeton University Press, 1977), 99.

inferiors, particularly as shorter leases and economically driven migration diminished tenurial longevity. Even at the upper reaches of the gentry there had long existed analogous constraints on the appeal to ancestry, such as the practice of strict primogeniture, which drove younger children off family estates; the alienation of parts of landholdings; and the tendency of cadet lines to relocate, sometimes at a great distance.

In the case of the Blundells, ancestry was inseparably tied to the manor itself, its buildings, and the exploits of various family members in defense of their faith. Sister Winifred ensured that her father's and grandfather's sufferings became a matter of record in her house's chronicle. Much later, William Blundell's great-great-grandson, Nicholas the diarist, would be fascinated by the career of his own grandfather, William II, the Cavalier, who had died at seventy-eight in 1698, when Nicholas was in his late twenties. It was William II who taught the diarist reading and arithmetic as a child living at the hall, before Nicholas was sent to the Jesuit college at St. Omer. The Cavalier also introduced Nicholas to the family's history, including the story of William I's tribulations (and his coins), ceaselessly chastised the boy for his poor memory, and reminded him that the descent in the male line had been unbroken for several centuries – a point that must later have galled Nicholas, who was unable to produce a son. Nicholas himself carried on this pursuit of the familial past, at one point searching the family muniments and manorial documents back to the twelfth century.[47]

Although the enthusiasm for researching, creating, and registering pedigrees peaked under Elizabeth and James, ordinary gentry, successful yeomen like Robert Furse of Devon, and even ambitious urban householders like Denis Bond of Dorchester remained busy during the middle and latter decades of the seventeenth century rifling through their evidences, sorting through the old and the recent, adding information, and having clearer, fancier copies made.[48] At the opposite end of both the country and the religious spectrum, successive generations of Blundells took note of their ante-

---

[47] *Great Diurnal of Nicholas Blundell,* 3:ix. For information on the later history of the family, see B. M. Whitlock Blundell, "Little Crosby and the Blundell Family," unpublished paper in possession of the author; I am indebted to Brian Whitlock Blundell for providing me with a copy of this paper.

[48] H. J. Carpenter, "Furse of Moreshead: A Family Record of the Sixteenth Century," *Reports and Transactions of the Devonshire Association for the Advancement of Science, Literature and Art* 26 (1894): 169; David Underdown, *Fire from Heaven* (New Haven: Yale University Press, 1992), 49. Blundell's family is an excellent example: the "Great Hodge Podge" includes, among other things, the births, marriages, and deaths of family members noted by William, his grandson William, and the latter's grandson Nicholas.

cedents and carefully recorded births, marriages, and deaths in the several "Hodge Podges" begun by William the recusant and continued by his grandson and great-great-grandson. Thus William the Cavalier, approaching middle age in the 1670s, determined to present a definitive family history building on his grandfather's exemplary record keeping, assisted by contributions from his mother. "All of this page & the following I W Bl [i.e., the Cavalier] extracted out of severall old deeds and from notes from my grandfather Blundells hand; most exactly, and scrupulously" the Cavalier remarked with due piety, "& I hope to bring up ye Pedegree successively to Sr Robert Blundell Kt who lived in ye dayes of King John."[49]

Once established and acknowledged by the heralds, or reconfirmed in state documents such as letters patent, a worthy ancestry was displayed boldly on various parts of family property more visible than parchment pedigrees. The coat of arms, originally devised by the medieval military aristocracy in order to assist battlefield recognition (a use it had largely lost with the advent of Tudor measures against liveries), became the most recognizable symbol of gentility, and the educated layman soon grew passably familiar with the arcana of heraldry through the Elizabethan and Jacobean manuals published by officers of arms like John Guillim, and by enterprising amateurs like Edmund Bolton, both of whose works appeared in 1610.[50] The blazons adorning architecture, funereal art, and decorative chattels from the period are further evidence of this particular survival of the past, and of the related phenomenon of turning the newest, blandest implement into a *bien inaliénable*. In January 1617, for instance, Richard Brownlow paid 2d. for "engraving the arms" on a basin and ewer he had purchased for £23 7s. 8d. The cost of such engraving was not high, and it protected an otherwise unremarkable object

---

[49] Lancs RO DDBl Acc. 6121, "Great Hodge Podge," fols. 76v–78r, including a reverse genealogy from the Cavalier back to ancestors in the late thirteenth century. Some of his very early material came from beyond the family sources: he consulted "Doctor Cureden" (Richard Kuerden, another Lancashire recusant antiquary, some of whose papers survive in Chetham's Library, Manchester), who "told me since, that he had made som further discoveryes of ye Antiquity of my Family, & that he had given his said discoveryes to Mr Dugdale, ye Herald, at our last visitation about ye year 1665." Cf. ibid., fol. 184r, for names of all the children of the Cavalier's father, Nicholas, and Jane, his wife (thirteen in all including a previous William who died in infancy). The names reinforce the impression that the Blundells stuck very firmly to a small range of Christian names: Margaret, William, Emilia, Anne, William (the Cavalier), Dorothy, Margaret, Anne, Elizabeth, Richard, Winifred (d. 1677), and Frances (d. 1711) ("she was buried in ye Harkerk"). The Cavalier derived this list (dated by him 21 February 1648/9) "out of a note under my mothers owne hand."

[50] John Guillim, *A Display of Heraldrie* (London: W. Hall for R. Mab, 1610); Edmund Bolton, *The Elements of Armories* (London: G. Eld, 1610).

against theft, projected a visible symbol of family history, and made even the most recently acquired trinket into a potential heirloom.[51]

   This brings us directly back to the matter of Blundell's coins. Unlike King Alfred or Cnut, the Harkirke hoard was a durable commodity imported from remote antiquity, a semipermanent collection of artifacts nearly immune from time – a few, Blundell tells us, were broken – if not beyond human transformation into pyx and chalice. We can sense from Blundell's account of their discovery that the coins represented many things to different people. His servants, from Thomas Ryse to Edward Denton, knew enough to recognize that they were not current, that they belonged to "old time." If stories had developed about these coins – as such tales attached to innumerable other archaeological discoveries in the sixteenth and seventeenth centuries – they would probably have involved some element of narrative fabrication with tenuous roots in the document-able: a king, a Viking, or a defeated Saxon burying his treasure to save capture by an enemy, or perhaps marking the site of a great battle with abandoned spurs, swords, and horse brasses. On the other hand, folk culture from ancient British times to the present century has also found more practical uses for such accidental discoveries, turning them from curiosity to implement like a monastic ruin reclaimed to provide shelter. A Saxon or Romano-British coin could not be spent in the same way that an old angel or shilling could be; but it might still be adapted for use in the present. Although Blundell's entry into the scene came moments too late to tell us for certain, there can be little doubt that some of the kitchen conversation among the servants with regard to young Thomas Ryse's coin had to do with the possible uses of the discovery. Any object may serve more than one function, even for a single owner. It is not impossible that Thomas and his father recognized these coins as potential historical evidence, but this was surely not the first thing that came to their minds, just as Blundell himself, in turning them into church plate, was simulta-neously both restoring the silver to a sacred use, at a cost to the coins'

---

[51] Elizabeth Bligh, Lady Cust, *Records of the Cust Family: Second Series, the Brownlows of Belton, 1550–1779* (London: Mitchell, Hughes and Clarke, 1909), 54. For some other examples see the index to H. M. Colvin, ed., *The History of the King's Works, III, 1485–1660* (London: HMSO, 1975–82), 1:441, sub. "Heraldic Decoration".) According to Malcolm Airs, initials, dates, mottoes, and heraldic devices emblazoned on buildings are "sufficient testimony to their builders' desire for immortality." Malcolm Airs, *The Making of the English Country House, 1500–1640* (London: Architectural Press, 1975), 8. They are also a sign of the respect for these ancestors among those who chose to dwell in the presence of such tokens of descent.

historical value, and creating in the pyx and chalice objects that had a functional existence in the present.

At the time of their discovery the coins were something more than salvageable chunks of silver to Blundell, and his interests, otherwise apparently in harmony with his social inferiors', here competed with theirs just as they competed with the implicit interests of the Crown in treasure rights. What to the servants were objects of mild curiosity and potential economic benefit were to the leisured Blundell a physical link to local, national, and providential pasts he had thitherto been able to commune with only textually, but of which he had a higher than average awareness. To put it another way, the past played its part in the mental horizons of all the denizens of Little Crosby, but only Blundell, and perhaps some members of his family, had the scholarly knowledge – the historical "literacy," one might say – to connect its deposits to a specific moment in history. Much later, in 1655, his grandson would express the conviction that coins such as these could provide even the poorest yokel with a sense of history not to be found in books. Writing to an absent Catholic friend on whose land a tenant had just unearthed a trove of Roman coins bearing the image of Vespasian and symbols such as "SPQR" and the Roman eagle, the Cavalier enthused about the tangible history lesson this could provide the illiterate, bringing the dead directly into their hands. "Thus, sir, you may see that your learned Worships poore tenants neigbours [interlined], without the trouble of Livie, Tacitus, Sueton, or any other of thos crabbed companions, are as conversant with the noble old heroes as your self."[52]

COMMUNICATING ANTIQUARIAN DISCOVERIES

Conversing with noble old Alfred through his coins was probably the furthest thing from the minds of Ryse, Marrall, and Denton on that brisk morning in 1611. Nevertheless, the manner in which the older Blundell had acquired his hoard testifies to the existence and snowball-like growth of what may be called the archaeological economy in early modern England, a commercial and intellectual loop along which artifacts and old objects in general were recovered, sold or traded, interpreted, and (as ultimately happened in this case) redeployed to other uses. This was an

---

[52] Lancs RO DDBl Acc. 6121, "Great Hodge Podge," 85v, William Blundell to James Scarisbrick, 29 April 1655; reprinted with modernized spelling in *Cavalier's Note Book*, 280.

exceptional case insofar as the precious objects, unearthed by accident rather than by conscious excavation, came to Blundell more or less directly. In numerous other incidents all across the English countryside similar discoveries met, from the virtuoso's perspective, with less happy results. What if Blundell's coins had not been found by a member of his household, but, as was often the case, by a stranger, or for that matter, had been unearthed outside his demesne? Ploughmen, shepherds, and laborers were perennially turning up odds and ends of antiquity, urns, coins, arrowheads, and armor, and not infrequently speculating as to their origins; and the items themselves did not always end up in the closets of the learned. Stories abound about the destruction of this or that historical treasure by superstitious or avaricious locals, and Joseph Levine has documented a good example of this in the ruin of the Stonesfield pavement at the start of the eighteenth century.[53]

Because they nearly always provide our only source for the circumstances of antiquarian discoveries, there is some risk in taking the intellectual and social snobbery of the historically minded humanist too far. More often than not, interesting antiquities first reached educated minds through rough hands and dirty jerkins. Many seventeenth- and eighteenth-century collectors would gloat in their letters and diaries of the yokels and bumpkins who had easily parted with a gold coin, bronze shield, or other valuable for a pittance. To read the accounts of some Restoration and Hanoverian antiquaries, these objects were almost invariably stumbled over by plain, frieze-clad rascals and simpletons who either destroyed them or, nearly as foolish, gave them up en route to the alehouse. The disparagement of the discoverer and procurer of antiquities as alternatively greedy or stupid is a mark of deteriorating cultural relations beginning in the second half of the seventeenth century. It is much less evident in the comments of Tudor and early Stuart antiquaries: Blundell's account conveys gratitude and even a hint of admiration for the quick-wittedness of young Thomas Ryse, rather than the sort of "see-the-silly-cowherd" contempt one reads in an Anthony à Wood or a Thomas Hearne fifty or a hundred years later.

An antiquity having been wrested from its initial finder, the further communication of such discoveries within the educated elite took place along both formal and informal lines, leaving more obvious traces from

---

[53] Joseph M. Levine, "The Stonesfield Pavement: Archaeology in Augustan England," in *Humanism and History*, 107–22.

which we can excavate regional and national intellectual networks. Not all of this activity can be attributed to the press. Print had certainly made possible cheap reproductions (like Blundell's copperplate) of texts and artifacts, but autograph transcripts of rare books and documents continued to travel across the English countryside by carrier, accounting for the enormous numbers of surviving sixteenth- and seventeenth-century copies of particular medieval documents and of entire books that had failed to reach the typesetter. Leland's *Itinerary* and a few of the early county chorographies, Sampson Erdeswicke's *Staffordshire* and Tristram Risdon's *Devon* (none of which books emerged from a press before the eighteenth century), are particularly notable in this regard.[54] The frosty climate of Sefton notwithstanding, religion was generally no impediment to contact with other antiquaries, scholarly interests crossing confessional lines with relative ease. Had Blundell been better known he might well have lent his coins out – we do not know, in fact, that he did not do so. This practice was less common in the late sixteenth and early seventeenth centuries than it would eventually become. The favored Jacobean and Caroline practice was to distribute workmanlike transcripts and drawings, just as pedigrees and coats of arms were similarly sketched and circulated; Blundell did just this in causing the coins to be engraved and having copies distributed in the countryside.

By the end of the seventeenth century a much improved public carriage system, better roads, and a superabundance of numismatic discoveries had made such items easier to disseminate and had substantially reduced both the monetary and the historical value of any single trove. Coins, urns, bronzes, and other objects changed hands in greater numbers, either on loan or as gifts.[55] A remarkable illustration of how such artifacts could circulate, given a network considerably more elaborate than Blundell's,

---

[54] For example, Cambridge University Library (CUL) Mm.4.23, an eighty-two-leaf copy, written in the late seventeenth century, of Erdeswicke, with three pages of the continuation (written c. 1673) of that author by Sir Simon Degge. The Staffordshire Record Office and William Salt Library each have several other manuscripts; several manuscript copies of Risdon's *Chorographical Description or Survey of Devon*, first printed by Edmund Curll in 1711 (in a bad edition), are held at the West Country Studies Library and in the Devon Record Office, both in Exeter. A further example would be "The Peregrination of Doctor Boorde," a copy of Andrew Boorde's topographical travels, in the hand of Laurence Nowell and passed on, via William Lambarde (who signed the work in Anglo-Saxon characters), to seventeenth-century users. Bodleian Library, Oxford, MS Top. gen. e. 62, fols. 7–54.

[55] Arjun Appadurai, "Introduction: Commodities and the Politics of Value," in *The Social Life of Things: Commodities in Cultural Perspective*, ed. Appadurai (Cambridge: Cambridge University Press, 1986), 3–63.

comes from the late 1690s, when some medals were found in Wallingford. According to Thomas Ford, writing about the discovery, "Tis suspected there were gold & pure silver peices amongst them, tho' concealed by the greedy discoverers. A great part of them they sent to London to be refined for the silver; some few were distributed to such country fellows as came to gaze & wonder at such strange money; the rest are ingrossed by an iron-monger in Wallingford who having heard how valuable single & particular medals are, sets extravagant rates on them, imagining al to be such." Ford himself had heard of these only at Christmas of 1699, while visiting rela-tions in the area, but by that point only a handful was still there. Ford's lament for the fate of this discovery echoes the "greedy ignorant country-man" motif common in such accounts by 1700, and casts further light on Blundell's rush, in 1611, to snap up the coins on his land. "Tis pitty," Ford remarks, "so many excellent monuments of antiquity should be so lost or that some curious person was not at the discovery who might have re-deemed many valuable pieces from the crucible & settled many contro-verted points of history by their most certain testimony."[56]

But there is an intellectual and not just a chronological gap between Ford's remark and Blundell's description of his own discovery nearly a century before. From Blundell's sharing in his tenants' sense of wonder, from the excitement of discovery and the challenge of explaining the Harkirke coins as an intellectual problem in itself, we come to Ford's more passive, scholarly, and cold evaluation of the Wallingford hoard as simply several lost bits of information for the incremental construction of a definitively "true" history of Britain, information nearly vitiated by the very vulgar sort whose traditions and beliefs continually conspired against the hegemony of the documentable past. For Ford, who never laid eyes on these particular coins, they were less artifacts to be collected and cherished, even donated as gifts, and certainly shown off to visitors, than they were pocket-sized ingots of information to be fitted into a historical picture and used to sharpen that picture around the edges, purging popu-lar error along the way. Of course there were elements of that implicit in Blundell's account also, but in his case the recourse to medieval and modern authorities was to the end of identifying the coins, not the other way around. The reliclike quality that the archaeological finds of the sixteenth century had possessed was much dissipated by the end of the following century, when both the depth and quantity of antiquarian and

---

[56] CUL MS Mm.6.50 (Covel letters), fol. 229, Ford to John Covel, 29 January 1699/1700.

numismatic scholarship had expanded. As one East Anglian scholar, Thomas Pocock, remarked to a friend, "I have so many affairs of importance on my hands, besides collecting rarities in art and nature, that I have no time for local words, or the usual catachreses of the vulgar."[57]

Once acquired by local antiquaries, coins and other artifacts often reentered circulation, either literally as gifts or loans, or intellectually through written descriptions and letters. Blundell published the coins locally, and without his historical deliberations on them, in the copperplate, and seems to have done so primarily for religious reasons. Had he lived sixty years later, he could easily have done as many rural squires and clerics with greater pretensions to citizenship in the *respublica litterarum* and submitted his work to the Royal Society or, later still, to the Society of Antiquaries, which was refounded in Queen Anne's reign.[58] But in 1611 there were few such outlets. Blundell was not a lawyer and did not have connections with the philological elite, which included Spelman, John Selden, John Dodderidge, John Davies, and other lawyer-scholars. The informal Elizabethan Society of Antiquaries had not met for several years, and would reassemble only briefly in 1614. But the existence of two copies of Blundell's account, one done up for the engraver, the other in a private notebook bound within another remnant of the family's medieval past, suggests that he entertained thoughts of having both his discovery and his ruminations on it survive his death.

This may be the reason why the notebook contains verbal descriptions and references to historical sources. It takes the bare depiction of the coins in the roll account and dresses it in the trappings of historical scholarship, in much the way that heralds and antiquaries from William Camden to William Dugdale converted raw familial evidences into learned accounts of gentry pedigrees buttressed by citations from chronicles and other records. The coins serve in the notebook – as they do not in the roll – as so many tiny, circular windows through which Blundell could peer into the past to construct mininarratives of various kings' reigns, while obliquely commenting on the present; but they figure promi-

---

[57] Essex RO D/Y/1/1/N-P, Pocock (in Danbury) to Rev. William Holman, 24 May 1723.
[58] The manuscript minute book of the Society of Antiquaries of London (SAL), Antiquaries MS 265 bulges with reports by eager fellows and correspondents of such discoveries as Blundell's, a century after the Harkirke coins appeared, but these are almost always less informative than the Blundell account, carrying little reference to the identities of the finders beyond their low class. I am indebted to Mr. Bernard Nurse, librarian to the Society of Antiquaries of London, for making this manuscript available to me.

nently in these accounts rather than merely decorating them. He endeavored, for instance, to explain the name Cudberht on the reverse of one of Alfred's coins, though he could "fynde written no espetiall cause or reason why this kinge shoulde set him in his coyne." Mindful of St. Cuthbert of Lindisfarne (mentioned in Bede) who is supposed to have appeared to Alfred in a vision during his darkest time, Blundell used his imagination to bridge the gap between coin and book. "I thinke it moste lyke and probable that K. Aelfred caused the coine so to be made in memorie of the fore said miracle." In this vision, Cuthbert had reassured Alfred that the English were suffering "by the swoorde of ye Danes" for their sins, but that the Lord would not allow their extinction "in respecte of so manie saintes that had been of yt nation."[59] In Blundell's Saxon "English" one can read Jacobean "Catholics"; perhaps it had not escaped his notice that the new king, who had so recently revived the persecutions of his predecessor, was in fact married to a Dane.

INTERPRETING THE DISCOVERY: ARTIFACT ENCOUNTERS TEXT

This brings us, at long last, to the point at which one might normally expect a historiographical study to have begun, namely Blundell's efforts to situate his find in history, to evaluate and then to exploit its potential as scholarly evidence of life in the past. Here we enter into an intellectual process that separates him, the somewhat learned enthusiast with a modicum of knowledge and an abundance of religious conviction, from his servants and family, who now fade from the story. The coins themselves had, in the space of a few hours, moved from lost treasure, to recovered objects of popular speculation, to family possessions transferred from tenurial outreach into the private household, to become, finally, the focus of critical, scholarly contemplation in the solitude of Blundell's study. Here he communed silently with the textual authorities represented in his library. The "living" past of the disgorged artifacts was now being mediated through and explained by the historical past, the unattainable realm of dead kings and chroniclers. Although the works to which Blundell refers in the notebook are a mixture of medieval and modern, antiquarian

---

[59] The story of King Alfred, complete with persecution by Danes, flight, and hunger, had particular appeal to the long-suffering Blundell, who saw in him an ancient model for faith under dire circumstances. *Crosby Records*, 50–1. Similar sentiments color his account of Edward the Martyr, ibid., 59.

and historical, he was reading them for other than the conventional exemplary or commemorative value. He was instead using them as props, aids to guide his historical imagination, in thinking about how and why the coins were made, by whom, and, perhaps, how they came to be buried where they were.

The exercise began with a "more dilligent revewe" of the coins' condition and their inscriptions, but soon ran up against Blundell's own rather limited linguistic ability: Several of the coins were not English but Danish, and by his own admission he was unable to "perfectly imitate and expresse" the "strange characters" on many of them. To proceed further he needed outside help, to be provided by his books. And even this help had its limits. Antiquarianism by 1611 had fixed its gaze more steadily upon Roman remains than medieval, though the Old English editions produced under Elizabeth by Archbishop Matthew Parker and his associates, the legal texts of William Lambarde, and language studies such as Richard Verstegan's *Restitution of Decayed Intelligence* (the work of another nostalgic Catholic) and Camden's *Remains* were together beginning to shift interest in the latter direction. If Blundell was successful in identifying most of the individual coins, however, he conspicuously failed to fit them into the broader picture of Anglo-Danish history, instead reducing them to biographical mininarratives of each depicted king's reign. Without the critical tools to generalize about life and events in the tenth-century north, he fell back on the genre he knew best, the formal history. In so doing he was following in reverse the very route being taken at exactly the same time, several hundred miles to the south, by the London historian John Speed, who in 1611 was preparing coins to decorate the heads of his reign-by-reign *History of Great Britain*.[60]

We know from Blundell's own account that his reading was wide and that he was better than usually acquainted with some of the major medieval and post-medieval authors of the past.[61] By 1611, printed editions existed of many of the medieval historians. Various works by William of Malmesbury and Roger of Hoveden (or Howden) had been available in Latin for little over a decade in the collection of chroniclers published by

---

[60] Henry Ellis, ed., *Original Letters of Eminent Literary Men of the Sixteenth, Seventeenth and Eighteenth Centuries*, Camden Society, o.s. 23 (London, 1843), 108–13; D. R. Woolf, *The Idea of History in Early Stuart England: Erudition, Ideology, and "The Light of Truth" from the Accession of James I to the Civil War* (Toronto: University of Toronto Press, 1990), 68.

[61] For the medieval historians, the indispensable work is Antonia Gransden, *Historical Writing in England*, 2 vols. (Ithaca, N.Y.: Cornell University Press, 1974–82).

Sir Henry Savile, while Bede, the most admired Anglo-Saxon historian, had been translated into English by the Catholic propagandist Thomas Stapleton in 1565, copies of his history having been known even earlier in private libraries such as those of Cambridge.[62] Blundell's familiarity with Bede, a northerner and a monk, is not surprising. The chronicles of Malmesbury and Hoveden were a bit more out of the way.[63] His source for Edward the Confessor's payment of Peter's pence is given as a life of the Confessor by "Alred." This is without doubt Ailred or Ethelred of Rievaulx (c. 1109–66), whose life of Edward was compiled after the king's canonization in 1161.[64] Acquaintance with this, and with Asser's life of Alfred, published by Archbishop Parker in a Latin and Anglo-Saxon edition in 1574, bespeaks a particular concern with the Anglo-Saxon era, one that contrasts with the usual Protestant veneration of Alfred as a kind of proto-Protestant monarch ruling free of papal tyranny, as exemplified in Robert Powell's 1634 comparison of that king with Charles I.[65]

Blundell's veneration of Alfred as a pious lawgiver is clear. The king was "of such pietie and devotion as Florent. Westmon. and others write that hee daihe heard masse, and in the night season unknowen to all his servants, hee frequented churches to here service. He wrote and promulgated most christian lawes." Alfred alone among England's kings, notes Blundell (from Foxe's *Acts* of all places!) "tooke his crowne and unction

[62] E. Leedham-Green, *Books in Cambridge Inventories,* 2 vols. (Cambridge: Cambridge University Press, 1986) lists four Tudor copies of Bede's *Ecclesiastical History.*

[63] The *Rerum Anglicarum Scriptores post Bedam,* ed. H. Savile (London: G. Bishop, R. Nuberie & R. Barker, 1606; 2d ed., Frankfurt: Typis Wechelianis apud C. Marnium & heredes I. Aubrij, 1601) included, in addition to Malmesbury and Hoveden, the *Chronicon Ethelwerdi* and a few other late Saxon–early Norman historical works such as the chronicle then attributed to Ingulph of Croyland (which was in fact a late medieval forgery but would not be exposed as such till the early nineteenth century). It is certain from Blundell's own page references to Ingulph that he used the Frankfurt edition of 1601, which paginates differently from the earlier London edition. Ingulph concludes with a reference to the Laws of Edward, the texts of which are not there included, but were easily available in Lambarde. Blundell also took extracts from Malmesbury out of a more modern and less direct source, Robert Parsons's *A Treatise of Three Conversions of England* (St. Omer, 1603).

[64] It was printed in a mutilated form in John Capgrave's *Legenda nova* (1516), and in a publication by Laurentius Surius at Cologne in the late sixteenth century. Blundell must have used the Capgrave volume, since the full text was first accurately printed by Roger Twysden in 1652 in his *Historia Anglicanae Scriptores Decem.*

[65] Robert Powell, *The Life of Alfred* (London: R. Badger for T. Alchorn, 1634); Aelfric of Eynsham's writings, published by Archbishop Parker's circle of Anglo-Saxon scholars as *A Testimonie of Antiquitie* (London: John Day, 1566), is another example of the Protestant attempt to find ancient roots for the reformed church in the Anglo-Saxon era. Asser was also published in Camden's edition of chronicles, *Anglia, Normannica . . . a veteribus scripta* (Frankfurt: I. Claudi, Marnij, & Haeredum, 1603).

of the pope."[66] The reference to "Florent. Westmon." is in itself of interest. There is no chronicler called "Florence of Westminster"; Blundell
probably meant to write "Florent. Wigorn.," in reference to the twelfth-
century Worcester chronicle which was then (and until recent times)
ascribed to one Florence, a monk of Worcester. Alternatively, he may
have intended the *Flores Historiarum,* a work now attributed to Matthew
Paris (continuing Roger of Wendover) but then thought to be by the
nonexistent "Matthew of Westminster." Both works begin with Creation
and therefore include the reign of Alfred, and both were in print by the
end of the sixteenth century.[67] But Blundell's confused reference suggests
that he had conflated the two books, and thereby helps to identify the
precise edition he used: not the first, 1592 edition of Florence, which was
edited by the northern Catholic antiquary William Howard of Naworth,
but rather the version of this appended to an edition of the *Flores Histo-*
riarum published at Frankfurt in 1601.[68]

Ranulf Higden's *Polychronicon* and the *Anglica Historia* of Polydore
Vergil are other obvious sources – Blundell was looking up "authorities,"
not doing "research" in the modern sense, and so did not discriminate
among his books as to "primary" and "secondary." The *Polychronicon,*
in the late-fourteenth-century English of John of Trevisa, was one of the
best-known potboilers of the later Middle Ages, printed by William Caxton in 1482 and republished several times in the early Tudor decades.
Vergil's *Anglica Historia,* though notoriously unpopular among its English critics for its doubt of Arthurian and other British myths (and its

---

[66] Lancs, RO DDBl Acc. 6121; *Crosby Records,* 52. Blundell also relies here on Richard
Verstegan's *Restitution,* published in 1605. It should be pointed out that relations between the Blundells and individual members of the pre-Reformation clergy had not
always been smooth. A bitter civil dispute in 1519 had occurred between William's
ancestor, another Nicholas Blundell, and Sir Edward Mulnes or Molyneux, parson of
Sefton. See Lancs RO DDBl 24/3 and 4 for "the wronges and ingerys that dame Anne
Mulnes and Sir Edvard Mulnes, clerke, person of the churche of Sefton, by thare gret
mygth and pawer have done to Nycholas Blundell and his wyff and chyldren"; the
matter finally had to be resolved by a decree in Star Chamber of 14 November 1527, for
which see Lancs RO DDBl 24/5. The Molyneuxs, whose seat was at Sefton within the
same parish, would prove formidable enemies to the Blundells over the ensuing century;
Sir Richard Molyneux led the search of William Blundell's house in 1598.

[67] See Gransden, *Historical Writing in England,* 1:143–4; and Richard Vaughan, *Matthew*
Paris (Cambridge: Cambridge University Press, 1958), 94.

[68] Florence of Worcester, *Chronicon ex chronicis, ab initio mundi usque ad annum*
MCXVII, ed. W. Howard of Naworth (London: T. Dawson for R. Watkins, 1592);
Flores historiarum per Matthaeum Westmonasteriensem collecti ... Et Chronicon ex
chronicis, ab initio mundi usque ad annum Domini MCXVIII, deductum auctore
Florentio Wigorniensi (Frankfurt: Typis Wechelianis apud Claudium, Marnium &
heredes Ioannis Aubrij, 1601), 459–696.

author's papal office), would no doubt appeal to a stubborn Catholic like the lord of Little Crosby.

Blundell resorted to books even more recent than Vergil's as well, since they could provide a guide to the contents of the older, less easily consulted medieval histories. It comes as no surprise to find John Stow among the authors consulted. By 1611, just four years before the second to last edition of Stow's *Annales* was to appear, his series of chronicles had become for most Englishmen the easiest point of access to their own history. More up-to-date than the earlier chronicles of Thomas Lanquet, Edward Hall, and Richard Grafton, and less bulky than the enormous and expensive Holinshed (Speed's *History,* we have seen, was still in press), Stow's *Summaries, Chronicles,* and *Annales* are frequently to be found in early-seventeenth-century book lists. Francis Godwin's book of bishops is a somewhat more peculiar choice, given that its account (which earned the author his own episcopal see) demonstrates the succession of archbishops and bishops free of papal suzerainty and under royal authority. But it, too, was often to be found in Stuart libraries, and its pre-Tudor emphasis lent it special relevance to Blundell's fixation on the Middle Ages; the Cavalier would make use of the same work in his own notes on bishoprics a few decades later.[69] John Caius's *De antiquitate Cantabrigiensis academiae libri duo* (a historical "proof" of the greater antiquity of Cambridge over Oxford) held similar information, making mention of Alfred's laws, and discussing ancient coinage and its values; this book also included a *catalogus* of major historians that Blundell would have found useful.[70] The presence of Foxe is tougher to account for, though Blundell may have wished to acquire a good sense of the enemy, and the Book of Martyrs contains informative narratives of the activities of Anglo-Saxon clergy and kings; his account of the coins makes frequent reference to *The Acts and Monuments* without any confessional sniping.[71] It is Foxe, along with Polydore and Roger Hoveden, whom

---

[69] Lancs RO DDBl Acc. 6121, "Great Hodge Podge," fol. 93r.

[70] See John Caius, *De antiquitate Cantabrigiensis academiae libri duo,* 328, for Alfred's laws, and 361–6 for his *catalogus.*

[71] In any case, Blundell was not alone among Elizabethan Catholics in citing Foxe to his own ends: in 1583 Lady Tresham recorded that her husband had cited Foxe's martyrs in defense of his refusal to acknowledge fault in concealing the Jesuit Edmund Campion. Hist. MSS Comm., *Various Collections,* 3:30. Indeed, Blundell almost makes Foxe look like a Catholic historian, writing of Athelstan's survival of a conspiracy: "In this king's tyme there befell a notable miracle recited by John Foxe, and registered by Malmesburie"; Foxe certainly did not record this as a "miracle." *Crosby Records,* 57; and Lancs RO DDBl Acc. 6121.

Blundell cites in support of his case for the continuity of payment of Peter's pence from early Saxon times, through the Danish invasions and the Norman conquest, up to the time of Henry VIII, who "brake off with the pope, and sea of Rome, for causes whiche all men knowe."[72]

But the most important book here, medieval or modern, is Camden's, for its examples and discussions of ancient and medieval coinage. Blundell himself was obviously able to read Latin, since he refers specifically to pages in the 1594 edition of *Britannia* (Philemon Holland's 1610 translation having apparently not yet found its way to Little Crosby).[73] In either language, Camden's was the book that more than any other equipped the would-be provincial scholar, dwelling far from libraries and official records and isolated from the conversation of the most learned, with the minimum of what he needed to know. Camden was to the island's prehistoric, Roman, and early medieval antiquities what his older contemporary Lambarde had been to JPs cutting their way through thickets of Elizabethan statutes, and what still another William, the fifteenth-century canonist Lyndewode, had been to pre-Reformation church lawyers. *Britannia* deserves a special place in the history of history in England, less for what its author did for historical method than for what the book itself did, in the century after its first publication in 1586, for the dissemination of a rudimentary knowledge of British antiquity, and the turning of many gentry minds toward the history and archaeology of their localities. It would be reedited in 1695 by a team of scholars led by Edmund Gibson, who invited contributions from gentry throughout the kingdom with regard to county antiquities and natural history – and one of these contributions would come from Blundell's eventual heir, William the Cavalier, who thereby put back into the changing text of *Britannia* something comparable to that which his grandfather had taken out eighty-four years earlier.[74]

Blundell's own synthesis of his reading from Camden with his own and his neighbors' knowledge is evident from his treatment of the Northumbrian king, St. Oswald, martyred at the hands of Penda, king of Mercia, in A.D. 642 (and more often associated with Whitchurch in Shrop-

---

[72] Lancs RO DDBl Acc. 6121; *Crosby Records*, 48.

[73] *Crosby Records*, 55.

[74] In the 1695 edition of *Camden's Britannia*, edited by Gibson (London: F. Collins for A. Swalle . . . and A. & J. Churchill), 802, an addition by the editor refers to the coins as having been found 8 April 1611 by Blundell "in a place call'd Harkirke," and mentions their having been printed in a "copper-plate"; it then goes on to acknowledge the assistance of the Cavalier, "to whom we are indebted for some particulars belonging to those parts."

shire, near the site of his death). Blundell transcribed from Camden some verses inscribed on the porch of Winwick Church, about thirty miles from Little Crosby:

Hic locus, Oswalde, quondam placuit tibi valde
Northanhumbrorum fueras Rex, nuncque Polorum
Regna tenes, loco passus Marcelde vocato.[75]

Rather than rest here, Blundell – who unlike Camden was eager to believe stories of Oswald's miraculous deeds – embellished his account with reference to oral tradition:

See Cambden, pag. 981, in ye impression at London of ye yeare 1594. More-o[ver], a Catholique gentleman and frend of myne whoe had dwelte heretofore nere to the saide place, beinge moved by my letter to certifie me what hee knewe thereof, writethe that the people thereaboute have yet in there mouthes (it may be by tradition) yt K. Oswalde being greevouslie wounded in a battell not farre from yt place, vowed yt if hee might wendequicke (or whicke according to there speache) hee wolde there builde a Churche, wherupon (as they saye) it was then called Wendwhicke, now Winwicke.

Moreover on yt syde of Newton parke wch is towards Winwick not eight roods (as I rem[em]ber saith this gentleman) from the pale, there is a little well walled with stone within, which ye people call St. Oswald's well, and neare therunto there was an olde tree standinge in my tyme which had (as the people say) a picture standinge in it, the place shewinge when I lived there yt it might fitlie be used for such a purpose, and further (as I remember saithe hee) I have hearde it there reported that there had bine a greate pilgremage to yt place. And thus I have thought good to take or rather seeke occasion here to write of ye place of this blessed K. and martir his death, because ye same is by wronge information saide in a late pious booke to have bine at Osestree.[76]

Limited and without context as it may have been, William Blundell's knowledge of medieval history and numismatics was not commonplace in 1611. Yet it was fast becoming so. Since Leland's exploration of the monastic ruins and his examination of English monuments seventy years earlier, and even more since the advent of the county chorographies and the publication of a number of Tudor chronicles, historical and antiquar-

---

[75] "This happy place did holy Oswald love / Who once Northumbria rul'd, now reigns above, / And from Marcelde did to Heaven remove." *Camden's Britannia* (1695), 790; The Latin version is from *Britannia* (London: G. Bishop, 1607), 612.

[76] *Crosby Records*, 56, 56n. For Camden's more meager account see the edition of 1607, 612; and the edition of 1695, 790. There is more on Oswald's miracles (which Camden regards as the "ridiculous" invention of medieval historians), and on his death, see *Britannia* 452, and *Camden's Britannia*, 854. The connection between Alfred and Oswald is that Blundell felt obliged to explain the difference between Alfred the Great and Alfred of Northumberland, the latter being a "nephew" to St. Oswald.

ian knowledge of the classical and medieval periods had achieved an unprecedented public prominence. From having once been the preserve of clerics and a few bookish aristocrats, it was now the common domain of the educated gentleman. The appearance of multiple historical genres in the late sixteenth century, as the chronicle yielded its virtual monopoly to the humanist "politic" history, the history play, and the historical verse narrative (from the *Mirror for Magistrates* to the minor epics of Michael Drayton and Samuel Daniel), reflects a rising level of historical literacy, a ready familiarity with and interest in the major episodes and personalities of the national and international past beyond the contents of classical historians studied for rhetorical purposes at the universities.

The speed of this change should be neither exaggerated nor denied. The real "revolution" in historical thinking came over a period of more than a century, and it is less discernible in the genres within which history was written than in the several ways in which and increasing frequency with which it was *read*. Were a graph to be drawn of the expansion of England's historical readership, it would ascend gently from as early as the 1470s, and a bit more vigorously after 1550; the sharpest rise, however, would come in the century after William Blundell's death in 1638, public interest driving and in turn fueled by a vastly increased number of published works about the past, of varying shapes, sizes, and descriptions. By the time of Nicholas Blundell the diarist, the boundaries between the oral and popular on the one hand, and the official, if partisan, versions of history contained in books on the other, were more firmly established than they had been in that of his great-great-grandfather a century earlier. The number of books on "history" of different sorts had increased to such a degree that something like a modern notion of proper historical literacy is evident, with historical episodes suffusing civilized discourse. This is concretely evident in the contents of libraries: Those for the sixteenth century generally contain few historical titles; even allowing for the greater numbers of books in print on a wide range of historical topics, the number of library lists, private catalogues, and publicly available copies of history books increased enormously during the seventeenth century.

What we would now call mainstream historical episodes from classical, medieval, and recent history, domestic and foreign – the material highlighted in humanist historiography – was becoming the stuff of daily conversation in the early seventeenth century, especially among the social and political elite: It saturates the writings of early Stuart miscellanists and letter writers such as Robert Burton and James Howell. The great event had still to compete with the marginal and trivial, whether jokes and anecdotes involving famous persons, or the more popular variety of local lore and tradition that made its way around the village community to be picked up by (and perhaps sometimes embellished or invented for) traveling scholars such as Leland, Camden, and their many seventeenth- and eighteenth-century successors. Like the historical reader, these informal, oral modes of historical discourse have been little studied, despite the fact that a majority of Tudor and early Stuart antiquaries thought them worth recording and believed them to be a legitimate supplement to written evidence. The historical and pseudohistorical anecdote remained, and indeed became more commonplace in verbal discourse about the past at the very time that it was fading, according to Annabel Patterson, from humanist historiography: It found a new home in informal history when exiled from the formal genre. The anecdote was a manageable, portable snatch of the past that could be dropped into the most mundane social situations by men or women.[77]

The conversational anecdote of the elite had its popular counterpart in village oral traditions of the sort that Blundell had heard about King Oswald. As late as the 1690s, Abraham de la Pryme, a Yorkshire vicar, boasted of his use of such sources at the beginning of his unpublished history of the town of Hatfield Chase. "I have searched & examined not onely all printed books & chronicles, in which I might expect to find any thing relateing there to, but have also examind all the most antient men liveing in the whole country round about." His historical practice follows this announced method, as he relies, during his recitation of regional history from the time of the Cimbri, on the popular sense of place and event to locate, in a small hill of earth near Hadham field, the battle of Heathfield (which Pryme thought was his own parish of Hatfield). Pryme's knowledge of history and chronology told him that this battle had occurred on 12 October 633 between the Deirans and Mercians, and that in it Edwin, king of Deira, and many of his nobles had perished. What he could not find from books was the precise location of the field of battle:

The country people know the aforesayd place very well, & will shew a place a little way of which they call Slei-Bur-Hill-Slac – where blood they say (by tradi-

---

[77] I am indebted to Annabel Patterson's essay in this volume for making me consider more thoroughly the matter of "portability."

tion) flow'd down in whole torrents unto the lower parts of the field and then ran like a river into the commonside to the southwards. . . . But when all this happend they do not know, but tis most certain & undoubted that it was after this great fight.[78]

Such beliefs were as much a part of the early modern sense of the past as impolitic comparisons between Elizabeth I and Richard II, parliamentary tributes to Magna Carta, or narratives of Cannae, Philippi, and Hastings. Nor were they, as the interest of a Hans Sloane or a John Locke demonstrates toward the end of the period, strictly for the ears of the vulgar. The scholarly, "modern" variety of history, socially sanctioned and documented, proved remarkably flexible in appropriating certain vestiges of previously local legends, turning select regional heroes into national figures. Robin Hood was one example, and Guy of Warwick another. William Jackson, the customs master of Yarmouth in the late seventeenth century, joined in attempts to domesticate and historicize Robin Hood by drawing up an elaborate pedigree for him. This made Robin the ancestor of the Devereux earls of Essex and of Jackson's own contemporary, Viscount Hereford. Jackson places Robin in Henry III's time and recounts his death seven miles from Wakefield, in a nunnery; "over [his] grave is a stone with some obsolete letters not to be read and now to be seene called Robin Hoods grave & formerly an arbour of trees and wood"; eager to fix this legendary figure in time, he even dates Robin's death to 50 Hen. 3 (1265), perhaps because he was familiar with the year as the date of the fall of Simon de Montfort.[79] The imaginative process could still, as it had for William Blundell many years before, tame even the wildest aspects of the past. Given a little outside reading and a memory for detail, an educated mind could take the unglossed, disorderly fuzz of inherited myth and tradition, much as it might take the more tangible but no less raw matter of a Saxon coin trove, and turn it into the comforting neatness of datable, chronological history.

This essay has raised several problems without pretending to do more than lay them open for further discussion. It may be time to cease picking over the carcass of early modern historiography for the origins of modern method, and to reexamine our own definition of the historical before we seek to impose it on the past. Future scholarship will have to take greater note of such matters as the perception of time and space, attitudes to

---

[78] BL MS Lans. 897, fol. 11r, 29r.
[79] CUL Oo.6.115, collections of William Jackson of Yarmouth.

ancestry, the sense of the continuity of past and present, and the ways in which history was read and imagined, as well as researched and written. Perhaps the techniques and sources of modern local social history can eventually show us how the inhabitants of our past went about the business of sorting out *their* past. The historical culture that produced and read Camden's *Britannia,* Foxe's *Acts and Monuments,* Stow's *Annales,* and Dugdale's *Monasticon* was unquestionably Camden's, Foxe's, Stow's, and Dugdale's. But it was also the culture of the curious landlord, William Blundell, his family, and their dawdling cowherd.

6

Murder in Faversham:
Holinshed's impertinent history

RICHARD HELGERSON

As its first entry for the year 1551, Holinshed's *Chronicles* (1577 and 1587) presents a detailed account of the murder of a certain Master Arden, a gentleman of Faversham in Kent, by his wife, her lover, and a host of accomplices. The entry is not unique. Leaving aside political assassinations, Holinshed's 1587 index lists some twenty-three murders. But its length does make it unusual. Where most of Holinshed's other murder stories get no more than a sentence or two, the Arden account goes on for a full seven tightly printed folio columns, nearly five thousand words, considerably more than he gives many events of state. Perhaps that's why he felt the need for a justification and apology: "The which murder, for the horribleness thereof, although otherwise it may seem to be but a private matter and therefore, as it were, impertinent to this history, I have thought good to set it forth somewhat at large."[1]

The "horribleness" Holinshed vaunts is obvious enough: a wife's adultery leading to the murder of her husband; servants rebelling against their master; neighbors turning against neighbor; the engagement first of a poisoner and then of "a notorious murdering ruffian" and his vagabond companion; a whole series of grotesque failed attempts, culminating in a successfully brutal murder in the victim's own parlor; and finally eight spectacular public executions. Nor was the horribleness only a matter of

---

[1] Raphael Holinshed, *The Third Volume of Chronicles* (London: J. Harison et al., 1587), sig. kkkkki^v. Holinshed's 1577 account of Arden's murder differs mainly in lacking the extensive marginal glosses that distinguish the posthumous 1587 edition. In this and other quotations, I have modernized both spelling and punctuation. I also modernize spelling and punctuation in titles mentioned in the text, but I retain the original spelling, regularizing i, j, u, and v, in titles cited in notes. One further procedural note: in referring to "Holinshed," I am referring to the editorial group that produced Holinshed's *Chronicles,* a group that included a number of people in addition to Holinshed himself.

sensational transgression and violence. It also served to prompt wonder and thus led to a reawakened sense of human depravity and providential design – a design signaled by the miraculous print of Arden's body still to be seen "two years and more" after he was slain in the field where the murderers dumped him. Both the horrible murder and the wonderful sign were prodigies of a sort that got much attention in medieval and early modern chronicles, where the doings of God were thought at least as germane to the historical enterprise as the doings of men. But by the time Holinshed wrote not even the exemplary horribleness of the Arden story was quite enough to fend off the fear of impertinence. As his apology makes clear, Holinshed held conflicting notions of historical selection: one that still valued horribleness, wherever it might be found; but another that considered "private matters," however prodigious, impertinent. And in succeeding decades, the second and more exclusionary of these notions, strongly backed by a new generation of politic and humanist historiographers, gained such authority that it made Holinshed's less decisive compilation look like a tissue of impertinence. "Voluminous Holinshed," the *Chronicles* was soon being called, "full of confusion and commixture of unworthy relations"; "trivial household trash"; "vast, vulgar tomes . . . recovered from out of innumerable ruins."[2]

That shift in historiographical focus is part – but only part – of what one discovers in attending to the fate of the Arden story. Yes, the sense of impertinence grew – grew, in fact, to such an extent that Arden's murder wholly lost its place in the formal writing of history. But the exile was neither immediate nor universal. On the contrary, the Arden story and its nearest rival in length, Holinshed's single-column account of the murder of Master George Sanders of London by *his* wife and *her* lover, went on being retold in edition after edition of John Stow's *Chronicles* and *Annals* (1580 to 1631), made it into Thomas Heywood's versified romp through English history, the *Troia Britannica* (1609), and even found a place on the London stage, where both were performed as plays: *Arden of Faversham* (1591) and *A Warning for Fair Women* (1599). Since then, the Arden story –

---

[2] Holinshed (1587), sig. kkkkkii and kkkkkiii^v. The phrases at the end of the paragraph come from Peter Heylyn, *Microcosmus, or A Little Description of the Great World* (Oxford: John Lichfield and James Short, 1621), sig. C1, John Donne, *The Satires, Epigrams, and Verse Letters*, ed. W. Milgate (Oxford: Clarendon Press, 1967), 17, and Edmund Bolton, *Hypercritica, or a Rule of Judgment for Writing and Reading our History's*, in *Critical Essays of the Seventeenth Century*, ed. J. E. Spingarn (Oxford: Clarendon Press, 1908), 1.97–8. I have borrowed them from the epigraph to Annabel Patterson's "Rethinking Tudor Historiography," *SAQ* 92 (1993): 185.

sometimes in the company of the Sanders murder, sometimes alone, sometimes in quite other company – has been so often and so variously retold that the story of its multiple retellings now deserves an account of its own. For what even Holinshed thought could be saved from impertinence only by its wonderful horribleness and what his more discriminating Elizabethan and Jacobean successors thought simply impertinent – trivial, trashy, and vulgar – can now be understood as a point of intersection for a whole range of once marginalized and still suspect historical interests, interests that were repressed by the post-Holinshed redefinition of history but that have lately returned in force to call that humanist enterprise into question.

Identifying those interests and the forces arrayed against them is one aim of this essay. But another is to suggest that the very terms of the opposition have – at least in the case of the Arden story – unnecessarily obscured the pertinence of that story to the broader aims of humanist historiography. On closer examination, Holinshed's "private matter" turns out not to have been quite so private as he claimed, and the exclusions and admissions based on that distinction – and on other distinctions like it – turn out not to have quite the compelling rationale they may seem to have had. But this gets us ahead of ourselves. Let's first see where and why the story has been valued and where and why it hasn't.

ON THE MARGINS

Any list of the historical hinterlands that have welcomed the Arden story is bound to have an element of the arbitrary. Their territories overlap so extensively that they are not easily distinguished. And any labeling that puts old tellings in new categories will fall, just as inevitably, into anachronism. The new labels speak of new interests that can never be neatly equated with the old. Yet, despite the arbitrariness and anachronism, some provisional sorting out is worth attempting for the sense it can give us of historiographical commonality and difference across time, of the shifting ways in which the limits of what counts as "history" have been configured and maintained. Whatever the accomplishment of early modern humanist historiography – and that accomplishment has certainly been considerable – it was won at the expense of stories like Arden's.

Where then has that story been felt to belong? I would identify seven relatively distinct provinces, all outside the usual bounds of serious historiography, as those bounds were coming to be established in the sixteenth and seventeenth centuries and as they remained in force, despite occasional realignments, well into the present century.

1. *"Vulgar" or popular history.* That the Arden story can now be seen as belonging to popular history – that is, to the history of common people – might have surprised Holinshed. He presents Arden as a "gentlemen" and his wife as a "gentlewoman" with "friends" powerful enough to advance her husband.[3] But that social distinction has not been much regarded in subsequent retellings, and the rest of the Arden cast is notably common, even by sixteenth-century standards. Alice Arden's lover was a mere "tailor by occupation," and the others charged with the murder were the lover's sister, "a painter . . . who had skill in poisons," a neighboring townsman, a goldsmith, two vagabonds, and two household servants.[4] If Arden's murder was an extraordinary event, those involved in it have generally been taken to be alarmingly ordinary: merchants, craftsmen, servants, and a couple of rogues. In marked contrast to the history of English kings and nobles that surrounds it in Holinshed and that continued to compete with it on the London stage, this story represents people from those less elevated ranks to which the vast majority of England's population belonged.

But more than just being *about* people of less than noble status, Arden's murder was apparently thought of particular interest to audiences of the common sort. Holinshed's "vulgar tomes" were quickly stigmatized as having a discreditable plebeian appeal – a charge in no way diminished by what one might think the prohibitive cost of his heavy folios – and that stigma attached still more strongly to the less imposing chronicles of John Stow and Thomas Heywood, the latter an especially notorious vulgarizer. The anonymous play *Arden of Faversham*, first performed in 1591 and printed in 1592, 1599, and 1633, claims not to have a lower-ranked audience specifically in mind. Its epilogue is addressed to gentlemen, but it

---

[3] Holinshed (1587), sig. kkkkki[v]. For a discussion of Arden's social status, see Lena Cowen Orlin, "Man's House as His Castle in *Arden of Feversham*," *Medieval and Renaissance Drama in England* 2 (1985): 57–89. Orlin argues that the play based on Holinshed's account "takes as its protagonist a gentleman, not a member of the middle class, nor a bourgeois hero, nor a citizen hero, as has often been posited" (81–2). That positing has, however, made the Arden story function as part of a popular history. Nor is this result simply a historical error. Placed next to the kings, nobles, and other high officers of state who fill most of Holinshed's pages and who dominate both humanist history and Elizabethan tragedy, even Arden's gentry status figures as popular. Peter Holbrook discusses *Arden* in these terms in *Literature and Degree in Renaissance England: Nashe, Bourgeois Tragedy, Shakespeare* (Newark, Del.: University of Delaware Press, 1994), 86–104.

[4] Holinshed, (1587), sig. kkkkki[v] and kkkkkii.

apologizes to the gentlemen for presenting such a "naked tragedy," as though gentle tastes and this base matter might be thought in conflict. And the one clear evidence of the play's early appropriation suggests a distinctly lower social register. By the 1630s, *Arden* had been transformed into a broadside ballad, "The Complaint and Lamentation of Mistress Arden." Nor did its descent stop here. In late-eighteenth-century Faversham, the play was being performed as a puppet show. There have in fact been adaptations for all social levels. While the townspeople of Faversham were seeing their favorite local murder reenacted by puppets, the patrons of Sadler's Wells were enjoying it danced as a ballet, and more recently it has reappeared as an opera.[5] But even when the genre is more elevated and the audience more socially select, the special *frisson* of the Arden story continues to come from the nonaristocratic ordinariness of its victim – a kind of provincial everyman – and from the still lower-ranked menace of those who surround and destroy him.

2. *The history of crime.* When the lower orders get noticed at all, it is specifically for their disruptiveness, for their engagement in rebellion or crime. And in the post-Holinshed era that notice has usually come in genres well removed from serious history. *Arden of Faversham* is the first of a large number of English plays based on actual crimes, and the similarly anonymous *Warning for Fair Women* (1599) is among its earliest imitators. The Sanders murder got still earlier attention in a pamphlet by Arthur Golding, *A Brief Discourse of the Late Murder of Master George Sanders* (1573), and was the lead piece in Anthony Munday's *View of Sundry Examples* (1580), and both the Sanders and Arden murders found a place in the "mass of murders" section of T. I.'s *World of Wonders* (1595). These genres – the murder play, the crime pamphlet, and the collection of wonders – all got going in the decade and a half following the publication of Holinshed's first edition and may owe something to the fascination exercised by its account of the Arden murder.[6] "Horrible-

---

[5] See M. L. Wine's survey of the stage history of *Arden* in the introduction to his Revels edition of the play (London: Methuen, 1973), xlv–lvii. The opera is Alexander Goehr's *Arden Muss Sterben* (1967). The phrase "naked tragedy" is found on p. 140 of Wine's edition.

[6] According to Victor E. Neuberg, the Arden story "set a pattern which was to be worked and re-worked, at least until the outbreak of the Civil War." *Popular Literature: A History and Guide from the Beginning of Printing to the Year 1897* (Harmondsworth, England: Penguin Books, 1977), 87. As a further indication of its effect on subsequent crime literature, P. D. James on a lecture tour in Canada a few years ago identified the Arden story as one of the principal sources of the genre to which she has contributed with such success, the detective novel. My thanks for this report to Professor Catherine Shaw.

ness," as Holinshed calls it, clearly had a market. And that market has continued to provide a demand for the numerous progeny of these early genres of crime literature, including the long-running and frequently updated *Newgate Calendar,* in whose multivolume twentieth-century incarnation Alice Arden is preceded in the roll of English criminals only by two medieval robber bands. To judge from *The Newgate Calendar,* Arden's murder is the first "modern" crime, the act that leads, discursively at least, to our own "true crime" magazines and tabloid newspapers.[7]

But what flourished in plays, pamphlets, and popular journalism has, until recently, been left out of serious historiography. As little as two decades ago, G. R. Elton could still call the history of crime "something like a wilderness."[8] That situation has changed rapidly. Just a few years after Elton's remark, J. A. Sharpe began a book entitled *Crime in Early Modern England* by declaring that "the history of crime is a major growth area of historical research,"[9] and since then publications have multiplied rapidly. Historians are keenly aware of the disreputable popular genres to which crime and its history have been largely confined – indeed, work in those genres supplies the historians with some of their richest sources – but the fact that they are regarding such material at all suggests a decisive break with the post-Holinshed redefinition of proper historical practice.

3. *Domestic history or the history of private life.* When literary scholars name the genre that begins with *Arden of Faversham,* they usually call it "domestic drama."[10] Closely related to that term is the one Holinshed used in apologizing for the impertinence of the Arden story: "but a private matter." "Domestic" and "private" name another, still more fun-

---

[7] J. L. Rayner and G. T. Crook, eds., *The Complete Newgate Calendar,* 5 vols. (London: Navarre Society, 1926). Other versions of *The Newgate Calendar* appeared in 1728, 1773, 1809, 1826, 1840, 1845, 1908, 1932, and 1951.

[8] G. R. Elton, "Introduction: Crime and the Historian," in *Crime in England, 1550–1800,* ed. J. S. Cockburn (London: Methuen, 1977), 1.

[9] J. A. Sharpe, *Crime in Early Modern England, 1550–1750* (London: Longman, 1984), 1. For an example of such work in an area where literary and historical study intersect, an example that includes extensive and valuable discussions of the Arden story, see Frances E. Dolan, *Dangerous Familiars: Representations of Domestic Crime in England, 1550–1700* (Ithaca, N.Y.: Cornell University Press, 1994).

[10] See, for example, Arthur Eustace Morgan, *English Domestic Drama* (Folcroft, Pa.: Folcroft Press, 1912); Michel Grivelet, *Thomas Heywood et le Drame Domestique Élisabethain* (Paris: Didier, 1957); Arnold Hauser, "The Origins of Domestic Drama," in *The Theory of the Modern Stage,* ed. Eric Bentley (Harmondsworth, England: Penguin, 1968), 403–19; and Andrew Clark, *Domestic Drama: A Survey of the Origins, Antecedents and Nature of the Domestic Play in England, 1500–1640,* 2 vols. (Salzburg: Institut für Englische Sprache und Literatur, 1975).

damental exclusion essential to the construction of humanist historiography. That construction depends on a sharp division of the private from the public, of the home from the larger world outside. Private and domestic matters became the province of literature rather than history – though in the sixteenth and seventeenth centuries even literature, as defined by humanist poetics, confined the domestic affairs of nonaristocrats to comedy. That is why *Arden of Faversham* and the other "domestic tragedies" that followed from it seem so anomalous. But in literature that anomaly went on to disrupt and eventually reorder the whole system of appropriate generic types. In the eighteenth century, domestic tragedy staged a remarkable comeback (including a rewrite of *Arden* by George Lillo, one of the most prominent "domestic" dramatists), and the novel, whose rise has been so often charted, gave still fuller scope to the representation of domestic and private events at all levels of society. (Not surprisingly, the Arden story has itself been the subject of a novel.[11]) But only recently has domesticity been thought to have a history deserving the professional historian's attention, attention it is now getting from many directions.[12] And with the new focus on domesticity and private life, the Arden murder has emerged as a prime historical example. Questions of household government, of the legal regulation of marriage, of domestic violence, of marital and extramarital sexuality, and of master–servant relations have all been discussed in terms of Arden's murder and its various early modern representations.[13] Preserved in literary and quasi-literary form, the Arden story has now returned to history.

4. *Women's history.* That return belongs, however, as much to the

[11] Diane Davidson, *Faversham* (New York: Crown Publishers, 1969).

[12] For an account of some eighteenth-century anticipations of this historiographical interest in domestic life, see Mark Phillips's essay in this volume. See also J. Paul Hunter's essay in this volume, which interestingly explores the eighteenth-century relation between the novel and formal historiography. Both Phillips and Hunter suggest complexities that the present essay, in its rapid jump from the sixteenth century forward, can do no more than acknowledge. But both also document the persistence of some of the exclusions I see developing in the late sixteenth century.

[13] See Catherine Belsey, "Alice Arden's Crime," *Renaissance Drama* n.s. 13 (1982): 82–102 (reprinted in Belsey's *The Subject of Tragedy: Identity and Difference in Renaissance Drama* [London: Methuen, 1985], 129–148); Lena Cowen Orlin, "Man's House"; Orlin, "Familial Transgressions, Societal Change on the Elizabethan Stage," in *Sexuality and Politics in Renaissance Drama*, ed. Carole Levin and Karen Robertson (Lewiston, NY: Edwin Mellen Press, 1991), 27–55; Frances E. Dolan, "Home-Rebels and House Traitors: Murderous Wives in Early Modern England," *Yale Journal of History and Law* 4 (1992): 1–31; Dolan, "The Subordinate('s) Plot: Petty Treason and the Forms of Domestic Rebellion," *Shakespeare Quarterly* 43 (1993): 317–40; and Betty S. Travitsky, "Husband-Murder and Petty Treason in English Renaissance Tragedy," *Renaissance Drama* n.s. 21 (1990): 171–98.

history of women as it does to domestic history or the history of private life. More than anything else, the recent surge of interest in *Arden* and other plays like it is due to the feminist insistence on attending to issues of gender and sexual difference. Once omitted from historical regard, except when inheritance endowed them with sovereign power, women have recently moved to the center of attention in literary and historical study. And the Arden story, particularly Alice Arden's part in it, has moved with them. "Alice Arden's Crime" is the title of the essay that has done most to get critics talking about *Arden,* and many of the subsequent studies have focused almost exclusively on the murderous wife.[14]

A similar sharpening of the focus on Alice marks the story's early transition from chronicle to play and from play to ballad. That Arden was murdered by his wife had much to do with the "horribleness" of the story for Holinshed, but the chronicle remained more interested in Arden than Alice. But on stage Alice emerged as the strongest and most active character, not only the driving force behind the play's action but also its most brilliant and troubling poet-rhetorician. The best lines are all hers. And in the ballad she is the only speaker; hers, the only motives that count. Even the *Newgate Calendar* chose Alice, over all the other con-spirators, including the sensational ruffians Black Will and Shakebag, to stand for this paradigmatic crime. As the Arden story moved further from the increasingly male and upper-class genre of history, it became more and more exclusively Alice's. Rejoining history under a feminist banner, it remains hers.

5. *Local history.* One place where the story has never been Alice's is Faversham. The earliest surviving record of Arden's murder is in the Faversham Wardmote Book, and in Faversham, where the play has been produced with such regularity over the last four centuries as to prompt one modern editor to call it "Faversham's . . . own 'passion play,' " the story still belongs to the town.[15] As recently as 1992, and for the second time in less than a decade, *Arden* was staged in the garden of what its current owners still call "Arden's House," and that same year the town's guildhall was taken over for "Arden 400: An Exhibition of Life in Faversham over 400 Years Ago." Local historians from Thomas Southouse in the seven-

---

[14] See the studies by Belsey, Orlin, Dolan, and Travitsky mentioned in the previous note. For a still more recent essay that discusses the play in terms of woman's history, see Julie R. Schutzman, "Alice Arden's Freedom and the Suspended Moment of *Arden of Faversham,*" SEL 36 (1996): 298–314.

[15] Wine, introduction to *Arden,* xlvii. For a transcription of the Wardmote Book account, see Wine, *Arden,* 160–3.

teenth century to Edward Jacob in the eighteenth to C. E. Donne in the nineteenth to Lionel Cust and Arthur Percival in the twentieth have regularly revisited the story, and the Faversham Heritage Center proclaims the importance of Arden's muder to local self-understanding not only by the pamphlets it sells on Arden but also by its location in the Fleur-de-Lis – Holinshed's "flower de lice" – where Alice's lover, Thomas Mosby, lodged on the night of the murder.[16] Nor is local speculation regarding Arden's death confined to those who publish in antiquarian journals and heritage society pamphlets. A few years ago, a Faversham agronomist assured me that Alice was a witch and that Arden was murdered in a ritual sacrifice.

This local attachment to Arden's murder owes much to the interest others have taken in it, particularly that anonymous other – tantalizingly identified from time to time as William Shakespeare, Thomas Kyd, or Christopher Marlowe – who made a play about it.[17] But the story has deeper roots as well, associated, as it is, with the most traumatic turning point in Faversham's long communal existence, the dissolution and destruction of its twelfth-century abbey and the town's subsequent rechartering under the sole jurisdiction of a secular corporation. By the time of his death, Thomas Arden – or Ardern, as contemporary records call him – had become the owner of nearly all the dissolved abbey's property, including more than two dozen of the town's houses; and his own house, in what had been the abbey's outer gate, was the only significant abbey building left standing. Furthermore, Arden seems to have been the town councillor – the "jurat" in local parlance – most responsible for securing the new charter and for establishing the new set of local statutes

---

[16] Thomas Southouse, *Monasticon Favershamiense in Agro Cantiano* (London: T. Passenger, 1671); Edward Jacob, *The History of the Town and Port of Faversham in the County of Kent* (London: J. Marsh, 1774); C. E. Donne, *An Essay on the Tragedy of "Arden of Faversham": Being the Substance of a Paper Read at a Meeting of the Kent Archaeological Society Held at Faversham in July, 1872* (London: Russell Smith, 1873); Lionel Cust, "Arden of Faversham," *Archaeologia Cantiana* 34 (1920): 101–38; and Arthur Percival, "Arden of Faversham: The Man and the Play," *Bygone Kent* 13 (1992): 187–92, 278–82. In 1770, Jacob also published an edition of *Arden* with an account of the murder "from authentic papers of the time." Among the mimeographed pamphlets for sale at the Faversham Heritage Center is Anita Holt's "*Arden of Faversham*: A Study of the Play First Published in 1592," *Faversham Papers*, no. 7 (1970).

[17] On the authorship question, see Wine, introduction to *Arden*, lxxxi–xcii; and Martin White, introduction to the New Mermaid edition of *Arden* (London: Ernest Benn, 1982), xiv–xvii. As both make clear, there is no external evidence regarding who wrote *Arden*, and the internal evidence is too weak to make a convincing case for any candidate. For reasons of local pride, sentiment in Faversham has generally favored Shakespeare or Marlowe over Kyd or any other contender.

that followed it. To call *Arden* Faversham's passion play is thus particularly apt, for Arden was the first to fill the large space that the dissolution of the Faversham monastic community opened.

But this local interest hardly counts as history. Since the seventeenth century, local antiquarian study has been a genre almost as distant from the high road of historiographical practice as murder pamphlets and domestic plays. But that too is changing quickly, and once again the Arden story is figuring in the change. Peter Clark in his *English Provincial Society from the Reformation to the Revolution* evokes Arden's murder for what it reveals concerning local religious and political conflicts, and Lena Cowen Orlin, in the remarkable first chapter of her recent book, *Private Matters and Public Culture in Post-Reformation England,* retells the story with an anthropological attention to small-town social dynamics.[18] In accounts like these, Alice moves into the background, to be replaced by a whole network of local patrons, tenants, and neighbors.

6. *Socioeconomic history.* Central to much local antiquarian study has been a fascination with questions of property ownership and revenues. Early modern county chorographies are full of information of this sort, and it figures largely in both Southouse's and Jacob's books on Faversham. Southouse prints, for example, the precise rents the Faversham abbey charged for the various houses it owned – including, as Southouse is at pains to point out, the house "where that fatal tragedy was really acted by Alice Arden and her wicked accomplices upon the body of her husband, Mr. Thomas Ardern (sometimes mayor of this town)."[19] Such matters – rents as well as murders – were of intense local interest. It is thus not surprising that the Wardmote Book account of Arden's murder ends with a detailed record of the sums realized from the apparel and moveable goods seized from the convicted murderers and forfeited to the town. But even Holinshed, though he includes no precise monetary figures, makes economic issues central to the understanding of Arden's murder. Not only is one of the murderers a neighbor from whom "Master Arden had wrested a piece of ground on the backside of the abbey," but God himself, moved by

---

[18] Peter Clark, *English Provincial Society from the Reformation to the Revolution: Religion, Politics and Society in Kent, 1500–1640* (Hassocks, Sussex: Harvester Press, 1977), 74, 82–4; and Lena Cowen Orlin, *Private Matters and Public Culture in Post-Reformation England* (Ithaca, N.Y.: Cornell University Press, 1994), 15–84.

[19] Southouse, *Monasticon,* sig. D6. This double interest persists. Patricia Hyde, a member of a group called the Faversham Historians, is currently combining a study of Faversham rent rolls with a new look at Arden. See Hyde's article on another sixteenth-century Faversham resident, "Henry Hatch and the Battle over his Will," *Archaeologia Cantiana* 102 (1985): 111–28.

"the tears of the oppressed," has wrought "vengeance" on Arden for the social and economic sin of preferring "his private profit before common gain."[20] Seen this way, Arden's death is less a domestic murder than a divine punishment, and the real criminal is not Alice but rather Arden himself.

Holinshed's providential morality is not shared by modern historians or critics. If it were, I would be including "providential history" as an eighth marginalized category, for certainly in the story's earliest tellings all seven of the interests that I am listing depended for their inclusion on the sense of prodigious horror and wonder that leads, in Holinshed at least, to an explicit recognition of divine intervention. But, after centuries of history writing in which the economic was largely ignored in favor of the political, Holinshed's accompanying sense that the Arden story also belongs to the realm of buying and selling, of property and exchange, now finds support. Lena Orlin's book pays detailed and careful attention to Arden's property dealings and shows how those dealings contributed to his violent death, and several recent studies of the play argue that it too understands Arden's death socially and economically. The most pointed of these, David Attwell's "Property, Status, and the Subject in a Middle-class Tragedy," reads the play in terms of "the ethics of property and the distribution of status attendant on changing patterns of ownership."[21] As

---

[20] Holinshed, *Chronicles* (1587), sig. kkkkkiii-kkkkkiii^v. Holinshed's language in this passage strikingly echoes Elizabethan attacks on courtier-monopolists, men whose royal grants brought, as Francis Moore charged, "the general profit into a private hand" (quoted by Sacks below, p. 130). Though, as I will show in the penultimate section of this essay, Holinshed conceals Arden's own court connection and thus obscures one aspect of this likeness, the similarity remains significant, for it reveals how easily reversible the association of those two slippery but nevertheless unavoidable terms, "private" and "public," really was, the "private" interests of "public" figures being played against the "general" or "public" good of "private" subjects. For a discussion of the monopolists and the parliamentary attack on them, see David Harris Sacks, "Private Profit and Public Good: The Problem of the State in Elizabethan Theory and Practice," in *Law, Literature, and the Settlement of Regimes,* ed. Gordon J. Schochet (Washington, D.C.: The Folger Institute, 1990), 121–42.

[21] Orlin, *Private Matters;* David Attwell, "Property, Status, and the Subject in a Middle-class Tragedy: *Arden of Faversham,*" *ELR* 21 (1991): 347. See also Wine, introduction to *Arden,* lxi–lxiv; White, introduction to *Arden,* xvii–xxx. White pushes Wine's socio-economic analysis considerably further than Wine, fearful of making *Arden* a "dramatized sociological tract" (p. lxiv), was willing to go. The socioeconomic dimension of *Arden* is also central to Frank Whigham's very interesting chapter on the play in *Seizures of the Will in Early Modern English Drama* (Cambridge: Cambridge University Press, 1996), and it gets a suggestive twist in the direction of the new practice of estate surveying in an article by Garrett A. Sullivan Jr., " 'Arden lay murdered in that plot of ground': Surveying, Land, and Arden of Faversham," *ELH* 61 (1994): 231–52. See also James R. Keller, "Arden's Land Acquisitions and the Dissolution of the Monasteries," *English Language Notes* 30 (1993): 20–4.

well as belonging to Alice and to Faversham, the Arden story now belongs to Marx, Weber, and R. H. Tawney.

7. *Anecdotal history.* When historians write of common people, of crime, of domesticity and private life, of women, of local experience, and of socioeconomic behavior, they try most often to rely on evidence that can be represented statistically or, at the very least, described as an aggregate. Individual cases, like Arden's, remain suspect. Their oddity – their singular horribleness – is what attracted notice, and if they are odd they can't be representative. Where the humanist historiography that displaced Holinshed's miscellaneous chronicling narrated events that were assumed to be significant because their actors were located at or near the summit of national power, the newer socially oriented historiography eschews narrative in favor of structure.

But even this reserve is giving way. The pegs on which many influential, if controversial, "new historicist" studies hang their interpretations of early modern English literature and culture are unabashedly anecdotal, and more and more historians are writing articles and books about local and domestic events the status and gender of whose actors would in the past have kept them from serious notice.[22] Perhaps it is unfair to call such history anecdotal. Much of it, including the story of Arden's murder, doesn't quite fit the usual definition of an anecdote.[23] This is the pejorative label stuck on such history by those who dislike it. "History as *petit recit*," which at least has the dignity of a foreign language, might do better. "Microhistory" is still another possibility. But the point remains that if a story like Arden's is to claim historical attention, it must be in terms that value its particularity and even its oddity, value them despite the humble station of its actors and the local and domestic setting of its action. The motives for that revaluation are not likely to resemble Holinshed's providentialism. The new historicist aim would, in fact, appear to be almost the opposite: not to mystify or resacralize seemingly unnatu-

---

[22] Lawrence Stone's *Uncertain Unions: Marriage in England, 1660–1753* (Oxford: Oxford University Press, 1992) and *Broken Lives: Separation and Divorce in England, 1660–1857* (Oxford: Oxford University Press, 1993) provide remarkable examples of anecdotal social history on a massive scale. The generic affiliation of such work is neatly suggested by the epigraph Stone takes from G. R. Elton and that Keith Thomas repeats in his *New York Review of Books* (4 November 1993) account of Stone's two volumes: "The dedicated social historian is second cousin to the tabloid journalist."

[23] See Annabel Patterson on Holinshed's use of anecdote elsewhere in this volume and in her *Reading Holinshed's* Chronicles (Chicago: University of Chicago Press, 1994), 42–7. Patterson's precise and quite unpejorative definition of "anecdote" would probably exclude a story as large and consequential, at least for its actors, as Arden's murder.

ral events, but rather to destabilize or defeat naturalistic explanations. And even the social historians, who do, after all, remain interested in turning anecdote to the ends of large-scale explanation, look for their explanations on earth rather than in heaven. But the very inclination to rely on anecdotal particularity, whatever the motive, does suggest a renewed commonality with Holinshed's kind of history writing.[24]

DRAWING BOUNDARIES

For more than half a century – from its first brief mention in the *Breviat Chronicle* of 1551 through the long and detailed account in Holinshed to the retellings in Stow and Heywood – Arden's murder was very much part of England's history. But then, as we have seen, it left history (or was forcibly ejected from it) to reappear in a succession of genres well off the main line of English historical writing – stage play, ballad, collection of wonders, calendar of crime, antiquarian treatise, puppet show, ballet, novel, and opera – before finally being readmitted under the aegis of those newly opened historiographical territories I list in the last section. This readmission has, it must be confessed, been more the work of literary scholars than historians. The cultural, political, and intellectual shifts that have redirected attention toward popular history, crime, domesticity and private life, women, local and socioeconomic history, and the sort of quotidian particularity that I have called "anecdotal" have affected historians and literary scholars alike. But not only are historians more inclined to deal with social aggregates than particulars, they also have a much fuller archive – one packed, for example, with thousands of legal records – to draw on. Literary scholars, whatever else they may do, still try to find a poem, play, or narrative fiction to anchor their work. And for the early modern period, *Arden of Faversham* has been a remarkably good anchor. If *Arden* hadn't existed, we would have had to invent it. Indeed, we have invented it, in the root sense of having both found and recreated it, just as Holinshed and the play's anonymous author and the many others who have followed them found and recreated the story to meet their own, very different generic and ideological needs.

---

[24] As further evidence of this commonality, one might cite the recent and enormously successful *New History of French Literature,* ed. Denis Hollier (Cambridge, Mass.: Harvard University Press, 1989), which adopts something like chronicle form to present a discontinuous and anecdotal account of French literature. Clearly, the aims of this volume are disruptively postmodern rather than providentially premodern, but the form that serves both is much the same.

But no less significant than the reasons for Arden's multiple reappropri-
ations over the last four centuries are the reasons for its early modern
exclusion from the main line of national history – from, that is, the generic territory where it made its first notable appearance – an exclusion
that until recently has remained firmly in place. In whose name was this
exclusion enforced? What were the interests that found a story like Arden's and a book like Holinshed's objectionable? I have been using the
terms "humanist" and "politic" to identify this exclusionary movement.
Who were the humanist and politic historiographers? And how and why
did they redefine the historical enterprise?

After the work of F. Smith Fussner, F. J. Levy, Arthur Ferguson, Antonia Gransden, Joseph Levine, and D. R. Woolf, it may seem unnecessary
to go over this ground once again, but the ground does reconfigure itself
when seen from the perspective of Arden's murder.[25] There has, for example, been a recent inclination to say that nothing very revolutionary happened in sixteenth- and seventeenth-century English historiography.[26]
From some points of view, that may be so. But if you are the Arden story,
appearing comfortably in chronicle after chronicle and then suddenly
dropped, the change would have seemed revolutionary enough. You had
been revolved right out of history. Certainly the humanist historiographers along with their friends and supporters thought the break very
sharp – even absolute. The kind of dismissive reference to the chroniclers
that I quoted at the beginning of this essay provides one testimony to
their sense of unbridgeable difference. Another comes from the still more
frequent complaint that English history had yet to be written. As Edmund
Bolton put it, "Many great volumes carry among us the titles of histories,
but learned men . . . absolutely deny that any of ours discharge that office
which the titles promise."[27] As history, chronicles simply did not count.

---

[25] F. Smith Fussner, *The Historical Revolution: English Historical Writing and Thought,
1580–1640* (London: Routledge, 1962); F. J. Levy, *Tudor Historical Thought* (San Ma-
rino, Calif.: Huntington Library, 1967); Arthur B. Ferguson, *Clio Unbound: Perception
of the Social and Cultural Past in Renaissance England* (Durham, N.C.: Duke University
Press, 1979); Antonia Gransden, *Historical Writing in England* (Ithaca, N.Y.: Cornell
University Press, 1974–82); Joseph M. Levine, *Humanism and History: Origins of
Modern English Historiography* (Ithaca, N.Y.: Cornell University Press, 1987); and
D. R. Woolf, *The Idea of History in Early Stuart England: Erudition, Ideology, and "The
Light of Truth" from the Accession of James I to the Civil War* (Toronto: University of
Toronto Press, 1990).

[26] "Few scholars would now agree that there was anything terribly revolutionary about the
developments in English historical writing [in this period]." Woolf, *Idea of History,* xi.

[27] Bolton, *Hypercritica,* 1:83. A year or two later, in his commendatory letter prefaced to
Augustine Vincent's *Discoverie of Errours* (London: W. Jaggard, 1622), John Selden

What would count was easily defined. "Histories," wrote Thomas Blundeville, "be made of deeds done by a public weal or against a public weal, and such deeds be either deeds of war, of peace, or else sedition and conspiracy."[28] In short, war, politics, and the state were the only proper subjects for history. Blundeville's treatise was published in 1574, three years before the first edition of Holinshed's *Chronicles,* and reflects views then current in Italy and France. Indeed, his book is, as he makes clear, little more than a translation from two Italian writers, Francesco Patrizzi and Giacomo Aconcio. Views of this sort had made a brief English appearance decades earlier in the work of Thomas More and Polydore Vergil – Vergil himself an Italian – but it was not for another quarter century, not until the historiographical emergence of John Hayward, Francis Bacon, William Camden, John Speed, Fulke Greville, and Samuel Daniel, that the newer understanding of history's proper scope took over in England. F. J. Levy has suggested – plausibly, I think – that the specific impetus for this sharper focus on politics came from the Essex affair in the late 1590s and early years of the seventeenth century.[29] Many of those involved in the shift in historical practice were also involved with Essex. The intense, heady, and frightening experience of near proximity to revolt focused attention on the need for heightened political awareness, an awareness informed by the past. Already, in an Italy overrun by the French, Niccolò Machiavelli and Francesco Guicciardini had come to a similar conclusion, and their example showed what might be done. And, of course, for the Italians and the English alike, a still broader prompting came from the humanist recovery of classical antiquity and from the model of ancient historians like Polybius and Tacitus. Taken together, these various lines of influence pushed toward a sharply redefined historical practice, a practice that would limit itself, in the words of A. P.'s address to the reader of Sir John Hayward's *Life and Reign of King Henry the IV,* to "either the government of mighty states or the lives and acts of famous men."[30]

Making history more useful was a goal these men shared, but they had

remarked that, with the exception of Camden's *Annals* and Bacon's *Henry VII,* "we have not so much as a public piece of the *History of England*" (sig. Ai^v).

[28] Thomas Blundeville, *The True Order and Methode of Wryting and Reading Hystories* (London: W. Seres, 1574), sig. Aiv^v.

[29] F. J. Levy, "Hayward, Daniel, and the Beginnings of Politic History in England," *Huntington Library Quarterly* 50 (1987): 1–34.

[30] Sir John Hayward, *The First Part of the Life and Raigne of King Henrie the IIII* (London: J. Wolfe, 1599), sig. A3.

a quite different notion of what constituted appropriate use than had been common before. History had long been thought a repository of moral example and a revelation of divine providence. Holinshed certainly thought of it that way. The humanist historians redefined both the lesson and the audience. Instead of general moral and religious teaching, history now taught politics. And instead of a universal audience, it now addressed princes and other great men of state. With a sharpened focus came a distinct elevation in status. Bacon talked of a hierarchy "of books no less than of persons, for as nothing derogates from the dignity of a state more than confusion of ranks and degrees, so it not a little embases the authority of a history to intermingle matters of lighter moment . . . with matters of state," and Camden clearly agreed. "It standeth," he wrote in the preface to his *Annales,* "with the law and dignity of history to run through business of highest weight and not to inquire after small matters." Similarly, Sir George Buck, in his *History of King Richard the Third,* bragged that he had "omitted nothing of great matter or moment, nor anything else but some slight matters, and such as are to be seen in the common and vulgar chronicles and stories and which are in the hands of every idiot or mere foolish reader and to no purpose and for the most part not worth the reading." Nor was it any surprise if chroniclers wrote of base matters for a base audience, they themselves being, as Edmund Bolton charged, "of the dregs of the common people."[31] Low writers, low subjects, low readers. This was the cluster the humanist historians were trying to replace with another, one made up of high writers, high subjects, and high readers. In this new configuration, a story like Arden's had no place.

But Arden's murder and stories like it were also squeezed out by a new insistence on narrative coherence, by what Lord Herbert of Cherbury called "an entire narration of public actions."[32] History was to contain the record of "things done" – the *res gestae,* whose "tyranny" over the early modern art of history has rightly bothered Arthur Ferguson – but not just any "thing" would do. History's "things" had to qualify for

---

[31] Francis Bacon, *De Augmentis Scientiarum,* in *The Works of Francis Bacon,* ed. and trans. James Spedding (London: Longman and Co., 1857–74), 4:310 (bk. 2, chap. 9); William Camden, *Annales, or the History of the Most Renowned and Victorious Princesse Elizabeth, Late Queen of England,* trans. Robert Norton (London: B. Fisher, 1635), sig. c3ᵛ; Sir George Buck, *The History of King Richard the Third (1619),* ed. Arthur Noel Kincaid (Gloucester: Alan Sutton, 1979), 7–8; and Bolton, *Hypercritica,* 96.

[32] Edward, Lord Herbert of Cherbury, *The Life and Raigne of King Henry the Eighth* (London: T. Whitaker, 1649), sig. A3.

arrangement in a firm causal order. This is clearly what Bacon sought in the "one just and complete history" that he told Lord Ellesmere England and Scotland should have, and it is essential to his idea of "perfect" history.[33] But not only does such narrative coherence distinguish humanist history from its chronicling rival, it also underlies its politic didacticism. Only if actions are seen in relation to their causes and consequences can a statesman learn from them how to act in a similar situation. John Hayward makes just this point in a dedication to Charles I. History, Hayward writes, is "the fittest subject for your highness's reading, for by diligent perusing the acts of great men, by considering all the circumstances of them, by comparing counsels and means with events [i.e., outcomes], a man may seem to have lived in all ages." Whatever didn't qualify as the circumstance, counsel, means, or event of a great man's act was simply to be left out. It is thus with considerable pride that Camden, one of the most influential of the new historians, announces: "Digressions I have avoided."[34]

Avoiding digression was a prime objective of humanist historiography. But to avoid a digression, you had to be able to recognize one when you saw it coming. John Trussell, in his continuation of Daniel's *History of England,* supplies a description, an elaboration of a list he borrowed from Bacon:

1. Matters of ceremony, as coronations, christenings, marriages, funerals, solemn feasts, and such like. 2. Matters of triumph, as tiltings, maskings, barriers, pageants, galley-foists, and the like. 3. Matters of novelty, as great inundations, sudden rising and falling of the price of corn, strange monsters, justice done on petty offenders, and such like executions, with which the *cacoethes* of the writers of those times have mingled matters of state."[35]

All three exclusions merit attention, for all three name areas that recent historical study has retrieved.[36] What the early modern ruled out, the

---

[33] Ferguson, *Clio Unbound,* pp. 3–27. Bacon, "A Letter to the Lord Chancellor, touching the History of Britain" and *De Augmentis Scientiarum,* in *Works,* 10:250 and 4:302.

[34] Sir John Hayward, *The Lives of the III Normans* (London: R. B., 1613), sig. A4; Camden, *Annales,* sig. c3ᵛ.

[35] John Trussell, *A Continuation of the Collection of the History of England* (London: E. Dawson, 1636), sig. A4. Compare Bacon's *Advancement of Learning:* "It doth not a little embase the authority of a history to intermingle matters of triumph or matters of ceremony or matters of novelty with matters of state" (*Works,* 3:339).

[36] The historical recovery of Trussell's "matters of ceremony" and "matters of triumph" has again been more the work of scholars whose training is in disciplines other than history: an art historian like Roy Strong or literary historians like Stephen Orgel, Richard McCoy, David Bergeron, and Patricia Fumerton. But history-department historians have not altogether shunned such "superfluous exuberances," as Trussell called them.

postmodern is systematically readmitting. But, of course, it is Trussell's third category, "matters of novelty," that most interests us here. "Justice done on petty offenders, and such like executions" catches the Arden story directly. Alice Arden and two of the household servants were executed specifically for the crime of "petty" treason, the murder of a husband or master. But from the perspective of humanist and politic history, any common murderer, even one whose crime did not fall under the technical definition of petty treason, was a "petty offender" and, as such, had no place in a proper historical narrative.

And no less significant than the simple fact of exclusion is the company in which the excluded finds itself. Trussell classes "justice done on petty offenders" with such other "matters of novelty" as "great inundations, sudden rising and falling of the price of corn, [and] strange monsters." This, however odd it may seem to us, was not an idiosyncratic classification. What Trussell excluded from history as a related cluster reappeared as a related cluster in publications like *A World of Wonders*, where Arden's murder shares space with famine and dearth, with a tempest of venomous beasts, with a precipitous drop in the price of wheat, and with a fish shaped like a man. These "wonders," these violations of nature – Arden's murder as much as the others – are "signs, threats, tokens of God's wrath," acts of divine retribution and admonitions against further sin.[37] Beginning with horribleness and ending with a wondrous sign of God's vengeance, Holinshed's Arden story functions, as I have already remarked, in much the same way. From this vantage point, the only fully coherent narrative would be the narrative of God's inscrutable will, and since God's will remains inscrutable it can only be represented in the fragmentary glimpses afforded by a "world of wonders" or a discontinuous chronicle.

The humanist historians were not ready to abandon all idea of divine providence working through time, nor were they immune to the lure of an occasional prodigy. But their primary aim was to explain human history – by which they meant the history of states and great men – in human terms. As a result, a gap opened between a world of state politics, of calculation and contingency, of human action and human effect, on the one hand, and a very different world of commoners and women, of

See, for example, Kevin Sharpe's *Criticism and Compliment: The Politics of Literature in the England of Charles I* (Cambridge: Cambridge University Press, 1987), which deals extensively with "maskings" and other matters of ceremony and triumph.
[37] *A World of Wonders* (London: W. Barley, 1595), sig. A2.

crimes and prodigies, of the local, domestic, social, and economic, on the other. Only the former belonged to history. The latter had its place in poetry, religion, and similar old wives' tales – which is where the Arden story takes refuge. When Samuel Daniel identified "improvement of the sovereignty" as a prime accomplishment of the sixteenth century, he pointed toward the cause of his own historical discourse and that of his fellow politic humanists. "The better to fit their use," Daniel wrote, "I have made choice to deliver only those affairs of action that most concern the government."[38] History followed sovereignty. Its purpose was to serve and describe the state. Anything else was, as Daniel's successor put it, a "superfluous exuberance."[39]

An apparent exception to this exclusion, the mention of the Arden story as late as 1643 in Richard Baker's *Chronicle of the Kings of England,* is actually further evidence of it. Baker lumps Arden's murder with a burnt church, an episode of the sweating sickness, the birth of a child with "two perfect bodies from the navel upward," and the taking of nine dolphins – all in a section devoted to the "casualties" of King Edward's reign. Alluding to the humanist historians in his epistle to the reader, Baker remarks that "where many have written the reigns of some of our kings excellently in the way of *history,* yet I may say they have not done so well in the way of *chronicle,* for whilst they insist wholly upon matters of state, they wholly omit meaner accidents, which yet are materials as proper for a chronicle as the other." As a chronicler, Baker includes such meaner accidents, but as someone writing in the wake of the humanist historians, he confines them to a section separate from his political narrative – acknowledging, in effect, their removal from history.[40]

BOUNDARY-BREAKING FACTS

In admitting that his account of Arden's murder might be considered impertinent, Holinshed anticipates this split. Though for him horrible-ness – a near neighbor of wonder and novelty – can still erase, as it couldn't for his humanist successors, the impertinence of an otherwise "private matter," he nevertheless recognizes that his most pressing obliga-

---

[38] Samuel Daniel, *The First Part of the Historie of England* (London: N. Okes, 1612), sig. A2ᵛ.

[39] Trussell, *Continuation,* sig. A4.

[40] Richard Baker, *Chronicle of the Kings of England from the Time of the Romans Government unto the Raigne of our Soveraigne Lord King Charles* (London: Daniel Frere, 1643), sigs. L113–3ᵛ, A2 (my emphasis).

tion is to write public and political history. But, curiously, when we set Holinshed's account against the various surviving documents concerning Arden and his murder, the conceptual divisions on which both his sense of significant difference and the subsequent enterprise of humanist historiography depended – the division of elite from popular, of law-abiding (or law-making) from criminal, of public from private, of men from women, of national from local, of political from socioeconomic, of the truly historical from the merely anecdotal – all crumble. At every point, Holinshed's "private matter" turns out to have had significant public entanglements, and Holinshed himself is revealed as having helped create the seeming impertinence for which he apologizes.

Consider, for example, these facts, most of them missing from Holinshed's account: Neither Arden nor his wife was a native of Faversham. They arrived just a decade before Arden's murder from London, where Arden had been clerk to Alice's stepfather, Edward North, and they came with a position and with property derived specifically from their official connections. North, soon to be Sir Edward North and eventually Baron North of Kirtling, was clerk of the parliament when Arden first appeared in his employ. From parliament, North moved quickly into the newly created Court of Augmentations, rising by 1546 to the post of its lord chancellor. It was Augmentations that administered land coming to the Crown from dissolved monasteries, and it was abbey land in Faversham, acquired from its first lay holder, Sir Thomas Cheney, that enriched Arden. Either North or Cheney, who was lord warden of the Cinque Ports, must have secured Arden's appointment to the lucrative post of king's customs officer for the port of Faversham and later to the position of king's comptroller of the neighboring Sandwich port. Supported by this abundant flow of governmental largess, Arden lived in Faversham as the Crown's officer and as the owner of most of what had been the Crown's land there, a man with connections that reached all the way to the privy council, where his stepfather-in-law sat in his ex officio capacity as chancellor of the Court of Augmentations. From the first, Arden was, in the words of Lena Orlin, who has described these relations in compelling detail, "a king's man in Faversham."[41]

Arden's Westminster connections may explain why he took a lead role in securing the town's royal reincorporation in 1544. And they may explain as well why the privy council showed such interest in his murder.

---

[41] Orlin, *Private Matters*, 31.

The king's chief councillors sitting in official session ordered one suspect brought to London for questioning, arranged for the pursuit and arrest of two others, and determined the precise place and mode of execution for the first group to be apprehended and convicted: "Cicley Pounder, widow, and Thomas Mosby to be hanged in Smithfield in London; Alice Arden to be burned at Canterbury, and Bradshaw to be hanged there in chains; Michael Sanderson to be hanged, drawn, and quartered at Faversham, and Elizabeth Stafford to be burned there"[42] – a particularly eerie decree if we notice that among the councillors who issued it was Alice Arden's stepfather, Lord North. For the humanist historians, these executions would rank among those digressive "matters of novelty," the sort of thing that should be left out of history. But clearly such acts of state, like the equally digressive matters of ceremony and triumph, figured significantly in a theater of power that the highest officers in the land thought it worth their while to stage. And, in this particular case, the victim of the crime whose perpetrators were being so spectacularly punished was (though it would be hard to guess it from Holinshed's account) himself a public man, a servant of the Crown, a man whose participation in the royally dictated dissolution of church property and in nationally determined partisan and sectarian conflict may have helped bring on his death.

Everywhere one looks national actors and national actions impinge on this seemingly local and domestic event. Alice's lover, Thomas Mosby, was Sir Edward North's steward; John Greene, another of the conspirators, was Sir Anthony Aucher's man; and George Bradshaw, the goldsmith Holinshed thought innocent of the complicity for which he was executed, had served under Sir Richard Cavendish. It is hard to know just what weight to give these connections. North, Aucher, and Cavendish were all men of considerable political standing, and at least one of them has been thought party to the crime. "The murder of Arden of Faversham," writes Peter Clark, "may well have been related to a dispute between him and . . . Aucher." And Clark also notes that "Arden's death was . . . interesting for another reason . . . Sir Thomas Moyle and other Catholics sought to exploit the murder for their own ends, by trying to implicate an innocent man 'hating [him] for the gospel.'"[43] Nor were

---

[42] *Acts of the Privy Council, 1550–52* (London: HMSO, 1891), 230.

[43] Clark, *English Provincial Society*, 83–4. In *Private Matters,* Lena Orlin adds still another distinguished name to the list of possible suspects, Arden's own patron Sir Thomas Cheney (53–62).

these the only public issues engaged in Arden's death. The hired killer, Black Will, was a soldier from King Henry's French war, one of hundreds of marauders who terrorized the Kentish countryside in those years. And even Alice, if one accepts the arguments of Catherine Belsey, was prompted in her crime by a crisis in the institutional basis of marriage that derived from state action.[44] In this tangle of intersecting forces, who is to say where the public ends and the private begins? Surely, to consider Arden's murder as history – even as the kind of political history the humanists favored – would be no impertinence.

Yet "impertinent" (except, of course, for its horribleness) is precisely what Holinshed calls it, and either he or the reporters on whom he depended – those unnamed investigators who, as Holinshed tells us, "used some diligence to gather the true understanding of the circumstances" – made sure the story's political pertinence would remain invisible.[45] As it happens, the manuscript from which Holinshed worked is preserved in the Stow papers at the British Library. Comparison of it with the printed account shows already some tactful obscuring of possible public implications. Though Holinshed says that Mosby was "servant to the Lord North," he leaves out that Alice was "the Lord North's wife's daughter," that Mosby "was made one of the chiefest gentlemen about the Lord North," and that Arden winked at their adultery "in hope of attaining some benefits of the Lord North by means of this Mosby, who could do much with him."[46] But both accounts fail to note that Arden himself had also worked for North, that he had been jurat and mayor of Faversham, that he was king's customer of Faversham port, and that his extensive land holdings came from patronage ties to the upper reaches of the governing hierarchy.

What Holinshed omits, the anonymous playwright restores with a truth-telling fiction. "Arden, cheer up thy spirits and droop no more," says Arden's friend Franklin in the play's opening lines, "My gracious lord, the duke of Somerset" – then lord protector of England –

Hath freely given to thee and to thy heirs,
By letters patents from his majesty,
All the lands of the abbey of Faversham.
Here are the deeds,
Sealed and subscribed with his name and the king's.
Read them, and leave this melancholy mood.[47]

---

[44] Belsey, *Subject of Tragedy*, 137–44.   [45] Holinshed (1587), sig. kkkkki[v].
[46] British Library, Harleian MS 542, fols. 34–7b.   [47] *Arden*, ed. Wine, 4–5.

No surviving document suggests that Arden received any part of the abbey lands as a direct grant from the lord protector or the king, but this speech does nevertheless give back to Arden's story a political dimension that Holinshed silently denies. And through the continuing presence of the fictional Franklin, who is identified as the lord protector's man, that dimension remains a dimly lit but clearly perceptible part of the play right up to the epilogue, which Franklin speaks and which once again alludes to the lord protector. But though *Arden of Faversham* pulls toward the national and thus toward history as both Holinshed and his humanist successors understood it, the play's very genre consigned it to the margins of Tudor historical writing, a place lacking the authority needed to establish a claim that would be recognized within the court of humanist historiography.

Why should the chronicler be so shy about the political implications of Arden's murder and the dramatist so bold? Both may have feared offending the North family. Holinshed greatly diminishes the connection, and the playwright substitutes another name. But where Holinshed keeps the story local and domestic, the playwright gives it a new tie to the king's government. The answer lies, I think, in generic aims and anxieties. Despite Holinshed's fear of impertinence, he had in the story's exemplary quality – its beginning in horribleness and ending in wonder – adequate grounds for its inclusion. Of the three ends to which Holinshed thought "chronicles and histories ought chiefly to be written" – namely, "their native country's praise . . . , the encouragement of their worthy countrymen by elders' advancements, and the daunting of the vicious by sore penal examples" – Arden's murder and the spectacular executions that followed from it richly satisfy at least the third.[48] And for this purpose a local and domestic story does quite as well as a national one. Indeed, it may do better, since it belongs to a sphere where ordinary morality has more obvious and unequivocal application than it does in the highest affairs of state. But for a dramatist, wanting to give tragic stature to a common and domestic murder, some connection, however remote, to the crown was needed – and was supplied. But whatever the motivation, the effect of Holinshed's choice was to mark off a private space that might be labeled impertinent to the public matter of politic history, while the effect of the dramatist's choice was to keep alive, if only barely, a sense of the early modern interpenetration of the public and private.

---

[48] Holinshed, *The First Volume of the Chronicles of England, Scotland, and Ireland* (London: John Hume, 1577), sig. iiii.

OECONOMICAL HISTORY

By now it should be clear that I am arguing for a historiographical inclusiveness that would attend to such sometimes marginalized matters as the popular, the domestic, the local, the social, and so on but that would also explore their various intersections with the so-called public and politic. Before ending, I'd like to have a final go at this argument with the help of an odd but suggestive early-seventeenth-century historiographical treatise, one that neatly underscores the points I've been making: first by confining the social and domestic to a sphere separate from the political and then by letting us discover once again how artificial that separation really is.

In his "intermixed discourse upon historical and poetical relations," *The Scholar's Medley* (1614), Richard Brathwait both follows humanist teaching and departs from it. His preliminary definition could not be more orthodox or more exclusionary: "The true use and scope of all histories ought to tend to no other purpose than a true narration of what is done or hath been achieved either in foreign or domestic affairs." But then he makes an unusual allowance: "To touch the manners and conditions of inhabitants, how they live, and to what trades most inclined, with who they have commerce, or the like, will not derogate anything from the scope of an history, or any way imply a digression." The sense of deliberate transgression we feel in Brathwait's overinsistent "anything" and "any way" is later enforced when he introduces the strikingly anomalous category – anomalous at least from the perspective of the newer politic history – of what he calls "oeconomical histories, teaching private families how to be disposed." In this area it does not matter, he says, whether the "histories" are true or feigned. What does matter is that "order" be "attained by examples": "The best government in private proceeds from histories and the serious reading thereof, the virtuous matron squaring her course by that modestest of Roman dames, Lucretia, making her *colum* her *thorum,* her distaff her best companion in her bed when her husband was absent. No vicious mind can deprave her; she is fighting at home with her own passions, whilst Colatine, her husband, fights in the field against his country's enemy."[49]

A vicious mind might guess that Brathwait was indulging his irrepress-

---

[49] Richard Brathwait, *The Schollers Medley, or, An Intermixt Discourse upon Historicall and Poeticall Relations* (London: G. Norton, 1614), sigs. B1, B2ᵛ, O4–4ᵛ.

ibly salacious wit in this passage. The Roman Lucretia stayed up spinning with her maids; she didn't take her distaff dildolike to bed. But more significant is the equation Brathwait makes almost automatically and repeats again and again, not only in this book but also in his *Good Wife* (1618) and his *Ar't Asleep Husband? A Bolster Lecture* (1640): the equation of domestic order with female chastity. Retelling stories of chastity defended and violated constitutes for Brathwait "oeconomical history." But when one examines the particular "history" he offers as his prime example, the history of the Roman Lucretia, the difference between the "oeconomical" and the "political," between "private government" and "public," proves impossible to maintain. Not only is there a likeness between Lucretia's fight at home and Colatine's fight in the field, but Lucretia's fight ends by remaking the state. As a result of her rape by the younger Tarquin, the son of the Roman monarch, "the state government changed," as Shakespeare put it in the dedication to his *Rape of Lucrece,* "from kings to consuls." Outraged by the prince's tyrannical act, Lucretia's husband and the other nobles drove the Tarquins from Rome and established a republic. The Roman republic was thus founded on Lucretia's domestic virtue.[50]

No comparable claim can be made for Alice Arden's domestic vice. The only thing that seems to have been founded on it is the genre of the true-crime story. Yet, like Lucretia's, Alice Arden's is an "oeconomical history" that has refused to stay at home. First brought to the London stage at the same time as the earliest "chronicle history" plays, Alice's murder of Arden has continued to stand for an alternative history of England, a history focused not on the court and the battlefield, as were those other plays, but on the household and the local community. This alternative history is not, however, indifferent to the court and the great affairs of state. On the contrary, it engages them at every point (though not necessarily in every telling), and in doing so suggests a new historiography, one that would combine the private and the public, the local and the national, the anecdotal, the constitutional, and the statistical.

Holinshed's apparently miscellaneous chronicling shows one way of doing this, though even he avoids revealing how his impertinent private matter is linked to his public history. Indeed, by presenting Arden's murder as a wonder, an example of horribleness, Holinshed removes it from

---

[50] On the relation of the Lucretia story to the development of early Italian civic humanism, see Stephanie H. Jed, *Chaste Thinking: The Rape of Lucretia and the Birth of Humanism* (Bloomington: Indiana University Press, 1989).

consequential politic history almost as effectively as do the humanist historians by their flat suppression, for such a definition denies the possibility that in first cuckolding Arden and then murdering him, Alice and the other conspirators performed a series of acts no less deliberate and no less political than many an act of state, denies them effective public agency. Having found our way behind that denial, we can at least imagine that their ultimate treason was not only "petty," that Arden was killed not only as an encumbering husband and grasping landlord but also as the king's man in Faversham. But whatever we conclude concerning this more radical possibility, the link between the public and the private is at least as firm in the story of Arden of Faversham as it is in the story of the Roman Lucretia. The state lived in Arden's life and death, and the state is known when his story is retold. The dissolution of the monasteries, the establishment of a state religion, the growth in royal sovereignty, the networks of national patronage and affiliation, the laws of marriage and divorce – all these are implicated in this local story of adultery and murder. To know Arden's story is to know these public events more concretely and more fully, to know not only what was done by the state but also how its doings were experienced and resisted. To know Arden's story is, in short, to know a significant bit of politic history – though official historiography, even of the pre- and post-humanist sorts, has not always let that fact be known.

7

Foul, his wife, the mayor, and Foul's mare: The power of anecdote in Tudor historiography

ANNABEL PATTERSON

We all know, or think we do, what an anecdote is, and in disciplines that assume or aspire to the scientific use of evidence the value of the anecdote has for centuries been low. In the late twentieth century, the aspirations of history to scientificity have risen, as witness the respect for statistics in social history, the lost prestige of intellectual history, and the avoidance in political history of large theoretical generalizations. Accordingly the phrase "only anecdotal," which has always implied unreliable information, has a comforting meaning in history, as it does also in law and medicine, conveying the notion that beyond the anecdotal lies objective and neatly serried fact.

Yet there are signs within history, as also within law and medicine, that the assumptions demanding the exclusion of the anecdotal from legitimate evidence are due for interrogation. Some of the pressure has been coming, of course, from the various attempts in literary studies to reinflect that discipline with historical knowledge. The so-called new historicism pioneered by Stephen Greenblatt is perhaps only recognizable as a movement by its reliance on the colorful anecdote, which (precisely because of these new historicist claims) can provoke protests from conservative literary critics. Thus Brian Vickers, after reproaching Greenblatt for misusing the anthropological techniques of Clifford Geertz, remarks: "The dangers of this elevation of the anecdotal to a central status are clear, encouraging as it does the use of interesting little stories not as ornaments to the text but as load-bearing props in the argument, a role to which they are unsuited."[1] While Vicker's complaint

---

[1] Brian Vickers, *Appropriating Shakespeare* (New Haven and London: Yale University Press, 1993), 229. See also Jean Howard, "The New Historicism in Renaissance Studies," *English Literary Renaissance* 16 (1986): 38–9; and Howard Dobin, *Merlin's Disci-*

is ostensibly procedural ("the New Historicists seldom declare what status they are claiming for the 'cultural samples' on display, an opportunistic silence which leaves their readers unable to know what weight to give this anecdotal material" [228]), his language seems infected by the contempt that has attached to the anecdote since its formal existence was recognized.

This essay offers two contributions to the growing debate about anecdotal evidence. The first is a brief excursus into the emergence of the term "anecdote" within historiography, itself an anecdote about the mysterious ways in which cultural history works. The second is an argument about the use of anecdotes in Tudor historiography, well before the term came into circulation. The interplay between the two sections of the argument is perverse, in that there can be no direct causal relation between the semantics of "anecdote" as they developed in the late seventeenth century and the work of historians a century earlier; but it is also intricate and compelling, in that, as I claim, the Tudor historians had grasped the function of the anecdote well before it was named, and used it to bolster a theory of history in which the unreliable, the eccentric, and the improper (or what society and its institutions may so designate) play a serious part in the analysis.

My own interest in the anecdote therefore differs in principle from that of other new historicists, if we may, for heuristic purposes only, imagine them as a collective. Whereas Greenblatt and others tend to choose their anecdotes from widely disparate sources, and to use them as symptoms of how early modern society conceived of itself, I am interested rather in how early modern writers chose their own anecdotes, and used them as symbols of their own social analysis and concerns. The theoretical difference resides in the degree of intentionality and self-consciousness attributed to those from the past whom we try to understand; the procedural difference resides in the fact that, while my choice of anecdotes from Holinshed's *Chronicles* is selective, it is rendered less arbitrary by the fact that the chroniclers themselves engaged in a prior act of selection. This approach represents the Tudor chroniclers as a cannier species than literary new historicism can accommodate; and it also makes them seem much more sophisticated than is conventionally allowed to Tudor historiography.

ples: Prophecy, Poetry, and Power in Renaissance England (Stanford: Stanford University Press, 1990), 8–16.

PART 1: SECRET HISTORY

Derived from *anecdota,* the Greek word for "things unpublished" (or, interestingly, with respect to women, "not given in marriage")[2] "anecdote" and its cognates entered historiography with the writing, c. A.D. 550, of Procopius's *Anecdota,* subsequently known as the *Secret History.* Procopius himself called the work *Anecdota,* indicating that he knew it was unpublishable, though presumably intended for quiet manuscript circulation. First mentioned by Suidas in the tenth century, the *Anecdota* remained in manuscript until discovered in the Vatican library by Alemanni, the papal librarian, and edited by him in 1623 under the title of *Arcana Historia.* One can infer its modern reputation from the Loeb edition of 1935, where we are informed that Procopius's

avowed purpose in writing this book was to tell the whole unvarnished truth which he had not deemed wise to set down in the seven books of the *Histories;* these had already been published and broadcast throughout the Empire. . . . [But here] the interest of Procopius has shifted suddenly from events to persons, and his one purpose comes to be to impugn the motives of Justinian and of the able Belisarius, and to cover with the vilest slander the Empress Theodora and Antonina, the wife of Belisarius.[3]

And, the modern translator added tartly, "The *Secret History* has been translated into modern languages by several hands, sometimes anonymously and with the manifest purpose of exploiting the salacious tone of some of its passages" (1:xxi).

In France, the *Histoire secrète* appeared in 1669. In England, one translation appeared in 1674.[4] The translator declined to be identified; but it is not difficult to recognize the parallel suggested between Justinian and Charles II, especially given the rendering of Procopius's own introduction to the work:

When I writ my first Histories, I thought it not expedient to be too particular, by reason the main Agents were then living; and I could not long have concealed, or secured my self against some exemplary punishment, if my Book should have

---

[2] Normally I deplore the habit of using the *Oxford English Dictionary* as a research tool. In this case, however, my attention was drawn to the unusually rich lexical history of "anecdote" by Margery Sabin, whose own work is on the anecdotal representation of suttee (widow burning) in the colonialist memoirs of Sir William Henry Sleeman.

[3] *Procopius,* trans. H. B. Dewing, 7 vols. (Heinemann), 1:vi–vii.

[4] *The Secret History of the Court of the Emperor Justinian* (London: for John Barkesdale, 1674).

been published; and I judged it very dangerous, to commit such a secret to any Friend whatsoever.

Now, however, that the primary subjects are deceased, the project may have some efficacy:

Nothing excited me so strongly to this work, as that such persons who are desirous to govern in an Arbitrary way, might discover, by the misfortune of those whom I mention, the destiny that attends them, and the just recompence they are to expect of their crimes. (sig. B1)

Two years later the term *anecdote* appeared in one of Andrew Marvell's polemical pamphlets, *Mr. Smirke, or the Divine in Mode,* itself published anonymously;[5] and in 1682, the year of the Popish Plot and the Exclusion Crisis, when the Whigs were, like their opponents, looking for new polemical weapons, the anonymous English translation of Procopius was re-issued under a more provocative title: *The Debaucht Court. Or, the Lives of the Emperor Justinian, and his Empress Theodora the Comedian.*

In 1685 a new component was added to this story, with the publication of Antoine Varillas's *Anecdotes de Florence,* which was promptly translated for English readers by Ferrand Spence as *Anecdotes of Florence, or the Secret History of the House of Medicis* (1686). In 1686, this was apparently to be understood in terms of James II's accession and Monmouth's rebellion.[6]

Varillas's preface, also translated, provided an elaborate defense of

---

[5] Andrew Marvell, *Complete Works,* ed. A. B. Grosart (1875), 4:70–1: "For that of the Savoy, in which he instances, it might almost as well have been in Piedmont. A man disinterested either way, might make a pleasant story of the anecdota of that meeting, and manifest how well his Majesties gracious Declaration, before his return, and his broad seal afterwards were pursued."

[6] Antoine Varillas, *Anecdotes of Florence, or the Secret History of the House of Medicis,* trans. Ferrand Spence (London, 1686). Spence mistakenly dedicated his translation to Henry, earl of Pembroke, instead of Thomas, eighth earl of Pembroke, who succeeded to the title in 1683, and whose career is alluded to in the dedication. Created lord-lieutenant of Wiltshire at the same time, Pembroke raised the militia of his county against Monmouth in 1585, in return for which he received a bounty of £1,000 in the late summer. Citing the *London Gazette,* 30 August–2 September 1686, Richard Ashcraft notes that a year later Pembroke was still in great favor with James II, who stayed at his house in August. Ashcraft, *Revolutionary Politics and Locke's* Two Treatises of Government (Princeton: Princeton University Press, 1986), 514 n. But Pembroke's cooperation with James's government ceased in 1687, when he refused to assist in "regulating" the municipal corporations, and was dismissed. After the revolution, to which he promptly transferred his allegiance, he was reappointed, and carried the sword of justice at the coronation. Spence's dedication had encouraged Pembroke to note that "these Anecdota may, perchance, by some Gentlemen, be tax'd with containing Reflections, injurious to a Soveraign House; but . . . what Stem, however Holy, what Dignities and Offices, however August and Sacred, but have been tarnish'd by unworthy Members" (n.p.).

anecdota as alternative history with rules of its own. It spoke of "the sad Destiny of *Anecdota,* that cannot indure anything mysterious, shou'd be left to Posterity without explaining it" (sig. a6). And it provided a distinction between publishable and unpublishable history in terms of the facts recorded:

The Historian considers almost ever Men in Publick, whereas the Anecdotographer only examines 'em in private. Th' one thinks he has perform'd his duty, when he draws them such as they were in the Army, or in the tumult of Cities, and th'other endeavours by all means to get open their Closet-door; th'one sees them in Ceremony, and th'other in Conversation; th'one fixs principally upon their Actions, and th'other wou'd be a Witness of their inward Life, and assist at the most private hours of their leisure. (sig. A5)

By the middle of the next century, Chambers's *Cyclopedia* provided the following definition: "*Anecdotes, anecdota,* a term used by some authors, for the titles of Secret Histories; that is, of such as relate the secret affairs and transactions of princes; speaking with too much freedom, or too much sincerity, of the manner and conduct of persons in authority, to allow of their being made public." From this sequence of events in the publishing and political worlds came the stigma that now hangs around the idea of the anecdote as something unreliable in history as a practice, something if not actually scandalous and underhanded, the move that dares not speak its name, then unverifiable, unscientific, and self-indulgently gossipy. Hence the pun attributed to John Wilkes, whereby writers entered their "anecdotage."

PART 2: HOLINSHED'S *CHRONICLES*

What does all this have to do with Tudor historiography? As far as concerns the history of the term "anecdote," nothing at all, since no sixteenth-century historian would have used it. Yet the Tudor chroniclers, and above all the group that collaborated on Holinshed's *Chronicles,* employed mininarratives that we would now call anecdotes, which had a good deal (but not everything) in common with the "secret history" later derived from Procopius. Read as deliberate insertions, rather than a sign of the chroniclers' lack of discipline or garrulity, these anecdotes reveal an agenda that runs, if not exactly counter to the stories of kings and battles, laws and punishments, in energetic counterpoint to it. Though by no means always concerned with the private lives of the powerful – the definition that Varillas gave of *anecdota* – the anecdotes deployed in Ho-

linshed's *Chronicles* were the symptoms and signals of resistance to the
generalizing and ordering impulses, both in historiography and in the
societies history tends to monumentalize. And one of their weapons of
resistance is a startling and often (it may seem to us) incongruous display
of humor.

This argument is part of a larger revisionary claim about the *Chronicles*
as a whole.[7] Usually considered only as an archaic form of history writing,
properly displaced by more selective, better-structured histories, the
Chronicles, like the anecdote, is due for revaluation. It responds brilliantly
to the kinds of questions posed by cultural history, which is no less committed to the rules of evidence than traditional history, but is also concerned
with the ways in which earlier societies processed their experience, and the
kinds of stories they told about it. Read as a massive archive packed with
information about sixteenth-century social experience – political, religious, economic, legal, and even sexual – the *Chronicles* also conveys unparalleled insight into the way the Elizabethan middle class, from whom
the chroniclers came, understood their society and wished to intervene in
it. Recognizing the crisis of disunity that resulted from the Reformation
and dynastic power struggles, they argued implicitly for an idea of the
nation that was more inclusive, multivalent, and multivocal than the models that successive Tudor governments, with their conflicting agendas, attempted to impose. Rather than being the author of a horrendous muddle,
as has repeatedly been charged, Raphael Holinshed developed a set of
historiographical protocols that could register shifts and strains in the
socioeconomic structure, uncertainty and even skepticism in the law and
its reception, and complications and danger inherent in life after four
dramatic changes of regime and hence of the official religion. His successors in the second edition, Abraham Fleming, John Stow, John Hooker,
and Francis Thynne, not only followed his lead but exaggerated some of
his protocols to the point where their intentions appear unmistakable.
Among these protocols were an emphasis on "verbatim" reporting, a preference for first-person, eyewitness record where possible, the inclusion of
original documents in full, ironic juxtaposition of the gruesome with the
celebratory, and the protocol I am here examining – the anecdote – which
is not unrelated in intention and effect to all of the above.

The anecdotes in the *Chronicles* are brief, independent narratives

---

[7] See my *Reading Holinshed*'s Chronicles (Chicago: Chicago University Press, 1994), where
much of the following material appears in fragments. For the present essay, I have gathered the anecdotes into a series and intensified the commentary upon them.

about individual human behavior, individual in the sense that the behavior narrated appears to interrogate the system – legal, economic, social, sexual. The typical story is short enough to be emblematic, independent enough of its surroundings to be portable, that is to say, relocatable from one chronicle to another, from a chronological to an achronological spot, from one style or even one ideological perspective to another. Sometimes the protagonists are historical figures in the conventional sense, though caught in an unusual posture, sometimes they are nameless; but their independence of spirit, their refusal to be absorbed into the unifying texture of a grand narrative, is evident nonetheless. The better anecdotes contain snatches of conversation, whose verisimilitude is a key to their memorability, the cause of their having remained in the cultural memory. The appearance of unusual, unpredictable detail is both a feature of the anecdote and related to the chroniclers' anthropological habits of observation. But there is also a politics involved, as well as anthropological fidelity. The anecdotes of Holinshed's *Chronicles* repeatedly feature rebels, victims, tricksters, skeptics, women. Their inclusion therefore lends credence to my claim that in 1577 Raphael Holinshed attempted to include within the boundaries of the nation those whom that centripetal concept is meant to exile, and that national history usually ignores.

Anecdotes are, moreover, *added* in the 1587 edition of the *Chronicles* to Holinshed's accounts of earlier reigns, having been carefully culled by his successors from the pages of Edward Hall's *Union*, John Foxe's *Acts and Monuments*, John Stow's *Chronicle*, and other sources. There is more at stake here than the provision of thick description or local color, although the chroniclers evidently felt that these were indispensable to their task. After one becomes familiar with the *Chronicles* the anecdotes begin to speak to each other across the vast expanses of military campaigns, state entertainments, and lists of officeholders, and the stories they tell come to acquire representative, because cumulative, force.

In order to substantiate these claims I shall now provide a series of examples, arranged in ascending order of complexity. For each of these I suggest an analogous literary genre, but with the very opposite intention from that attributed to postmodernism; for to observe that an anecdote may have one of a range of plots and tones does not render it merely textual, or blur the boundaries between history and fiction. Rather it acknowledges that history, if it scrupulously attends to the particular and the peculiar, is unable to achieve a reliably even tone.

The first in my series is a story attributed to William of Malmesbury about William Rufus, first son of William the Conqueror. Despite its antiquity, it could easily have recurred in the sixteenth century: "I find," wrote Holinshed (meaning, I find in my source),

that in apparell he loved to be gaie and gorgeous, & could not abide to have anie thing (for his wearing) esteemed at a small valure. Whereupon it came to passe on a morning, when he should pull on a new paire of hose, he asked the groome of his chamber that brought them to him what they cost? Three shillings saith he; "Why thou hooreson (said the king) doth a paire of hose of three shillings price become a king to weare? Go thy waies, and fetch me a paire that shall cost a marke of silver." The groome went, and brought him another paire, for the which he paid scarselie so much as for the first. But when the king asked what they stood him in, he told him they cost a marke: and then was he well satisfied, and said; "Yea marie, these are more fit for a king to wear," and so drew them upon his legs.[8]

It is impossible to read this anecdote without recognizing its irreverent intentions, its willingness to display the upstaging of a vain and silly monarch by a shrewd and witty servant. Its underlying structure is that of the Aesopian fable, the king of beasts outwitted by the fox; and Holinshed's translation has not only brought out the liveliness of Malmesbury's anecdote (which would be sadly obscured by his nineteenth-century translator John Sharpe), it has also pruned the anecdote of elements that originally pointed the reader in different directions. For Malmesbury had buried the anecdote in a complex discussion of William's legendary generosity, about which he was entering a series of moral qualifications; and he had concluded it as follows:

Thus his chamberlain used to charge him what he pleased for his clothes; acquiring by this means many things for his own advantage. The fame of [William's] generosity, therefore, pervaded all the West, and reached even to the East (2146).

Holinshed selected only the anecdote, suppressing the servant's venality. Rather than functioning as an exemplum in a philosophical discussion of what constitutes true largesse, it becomes an item in the *Chronicles*' much longer if discontinuous story of prices, economic disparity between the classes, and conspicuous consumption at court; and the direction of its moral sympathy has been delicately shifted from what William of Malmesbury intended.

My second example is self-evidently a pastoral, though blended uncom-

---

[8] *Holinshed's* Chronicles, ed. Henry Ellis (London, 1807; reprint New York: AMS Press, 1965), 2:46.

fortably (as the pastoral often was in Elizabethan literature) with satirical antipastoral. It appears as a detail within an extensive account provided by Holinshed of the floods that overtook the northeast coast in October 1570:

> Also between Hum[b]erston and Grimsbie were lost eleven hundred sheepe of one master Spensers, whose sheepherd about middaie, comming to his wife, asked his dinner: and she being more bold than manerlie, said, he should have none of hir. Then he chanced to looke toward the marishes where the sheepe were, and saw the water breake in so fiercelie, that the sheepe would be lost, if they were not brought from thense, said, that he was not a good sheepherd that would not venture his life for his sheepe, and so went streight to drive them from thense, but he and his sheepe, were both drowned, and after the water being gone, he was found dead, standing upright in a ditch. (4:256)

Why are we told this story, when the statistics of the devastation to sheep farming that Holinshed provided would seem adequate for agricultural history, the business in hand? Perhaps to people the drowned landscape, to offer something other than an economic accounting of the nature of loss. But such old-fashioned humanism does not exhaust the anecdote's own economy of suggestiveness, of which the most striking is that gratuitous and circumstantial detail, "standing upright in a ditch." How deeply should we interpret its symbolism? Is the uprightness of the corpse a proof of the shepherd's integrity and a tribute to his humanity, or does it transform him into a mute signpost of unresolved domestic conflict and social disadvantage? Where does Holinshed stand on the "more bold than manerlie" woman who refused her husband his dinner? Was her refusal intended to remind him of his charge, or was it merely mean-spirited? If the latter, did it serve nevertheless to render him obstinately selfless? Indeed, what was his duty? Should a wage laborer have given his life for Master Spenser's sheep? In the margin beside his presumably verbatim assertion that "he was not a good sheepherd that would not venture his life for his sheepe" stands Holinshed's only interpretive key: "Scripture abused." At the least, the reader is being encouraged to consider wherein the abuse consists, a question that might send ripples of unease in ever-widening circles.

The next anecdote in my series is still more complex in tone and function. It also involves an unfortunate marriage, but one contained in the larger tragedy of church and state set in motion by Henry VIII's marital barbarism. It occurs in Francis Thynne's catalogue of archbishops, which was originally inserted into the *Chronicles* under the

year 1586, although the chronological moment the anecdote recalls was
actually 1540. The anecdote has laughter within it, but it is not told
facetiously. We can be confident that its protagonists, Henry himself and
Archbishop Cranmer, were historical figures; and Thynne was able to
translate it verbatim from an unexceptionable source, the Latin history
of the English archbishops by Matthew Parker, himself a holder of that
pastoral office. But the anecdote renders "official" policy shameful
nevertheless, an inference certainly not contradicted by the fact that
Thynne's catalogue of archbishops was deleted from the second edition
of the *Chronicles*, when the work was called in by the Privy Council in
January 1587.

The anecdote belongs to that late stage in the Henrician Reformation,
after the death of Thomas Cromwell and the passing of the fearsome Six
Articles in 1539, when Counter-Reformation would be a more appropriate term. "Some of the nobilitie and councell" who were religious conser-
vatives attempted to persuade Henry to exclude Cranmer, as a danger to
the old religion, from the Privy Council, and to send him to the Tower:

For so long as he sat present in the councell, everie one there would be afraid to
speak what they knew against him. Whereupon rumors were spread, that Cranmer by the *secret* judgement of the king should be condemned, and loose his hed,
as Cromwell had doone . . . wherfore Cranmer *secretlie* with tears bewailed the
times, though outwardlie he shewed a merie countenance. (4:737; italics added)

Henry, therefore, "perceiving whereunto tended this drift of the pontifi-
cals (which favored the Roman religion), after supper for recreations
cause tooke barge to row up and downe the Thames," and to steer
toward Lambeth Palace. Informed by some of his men who stood on
Lambeth Bridge of the king's approach, Cranmer

speedilie came to the bridge to salute the king either passing by, or else to receive
him on shore, and to lead him to his house. But the king commanded him to come
into his bote and to sit down by him, with whom he had long and *secret talke*, the
watermen stil hovering with the bote on the river. (4:737; italics added)

This is indeed, in Thynne's translation, secret history, as the three "secret's" italicized above make clear, only one of which appears in Parker's
Latin. The suggestion is that the king himself, in need of privacy for a
delicate negotiation, has had to move onto no-man's-land for the
purpose – a suggestion assisted by Thynne's translation, which makes a
single sentence out of Parker's two, permitting a conscious connection
between Henry's insight into the "drift" of Cranmer's enemies and his

own decision to take to the water. There was "long and secret talke" between them, the "watermen stil hovering with the bote on the river," and Henry pretended to ask Cranmer's advice about how to identify and capture a dangerous archheretic. This is the game of cat and mouse:

Whereunto Cranmer (although he was in great feare) answered with a good countenance that the same counsell pleased him well, being verie glad to hear thereof, because by the punishment of that archheretike the rest of the flocke of heretikes would be bridled. But with this speech he did yet with a certain fatherlie reverence toward the king, modestlie admonish the king, that he shuld not judge them to be heretickes, who with the word of God strived against mens traditions. Whereunto the king said; It is rightlie spoken by you, for you are declared to us by manie to be that archhereticke of all our kingdome, who in Kent and in all your province doo so withstand us, that the beleefe of the six articles established in parlement be not received of the common people; wherefore openlie declare unto us what you thinke, and what you have doone of and in the same. Cranmer replied, that he was still of the same mind which he openlie professed himselfe to be at the making of that law [i.e., opposed to it], and that yet he had not offended anie thing since the same was made.

This courageous temporizing evidently strikes the right note:

Then the king somewhat leaving this grave talke, merrilie asked of him, whether his inner and privie bed were free from those articles. To which Cranmer (although he knew it dangerous by that law for priests to have wives, and that he certeinlie understood that the king knew that he was maried) answered, that he contracted that marriage before he was archbishop . . . but now because he would not offend so rigorous a law, he had not touched his wife since the making thereof, because he had presentlie sent hir unto hir freends in Germanie. By which plaine answer he wan such favor with the king, that the king incoraged him to be of good comfort. (4:737)

"Hovering" on the river, itself a wonderful locution for negotiation, king and bishop play out the game of mutual understanding and acceptable speech, in the frame of the dangerous politics of the day.

The genre of this piece is also, surely, antipastoral (note "the flocke of heretickes") but in the religious rather than the economic register with a corrosive irony (given the king's own marital history, past and future) exuding from the sexual register also. Within its own frame it is also a comedy of manners – political manners – that ends with a reconciliation between wit and threat, temerity and authority; but Cranmer's "good comfort" did not last. As Thynne ironically summed up the end of his larger story pages later, in Mary's reign "he was consumed to ashes": "a death not read before to have happened to anie archbishop, who as he was the first that publikelie impugned by established lawes the popes authoritie in England, so was he the first metropolitane that was burned for the same" (4:744). The elegant structure of this sentence mocks the reversals of ecclesiastical fortune in post-Reformation England, perhaps all the more effectively for Thynne's (and Parker's) withholding of overt expressions of sympathy and regret.[9] Indeed, the entire story highlights the difficulties of interpretation, but also its necessity, given the need to conceal one's true opinions in a climate of political hypocrisy; and though, like the stories of William Rufus's stockings and Master Spenser's shepherd, it reveals the complex interaction between classes, we may welcome the subtle perspective by which Henry is both Cranmer's master and friend, and Cranmer's servants are evidently concerned for his welfare.

The Cranmer story is clearly secret history as defined by Procopius and Varillas, especially in its focus on the "inner and privie bed." It lacks, however, one condition of the anecdote as I have defined it: portability, or rather the proof of its portability as seen in its relocation. Though it seems freestanding in this essay, it appears in Thynne's translation of Parker as deeply implicated in and congruous with its historical context. Not so with the following story about Lady Jane Grey that Abraham Fleming discovered and transplanted into the *Chronicles,* in order to substantiate his personal animus against Mary Tudor. In expanding on Holinshed's account of Mary's reign, he turned to Foxe's *Acts and Monuments* and produced the story of how Lady Jane had lost Mary's sympathy some years before they became rivals for the throne, by casually demonstrating disbelief in the Real Presence in the Eucharist. "Touching this ladie Jane in the high commendation of her goodlie mind," wrote Fleming,

I find this report in maister Foxes appendix: namelie that being on a time when she was verie yoong at Newhall in Essex at the ladie Maries, was by one ladie Anne Wharton desired to walke, and they passing by the chapell, the ladie Wharton made low curtsie to the popish sacrament hanging on the altar: Which when the ladie Jane saw [she] marvelled why she did so, and asked hir whether the ladie Marie were there [i.e., watching them] or not? Unto whome the ladie Wharton answered no, but she said that she made hir curtsie to him that made us all. Why quoth the ladie Jane, *how can he be there that made us all, and the baker made*

---

[9] Presumably the source of the anecdote was Cranmer himself, who had licensed Parker to preach in 1533. Parker's sympathies in this case may be inferred not only from the tone of the anecdote, but from the fact that he was himself married, and virtually in hiding during Mary's reign as a consequence of his support of Lady Jane Grey. Though aspects of his history of the archbishops infuriated the Puritans, it appears that he was a moderate Reformer.

him. This hir answer comming to the ladie Maries eares, she did never love hir after, as is credibly reported. (4:23; italics added)

Fleming's selection of this anecdote, hidden away in the appendix to the 1563 edition of the *Acts and Monuments,* is particularly revealing of the potency he and his colleagues perceived in the anecdote. As an ardent anti-Catholic (and in this he was exceptional in the group that produced the *Chronicles*) Fleming could have chosen the more solemn dialogue between Lady Jane and Dr. Feckenham, Queen Mary's personal confessor, whose mission was to "reduce" her to Catholicism before her execution; instead we have a story of female wit, or at least of female playfulness, which when read as blasphemy by a powerful member of a rival church leads, it is suggested, to a secret motive for later and final retribution. And the historian's mark of self-consciousness, "as is credibly reported," indicates that Fleming, following Foxe, was aware that his choice of material would be noted, and its historical status interrogated.

In my larger argument about the *Chronicles* I propose that Holinshed and his successors were visibly concerned with issues of justice and fairness in church and state, in the economy and the family, but especially before the law. Here are two related anecdotes added in 1587 that together speak to the theme of justice in a specifically legal context. They are paired also by virtue of giving conflicting images about the respective status of women and men within the legal system. The first deals with a trial and execution for witchcraft, a topic to which on the whole the *Chronicles* paid remarkably little attention, given what we have subsequently learned about the intensity with which witchcraft was criminalized during the period of compilation. According to Keith Thomas, home circuit trials for witchcraft "were at their zenith" during Elizabeth's reign, "when 455 out of the 790 known indictments were made, the majority during the 1580s and 1590s." And, he adds, "it is probable that there were more trials everywhere under Elizabeth than during the whole of the subsequent century."[10] Holinshed himself did not even record the passing of the 1563 statute making it a felony to invoke evil spirits for any purpose, whether or not *maleficium,* damage to others, was charged.[11] But the anecdote of Joan Cason added by Fleming to the second edition more than makes up for this omission, despite the fact that there is no logical (historical) reason, in the surrounding context of 1586, for its inclusion.

---

[10] Keith Thomas, *Religion and the Decline of Magic* (New York: Scribner, 1971), 451.
[11] 5 Eliz. cap. 16. See *Journals of the House of Commons,* 1:59. This act replaced the one passed by Henry VIII in 1542 and repealed by Edward VI in 1547.

Fleming may well have become interested in the topic of witchcraft by his collaboration with Reginald Scot in his *Discoverie of Witchcraft*,[12] published in 1584 in an attempt to defuse the witch craze with a heavy dose of rational sociology and a mild reproach to the 1563 statue.[13] Fleming here depended for his information upon, as the marginal note states, "The note of John Waller," who may have been the person mentioned by Anthony à Wood as an Oxford undergraduate magician.[14] In other words, Waller sent him an account of the trial, perhaps from his own eyewitness experience, and the role of the chronicler is "verbatim" reporting. Joan Cason was tried on 19 April 1586, before Thomas Barming, mayor of Faversham, in Kent, because Faversham was a Cinque Port, and therefore out of the normal judicial circuit.[15] Cason was a widow, "late the wife of one Freeman," and accused of having bewitched a three-year-old girl, Jane Cooke, who subsequently "languished and died." Seven women and one man gave evidence against her, who "though they were all verie poore people, yet were they the rather admitted to accuse her, for that they were hir neere neighbors, and hir offense verie odious" (4:891).

---

[12] Reginald Scot, *The Discoverie of Witchcraft,* ed. Hugh Ross Williamson (Carbondale, Ill.: Southern Illinois University Press, 1964). The *Discoverie* is lavishly illustrated with literary examples from Vergil, Ovid, Lucretius, and others, and with examples of Catholic ritual, such as the Latin verses of the *Agnus Dei*. These are provided with English verse translations by none other (the margins inform us) than Abraham Fleming. Fleming's contributions to the *Discoverie* are briefly mentioned by William E. Miller, "Abraham Fleming: Editor of Shakespeare's Holinshed," *Texas Studies in Language and Literature* 1 (1959): 93, but without attributing any significance to the collaboration.

[13] Like Keith Thomas, Scot analyzed the psychosocial complex involved in the so-called confessions; but unlike Thomas, Scot believed that the law, thanks to the 1563 statute, had made itself complicit with poverty and ignorance in a massive exercise in credulity and injustice. He regarded the trials themselves as the cause of the confessions: "*being called before a Justice, by due examination of the circumstances is driven to see hir imprecations and desires, and hir neighbors harmes and losses to concurre, and as it were to take effect*: and so confesseth that she (as a goddes) hath brought such things to passe. Wherein not onelie she, but the accuser, and also the Justice are fowlie deceived and abused" (29–30). And Scot took up expressly the question of the law's responsibility for such abuses. Although the Henrician and the Elizabethan statutes may have qualified the "old rigor" of the Catholic Church, he suggested, they left intact the *concept* of witchcraft: "the estimation of the omnipotencie of their words and charmes seemeth in those statutes to be somewhat mainteined, as a matter hitherto generallie received; and not yet so looked into, as that it is refuted and decided" (36).

[14] See Thomas, *Religion,* 226 n, citing Wood, *Athenae Oxonienses,* ed. P. Bliss (Oxford, 1813–20), vol. 1, cols. 188–9.

[15] C. L'Estrange Ewen, who compiled all the Tudor and Stuart witchcraft indictments, listed this case in an appendix containing trials mentioned in texts for which no indictments could be found in the records. See C. L'Estrange Ewen, *The Indictments for Witchcraft from the Records of 1373 Assizes Held for the Home Circuit. A.D. 1559–1736* (London: K. Paul, Trench, Trubner, and Co., 1929), 282.

The first deposition in the case was made by Sara Cooke, mother of the dead child:

that after hir said child had beene sicke, languishing by the space of thirteene daies, a travellor came into hir house, to the end to drinke a pot of ale (for she kept an alehouse) who seeing the lamentable case and pitious griefe of the child, called hir unto him saieng; Hostesse, I take it that your child is bewitched. Whereunto she answered, that she for hir part knew of no such matter. (4:891–2).

The traveler proposes that Cooke take a tile from over the lodging of "the partie suspected," and place it in the fire, and if that person has bewitched the child, the fire "will sparkle and flie round about the cradle." And she, "conceiving that travellors have good experience in such matters," proceeded to make the test, successfully. Suspicions were confirmed by the fact that Cason shortly afterward entered Cooke's house to ask after the sick child, who gazed up at her (having not opened her eyes all the previous night) and died four hours later.

Seven of her neighbors also gave evidence; but this had nothing to do with the death of the child, and was all focused on "a little thing like a rat (but more reddish) having a brode taile, which some of them had seene, and some had heard of" (893). This, of course, was the so-called familiar, necessary to establish in the minds of the jury a suspicion of supernatural dealings. The prisoner, however, unlike the many old women who confessed to a *maleficium* for the reasons Scot had analyzed two years earlier, steadfastly refused to admit any curse or ill-will, "anie thing doone, or purposed by hir to have beene doone in this behalfe" (4:892). (She had, after all, visited the child out of neighborly solicitousness.) She firmly continued to assert herself not guilty; and she gave examples of the malice her neighbors held toward her, "reciting also certaine controversies betwixt hir and them, wherein they had doone hir open wrong." In fact, she satisfied "the bench and all the jurie touching hir innocence for the killing of hir child."

However, at this point something went seriously wrong with her testimony. Cason admitted that

a little vermin, being of colour reddish, of stature lesse than a rat . . . did diverse yearses since (but not latelie) haunt her house, and manie other houses in the towne, and further, that she (*as she imagined*) heard it crie sometimes; Go to, go to, go to; sometimes, Sicke sicke; sometimes, Come, come. Whereby she gathered, that it charged hir to see hir maister Masons will performed; which she had not executed according to the confidence he had in hir; to the trouble of hir conscience, and vexation of her mind. And she honestlie confessed, that he had the use of hir bodie verie dishonestlie, whilest she was wife to hir husband Freeman. (4:892; italics added)

A guilty conscience, for personal matters quite irrelevant to the charge at hand, made Cason susceptible to the same superstitions as those that her neighbors invoked against her. The existence of a witch's familiar is therefore taken to be established by her own "confession." The chronicler, however, may reveal his skepticism in his asides ("as she imagined"); and the members of the jury were themselves, if not skeptical, sympathetic: "being loth to condemne hir of witchcraft, which they knew to be a fellonie, they acquitted hir thereof, and found hir giltie upon the said statute, for invocation of wicked spirits; thinking therefore to have procured her punishment by pillorie, or imprisonment, and to have saved hir from the gallowes" (4:892).

But the story is not to have a happy ending. For after Mayor Barming had pronounced the verdict, with the appropriate moralizations ("render most humble thanks to God and the queene, and hereafter . . . beware that you give no such occasions of offense againe"), there is an intervention:

A gentleman (being a lawyer, and of counsell with the towne, sitting upon the bench with the maior, to assist, or rather to direct him in the course of law and justice) hearing this mild judgement to proceed out of the maiors mouth, stept unto him, and told him, that (under correction) he thought him to erre in the principall point of his sentence (that is to saie) that instead of life he should have pronounced death; because invocation of wicked spirits was made fellonie by the statute whereupon she was arreigned. (4:893)

The mayor thereupon reversed his sentence, despite the fact that a mistrial had obviously occurred, "because there was no matter of invocation given in evidence against hir, nor proved in or by anie accusation, whereby the jurie might have anie colour to condemne hir therfore" (4:893). The jurors, in their well-meaning ignorance, misunderstood what verdict was possible; the mayor failed to correct them; and the interfering lawyer (supposedly expert) influenced judge and jury only in the direction of unjust severity.

Everyone knew that something had gone wrong; but the ony response was to stay the execution for three days, during which preachers attempted to persuade Joan Cason to confess to the invocation of wicked spirits, in order to clean up the record. "But no persuasion could prevaile, to make hir acknowledge anie other criminall offense, but hir lewd life and adulterous conversation" with Mason, and that when he died she had abused his trust in her with respect to the terms of his will. She went to the gallows still berating herself for this conflicted relationship, for which, she said, "the judgement of God was in such measure laid upon her." And so, the chronicler concluded, she made

> so godlie and penitent an end, that manie now lamented hir death, which were (before) hir utter enemies. Yea some wished hir alive after she was hanged, that cried out for the hangman when she was alive: but she should have beene more beholding unto them that had kept hir from the gallows, than to such as would have cut the rope when she was strangled. (4:893)

What role did Cason's adultery play in this mockery of justice? The story provides no editorial guidance; but neither is there a trace of a moralizing voice, outside of Mayor Barming's initial sentencing. "Being called before a Justice, by due examination of the circumstances," as Reginald Scot had put it in his sardonic account of why persons accused of witchcraft confessed, Cason is driven to search her conscience for guilt, and unsurprisingly she finds it.

Although somewhat more extensive than usual for an anecdote, Cason's case retains all of the features of my original definition: a self-standing narrative illustrative (representative) of strain in the sociopolitical structure, and with one or more colorful individuals at its center. We come to know the bumbling mayor and the troubled Cason all too well. As for conversation, surviving here in the form of legal testimony, it is unusually vivid, even for the *Chronicles*. Joan Cason's recall of the ratlike creature's injunctions ("Go to, go to," "Sicke sicke," "Come, come") is especially likely to stick in the reader's memory.

But surely these snatches of conversation are also simultaneously comic and tragic, an unstable mixture in any narrative, and inarguably so in the most important Tudor chronicle. I venture to say that it is not only the modern reader who would question a system in which such a mockery (in all senses of the word) of justice could occur. I suspect that comparable anecdotes could be retailed today by skeptical spectators at the trials of nursery school teachers accused of bizarre assaults on children. But they would not be included in a national history. What sort of history is it that does provide such material for inspection, and what deductions from it are we invited to draw?

In this case I believe we are provoked to interrogate not only the Elizabethan witchcraft statute but also its treatment by modern historians. Keith

Thomas, who made the most persistent inquiry into the causes of the Elizabethan witchcraft prosecutions, provided a materialist-psychological explanation, rather than a politico-legal one: a combination of religious depression (caused by the withdrawal of Catholicism's psychological supports); extreme poverty, especially on the part of those who became the victims of witchcraft trials, and who may have annoyed or embarrassed their neighbors by begging; the general inadequacy of medicine; and the "tyranny of local opinion," especially in rural environments, as to what constituted socially acceptable behavior. The trials, he thought, were fueled primarily by the same fears and misfortunes as in the past, and witch persecution was an essentially grassroots phenomenon, not one created by either churchmen or lawyers; he thus left himself finally with no satisfactory explanation for the extraordinary increase of trials in Elizabeth's reign. And a central part of his argument was that the legal machinery – the statutes that made prosecution by the state available as an option – was not to blame.[16] Yet the anecdote related by Abraham Fleming is eccentric in terms of these generalizations. Joan Cason exhibited none of the extreme poverty or antisocial behavior of the typical rural scapegoat. The idea of bewitchment is not a local grassroots response but is imported into the rural community by a stranger (male); and a second stranger – the interfering "gentleman" who prevents the mayor and the jury from applying their merciful if legally illiterate common sense – is the instrument of state intolerance in the broader sense.

In the narrower sense the problem of how the law shall be applied is exacerbated by the fact that Faversham is a port, with liberties that may collide with the liberty of the subject. And the story of Joan Cason is accordingly followed by another anecdote deliberately misplaced chronologically (since it belonged to the year 1547) on the grounds that both tales illustrate "*one* kind of government, for they are of the ports." The chronicler (presumably Fleming) himself draws an analogy between Joan Cason and one Mr. Foul of Rye, for whose story he cites no marginal source. We must therefore assume that the story derives from popular local knowledge.

Mr. Foul seems a fitting ending to my series, not only because here the man is the victim, but also because, in contrast to the tragic tone of Joan Cason's story, its tone is, at least initially, unmistakably comic:

---

[16] Thomas, *Religion*, 460–1.

There haunted to the house of this Foule, in respect of the good will he bare his wife, a little honest man, whose name I will not discover, who committed unto hir custodie a bag of monie, amounting to the sum of ten pounds stearling. Fouls wife locked it up in hir cupboord. Howbeit, she handled not the matter so covertlie, but hir convert baron espied it, and (in hir absence) either picked or brake open the locke, and tooke out the monie; wherewith afterwards he plaied the good fellow all the daies of life. For immediatelie his wife accused him (not of subtill dealing) but of plaine theft, regarding more hir friends losse, than hir husbands life. Hereupon the maior of Rie (at the next sessions) caused him to be indicted and arreigned, and being convinced of the fact, he was condemned and adjudged to death. For whose better execution, there was presentlie a new paire of gallowes erected, whereupon without further delaie he was hanged untill he was dead; which gallowes hath beene ever since called by the name of Fouls mare. And now he cared not so much for the maior, as the maior did for him. For Foule was skant cold, but manie murmured at the maior's hastie proceedings; which moved them to doubt and whisper, that Fouls fault was no fellonie. (4:893–4)

The zest with which this tale is told (to this point) belongs to the genre of the *fabliau*. It has a secret, sexual subtext; and it is packed with verbal jokes, whose point is increased by alliteration. "He plaied the good fellow all the daies of his life" plays right into the announcement of Foul's speedy execution, which made the days of his life extremely few; his very name is an emblem of foul play; and the relation between "Fouls mare" and the mayor who placed him on it is almost too good to believe. One would be tempted to read this as etiological fable, folk embroidery on a local place-name, or a modern marital satire (entitled "Foul, his wife, the mayor, and Foul's mare") were it not for what follows:

But now the maior (although it be said that portsmen maie tell their tale twise) could not now devise, how (Foule being dead) he might reverse this *foule* sentence. Nevertheless, he sent up with all speed to one maister Ramseie of Greies Inne, who was of counsell with the towne, to learne what the law was in that case: who having fully weied and conceived thereof, told the partie directlie, that the matter was without the compasse of fellonie. Whie sir (quoth the messenger) goodman Foule is alreadie hanged. . . . But what was he for a man (said maister Ramsie?) A bad fellow (said the messenger). Well (quoth he) go thou thie waies home, and then there is but one knave out of the waie. (4:894; italics added)

This tale does have a moral, but it is not, perhaps, the one the reader has been led to expect by its earlier comic, parodic tone. "Such conclusion," the chronicler wrote, showing his hand somewhat, "are manie times made in the ports, who sometimes use the privilege of their liberties, not as they ought, but as they list, seldome times applieng their authoritie to so good purposes as they might: for commonlie they use more circumspection in their expenses, than in their sentences" (4:894). This anecdote offered its Elizabethan readers an unofficial view of the system of justice in all its human fallibility, which the ordinary citizen could grasp even, or especially, as he laughed.

At the beginning of this paper, I asserted that other disciplines beside history were beginning to question the stigma attached to the anecdote. In *Doctors' Stories,* Kathryn Hunter remarks that whereas physicians today are likely to associate medical anecdotes "with unenlightened, pre-scientific practice," early modern medicine, like historiography, recognized the importance of single cases. Thus Sir Thomas Sydenham's case histories in the seventeenth century were themselves a reform of "a practice so tied to theory that physical examination was rarely undertaken and diagnosis by mail was widespread." In the next reform, however, physiological studies and pathological correlations took over from single clinical accounts and "ultimately enabled physicians to correct and extend their understanding of disease and its treatment."[17] Thus medical history, like the history of historiography, shows that the relation between individualization and generalization is in constant need of inspection; and it, too, is perhaps on the verge of a correction in favor of the anecdotal. Apart from their mnemonic value in medical education, anecdotes are useful, Hunter suggests, "not only in locating research problems but also in keeping alive a skepticism about new knowledge claims in a hierarchical, authoritarian discipline. As rough accounts of the unexpected and occasionally the improbable, they are frequently the as-yet-unorganized evidence at the forefront of clinical medicine" (75). And she concludes with a message therapeutic to disciplines other than her own: "Anecdotes represent and preserve the recognition of [the] intractable particularity of the individual . . . the irreducible knot at the center of a discipline of human knowledge . . ."(82).

---

[17] Kathryn Hunter, *Doctors' Stories: The Narrative Structure of Medical Knowledge* (Princeton: Princeton University Press, 1991), 71–2. I owe this reference to Diane Sadoff, who herself encountered it in connection with work on that notorious storyteller, Sigmund Freud.

8

Experience, truth, and natural history in early English gardening books

REBECCA BUSHNELL

> For I consider history and experience to be the same thing, as also philosophy and the sciences . . . History is either Natural or Civil. Natural History treats of the deeds and works of nature; Civil History of those of men.
> – Francis Bacon, *The Advancement of Learning*

In the twentieth century, natural history is understandable as history when it narrates the slow change of species over the millennia. In the early modern period, however, a history of nature meant something different: the story of nature's "deeds and works" seen through the human experience of them.[1] As such, early modern natural history may have been

Excerpted from Rebecca Bushnell, *A Culture of Teaching: Early Modern Humanism in Theory and Practice.* Copyright 1996 Cornell University Press. Used by permission of the publisher, Cornell University Press.

I owe many thanks to Suzanne Daly for her incomparable research assistance, and to David Sacks, Don Kelley, Phyllis Rackin, and David Boyd for their criticism of earlier drafts of this essay.

[1] See D. R. Woolf, *The Idea of History in Early Stuart England: Erudition, Ideology, and "The Light of Truth" from the Accession of James I to the Civil War* (Toronto: University of Toronto Press, 1990), on the notion of "history" implicit in natural history as a form of "inventory": "The natural historian was one who surveyed and drew up an inventory or list of natural life and of the composition of the world or the cosmos. Since there was as yet no notion of evolution, such an inventory inevitably depicted a world of stasis, not one of long-term change; it made no distinction between past and present. The absence of a temporal dimension is reflected in the synchronic – that is, non-narrative – form of all natural histories" (16). Yet, as I argue, this did not mean that writers did not argue about the temporal and national differences in the perception and writing of natural history. See also Joseph M. Levine, "Natural History and the History of the Scientific Revolution," *Clio* 13 (1983): 57–73, on the importance of tracking the development of natural history in this period. On the European development of natural history, and the argument that "the historicization of nature was already underway within the scope of the *Kunstkammern* from the sixteenth to the eighteenth centuries" (9), see Horst Bredekamp, *Antikensehnsucht und Machinenglauben: Die Geschichte der Kunstkammer und die*

179

atemporal in form, describing in the moment of writing natural phenomena as people knew them. Yet the writers of those histories understood that people had written differently of nature in past times and separate places. By the seventeenth century, natural historians were asking the same questions that the recorders of civil history posed: What constituted evidence of "historical" truth? Whom should one believe? Was it possible to write a universal history, or did history reside, like truth, only in the particulars?[2]

When Francis Bacon linked history with experience in his *Advancement of Learning,* he cut to the heart of this debate over truth, imagination, and authority in the writing of natural as well as civil history in England.[3] Bacon himself narrowed the field of authorities on natural history by cutting off both Greek philosophy (for "at that period there was but a narrow and meagre knowledge either of time or place,"[4]) and folk wisdom about the natural world. In *The Great Instauration* Bacon claimed to be

a more cautious purveyor than those who have hitherto dealt with natural history. For I admit nothing but on the faith of eyes, or at least of careful and severe examination; so that nothing is exaggerated for wonder's sake, but what I state is sound and without mixture of fables or vanity. All received or current falsehoods also (which by strange negligence have been allowed for many ages to prevail and become established) I proscribe and brand by name; that the sciences may be no

---

Zukunft der Kunstgeschichte (Berlin: Klaus Wagenbach, 1993), published in English as *The Lure of Antiquity and Cult of the Machine: The Kunstkammer and the Evolution of Nature, Art, and Technology,* trans. Allison Brown (Princeton: Markus Weiner, 1995).

[2] For a general discussion of the links between history and natural history in the seventeenth century, see Barbara J. Shapiro, *Probability and Certainty in Seventeenth-Century England: A Study of the Relationships between Natural Science, Religion, History, Law and Literature* (Princeton: Princeton University Press, 1983), chap. 4.

[3] See Francis Bacon, *Of the Dignity and Advancement of Learning* (translation of "De Augmentis"), in *The Works of Francis Bacon,* ed. James Spedding, Robert Leslie Ellis, and Douglas Denon Heath (London: Longman and Co., 1857–74), 4:293. Woolf writes that "Bacon's equation of history with experience has important implications for the history of scientific empiricism. Arno Seifert has argued persuasively that Bacon's thought is the culmination of a Renaissance tendency to reduce all empirical knowledge (cognitio) to various types of 'history.' In fact, this tendency can be seen at work decades before Bacon, in Bodin's use of the term *historia naturalis* and in other *artes historicae.* According to Seifert, 'history' becomes in Bacon a paradigm for all empirical inquiry." Woolf, *Idea of History,* 147–8; the reference is to Arno Seifert, *Cognitio Historica: Die Geschichte als Namengeberin der fruhneuzeitlichen Empire* (Berlin: Duncker and Humbolt, 1976), 52, 98 ff., 116–38.

[4] Francis Bacon, *Novum Organum,* in *Works,* 4:73. See Woolf: "The poverty of ancient philosophy can be ascribed directly to its lack of a proper sense of the past, which implies a consciousness of chronological and spatial order. . . . Natural history and civil history thus walk hand in hand." *The Idea of History,* 148.

more troubled with them. For it has been well observed that the fables and superstitions and follies which nurses instil into children do serious injury to their minds.[5]

In this passage, the wisdom of the ages and the follies of nurses are collapsed into the same imaginative fables. (Similarly, Sir Thomas Browne believed that classical writers were ultimately responsible for the errors of rural folks and for what many of the writers I will discuss refer to as "old wives' tales."[6]) The distrust of such "errors" accompanies Bacon's defense of depending on "the experiments of the mechanical arts," however "low and vulgar . . . men may think [them]."[7] Clearly, he differentiated acceptable "mechanical" (implicitly masculine) vulgarity from the unacceptable vulgarity of nurses.

Early modern English manuals and treatises on horticulture and husbandry, which constitute a subgenre of natural history, reveal the social and political stakes in such distinctions. These gardening books may at first appear prescriptive rather than historiographic, instructing the reader what to make of his or her land in the present and future, rather than telling of the land's past. Yet all the gardening rules found in these books are inevitably linked to the natural history of that land. In turn, gardening books reveal an awareness that the story of England's land may be told variously in different texts, including classical or foreign treatises, reports of customary practice, and books containing the "daily knowledge" of self-proclaimed professional gardeners. As it intersects with historiographic and scientific discourse, as well as controversies about the proper English rhetoric and aesthetics, the language of these gardening books engages in the social and political conflicts common to those discourses. These were conflicts that pitted the gentleman farmer against the "plain English husbandman," the man of science against the rural folk, and especially against women, while all claimed to speak for the English land and nation. In *A Social History of the Truth*, Steven Shapin has argued that seventeenth-century notions of gentility were closely linked to scientific credibility: According to Shapin, while "gentle" empirical scientists admitted their dependence on the common people's knowledge and manual labor, they distrusted them as informants, both because, as Shapin puts it, they might be "perceptually insensitive or

---

[5] Bacon, *The Great Instauration,* in *Works,* 4:30.
[6] On the connection between classical and folk errors, see Keith Thomas, *Man and the Natural World: A History of the Modern Sensibility* (New York: Pantheon Books, 1983), 77; Thomas Browne, see *Pseudodoxia Epidemica* (London: 1646), bk. 1, chaps. 6–9.
[7] Bacon, *Great Instauration,* 4:29.

incompetent," and because "greed, ignorance, and bias" could interfere, "transforming direct experience into deceit or delusion."[8] But this linking of class with credibility is not only true of what we would more narrowly construe as works of science: It crossed over into a wide field of writings that spoke to the question of human observation and experience.

Natural and human history meet in gardening books in two ways: They both connect people with the land, and they both are concerned with the truthful description of that relationship. Herbals are primarily taxonomic, concerned with the description and classification of plants; gardening books, however, tell how people worked the land, and the English land in particular. When gardening books described differences in soil and cultivation in separate parts of England, at stake was how the English man or woman was tied to a particular place, and through it linked to the nation as a whole. The gardening books thus functioned as a companion literature to the genre of chorography, sharing its aims and methods. At the same time, however, as these gardening books described and recommended specific practices of cultivation, they also diverged in their accounts of them. Different writers, all claiming to speak from experience, argued that they could prove – or disprove – limits on the human power to transform nature through cultivation. Some confidently described their own transformative powers, while others scoffed at these claims as vain lies or boasts. The question of art's domination over nature here neatly dovetailed with the debate over the role of art or imagination in presenting natural history: Precisely because these "experimental" manipulations seemed artful and ambitious to the point of being fantastic, critics insisted that they were merely imaginary. Where natural and human history were linked, the connections between truth, art, imagination, and experience were all mediated by the social position and desires of the writer, his sources, and his audience. The argument brings to the surface what is sometimes only implicit in other forms of early modern history writing: that a writer's claim to speak the truth, whether about nature or men, was inextricably linked to how he saw his own place in the world.

---

[8] Steven Shapin, *A Social History of the Truth: Civility and Science in Seventeenth-Century England* (Chicago: University of Chicago Press, 1994), 264–5. I have also been enlightened by Julie Solomon's work on the rhetoric of "disinterest" in Baconian empirical science, where she follows the links between the new science and "commercial class discourse" that "preserves a central place for self-interest but renders it fluid, unformulaic, and powerfully invisible." See Julie R. Solomon, "'To Know, To Fly, To Conjure': Situating Baconian Science at the Juncture of Early Modern Modes of Reading," *Renaissance Quarterly* 44 (1991): 522.

THE PLAIN ENGLISH HUSBANDMAN

When gardening books began to proliferate in the early sixteenth century, many wealthy landowners were undertaking the study of husbandry and horticulture, but the burgeoning field of gardening books was mostly stimulated by the increasing numbers of less-privileged gardeners. As economic pressures, including rising prices, food shortages, and a falling income from rents, brought some gentlemen to attend to their own demesnes, a literature developed to underwrite that enterprise.[9] In some gardening manuals the land's master himself was addressed as the "gardener" (although he was certainly not imagined as using the spade and knife himself).[10] Other books fashioned the gardener as the ideal gentleman's servant: William Lawson, in *A New Orchard and Garden* (1618), recommends finding

a fruicterer, religious, honest, skilfull in that facultie, and therewithall painfull. . . . Such a Gardener as will conscionably, quietly and patiently travell in your orchard, God shall crowne the labors of his hands with joyfullnesse, and make the cloudes droppe fatnesse upon your trees, hee will provoke your love, and earne his wages, and Fees belonging to his place. . . . If you bee not able, nor willing to hyre a Gardener, keepe your profites to your selfe, but then you must take all the paines.[11]

But, increasingly, gardening manuals were written to appeal primarily to yeomen, country housewives, and the poorer sort set on self-improvement.[12] Gervase Markham identified his intended audience as the "plaine

---

[9] Joan Thirsk, "Making a Fresh Start: Sixteenth-Century Agriculture and the Classical Inspiration," in *Culture and Cultivation in Early Modern England: Writing and the Land,* ed. Michael Leslie and Timothy Raylor (Leicester and London: Leicester University Press, 1992), 16–17.

[10] For an example of this genre, see *Foure Bookes of Husbandry, collected by M. Conradus Heresbachius, Counseller to the hygh and mighty Prince, the Duke of Cleve: Conteyning the whole arte and trade of Husbandry, with the antiquitie, and commendation thereof, Newly Englished, and Increased, by Barnabe Googe, Esquire* (London, 1577). For comments on such books, see Andrew McRae, "Husbandry Manuals and the Language of Agrarian Improvement," in *Culture and Cultivation,* ed. Leslie and Raylor, 38; and McRae, *God Speed the Plough* (Cambridge: Cambridge University Press, 1996).

[11] William Lawson, *A New Orchard and Garden* (London, 1618), 1–3.

[12] See, for example, Thomas Tusser, *Five Hundreth Points of Good Husbandry* (London, 1573); Reynolde Scot, *A Perfite Platforme of a Hoppe Garden* (London, 1578); and Leonard Mascall, *The First Book of Cattell* (London, 1596), among many other texts. McRae, "Husbandry Manuals," discusses the importance of these books, arguing that "the direction of husbandry writing towards the lower socio-economic orders gradually became the norm for English manuals" as "they appeal[ed] directly to 'thrift-coveting' farmers throughout the social order, and depict[ed] an economic structure sufficiently malleable to accommodate the desires and aspirations associated with individual 'improvement'" (44, 47).

English husbandman," as opposed to "great personages"; this "husband-man," distinct from the gentleman farmer, seems to have the status of a yeoman, or of someone just one step below a yeoman, a man bent on self-improvement in an economy that allowed for his advancement.[13] William Lawson's *The Country Housewifes Garden* (1617), in turn, was written specifically for an audience of women who had their own small plot of land to tend. Reynolde Scot's treatise on hop-gardens was aimed even lower, supposedly directed "plainely to playne men of the Countrye," those men who had not been "brought uppe in a close studye to discipher the Arte of Rhetoricke wyth theyr wyttes, but have been trayned in the open Fieldes to practyse the Art of Husbandrie wyth their Lymmes, as being placed in the frontyers of povertie, to beare the brunt of traveyle and labour."[14] All these books of instruction reflected the changing agrarian economy, which con-tributed to the developing consumer economy. New agricultural products, such as hops, pippins, and flowers, were being introduced and promoted as consumer products, while at the same time innovative agricultural proj-ects, such as woad-and-flax growing, took over in the countryside.[15] The gardening books themselves proliferated in conjunction with the changing agricultural markets, and with the rise of what Jack Goody has called "the professional nurseryman," as well as husbandmen.[16]

[13] Gervase Markham, *The English Husbandman* (London, 1613; reprint, New York: Gar-land Publishing, 1982). In *The English Yeoman Under Elizabeth and the Early Stuarts* (New Haven: Yale University Press, 1942), Mildred Campbell points out the controversy over whether the term "husbandman" was tied more closely to rank or occupation; she cites John Norden, Markham's contemporary, who ranked the husbandman next below the "yoman," and argues that the term was more generally used to apply to those who engaged in husbandry and for whom no other term of rank superseded (27–32). (But Markham, who was by birth a gentleman, describes himself as having lived as a husband-man for nine years.) More recently, it has been argued that the expansion of agrarian capitalism in this period with the rise of grain prices would have favored the "yeoman farmer," to the disadvantage of poorer farmers. (Thirsk, "Making a Fresh Start," 16). See J. A. Sharpe, *Early Modern England: A Social History, 1550–1760* (New York: Routledge, 1988), 132, on the ways in which the grain-price rise had different effects on different farmers, tending to favor the yeoman farmer; Sharpe describes agriculture in England in this period as "very capitalistic" (135).

[14] Reynolde Scot, *A Perfite Platforme of a Hoppe Garden* (London, 1578), sig. b2v.

[15] See Joan Thirsk, *Economic Policy and Projects: The Development of a Consumer Society in Early Modern England* (Oxford: Clarendon, 1978), on the introduction of the grow-ing of hops, pippins, apricots, licorice, and tobacco in the sixteenth century (13); the woad-growing projects; and the commercial flower market (46).

[16] Jack Goody notes the increase in the number of books in the late sixteenth and early seventeenth centuries and "the rise of the professional nurseryman and a huge expendi-ture on plants and seeds," Goody, *The Culture of Flowers* (Cambridge: Cambridge University Press, 1993), 184. See also Ronald Webber, *The Early Horticulturalists* (New-ton Abbot, Devonshire: David and Charles, 1968), for the emigration of continental horticulturists to England in the 1550s, the response of the Gardener's Company, and the

Not only did the gardening books provide practical advice for those who wished to improve themselves through agriculture, but the men who wrote them also used these books to fix their own social status. Like surgeons and teachers, gardeners were reaching toward a self-identification as "professionals" (no matter how little respect they may have in fact been given in economic or status terms).[17] That prolific writer of popular manuals on all subjects, Gervase Markham, boasted self-defensively in his book, *The English Husbandman,* that

I am not altogether unseene in these misteries I write of: for it is well knowne I followed the profession of a Husbandman so long my selfe, as well might make mee worthy to be a graduate in the vocation: wherein my simplicitie was not such but I both observed well those which were esteemed famous in the profession, and preserved to my selfe those rules which I found infallible by experience.[18]

Markham's appeal to his "profession" stakes out the position of husbandman in terms of then inchoate notions of professionalism, in particular the acquisition of a specific body of learning and inclusion in a select group of practitioners. His use of the term "vocation" here suggests the kind of secularization of sacred vocation that, when applied to lay occupations, was key to defining a new "profession."[19] At the same time, his claims to know the "misteries" of this art through observation and "experience" transformed the notion of professional learning by including the rules "found infallible by experience."[20] In his *Floraes Paradise,* Hugh Platt, too, wrote of "having out of mine owne particular experience, as also by long conference with diverse gentlemen of good skill and practice, in the altering, multiplying, enlarging, planting, and transplanting, of sundry sorts of fruites and flowers, at length obtained a pretty volume of

---

professionalization of nurserymen and seed sellers (19–22); and Thomas, *Man and the Natural World,* 224, for a discussion of the plant and flower market.

[17] On the controversy concerning the existence of "professions" in early modern England, see Rosemary O'Day, "The Professions in Early Modern England," *History Today* 36 (1986): 52–5; Wilfrid Prest, ed., *The Professions in Early Modern England* (London: Croom Helm, 1987); and Harold J. Cook, "Good Advice and Little Medicine: The Professional Authority of Early Modern English Physicians," *Journal of British Studies* 33 (1994): 1–31. Prest provides an overview of the changes over time in the study of the history of the professions.

[18] Gervase Markham, *The English Husbandman,* "former part of the first part," sig. a2r. This text is a bibliographic patchwork of collected, separately paginated "books" and "parts." I have cited passages using the terminology of the running heads.

[19] See O'Day, "The Professions," 53.

[20] See Thomas, *Man and the Natural World,* 224; and Thomas Hill (writing as "Dydymus Mountain"), *The Gardeners Labyrinth* (London, 1594; reprint New York: Garland, 1982), 3, 43, for the importance of the gardener's learning as well as his labor.

experimentall observations in this kinde." While Markham contrasted his work with the classical treatises, Platt opposed his "substantiall and approved matter" to that of the Schoolmen, "who have alreadie written many large and methodicall volumes of this subject (whose labours have greatly furnished our Studies and Libraries, but little or nothing altered or graced our Gardens and Orchards)." Platt claimed that he was not a "theorist" but rather one who "seeke[s] out the practicall, and operative part of Nature."[21] His own professionalism, like Markham's, was closely tied to practice of what others would call a mere occupation.

These different "gardeners" – master, servants, and in between – and their social standings are reflected in these texts' different claims to tell the truth, and in particular, in their appeal to experience. Especially in the sixteenth century, books directed toward the gentleman farmer were influenced by the classical texts that formed the basis of a humanist education. These books are studded with citations of classical treatises on agriculture (by authorities such as Varro, Columella, and Pliny), which were used as a source of practical information and description of horticultural practice – however inappropriately for sixteenth-century England, since the classical texts originated in a Mediterranean climate. As Joan Thirsk has argued, while the new attention to farming among the gentry was certainly stimulated by economic conditions, the justification for the change was underwritten by these classical authorities on farming.[22]

Later manuals directed toward the "plaine English Husbandman" and the poor displayed a more uneasy relationship to classical authority, similar to that seen in some English writing on poetics in the same period. The writers of these books seem impelled to cite the classics, but they also tried to distinguish particularly English agricultural practices from classical or foreign ones. Leonard Mascall, in his *Booke of the arte and maner, howe to plant and graffe all sortes of trees,* made a typical double move. He first justified both the art of grafting, and of writing about it, in terms of classical precedent, calling grafting an art that "hath bene put in writing of many great and worthie personages, in divers kinde of languages, as in Greke by Philometor, Hieron, Acheleus, Orpheus, Musceus, Homer, Hosiode, Constantine, Cesar: and in Latin, by Verron, Caton,

---

21 Hugh Platt, preface to the reader to *Floraes Paradise, Beautified and Adorned with sundry sorts of delicate fruites and flowers* (London, 1608), sigs. a3v–a4r.
22 Thirsk, "Making a Fresh Start," 19.

Columella, Paladius, Vergill, Amilius Macer." Yet, a few lines later, Mascall repositioned himself against this tradition, by insisting that all this had very little relevance for English gardeners:

for every one hath written according to the nature of his countrey. The Greekes for Greece, the Barbarians for Barbarie, the Italians for Italy, the French men for Fraunce &c. which writing without the order and practice, doth very small profite for this our Realme of England, the which I can blame nothing more than the negligence of our nation, which hath had small care heretofore in planting and graffing.[23]

Gervase Markham severed himself more resolutely from the classics, claiming in his *English Husbandman* that in his writing and gardening, "contrary to all other Authors, I am neither beholden to Pliny, Vergil, Columella, Varo, Rutillius, Libault, nor any other Forainer, but onely to our owne best experienst Countreymen, whose daily knowledge hath made them most perfect in their professions." These men, he insisted, are better qualified to teach, "being men of our owne neighbourhood, acquainted with our Climate and Soile": Why, for example, should we resort to "strangers helpe," which recommends we use asses' dung for manure, when England has few such animals?[24] Just as his conception of his "profession" was tied to his "observation" and "experience," Markham's claim to tell the truth was also linked to his sense of himself as an Englishman, one who had gained his knowledge from other Englishmen who in turn knew their own land through working it.

Markham's letter of dedication in *The English Husbandman* to Lord Clifton, baron of Leighton, suggests his awareness of the dangers of claiming to speak the truth on these grounds, especially when writing for a double audience of noble patron and English husbandman: what served as authority for one audience might not work for another. In his letter, Markham presented his book as "an account of the expence of my idle time," while protesting that

---

[23] Leonard Mascall, epistle to *A booke of the Arte and maner, howe to plant and graffe all sortes of trees, howe to set stones, and sowe Pepines to make wylde trees to graffe on, as also remedies and medicines* (London, 1572), sigs. a3r–v.

[24] Markham, *English Husbandman*, "second book," 13. For Markham's additional comments on these matters, see "second part of the first book," 89, where he insists that in the matter of hop growing, "I thus farre consent with Maister Scot, that I doe not so much respect the writings, opinions, and demonstrations, of the Greeke, Latine, or French authors, who never were acquainted with our soyles, as I doe the dayly practice and experience which I collect, both from my owne knowledge, and the labours of others my Countrymen, best seene and approved in this Art."

if your Lordship shall doubt of the true tast of the liquor because it proceedeth
from such a vessell as my selfe, whom you may imagine utterly unseasoned
with any of these knowledges, beleeve it (my most best Lord) that for divers
yeers, wherein I lived most happily, lived a Husbandman, amongst Husbandmen of most excellent knowledge; during all which time I let no observation
over-slip me.[25]

Markham thus attempted to describe himself as having "idle time," ally-
ing himself (as a gentleman by birth) with the aristocrat he addressed as a
patron, while also grounding his authority to speak on this matter in his
"observation" and work as a husbandman.[26] (In fact, Markham himself
came from a decayed gentry family and turned to farming to support his
own large family, while also producing a prodigious number of instruc-
tional manuals as well as some poetry and plays.)

Mascall's, Markham's, and Platt's appeals to order, practice, and experience were indirectly connected to the different empiricist turns taken in
the philosophical writings of Juan Luis Vives and Michel Montaigne
(Vives, for example, recommended that scientists consult "gardeners,
husbandmen, shepherds and hunters"), but they were more directly
linked with the "science" treated by the kind of technological writers on
exploration, astronomy, and navigation to whom Bacon turned.[27] As
Markham's frequent appeals to the plain English husbandman and Platt's
rejection of the Schoolmen indicate, such a position attempted to fashion
the unlearned man's claim to knowledge. The claim, however, was also
specifically national, separating English custom and present practice from
the classical rule, as well as from other "outlandish" or foreign models.
Like Samuel Daniel, who defended English poetry by arguing that "all
our understandings are not to be built by the square of Greece and Italie,"
men such as Markham and Mascall were attempting to create a new
authority for gardening description and advice that emanated from the
present experience of England.[28]

---

[25] Markham, epistle dedicatory to *English Husbandman*.

[26] See the biography of Markham by F. N. L. Poynter in *A Bibliography of Gervase Markham, 1568?–1637* (Oxford: Oxford Bibliographical Society, 1962), 1–34.

[27] *Vives: On Education: A Translation of the De Tradendis Disciplinis of Juan Luis Vives*, trans. Foster Watson (Cambridge: Cambridge University Press, 1913), 169–70.

[28] Samuel Daniel, "A Defence of Ryme," in *Poems and A Defence of Ryme*, ed. Arthur Colby Sprague (Chicago: University of Chicago Press, 1965), 139. For the argument in English poetics about vernacular vs. classical models, and how this debate might be correlated with political conflict over local vs. centralized authority, see Richard Helgerson, *Forms of Nationhood: The Elizabethan Writing of England* (Chicago: University of Chicago Press, 1992), chaps. 1, 3. While I would argue that the parallels between poetics and politics are not as strict as Helgerson suggests, I am much indebted to his

For gardening writers, England's particularity and their experience of it were directly linked to local and national identity. As in other European countries, English herbals and horticultural books focused on the depiction and cultivation of native plants. After its beginnings in the late medieval period, when herbalists added descriptions of local plants to classical manuscripts and assigned vernacular names to already listed herbs,[29] the vernacular movement gained nationalist momentum in the sixteenth century.[30] William Turner wrote his *Great Herbal* and *A New Herball* in English about English plants so that they would be useful for English physicians.[31] In his preface to *The Names of Herbes* (1548), he neatly delineated the connection between writing in the vernacular, describing English flora, and experiencing a specific English place: after he had

axed the advise of Phisicianes in thys matter [of whether to write in Latin or in English], their advise was that I shoulde cease from settynge out of this boke in latin tyll I had sene those places of Englande, wherein is moste plentie of herbes, that I might in my herbal declare to the greate honoure of our countre what numbre of sovereine and strang herbes were in Englande that were not in other nations, whose counsell I have folowed deferryng to set out my herbal in latin, tyl I have sene the west contrey, which I never sawe yet in al my lyfe, which countrey of al places of England, as I heare say is moste richly replenished wyth al kindes of straunge and wonderfull workes and giftes of nature, as are stones, herbes, fishes and metals.[32]

discussion of the politics of "localism" in early modern England. See also Wendy Wall, "Renaissance National Husbandry: Gervase Markham and the Publication of England," forthcoming in *Sixteenth Century Journal,* for an excellent reading of Markham that focuses on his local conception of national identity; Wall also analyzes Markham's competition with as well as his appropriation of foreign writers.

[29] See A. G. Morton, *History of Botanical Science: An Account of the Development of Botany from Ancient Times to the Present Day* (London: Academic Press, 1981), 96–8, 118.

[30] See Morton, *History of Botanical Science,* 118; for an example of such "vernacular" herbals, see Otto Brunfels's *Herbarum vivae eicones,* 3 vols, (Strasburg 1530–6), which was notable for its illustrations drawn from life. On Brunfels, see Blanche Henrey, *British Botanical and Horticultural Literature Before 1800* (London: Oxford University Press, 1975), 7.

[31] Frank J. Anderson, *An Illustrated History of the Herbals* (New York: Columbia University Press, 1977), writes of Turner:

Over 200 species native to England are described in Turner's pages, and some of them were first named by him. Like other physicians of his time, Turner was concerned with the proper identification of the medicinal materials of Dioscorides, but he was by no means overawed by his predecessor's authority, and differed with him on more than one occasion. Turner was well aware that the local northern floras did not agree with those written about by Dioscorides, Galen, and Pliny, and that the British flora was often distinct from the Continental floras. (152)

[32] William Turner, *The Names of Herbes in Greke, Latin, Englishe, Duche & Frenche wyth the commune names that Herbaries and Apotecaries use* (London, 1548; reprint, The

This passage joins the values of direct observation with a sense of the uniqueness of the "sovereine and strang" botanical riches of England, which are further narrowed to the specific locality of the West Country.

The gardening books at first may appear to tend toward generality rather than specificity, insofar as they offer uniform rules for cultivation that will impose order and form on a diverse nature: William Lawson boasted in his *New Orchard and Garden* that while "trees have their severall formes . . . neyther let any man ever so much as thinke, that it is unprobable, much lesse unpossible, to reform any tree of what kinde soever. For (believe mee) I have tried it. I can bring any tree (beginning by time) to any forme. The Peare and Holly may bee made to spread, and the Oake to Close."[33] At the same time, however, all the writers looked to regional differences. As John Norden put it, even if "there is no kinde of soile, be it ever so wilde, boggy, clay or sandy, but will yeeld one kind of beneficial fruit or other," every place should be cultivated "to its fittest fruit."[34] Markham thought that it was the husbandman's duty to "consider the nature of his grounds" before "he put his plough into the earth," because one could not generalize about the land, and "every man in his owne worke knowes the alteration of clymates." In short, the knowledge that the husbandman needed in working with soil was a knowledge of differences, as well as of rules of order and form, and these differences would affect one's relationship with the land. As Markham concluded,

The reason why I have thus at large discoursed of every severall soyle, both simple and compounded, is to show unto the industrious Husbandman, the perfect and true reason of the generall alteration of our workes in Husbandry, through this our Realme of England: for if all our Land, as it is one kingdome, were likewise of one composition, mixture, and goodnesse, it were then exceeding preposterous to see those diversities, alterations, I, and even contrary manners of proceedings in Husbandry, which are daily and hourely used.[35]

English Dialect Society, no. 34, London, 1888; reprint, Vaduz, Liechtenstein: Kraus Reprint Ltd., 1965), sig. a2r.

[33] Lawson, *New Orchard and Garden*, 35.

[34] John Norden, *The Surveiors Dialogue, Very Profitable for all men to peruse, but especially for all Gentlemen, or any other farmer, or Husbandmen, that shall either have occasion, or be willing to buy or sell lands . . .* (London, 1610), 167. McRae comments on this passage: "These attitudes inevitably promoted the acceptance of regional specialization. England could not henceforth be represented as a patchwork of self-sufficient manors, because the 'rule of reason' dictated specific uses for land in different regions. . . . This model would embrace regional specialization in the cause of 'reason,' and depict a nation bound by the 'rational' networks of a market economy." "Husbandry Manuals," 51. See also Thirsk, "Making a Fresh Start," 27.

[35] Markham, *English Husbandman*, "the first part," 2, 9.

The natural history practiced in horticultural books and herbals thus often offered an image of England in its particulars, as well as its ideal order. In his *English Husbandman,* Markham took care to specify different soils and their cultivation in a multitude of places. If your soil is generally of good condition, he wrote, "in this case it is best to lay your lands flat and levell, without ridges or furrowes, as is done in many parts of Cambridge-shire, some parts of Essex, and some parts of Hartford-shire"; if it is somewhat wet, "then you shall lay your lands large and high, with high ridges and deep furrows, as generally you see in Lincolne-shire, Nottinghamshire, Huntington-shire, and most of the middle shires in England"; but if it is very wet and heavy, then "you shall lay your land in little stitches, that is to say, not above three or foure furrowes at the most together, as is generally seene in Middlesexe, Hartford-shire, Kent and Surrey."[36] We are told, along the way, how people used peas for bread in Leicestershire, Lincolnshire, and Nottinghamshire,[37] and of the different characteristics of the cattle across England.[38] Similarly, amid his rules for ordering the orchard in his *New Orchard and Garden,* Lawson described the planting of fruit trees in hedges in Worcestershire and told the tale of a giant toppled oak in Brooham Park.[39] Norden's *Surveiors Dialogue* consistently blends advice about husbandry with a description of the ways in which each particular climate and soil of England could lend itself to cultivation: "For the first, namely your low and spungie grounds, trenched, is good for hoppes, as Essex, and Surrey, and other places do find to their profit. The hot and sandy, (omitting graine), is good for Carret roots, a beneficial fruit, as at Oxford, Ipswich, and many sea townes in Suffolke."[40]

This habit of gardening books had its closest analogues in chorography and topography, genres of writing that focused, as Richard Helgerson suggests, on places and the differences among them in both civil and natural history.[41] Like many contemporary descriptions of En-

---

[36] Ibid., "the former part," sig. e2v.

[37] Ibid., "the former part," sig. f3v.

[38] Ibid., "second book," 88–9. See also *Markham's Farewell to Husbandry, or the inriching of all sorts of Barren and Sterill Grounds in our Kingdome, to be fruitfull in all manner of Graine, Pulse, and Grasse as the best grounds whatsoever . . . attained by Travell and Experience, being a Worke never before handled by any Author* (London, 1620); this book also contains exact observations of the soils all over Britain.

[39] Lawson, *New Orchard and Garden,* 10, 42.

[40] Norden, *Surveiors Dialogue,* 168.

[41] See Helgerson, *Forms of Nationhood,* chap. 3. See Shapiro, *Probability and Certainty,* 128–30, on chorographic and topographical literature that "slid back and forth between

gland, whether they tended more toward natural history or to the description of its antiquities, the gardening books offered history as inventory rather than narrative, organized spatially rather than temporally, but as at the same time relating the "deeds and events" of the English land. The methods for assembling all these histories were also comparable: They relied a great deal on direct observation and the information gathered from local informants.[42] In chorographic texts we find detailed discussions of the practice of husbandry in different shires that echo what is seen in the contemporary gardening books. In Richard Carew's *Survey of Cornwall*, we not only hear about the nature of the Cornish soil, but we also are informed of the characteristic practices of tillage, a process of "beating, burning, scoding and sanding."[43] William Lambarde also opened his *Perambulation of Kent* with a consideration of its air, soil, and typical produce. Each of the county descriptions in Camden's *Britannia* begins with an estimate of that county's soil (which often differs in its parts). Michael Drayton's *Poly-Olbion*, too, mentions the "sundry various soyles" as the very first of Britain's wonders.[44] Both *Britannia* and *Poly-Olbion* weave images of the soil's fertility and cultivation together with the human history of the land. Drayton's poet imagines his muse taking flight over the English countryside, surveying its riches: She

Now, in the finnie Heaths, then in the Champains roves;
Now, measures out this Plaine; and then survayes those groves;
The batfull pastures fenc't, and most with quickset mound,
The sundry sorts of soyle, diversitie of ground;

natural history, chorography, history and simple description without any sense that these subject matters should not be mixed together" (130).

[42] William Camden, *Britannia sive florentissimorum regnorum Angliae, Scotiae, Hiberniae . . .* (London, 1594). Just as Turner was encouraged to visit the West Country when he wrote his herbal, when William Camden undertook to write his *Britannia*, he took to the road. As F. J. Levy describes Camden's method, "when he came to a spot suspected of hiding a Roman town, he looked for walls, for fragments of pavements, for coins, even for cropmarks. He spoke to the inhabitants to learn what they had discovered and to find any old legends still hanging over the town." *Tudor Historical Thought* (San Marino, Calif.: Huntington Library, 1967), 150. For examples of Camden's comments on the soil, see pp. 347–8, where he describes the soil in Suffolk ("sola nisi ad Orientum, admodum pingui, utpote ex argilla et marga composita"); and p. 358, where he describes that in Norfolk ("Solum pro locurum diversitate varium, alicusi pingue, luxurians, et succulentum, scilicet in Mershaland et Fliggi; alibi, maxime qua occasum spectat tenue, leve, et sabulosum, alibi argillosum et cretaceum").

[43] Richard Carew, *The Survey of Cornwall*, in *Richard Carew of Anthony: The Survey of Cornwall, &c.*, ed. F. E. Halliday (London: Andrew Melrose, 1953), 86, 102.

[44] "Of Albions glorious Ile the Wonders whilst I write, / The sundry varying soyles, the pleasures infinite . . . " Michael Drayton, *Poly-Olbion*, in *Michael Drayton: Tercentenary Edition*, ed. J. William Hebel (Oxford: Basil Blackwell, 1961), 4:1 (song 1, ll. 1–2).

Where Plow-men cleanse the Earth of rubbish, weed, and filth,
And give the fallow land their season and their tylth:
Where, best for breeding horse; here cattell fitst to keepe;
Which good for bearing Corne; which pasturing for sheepe:
The leane and hungry earth, the fat and marly mold,
Where sands be alwaies hot, and where the clayes be cold;
With plentie where they waste, some others toucht with want:
Heere set, and there they sowe; here proine, and there they plant.[45]

Drayton's muse, in her careful consideration of the fitness of the land and the traditions of its cultivation, sounds as if she is preparing to write a gardening book as much as a poem about Britain.

The kind of history practiced in chorography and the natural history of the gardening books thus shared common purposes and methods. They would tell the story of England, not through an account of its dynasties or wars, but rather through the experience or observation of its particularities. In the push to define a vernacular discourse of the landscape, both kinds of writers were driven to use local knowledge and experience to supplement or even supplant the information to be gained from books. As Keith Thomas tells the story, "It is not surprising . . . that natural history at first depended for its progress on absorbing much popular lore . . . Sir Joseph Banks, the future President of the Royal Society, as a schoolboy paid herb-women to teach him the names of flowers. Physicians and apothecaries had long depended for their supplies upon such persons, what William Turner called 'the old wives that gather herbs.' "[46] At the same time that story would be framed by a broader order, the ideal order of the English landscape, mixing beauty and profit, which served the political order of the English nation. Richard Helgerson has persuasively demonstrated how chorography, attending to the details of England's landscape, helped to construct a sense of nationhood,[47] if

---

[45] Ibid., 57 (song 3, ll. 347–58). For other relevant passages from *Poly-Olbion*, see the description of the Hermit's herbal practice (280–1), where Gerard is mentioned; the discussion of production of pear trees and perry in Worstershire (296; Camden also mentions this in *Britannia* [300]); the wonderful description of wild and cultivated flowers in the marriage of the Thames and the Isis (307–8); the description of the meal in Peryvale, in Middlesex (319); and an account of English produce (410).

[46] Thomas, *Man and the Natural World*, 73–4. Thomas cites William Turner, *A New Herball* (London, 1551), sig. a3v.

[47] "Proper names do much of the work of distinguishing, and it is on them that the chorographers most heavily rely. But many undertook differentiation of a more pointed sort. Reading them, we learn that 'the cordage or ropes for the navy of England should be twisted and made nowhere else' but in Dorset, that there is 'in all England . . . [no place] where the ground requireth greater charges' than in Devon, that the catch of pilchard is particularly abundant in Cornwall, that the common people are the 'shrub-

one believed that "the nation, unlike the dynasty, [was] strengthened by its very receptiveness to such individual and communal autonomy."[48] In this sense horticultural manuals, herbals, and chorography all functioned to define the parts that would be built up into England's story.

However, in the writing of natural history the recourse to local knowledge was inevitably valued differently according to one's social rank and profession. We have already seen how Markham's preface betrays some anxiety in balancing the expectations of an aristocratic patron with those of the "common" reader (bridging Markham's own complex social status). When natural history developed as a science not linked to practice and profit, rural informants were less appreciated.[49] What might in other contexts be considered another sign of England's great diversity – the variety of English regional names for plants and their culture – came to be considered a liability in the pursuit of science (not to speak of the market pressures for standardization).[50] By the end of the seventeenth century, by all accounts, rural knowledge of natural history stood in disrepute. When Bacon cheerfully admitted his dependence on the "low and vulgar" mechanical arts, while he dismissed antiquities, "citations or testimonies of authors," and "all superstitious stories" and "old wives' fables,"[51] he marked a middle point in the process of change. By the end of the century, it had become necessary to reject these superfluities in favor of the "chastity and brevity" of scientific truth.[52] Experience associated with local knowledge was more likely to be seen as vulgar error, in contrast with the scientists' controlled and carefully circumscribed trials. Gender, social position, education, and method all served to define and limit the role of experience in natural history and its relation to the truth.[53]

---

biest' in Pembroke, that Plymouth is 'second to no town in England for worth every way.'" Helgerson, *Forms of Nationhood,* 131. On chorography, see Levy, *Tudor Historical Thought,* chap. 4.

[48] Helgerson, *Forms of Nationhood,* 138.

[49] As Thomas puts it, "popular knowledge was soon eclipsed by the more thoroughgoing inquiries of the scientists, whose viewpoint was not narrowly utilitarian and who rapidly became disillusioned to discover that there were limits to rural curiosity." *Man and the Natural World,* 74.

[50] Thomas, *Man and the Natural World,* 83–4.

[51] Bacon, *Preparative towards a Natural and Experimental History,* in *Works,* 4:254–5.

[52] The phrase is from Bacon, *Advancement,* 3:255. On "weeding" natural history of "fables, antiquities, quotations, idle controversies, philology and ornaments," see ibid., 299.

[53] My thanks to Meredith Galman for pointing out, in an unpublished essay entitled "Petticote Surgeons and She-Physicians: The Professionalization of Medicine and the Displacement of Women," that the conflict over herbal medicine was also gendered.

FANCIES IN NATURE

When Bacon rejected the former errors of natural history, he rejected them as fictions – superstitions and "old wives tales." In contrast, his own experiments were meant to reveal the truth of nature by subjecting it to unnatural pressures, that is, to the conditions of the scientist's art. This experimental approach parallels Bacon's practice of civil history. In theory Bacon separated history from art or the imagination. Yet his writing of "politic" civil history entailed the use of the imagination as well as memory and reason in the manipulation of the materials of history to reveals its truths about human nature.[54] Art and nature, and art and history, are thus not easily divided, either in Bacon's writing or in much of early modern forms of history, natural and civil.

The second half of this essay examines how gardening books negotiated telling the truth about the horticultural practice of altering the color, scent, and shape of plants. Just as the practice of altering plants might be seen to balance the claims of nature and art, the process of writing about it vacillated between truth and fiction. As I have suggested was true for any claims to speak authoritatively about English nature and culture, beliefs about the validity of altering nature – and writing about it – were mediated by concerns about social stability and position. Just as changing nature through grafting or culture had a social resonance, the act of recording or reporting such acts was bound up with social concerns. To some, the act of grafting and writing about it marked a new confidence in the possibility of self-improvement. To others, these acts and reports were but the fancies and vain boasts of upstarts. In this sense, the denigration of local knowledge and stories could also be extended to the work of the practical or "mechanical" men to whom Bacon had professed his debt.

In Bacon's discussion of artificial nature, the complex link between technological art and the works of the imagination became manifest. Bacon insisted that his natural history would treat "not only of nature free and at large . . . but much more of nature under constraint and vexed; that is to say, when by art and the hand of man she is forced out of her natural state, and squeezed and moulded."[55] (As Evelyn Fox Keller has noted, the

---

[54] Levy, *Tudor Historical Thought*, 257–8.
[55] Bacon, *Great Instauration*, 4:29. On the value of the vexations of art, see also Bacon, *Preparative*, 4:257; in this text he sets out more directly the three branches of natural history, which treat nature "free," "perverse" (e.g., monsters), and "constrained and moulded by art and human ministry" (253). On Bacon on art and nature, see Bredekamp, *The Lure of Antiquity*, chap. 4.

Baconian method was gendered as masculine here, while its results were meant to invalidate "old wives' tales."[56]) He deplored the error of "considering art as merely an assistant to nature, having the power indeed to finish what nature has begun, to correct her when lapsing into error, or to set her free when in bondage, but by no means to change, transmute or fundamentally alter nature." On the contrary, Bacon insisted that "the artificial does not differ from the natural in form or essence, but only in the efficient; in that man has no power over nature except that of motion; he can put natural bodies together, and he can separate them; and therefore that wherever the case admits of the uniting or disuniting of natural bodies . . . man can do everything."[57] As Michèle Le Doeuff has argued, such a passage suggests Bacon's ambivalence on the question of art and nature, his effective blurring of the distinctions between them, where art can do all and nothing in nature.[58]

But a similar slippage occurs in Bacon's drawing of a difference between history – including natural history – and "poesy." History, the text says, is related to the memory, and "is properly concerned with individuals"; poesy "is also concerned with individuals," but "with this difference, that it commonly exceeds the measure of nature, joining at pleasure things which in nature would never have come together, and introducing things which in nature would never have come to pass. . . . This is the work of Imagination."[59] The terms of this passage effectively link the experimental practices in natural history that Bacon outlined in *Great Instauration* and described in *Sylva Sylvarum* with the effect of the imagination, or "poesy." *Sylva Sylvarum* repeatedly advises its reader how "to bring things together." It does not deny the possibility of "the transmutation of plants one into another"; "certainly it is a thing of difficulty, and requireth deep search into nature; but seeing there appear some manifest instances of it, the opinion of impossibility is to be rejected, and the

---

[56] See Evelyn Fox Keller, *Reflections on Gender and Science* (New Haven: Yale University Press, 1985), chap. 2.

[57] Bacon, *Advancement*, 4:294–5.

[58] Michèle Le Doeuff, "Man and Nature in the Gardens of Science," in *Francis Bacon's Legacy of Texts: "The Art of Discover Grows with Discovery,"* ed. William A. Sessions (New York: AMS, 1990), 128–34. Le Doeuff argues that we misread Bacon if we see him as "the philosopher of a triumphant domination of man over nature": rather, her view is that "Bacon challenges both the minimalist idea that the power of art is restricted to the perfecting of that which nature has already almost completed on her own, *and* the maximalist idea of art's discretionary power of transfiguration" (122–3). In this context, gardening is "that supreme craft which consists in denaturing things with nature's assistance" (126).

[59] Bacon, *Advancement*, 4:292.

means thereof to be found out."[60] In general, Bacon's "experiments" in horticulture (many borrowed from Giambattista della Porta's *Natural Magic*), like his other scientific efforts, explore ways of making things that would never have come to pass in nature, including the "curiosities" of several types of fruit upon one tree, "fruits of divers shapes and figures," "inscriptions or engravings in fruits or trees," and changes in the color and the nature of flowers.[61]

In his analogy between poesy and horticulture in *The Arte of English Poesy,* George Puttenham similarly blurred the fine distinction between what the human hand can and cannot do in nature, in effect suggesting the identity rather than dissimilarity of poetics and natural history.[62] In some cases, Puttenham wrote,

we say arte is an ayde and coadiutor to nature, and a futherer of her actions to good effect, or peradventure a meane to supply her wants . . . as the good gardiner seasons his soyle by sundrie sorts of compost . . . and waters his plants, and weedes his herbes or floures, and prunes his branches, and unleaves his boughes to let in the sunne, and twentie other waies cherisheth them and cureth their infirmities;

so the same is true of the poet's use of language. However, in turning again to horticulture, he argued further that art may also "surmount" and "alter" nature's

skill, so as by meanes of it her owne effects shall appeare more beautifull or straunge and miraculous. . . the Gardiner by his arte will not onely make an herbe, or flowr, or fruite, come forth in his season without impediment, but also will embellish the same in vertue, shape, odour, and taste, that nature of her selfe woulde never have done, as to make single gillifloure, or marigold, or daisie,

---

[60] Bacon, *Sylva Sylvarum,* in *Works,* 2:507.

[61] Ibid., 501–3. It is significant here that we do not necessarily see Bacon putting his own principles into practice; see Le Doeuff on *Sylva Sylvarum,* "Man and Nature," 132–4. The prefatory letter from William Rawley does try to reconcile the experiments described in *Sylva Sylvarum* with the plan of *The Great Instauration,* while pointing up the "baseness" and "vulgarity" of some of the experiments. See also Robert Leslie Ellis's apologetic introduction to the *Sylva* in vol. 2 of Bacon, *Works;* he notes that a large part of it amounts to stuff collected from "a few popular writers" (325), including della Porta. This inconsistency is comparable to what commentators have noted in the method of the *History of Henry VII.* See William Eamon, *Science and the Secrets of Nature: Books of Secrets in Medieval and Early Modern Culture* (Princeton: Princeton University Press, 1994), 285–91, on Bacon's attitude toward the "books of secrets" and natural magic.

[62] On Puttenham on nature and art, see Derek Attridge, "Puttenham's Perplexity: Nature, Art, and the Supplement in Renaissance Poetic Theory," in *Literary Theory/Renaissance Texts,* ed. Patricia Parker and David Quint (Baltimore: Johns Hopkins University Press, 1986), 257–89.

double, and the white rose redde, yellow, or carnation, a bitter mellon sweete, a sweete apple soure, a plumme or cherrie without a stone, a peare without core or kernell, a goord or coucumber like to a horne or any other figure he will: any of which things nature could not doe without mans helpe and arte.[63]

In speaking of the poet's art in comparison with that of the gardener, Puttenham's text, like Bacon's, glides over the unstable boundary between art's simply improving or bringing nature to its full expression and its bringing forth "things nature could not doe without man's helpe and arte," the creation of the beautiful, strange, and miraculous. The cultivation or refinement of what exists and the creation of something new are the same in language and in natural history, just as the distinction between them seems similarly unimportant.

Even Sir Philip Sidney's well-known formulation of the difference between poetry and nature draws them together through the language of natural history. In separating the poetic art from philosophy, history, and the sciences, which are restrained by nature, Sidney celebrated the autonomy of the poet who

disdaining to be tied to any such subjection [to nature], lifted up with the vigour of his own invention, doth grow in effect another nature, in making things either better than nature bringeth forth, or, quite anew, forms such as never were in nature, as the Heroes, Demigods, Cyclops, Chimeras, Furies, and such like: so as he goeth hand in hand with nature, not enclosed within the narrow warrant of her gifts, but freely ranging only within the zodiac of his own wit. Nature never set forth the earth in so rich tapestry as divers poets have done; neither with so pleasant rivers, fruitful trees, sweet-smelling flowers, nor whatsoever else may make the too much loved earth more lovely.[64]

Sidney's beginning might seem to oppose the poet to nature, freeing him from nature's dominion, but the language here in fact evokes an admiration of horticulture. It represents the poet as one who, like the consummate gardener, makes "the too much loved earth more lovely," fashioning what was never before in nature by going "hand in hand" with her. Throughout *A Defence of Poetry,* indeed, while Sidney tries to set the poet free, he also binds him to nature through an obligation to observe decorum.[65] The tension is analogous to that Sidney held to exist between

---

[63] George Puttenham, *The Arte of English Poesie,* in *Elizabethan Critical Essays,* ed. G. Gregory Smith (Oxford: Clarendon Press, 1904), 2:187–9.

[64] Philip Sidney, *A Defence of Poetry,* ed. Jan Van Dorsten (Oxford: Oxford University Press, 1966), 23–4.

[65] On this conflict in Sidney, see Phyllis Rackin, "Shakespeare's Boy Cleopatra, the Decorum of Nature, and the Golden World of Poetry," *PMLA* 87 (1972): 201–12. See also

poetry and history. Sidney may have mocked the historian "laden with old mouse-eaten records, authorizing himself (for the most part) upon other histories."[66] But his poet may also take the events of history as his material, while he also transforms them: "for whatsoever action, or faction, whatsoever counsel, policy, or war stratagem the historian is bound to recite, that may the poet (if he list) with his imitation make his own, beautifying it for further teaching, and more delighting, as it please him: having all, from Dante's heaven to his hell, under the authority of his pen."[67] The poet is the master, history the subject, like nature; but history, like nature again, is also the stuff from which the poet fashions his art.

Thus, Sidney and Bacon may both seem to oppose imagination and art to nature and history, insofar as they try to define poesy as unrestrained by either of them. But their analogies between poetry and horticulture, with their implicit equation of history and nature, undermine these oppositions. In Renaissance poetics, the notion that expresses this coalescence of nature and art is "invention," which uses reason to construct images never thought of before but preexisting in nature. These are found or "invented," discovered rather than created, and at the same time they are new.[68] The equivalent in Bacon's practice of natural history is experimentation that produces a new image of nature through "vexation," or the altering of its conditions. "Invention" is thus as important to natural history as it is to poetry: Both make something new of the true nature that was always there. For Bacon, invention in turn also served for the writing of civil history. As several commentators have noted, in writing his *History of Henry VII,* Bacon did not work with documents or artifacts, as an antiquarian might; rather he undertook the analysis of the raw materials of the report of men's characters and actions to produce the truth of human nature. As Stuart Clark puts it, "in reducing all sciences to natural science, Bacon in effect transformed all history into

Edward William Tayler, *Nature and Art in Renaissance Literature* (New York: Columbia University Press, 1964), on the parallels between poetics and gardening literature; he compares Puttenham with the preface of Lawson's *New Orchard and Garden* (17–19).
[66] Sidney, *Defence,* 30.   [67] Ibid., 37.
[68] So we find James VI telling poets "that ze may find in zour self sic a beginning of Nature, as ze may put in practise in zour verse many of thir foirsaidis preceptis, or ever ze sie them as they are heir set doun." "Ane Schort Treatise, Conteining Some Reulis and Cautelis to be Observit and Eschewit in Scottis Poesie," in *The Essayes of a Prentice, in the Divine Art of Poesie* (Edinburgh, 1585); I cite the reprint edited by Edward Arber (London: Constable and Co., 1870; reprint, New York: AMS, 1966), 55. See Grahame Castor, *Pléiade Poetics: A Study in Sixteenth-Century Thought and Terminology* (Cambridge: Cambridge University Press, 1964), on the subject of invention.

natural history": In doing so, he reordered and rejoined the data of history as a form of nature, using memory, reason, and imagination to "invent" the story of the past.[69]

However, for some natural historians (as for the enemies of poetry), imagination and invention were linked neither with the poet's golden world nor the experimentalist's vexed nature, but rather with lies, superstition, and vanity. Depending on the context, the object of attack might be the follies of old books, the boasts of practical writers, or the much-despised "old wives' tales," all rejected in the name of the truth of experience (even though most natural historians had turned to all these sources at some time). Paralleling the neoclassical poetic treatises, which opposed the purified vernacular of the neoclassical but native poet to the crude practices of a folk vernacular,[70] horticulturists who allied themselves with aristocratic aims and tastes turned against both rural practices *and* the "rude mechanicals" who boasted of their extraordinary transformations of nature. As I have suggested, in some gardening books a claim to tell the truth of natural history might be based on experience and made in the name of the "plain English husbandman," that is, in the name of local, professional, and national loyalty. In other books, however, the authority of experiential truth might be claimed in the name of a more abstract science, against the boasts of the "low" mechanical arts and their praise of artifice.[71] Both types of books based their claims to tell the truth about nature in social position and profession, which frame the appeal to observation and experience.

The kinds of truth particularly at stake in horticulture and husbandry were the truths of names, forms, and the nature of nature itself. The horticultural literature mostly debated the reliability of gardeners' claims to have altered nature. Some writers boasted of their ability to manipulate almost any plant to serve human needs and tastes. Others, however, insisted that the "property" of a living thing cannot be changed by art, while a few argued both ways at once, divided between a respect for the natural properties of plants and a desire to control them. Thomas Hill, Mascall,

---

[69] Stuart Clark, "Bacon's *Henrie VII*: A Case-Study in the Science of Man," *History and Theory* 13 (1974): 104.

[70] See, for example, Joachim Du Bellay, *La deffence et illustration de la langue françoyse* (1549), ed. Henri Chamard (Paris: Marcel Didier, 1948), 108–9.

[71] For a discussion of distinctions in notions of empiricism, and of the links between empiricism and theory, see Frederick O. Waage, "Touching the Compass: Empiricism in Popular Scientific Writing of Bacon's Time," *Huntington Library Quarterly* 41 (1978): 201–16.

and Markham all offered recipes for changing by artificial means the tastes of fruit, the colors and appearance of flowers, and the times of ripening.[72] For example, Markham praised "the effects of grafting" whereby you will have fruits "to ripen earely, as at the least two months before the ordinary time." Further, he advised that "if you will have the fruit to tast like spice, with a certaine delicate perfume, you shall boyle Honey, the powder of Cloves and Hoare together, and being cold annoynt the grafts therewith you put them into the cleft." If you want to change the color, bore a hole in the body and fill the hole with saffron to produce a yellow fruit.[73]

Yet even the industrious Markham was somewhat critical of such "conceits and experiments," which "concerne the curious rather then the wise,"[74] and other gardeners were still more doubtful of these efforts. Hugh Platt, who himself published compendia of "secret" ways to master the unreliability and mystery of just about everything, wavered between his admiration of Hill's "experience" in these matters of "changing the colour, taste, or sent, of any fruite, or flower" and his belief that "though some fruites and flowers seeme to carrie the sent, or tast, of some aromaticall bodie; yet that doth rather arise from their own naturall infused qualitie, then from the hand of man."[75] By 1629 John Parkinson contended much more strongly that the human hand has only a limited power over the plants. He insisted that "all double flowers were so found wilde, being the worke of nature alone, and not the art of any man," and that "there is no power or art in man, to cause flowers to shew their beauty divers moneths before their naturall time, nor to abide in their beauty longer then the appointed natural time for every one of them." He emphatically declared that any recipes for changing color or scent "from that they were or would be naturally, are meere fancies of men, without any ground of reason or truth."[76]

---

72 See Thomas Hill, *The Art of Gardening,* (London, 1608), 97, on lilies, for example.
73 Markham, *English Husbandman,* "second part of the first book," 57; see also his *Countryman's Recreation* (London, 1640), on "how one may Graffe, Plant, and Garden, subtile or artificially, and to make many things in Gardens very strange" (53).
74 Markham, *English Husbandman,* "second part of the first book," 129–30; also "second book," 41. In the "second part of the first book," he notes: "And some great persons I know, that with infinit cost, and I hope prosperous successe, hath planted a Vineyard of many Acres, in which the hands of the best experienced French men hath beene imploied: but for those great workes they are onely for great men, and not for the plaine English Husbandman, neither will such workes by any meanes prosper in many parts of our kingdome" (130).
75 Hugh Platt, *Floraes Paradise, Beautified and Adorned with sundry sorts of delicate fruites and flowers* (London, 1608), 141–2.
76 John Parkinson, *Paradisi in Sole, Paradisus Terrestris, A Garden of all sorts of pleasant flowers, which our English ayre will permitt to be noursed up . . .* (London, 1629), 25.

The ongoing argument over cultivating gillyflowers neatly demonstrates how such claims for and against art generated a quarrel about truth-telling in natural history that had a distinct social orientation. Markham and Platt both suggested that you could change a gillyflower from a single to a more valued double bloom, or change its color, through careful culture. Platt directed the gardener to make a plant double in the following way:

Remove a plant of stock gilliflowers when it is a little woodded, & not too greene, and water it presently; doe this three daies after the full [moon], and remoove it twice more before the change [of the moon]. Doe this in barraine ground, and likewise three daies after the next full moone, remove againe; and then remove once more before the change: Then at the third full moone, viz. 8. dayes after, remove againe, & set in very rich grounde, and this will make it to bring forth a double flower.[77]

Markham instead recommended grafting to change the color, size, and form of gillyflowers:

These Gilliflowers you may make of any colour you please, in such sort as is shewed you for the colouring of Lillyes, and if you please to have them of mixt colours you may also, by grafting of contrary colours one into another: and you may with as great ease graft the Gylliflower as any fruit whatsoever, by the joyning of the knots one into another, and then wrapping them about with a little soft sleav'd silke, and covering the place close with soft red Ware well tempered. And you shall understand that the grafting of Gylliflowers maketh them exceeding great, double, and most orient of colour.[78]

In each case, the writer's rhetoric is self-assured, celebrating the gardener's transformative skill, and conveying through exact detail experience in the field (whether he had such experience or not). The texts suggest, in Platt's case, the intricacy and difficulty of the procedure, and in Markham's, the necessary tenderness and delicacy by which the gardener can make the single, small, or plain gillyflower change its nature. That is, in both cases the text draws attention to the garden master's

---

[77] Platt, *Floraes Paradise*, 78–9.

[78] Markham, *English Husbandman*, "second book," 36. Markham goes on to make an interesting "class" distinction between general gillyflowers and wall-gillyflowers: while the former is tender, and thus alterable, the latter appears more like a weed, insofar as it "delighteth in hard rubbish, limy, and stonie grounds. . . . It would be sowen in very small quantity, for after it have once taken rote, it will naturally of it selfe over-spread much ground, and hardly ever after be rooted out. It is of it selfe of so exceeding a strong and sweet smell, that it cannot be forced to take any other, and therefore is ever preserved in its owne nature." *English Husbandman*, "second book," 37. What is interesting here is that the tough wall-gillyflower cannot be altered, whereas the tender one can.

artistry and confidence. In so doing, the rhetoric of instruction itself implies the truth of the description in its prescription.

In 1629, however, in his *Paradisi in Sole,* John Parkinson argued quite differently, also supposedly using experience and observation, but this time against the claims of the "plain English husbandman." More elevated than Markham and Platt, Parkinson was apothecary to James I and Charles I, and his book was dedicated to Henrietta Maria. In his dedication, Parkinson addressed the queen as the most eminent of gardeners: Insofar as she "furnished with them [flowers] as farre beyond others, as you are eminent before them," he asked her to accept "this speaking Garden, that may informe you in all the particulars of your store."[79] The whole of the English landscape, this implies, was hers to inventory and enjoy. The shift here from the plain English husbandman to the aristocratic gardener prepares the reader for the text that follows, which depicts a natural aristocracy in the world of plants, one that cannot be altered by artificial means.[80]

Against Markham and others, Parkinson claimed that you could not propagate gillyflowers by grafting, denying that such reports were "of any more worth than an old Wives tale, both nature, reason, and experience, all contesting against such an idle fancy, let men make what ostentation they please." He mocked any claims that gardeners made to achieve such results, deploring "the wonderfull desire that many have to see faire, double, and sweete flowers, [which] hath transported them beyond both reason and nature, feigning and boasting often of what they would have, as if they had it." He accused them of spreading "false tales and reports" of altering flowers. Some of these errors may be "ancient, and continued long by tradition, and others are of later invention: and therefore the

---

[79] Parkinson, epistle dedicatory *to Paradisi.*

[80] In contrast, Platt had marked the potential different concerns of these two audiences when he pitched his book for delight as well as profit: "to the profit of some, who by their manuall workes, may gaine a greater imployment, then heretofore in their usuall callings: and to the pleasuring of others, who delight to see a raritie spring out of their owne labours, and to provoke Nature to play, and to shew some of her pleasing varieties, when she hath met with a stirring workman"; sig. a3r–v. While Platt's book seems to be primarily directed toward the practical or "manual" uses, yet it also justified itself for those who appreciate pleasure and play in the interplay of art and nature, implicitly those who did not need to work but who derived pleasure from the manipulation of nature. See Bredekamp, *The Lure of Antiquity,* chap. 4, on "playfulness." See Terry Comito, *The Idea of the Garden in the Renaissance* (New Brunswick: Rutgers University Press, 1978), 21–2, on the distinction between books oriented toward the aristocracy and the practical gardening manuals; I disagree with Comito's view, however, that the former recognized no weeds in nature's treasury.

more to be condemned, that men of wit and judgement in these dayes should expose themselves in their writings, to be rather laughed at, then beleeved for such idle tales." Parkinson considered himself brave in countering these tales and expected to "undergo many calumnies," but he still hoped "by reason [to] perswade many in the truth."[81]

Most important, Parkinson insisted that he knew these tales to be false from "mine own experience in the matter." He asked if anyone could prove such claims, "but I never could finde any one, that could assuredly resolve me, that he knew certainly any such thing to be done: all that they could say was but report." As for planting at the change of the moon, he ruefully told his reader, "I have made tryall at many times, and in many sorts of plants, accordingly, and as I thought fit, by planting & transplanting them, but I could never see the effect desired, but rather in many of them the losse of my plants." Similarly, regarding the changing of colors and scents, such as Hill described, Parkinson scoffed that such claims did not hold up to trial, for

the many rules and directions extant in manie mens writings, to cause flowers to grow yellow, red, greene, or white, that never were so naturally, as also to be of the sent of Cinamon, Muske, &c, would almost perswade any, that the matters thus set downe by such persons, and with some shew of probability, were constant and assured proofes thereof: but when they come to the triall, they all vanish away like smoake.

All these claims "are mere idle tales & fancies, without all reason or truth, or shadow of reason or truth."[82]

Parkinson's reaction against writers like Hill, Platt, and Markham, who offered the opportunity for self-advancement through improving nature, repositioned the social significance of gardening and reoriented the connection between experience and truth in natural history. Parkinson's argument reflected a conservative position on social mobility, where nature's ranks served as an allegory of human society. Parkinson particularly valued his own books for distinguishing the common from the rare flowers, whereas earlier herbal and botanical works had not made such a distinction. He criticized Turner and John Gerard for not having "particularly severed those that are beautifull flower plants, fit to store a garden of delight and pleasure, from the wilde and unfit: but have enterlaced many,

[81] Parkinson, *Paradisi*, 21–2.   [82] Ibid., 23–4.

one among another, whereby many that have desired to have faire flowers, have not known either what to choose, or what to desire." His own book, in contrast, was written for those who wanted to choose according to ranks and differences of beauty and rarity: "To satisfie therefore their desires that are lovers of such Delights, I took upon me this labour and charge, and have here selected and set forth a Garden of all the chiefest for choyce, and fairest for shew, from among all the severall Tribes and Kindreds of Natures beauty, and have ranked them as neere as I could, in affinity one unto another."[83] While the earlier husbandry and horticultural manuals scrupulously identified the most useful herbs (in distinction to weeds), they also believed in the mixture of profit and delight, the practical and the beautiful.[84] Parkinson, however, was more concerned to order the society of his garden, with the species set in aesthetic "ranks."

Parkinson's explanation of what constitutes a plant's nature, drawing on a notion of an inalterable "spiritual" essence, has a similar social inflection. In answer to the question of how some gillyflowers came to be double, "if they were not made so by art," Parkinson crisply replied that we just do not know, but that they were naturally so: "we onely have them as nature hath produced them, and so they remaine." He speculated that something added to a plant cannot change it permanently, for such added substances were "corporeal . . . and whatsoever should give any colour unto a living and growing plant, must be spirituall: for no solide corporeall substance can joyne it self with the life and essence of an herbe or tree. . . . For no heterogeneall things can bee mixed naturally together."[85] Whereas in works directed to the middling sort, the gardeners expressed confidence in the human ability to manipulate or improve nature, Parkinson posited for an audience of the better sort a nature resistant to interference while defining a natural "aristocracy" in the botanical world. In this view, which sorts out the better

---

[83] Ibid., epistle to the reader.

[84] See, for example, Lawson's *New Orchard and Garden,* which reiterates the ways in which an orchard offers both "unspeakable delight and infinite commoditie" (54). See also Parkinson on the importance of decorum in the planning of gardens: "I persuade my selfe, that Gentlemen of the better sort and quality, will provide such a parcell of ground to bee laid out for their Garden, and in such convenient manner, as may be fit and answerable to the degree they hold." *Paradisi,* 3.

[85] Ibid., 23, 24. The text continues: "For sents and colours are both such qualities as follow the essence of plants, even as formes are also; and one may as well make any plant to grow of what forme you will, as to make it of what sent or colour you will; and if any man can forme plants at his will and pleasure, he can doe as much as God himselfe that created them."

flowers from the unfit, the plants can be nurtured or killed, but their place in the aesthetic and "social" order cannot be changed.[86]

Thus, when Parkinson condemned the false tales and reports of the horticulturalists in the gardening manuals, and when he offered to tell the truth of his own experience, his contention cannot be separated from his own view of the natural world. The writers' "feigning and boasting" of "what they would have, as if they had it" seems to refer as much to the writers' own social ambition as it does to their tales of extraordinary improvements in nature. For Parkinson, trial and experience are tied less to a claim to know something because of daily labor than they are to the imposition of scientific trial for the sake of establishing the truth. The representation of the earlier horticulturists' reports as "idle" fancies undercuts both their claims of practice and their masculine rhetoric of instruction. Their reports become no better than the "old wives' tales" that Bacon rejected in favor of technical experience.

In his own discussion of altering gillyflowers in *Sylva Sylvarum*, Bacon himself tried to find the middle ground between respecting an immutable aristocracy in nature and retaining the right to change it: This balance, in turn, reflects his complex negotiation of the writing of all kinds of histories, whether of people or nature. Like Parkinson, Bacon contended that "the altering of the scent, colour, or taste of fruit, by infusing, mixing, or letting into the bark or root of the tree, herb, or flower, any coloured, aromatical, or medicinal substance, are but fancies."[87] Yet then the text goes on at length to consider all sorts of horticultural curiosities (even though its author may "hate impostures, and despise curiosities"[88]). Bacon cared to speculate why gillyflowers might be either double or single, whereas Parkinson was just content that they were so:

Take gilly-flower seed, of one kind of gilly-flower, ... and sow it; and there will come up gilly-flowers, some of one colour, and some of another, casually, as the seed meeteth with nourishment in the earth; so that the gardeners find that they may have two or three roots amongst an hundred that are rare and of great price; as purple, carnation of several stripes: the cause is (no doubt) that in earth, though it be contiguous and in one bed, there are very several juices; and as the seed doth casually meet with them, so it cometh forth.[89]

---

[86] For a discussion of the passage from Shakespeare's *The Winter's Tale* on grafting gillyflowers, see Rebecca W. Bushnell, *A Culture of Teaching: Early Modern Humanism in Theory and Practice* (Ithaca, N.Y.: Cornell University Press, 1996), chap. 3.

[87] Bacon, *Sylva Sylvarum*, 2:498–9. [88] Ibid., 501.

[89] Ibid., 504. Bacon also suggests that culture can change the color of a flower: "Amongst curiosities I shall place coloration, though it be somewhat better; for beauty in flowers is

Such an explanation thus implies at once rarity by nature and a random material causation, which could then lend itself to manipulation. This practice Bacon eagerly advocated: "It is a curiosity also to make flowers double; which is effected by often removing them into new earth: as, on the contrary part, double flowers, by neglecting and not removing, prove single. And the way to do it speedily, is to sow or set seeds or slips of flowers; and as soon as they come up, to remove them into new ground that is good."[90] Bacon thus delicately balanced a notion of fixed nature (set in the seed) with recognition of the influence of local conditions, which permited the intervention of the human hand.[91] At the same time, Bacon's experimental "curiosity" is meant to be contrasted with other "fancies" of manipulating nature: The rhetoric implies that while their fancies are mere effects of the imagination, reporting what might only be possible in nature, his "curiosity" is grounded in an analysis of natural processes and causality. Like the Baconian civil historian, who distilled the order of men's lives by systematizing and interpreting the data of human experience, the Baconian natural historian could be a "maker" of nature while still bound to what is given.

When Bacon tentatively and Parkinson vehemently turned against men like Hill and Markham in defying their claims to alter nature, they thus

---

their preeminence. It is observed by some, that gilly-flowers, sweet-williams, violets, that are coloured, if they be neglected, and neither watered, nor new moulded, nor transplanted, will turn white. And it is probable that the white with much culture may turn coloured" (502).

[90] Ibid., 505.

[91] In his essay "Of Gardens" Bacon veered between a naturalist aesthetic (suggested in his distaste for topiary and admiration of a heath) and his effort to create a *ver perpetuum* or perpetual spring in a "Royall Ordering of Gardens." Francis Bacon, "Of Gardens," in *The Essayes or Counsels* (London, 1625), 266. In his *New Atlantis* gardens prosper through the art of grafting and "inoculating," so that they are "by art greater much than their nature." *New Atlantis,* in *Works,* 3:158. It could be argued that aristocrats might see in the improvement of nature "a new freedom based on the power they effortlessly wield over the world" (Comito, *Idea of the Garden,* 2); yet, at the same time, the naturalism of Bacon's ideal garden itself marks an emerging aristocratic aesthetic, at a time when "improvement" might as well be associated with the ambitions of the socially mobile. Tayler writes:

> The "natural garden" is for most historians of taste identified with the eighteenth century, and yet one suspects that the ideal order of the axial pattern decried by the eighteenth century must have seemed nothing so much as natural to the Elizabethan who could see formal order everywhere in Nature. In this sense many painters, gardeners, and writers may be said to anticipate the "natural" *furor hortensis* that agitated later generations. Even Milton, given propitious prelapsarian circumstances, was ready to describe the truly "natural" garden. (*Nature and Art,* 16)

I thank Barbara Riebling for her helpful remarks about Bacon's writing on gardens. See also Le Doeuff, "Man and Nature," 125–6.

signaled a shift in a conflict in the practice of natural history and its uses
of truth and experience. Bacon occupied a middle position: He professed
his dependence on such practitioners of the mechanical arts, just as he
also advocated their kind of experimentation and named it "experience."
Yet he also suggested his suspicion of some of these claims as "fancies."
Bacon's attack on a wide class of human errors in natural history caused
by the imagination, superstition, and tradition came close to demystifying
the claims of the gardener's art; this move accompanied his position that
"man has no power over nature except of motion." At the same time, he
himself sought to tell the story of the transformation in a new way in an
effort to seize its power for himself.

When Parkinson took a further step by attacking the "mechanicals'"
art in telling their story of nature, as well as their practice, he foreshad-
owed the direction taken by later books, such as Robert Sharrock's *The
History of the Propagation and Improvement of Vegetables by the Concurrence of Art and Nature* (2d ed. 1672) and Stephen Blake's *The Compleat Gardeners Practice* (1664), which were also to turn against the
claims of writers of an earlier generation, explicitly comparing their accounts of practice with an older form of historiography and with imaginative literature, whereas Parkinson had been merely allusive. Sharrock,
who was Robert Boyle's publisher and who recognized Bacon as his own
model, complained that he found in the earlier books "a multitude of
monstrous untruths, and prodigies of lies, in both Latine and English, old
and new writers, worse in their kind then the stories in Sir John
Mandevel's Travels or in the History of Fryer Bacon and his man Miles;
or else what may be more, ridiculously removed not only from the truth,
but from any semblance therof." Among these "few writings extant on
these subjects," he says, "some prove altogether useless; as being so full
of their natural Magick and Romantic stories, that we know no more
what to credit in those relations, in the Natural, then what in civil history
we may believe of King Arthur, Guy of Warwick in ours; or of Hector
and Priam in the Trojan story."[92]

Stephen Blake, who protested that his own intent in writing was merely
for the "preventing of publick dangers, not for the gaining of filthy lucre,
or the purchasing of vain glory, but for the gaining of a free conscience, and
purchasing of the society and love of just and wise men," also saw the

---

[92] Robert Sharrock, *The History of the Propagation and Improvement of Vegetables by the
Concurrence of Art and Nature*, 2d ed. (London, 1672), epistle dedicatory, 2.

earlier books on the subject as full of "vanities and ostentation."[93] Some books, he said, were as "uncreditable as the stories of Robin Hood."[94] Like Parkinson, Blake, too, was to object that "some men are of the opinion when they see this beautifull Flower [the gillyflower], as to think it of an art of their own, or others, but they are mistaken, [for] all the art of man is to find out the art of nature itself, for if any thing be not used in its own nature and season it will come to no effect."[95] He discussed in turn each of the claims that earlier writers had made to alter color, scent, and form, and rejected them; about claims that grafting would produce a flower of mixed color, for example, he wrote: "I could not give any credit to their words, as to believe them, for why, each of them keeps their own nature."[96] In response to those readers who might complain that he gave no rules for such practices, Blake made this retort: "That these intercisions and supplies, are but conceits took up upon trust, and never made good by practice, and therefore I shall not dispense with the time to answer them in particular, and swell up my Book about such uncertain, vain, and needlesse curiosities which are unpractical, and that is more, they were never affected, and so I wave the Discourse."[97] Experience and trial were thus turned against the men who had claimed them as the basis for their own authority. Their stories, in turn, became for Parkinson, Blake, and Sharrock, with many others who followed, no better than "old wives' tales," where social status was collapsed with the category of gender in an act of dismissal. Crucial to this move was the control of the alteration of "nature," whether construed literally, in the plant world, or metaphorically, as the social status quo. The recounting of early modern natural history, which depicted nature through both human uses and human social models, thus was itself indelibly marked with the social struggles of the men who unfolded it.

---

[93] Stephen Blake, preface to the reader to *The Compleat Gardeners Practice, Directing the Exact Way of Gardening in Three Parts* (London, 1664).

[94] Blake, *Compleat Gardeners Practice*, 71.   [95] Ibid., 26.   [96] Ibid., 23.   [97] Ibid., 65.

9

Thomas Hobbes's Machiavellian moments

DAVID WOOTTON

> ... and the weak yield to such conditions as they can get.
> – Thomas Hobbes's translation of *The History of the Grecian War*
> *Written by Thucydides* (1629)

Behemoth was written in or around 1667; *Leviathan* was published in 1651. But I want to start earlier. Just how early one can safely start is, as we will shortly see, a difficult question. For now let us stay on safe ground. In 1629 Hobbes published his translation of Thucydides, including that most compact of all analyses of power politics, the Melian dialogue. There the Athenian ambassadors swiftly reject arguments from right, justice, or principle as irrelevant, and assume such arguments will be recognized to be so:

But out of those things which we both of us do really think, let us go through with that which is feasible; both you and we knowing, that in human disputation justice is then only agreed on when the necessity is equal; whereas they that have odds of power exact as much as they can, and the weak yield to such conditions as they can get.[1]

There is an evident similarity between the Athenian view and Hobbes's insistence over twenty years later in *Leviathan* that there could be neither contract nor justice without a sovereign authority. Yet recent scholarship has tended to take Hobbes at his word when he insists that *Leviathan* is a work of geometrical and not historical argument, written under the influ-

---

[1] Thomas Hobbes, trans., *The History of the Grecian War Written by Thucydides*, in *The English Works of Thomas Hobbes*, ed. W. Molesworth (London: John Bohn, 1839–45), 9:99. The dialogue is discussed by Hobbes in "Of the Life and History of Thucydides," in *English Works*, 8:xxviii–xxix.

ence of Euclid and not Thucydides.[2] Consequently hardly anyone refers
to the Melian dialogue when interpreting *Leviathan*.[3] Hobbes the translator of history is presumed to be irrelevant to Hobbes the theorist of
politics. Yet Hobbes was more than a mere translator of history, for he
was, in his mature years, a historian, and a student, therefore, of "that
which is feasible," of might as well as right.

It is with this practical Hobbes that I am concerned here. My concern
is not with Hobbes as a teller of true stories, but with Hobbes as a reader
of history and analyst of human behavior. I believe the structure of *Leviathan* conceals the extent of Hobbes's debt to a reading of Thucydides,
Tacitus, Niccolò Machiavelli, and Justus Lipsius, to a tradition of philosophical history. Resituating him in that context serves, I hope, to illustrate the power and range of historical thought in the early modern
period. Hobbes is conventionally associated with the new science, but he
was also deeply imbued with the humanist culture of his day, and it is in
the terms provided by this culture that he thought about practical politics. Hobbes may have condemned the reading of "the books of Policy,
and Histories of the antient Greeks, and Romans" as being responsible
for tyrannophobia,[4] but there was nowhere else one could turn if one
wanted to discover the practical policies that would enable a ruler to
acquire unchecked power, and this question is one to which Hobbes must
have given considerable thought. As Leo Strauss put it, "in the new
political philosophy, history is "taken up" and conserved."[5]

I have two main arguments to put forward: first, that Hobbes's politics were Machiavellian,[6] and second, that they were, consequently, ex-

---

[2] See, however, Quentin Skinner, "*Scientia Civilis* in Classical Rhetoric and in the Early
Hobbes," in *Political Discourse in Early Modern Britain,* ed. Nicholas Phillipson and
Quentin Skinner (Cambridge: Cambridge University Press, 1993), 77–80; Gabriella
Slomp, "Hobbes, Thucydides and the Three Greatest Things," *History of Political Thought*
11 (1990): 565–86; and the literature cited by Slomp, 565–6.

[3] Although Quentin Skinner's *Reason and Rhetoric in the Philosophy of Hobbes* (Cambridge: Cambridge University Press, 1996) places a salutary emphasis on Hobbes's humanist preoccupations, it pays little attention to the role of force and fear in Hobbes's thought
(though note pp. 388–9). Skinner's discussions of Hobbes's Thucydides (161, 229–30,
242, 244–9, 282–3, 286–7, 342–3) and his *Behemoth* (431–6) consequently concentrate
on different aspects from those emphasized here, and he does not mention the Melian
dialogue, or offer a Machiavellian reading of Hobbes.

[4] Thomas Hobbes, *Leviathan,* ed. C. B. Macpherson (Harmondsworth, England: Penguin
Books, 1968), 369–70.

[5] Leo Strauss, *The Political Philosophy of Hobbes* (Oxford: Clarendon Press, 1936), 96.
Chap. 6 of this book is one of the few serious discussions of my subject.

[6] I owe my title, of course, to J. G. A. Pocock's *The Machiavellian Moment* (Princeton:
Princeton University Press, 1975). That *Leviathan* marks a Machiavellian moment is

tremely illiberal. The first argument is a new one.[7] It remains valid, I believe, even if one confines oneself (as I will not) to the evidence to be found in the texts of *Leviathan* and *Behemoth*. The second is an old one that, given the character of much of the recent literature on Hobbes, needs to be restated.

In an exam paper on the history of political theory, "Compare the political thought of Machiavelli and Hobbes" would be a reasonable question. Some students might welcome the opportunity to discuss the supposedly secular nature of both Machiavelli's and Hobbes's thought, their views on self-interest and violence, their attitudes toward absolutism, and the hostile responses of contemporaries to their work. Having discussed "Hobbes's affinities with Machiavelli," a good student would seek out the contrasts between them, arguing, perhaps, that Machiavelli's values are "masculine," Hobbes's "feminine."[8] A stylish answer would contain comments like Alan Ryan's: "Hobbes resembles Machiavelli in writing with great zest of a grim business."[9] But a student who went too far and argued that Hobbes was essentially Machiavellian would quickly be dismissed as "wayward."[10]

"Discuss Hobbes's use of Machiavelli," by contrast, would not be regarded as a reasonable question, for a student could rightly complain that it was impossible to answer. Yet a discussion of Hobbes as historian requires, I believe, that we address this question, even if Hobbes never once mentions Machiavelli.[11] Not surprisingly, the average book on Hobbes contains one or more passing references to Machiavelli, but con-

admitted (but only so the point can be dismissed) by Conal Condren, "Casuistry to Newcastle: *The Prince* in the World of the Book," in *Political Discourse in Early Modern Britain,* ed. Phillipson and Skinner, 184.

[7] But see now Arlene W. Saxonhouse, "Hobbes and the Beginnings of Modern Political Thought," in Thomas Hobbes, *Three Discourses,* ed. Noel B. Reynolds and Arlene W. Saxonhouse (Chicago: University of Chicago Press, 1995), 123–54.

[8] Mary G. Dietz, "Hobbes's Subject as Citizen," in *Thomas Hobbes and Political Theory,* ed. Dietz (Lawrence, Kans.: University Press of Kansas, 1990), 116.

[9] Alan Ryan, "Hobbes and Individualism," in *Perspectives on Thomas Hobbes,* ed. G. A. J. Rogers and Alan Ryan (Oxford: Clarendon Press, 1988), 104.

[10] "It would of course be just as wayward to claim that Hobbes too was essentially Machiavellian." Condren, "Casuistry to Newcastle," 184. See also the way in which Hobbes and Machiavelli are taken to stand for opposite values in Jonathan Scott, "The Rapture of Motion: James Harrington's Republicanism," in *Political Discourse in Early Modern Britain,* ed. Phillipson and Skinner, 162.

[11] He does mention the more respectable Lipsius in his "Life and History of Thucydides," 8:xxxi–xxxii. A more moderate version of my argument would claim that Hobbes was influenced by the reason-of-state literature that descended from Machiavelli. I do not adopt this line of argument because I am impressed by Hobbes's refusal to moralize his Machiavelli along the lines recommended by authors such as Lipsius.

tains no discussion of Hobbes's use of Machiavelli.[12] Books that one might expect to address the question – Felix Raab's *English Face of Machiavelli,* or J. G. A. Pocock's *Machiavellian Moment* – have nothing to say about it.[13] Our greatest Hobbes scholar, Quentin Skinner, is also our leading Machiavelli scholar: But he, too, has had nothing to say on Machiavelli *and* Hobbes. If one substitutes Leo Strauss's name for Quentin Skinner's in the previous sentence the conclusion still follows.[14] Or one can turn to a conventional textbook, such as John Plamenatz's *Man and Society*: There comparisons between Machiavelli and Hobbes are made in passing, but the assumption is that Machiavelli is interested in history, Hobbes in theory; Machiavelli in social man, Hobbes in presocial man; and that consequently the two exist in different worlds.[15]

In this essay I will argue that there are echoes of Machiavelli in Hobbes. In principle my undertaking is similar to that of Skinner when he finds echoes of Quintilian and Cicero in Hobbes, or that of Blair Worden when he finds echoes of Machiavelli in Milton.[16] Unfortunately my case is not as conclusive as theirs because, for the most part, I will be pointing to similarities in ideas, arguments, and preoccupations, rather than similarities in language or turns of phrase. I believe the similarities I identify are sufficiently evident as to justify the claim that Hobbes was using Machiavelli; and, as we shall see, my argument is strengthened by (although it is not dependent on) further evidence of a preoccupation with reason-of-state theory, certainly in Hobbes's circle, and perhaps on the part of Hobbes himself.

---

[12] Condren thinks Machiavelli is widely assumed to have influenced Hobbes, but the examples he cites hardly establish this, although one could obviously add to them: e.g., Gary B. Herbert, *Thomas Hobbes: The Unity of Scientific and Moral Wisdom* (Vancouver: University of British Columbia Press, 1989), 13, 18, 171; and (more significantly) Paul Rahe, *Republics Ancient and Modern* (Chapel Hill: University of North Carolina Press, 1992), 266, 369, 372, 380. Nevertheless, Condren's own view, far from being iconoclastic, is, I believe, dominant: "If when dealing with the possible relationships between Hobbes and Machiavelli, inquiries had been organized around the category of usage rather than influence, it is difficult to see how the fact that Hobbes gives no evidence of using Machiavelli could have been so often overlooked." Conal Condren, *The Status and Appraisal of Classic Texts* (Princeton: Princeton University Press, 1985), 136.

[13] Felix Raab, *The English Face of Machiavelli. A Changing Interpretation, 1500–1700* (London: Routledge and Keegan Paul, 1964). For Pocock, see above, n. 6.

[14] For Skinner, see above, n. 4. For Leo Strauss, see *The Political Philosophy of Hobbes: Its Basis and its Genesis,* trans. E. M. Sinclair (Chicago: University of Chicago Press, 1963); and *Natural Right and History* (Chicago: University of Chicago Press, 1953).

[15] John Plamenatz, *Man and Society* (London: Longmans, 1963), 1:1–7, 18–19, 24–5.

[16] Blair Worden, "Milton's Republicanism and the Tyranny of Heaven," in *Machiavelli and Republicanism,* ed. Gisela Bock, Quentin Skinner, and Maurizio Viroli (Cambridge: Cambridge University Press, 1990), 225–45.

It would be pedantic to point out that the libraries in which Hobbes worked contained the works of Machiavelli.[17] Of course they did, and we must assume that at some point or other Hobbes read Machiavelli, and decided what he thought of him. That Hobbes never bothers to refer to Machiavelli might lead one to think that the reading was desultory, the judgment summary, but I rather doubt it. Remember that Francis Bacon, Hobbes's friend and employer, was a careful student of Machiavelli. Remember that James Harrington, long before Strauss, first declared that Machiavelli and Hobbes were the founders of modern political theory: if Hobbes had paid little attention to Machiavelli beforehand, it is hard to imagine his not pausing to assess Harrington's claim, if only for reasons of vanity. Remember, too, that Harrington was not alone in turning to Machiavelli in the 1650s: the earl of Clarendon and Marchamont Nedham, John Lilburne and Edward Sexby, John Milton and Andrew Marvell, anybody and everybody read him in order to understand how a new prince, Oliver Cromwell, had come to seize power. In the 1650s (and again during the Exclusion Crisis, when Machiavelli could be described as an author "much studied of late"[18]) Machiavelli was not a mere classic. He had all the relevance of an analyst of contemporary politics. Hobbes had, at the least, the same motives for reading Machiavelli as everyone else did.

For whatever reason and at whatever moment Hobbes turned to Machiavelli, he did more, I want to argue, than passively read him. He taught himself to think like him, and persuaded himself that Hobbism and Machiavellism went hand in hand. This should be evident to anyone who accepts the recent claim that Hobbes wrote three discourses published in 1620 in an anonymous work, *Horae Subsecivae*.[19] We know that the majority of the essays in this volume were written by William Cavendish, Hobbes's pupil and, from 1626 until his death in 1628, second earl of

---

[17] See Richard Tuck, *Philosophy and Government, 1572–1651* (Cambridge: Cambridge University Press, 1993), 282; and Rahe, *Republics Ancient and Modern*, 366.

[18] Edward Cooke, *Memorabilia* (1681) cited in Condren, "Casuistry to Newscastle," 171.

[19] Noel B. Reynolds and John L. Hilton, "Thomas Hobbes and Authorship of the *Horae Subsecivae*," *History of Political Thought* 14 (1993): 361–80. See my discussion of the *Horae Subsecivae* in "A Perpetual Object of Hatred to All Theologians," *London Review of Books* (20 April 1995); and Richard Tuck, "Hobbes's Moral Philosophy," in *The Cambridge Companion to Hobbes*, ed. Tom Sorrell (Cambridge: Cambridge University Press, 1996), 199. I am grateful to Fritz Levy for first drawing the *Horae* to my attention. The Hobbesian material in the *Horae* has now been reprinted in Hobbes, *Three Discourses*, but I continue to cite the 1620 edition, whose pagination is reproduced in the edition of Reynolds and Saxonhouse.

Devonshire.[20] Computer analysis suggests that three of the longer essays, the "Discourse upon the Beginning of Tacitus," the "Discourse of Rome," and the "Discourse of Laws," are written in a different style, and that this style is indistinguishable from that of Hobbes. There is some internal evidence to support the claim that these essays have a different author from the others in the book. Not only does the style seem different, but their author has none of the aristocratic self-esteem of Cavendish, nor is he so prompt to express conventional religious opinions. (Indeed, his views seem distinctly unconventional: Natural scientists, he tells us, are bound to "count the manifestation of religion foolishness," while he himself has no patience with those who "turn the image of an *incorruptible* God into the likeness of a corruptible man. . . . I dare walk no further in this labyrinth, for fear of growing too infinite.") Both the opinions and the style seem to be those of Thomas Hobbes. I offer one phase to stand for many: "all men being of this condition, that desire and hope of good more affecteth them than fruition, for this induceth satiety, but hope is a whetstone to men's desires, and will not suffer them to languish."[21]

If this attribution is correct, then the claim that Hobbes was a close student of Machiavelli follows straightforwardly, for the "Discourse upon the Beginning of Tacitus" constantly echoes Machiavellian themes and problems. Its subject is a quintessentially Machiavellian one, the steps that should be taken by a new prince (in this case, Augustus) to hold on to power, explored in the light of a perception never spelled out by Machiavelli but present throughout his work: "though violence cannot last, yet the effects of it may; and that which is gotten violently, may be afterwards possessed quietly and constantly."[22] Throughout it focuses on problems identified by Machiavelli, such as the problem of how a prince should deal with a general in his service who is all too successful: "great services procure many times rather the hatred than the love of him they are done unto." In this context both Machiavelli and Hobbes are struck

---

[20] This point is not recognized by Arlene W. Saxonhouse, "Hobbes and the *Horae Subsecivae*," *Polity* 13 (1981): 541–67; and Friedrich D. Wolf, *Die neue Wissenschaft des Thomas Hobbes* (Stuttgart: Friedrich Fromann, 1969). See Douglas Bush, "Hobbes, William Cavendish and "Essayes,"" *Notes and Queries,* new series 20 (May 1973): 162–4; and Noel Malcolm, "Hobbes, Sandys, and the Virginia Company," *Historical Journal* 24 (1981): 320–1. Strauss, who first drew attention to those essays by Cavendish, had the good sense not to attribute them to Hobbes, while at the same time finding them Hobbesian in character. *Political Philosophy of Hobbes,* xii–xiii.

[21] Anon., *Horae Subsecivae* (London, 1620), 361–3, 291.

[22] Ibid., 234. Niccolò Machiavelli, *Discorsi sopra la prima deca di Tito Livio*, ed. Corrado Vivanti (Turin: Einaudi, 1983), 116.

by the same sentence from Tacitus's *Histories:* "benefits received are pleasing so long as they be requitable."[23] Its arguments are those of someone steeped in reason-of-state discourse. For example: "To whomsoever comes the profit of strange and unexpected accidents, to him also, for the most part, is imputed the contriving and effecting of them, if they be thought able," or "For there is no man that doth an injury to another, and scapeth with it, but will attribute his impunity to want of power in his adversary (for there be few that want will to revenge disgraces)."[24]

That the author of these discourses is familiar with Machiavelli seems evident. If he is Hobbes, then long before he published his translation of the Melian dialogue, Hobbes was wedded to Machiavellian modes of analysis. It was, it would seem, in the context of the humanist preoccupation with history and the Machiavellian study of politics that Hobbes developed those rudiments of his political philosophy that we find in the discourses. The "Discourse of Laws" in particular contains a striking premonition of the argument of *Leviathan,* written long before Hobbes's famous encounter with Euclid, and probably long before his development of a systematically materialist natural philosophy, both of which are normally supposed to be preconditions for Hobbism:

If men were not limited within certain rules, such confusion would follow in government that all the differences in right and wrong, just and unlawful, could never be distinguished; and that would cause such distraction in the people, and give so great an overthrow to conversation and commerce amongst men, that all right would be perverted by power, and all honesty swayed by greatness: So that the equal administration of justice is the true knot that binds us to unity and peace amongst ourselves, and disperseth all such violent and unlawful courses as otherwise liberty would insinuate, preserving every man in his right, and preventing others, who if they thought their actions might pass with impunity, would not measure their courses by the rule of Aequum and Justum, but by the square of their own benefit, and affections. And so, not being circumscribed within reasonable bounds, their reason becomes invisible; whereas when they find that Justice hath a predominant power, they are deterred from proceeding in those acts that otherwise their own wills and inclination would give them leave to effect.[25]

Present in embryo in this passage is the notion of a state of nature in which individuals have a right to all things; and the insistence that justice must have "a predominant power" is an important step toward Hobbes's portrait of the state as Leviathan.

---

[23] Anon., *Horae Subsecivae,* 280, 279. For evidence of Cavendish's (and by implication Hobbes's) familiarity with reason-of-state theorists, see the essay by Cavendish "Of Affectation" in *Horae Subsecivae,* 30–51.

[24] Ibid., 289, 302. [25] Ibid., 507–8.

One can reasonably suspect that Hobbes is indeed the author of the three discourses, but no final proof of this is likely to be forthcoming. Consequently, I will avoid relying upon this attribution hereafter. I want instead to turn to a text that is unquestionably by Hobbes, *Behemoth*. *Behemoth* is not only a study in "that which is feasible" but is also, I will argue, a self-consciously Machiavellian text. Failure to recognize this has been an obstacle to understanding what Hobbes is doing in writing history. If these claims are correct, then we should also be prepared to talk about Machiavelli's influence on *Leviathan,* and about the intimate relationship between Hobbes's political philosophy and Machiavelli's.

Behemoth was probably written in 1667, around the time of the fall of Clarendon, when the Restoration regime was experiencing its first major crisis. "In that year, when the Dutch fleet penetrated the Medway, and when Englishmen nostalgically recalled the foreign exploits and the healthy frugality of Puritan rule, the restored monarchy looked to be in serious trouble."[26] Republicanism, apparently decisively defeated in 1660, was getting its second wind. Charles II, at Hobbes's request, read *Behemoth* in manuscript. Hobbes can scarcely have been surprised when he forbade its publication. Five editions, however, appeared in 1679–80, at the height of the Exclusion Crisis, when a new civil war was widely forecast and feared.[27] In 1682, after Hobbes's death, his publisher (who had been forbidden by Hobbes to have anything to do with publication of a work banned by the king) was free to produce a corrected edition, which was printed the same year in a collection entitled *Tracts of Mr Thomas Hobbes*. With seven editions in four years, *Behemoth* was off to a flying start, and it would surely have been hard to predict its future failure, but the record from this point is bleak: Included in various editions of collected works and selected tracts (1750, 1815, and 1839–45), *Behemoth* was not to be republished in its own right until the Tönnies edition of 1889, an edition reprinted in 1969 with an introduction by Maurice Goldsmith and in 1990 with an introduction by Stephen Holmes.[28] Eventually a scholarly edition will appear in the Clarendon series, but in the meantime the nearest thing to such an edition is the

---

[26] Blair Worden, "Republicanism and the Restoration, 1660–1683," in *Republicanism and Commercial Society,* ed. David Wootton (Stanford: Stanford University Press, 1994), 139.

[27] One contemporary refutation was also published, J. Whitehall's *Behemoth Arraigned* (London, 1680).

[28] I cite this last edition, Thomas Hobbes, *Behemoth or The Long Parliament,* ed. Ferdinand Tönnies, introd. Stephen Holmes (Chicago: University of Chicago Press, 1990); the pagination is that of the original Tönnies edition.

French translation (1990), and the most careful historical introduction is that accompanying the Italian translation (1979).[29]

The conclusion is inescapable. This is a work that, at least until recently, has attracted neither scholars nor a wider public. Modern scholarship on *Behemoth*, indeed, began only in 1970, with the publication of an article by Royce MacGillivray. The library shelves groan under the weight of commentaries on *Leviathan,* but the literature on *Behemoth* fits neatly into a small folder. At least there is now a literature, however slight. Over the last few years, indeed, a number of scholars have argued that *Behemoth* ought to be central to any understanding of Hobbes. In 1978 Richard Ashcraft claimed that *Behemoth* showed that Hobbes understood clearly the role of class and ideology in the political process: If the world of *Leviathan* appeared to be a world of isolated individuals this was because Hobbes was deliberately seeking to turn people's minds away from the real-life political conflict he so accurately described in *Behemoth*. In a pair of articles and a book Robert Kraynak has argued that the ahistorical character of the argument of *Leviathan* has prevented people from recognizing that Hobbes's views were grounded in a historical analysis of conflict, an analysis epitomized in *Behemoth*. In his valuable introduction to the Chicago reprint of the Tönnies edition, Stephen Holmes stresses that a reading of *Behemoth* forces us to rethink conventional interpretations of *Leviathan* as an account of how rational utility-maximizers ought to behave: Hobbes's psychology is far too complex and subtle to reduce human behavior to such simple terms. Best of all, I think, S. A. Lloyd has argued that conventional interpretations of *Leviathan* underplay Hobbes's central preoccupation with religion. She employs *Behemoth* to validate a substantial reinterpretation of *Leviathan* as an attempt to resolve conflict, not between rational utility-maximizers, but between people with differing views about transcendent principles.[30]

---

[29] The Clarendon edition will be edited by Paul Seaward. The French translation is *Béhémoth ou le long parliament,* ed. and trans. Luc Borot (Paris: Librairie Philosophique J. Vrin, 1990); the Italian is *Behemoth,* ed. and trans. Onofrio Nicastro (Rome: Editori Laterza, 1979).

[30] The article by Royce MacGillivray is "Thomas Hobbes's History of the English Civil War: A Study of *Behemoth,*" *Journal of the History of Ideas* 31 (1970): 179–99. See also R. MacGillivray, *Restoration Historians and the English Civil War* (The Hague: Marinus Nijhoff, 1974). The article by Richard Ashcraft is "Ideology and Class in Hobbes's Political Theory," *Political Theory* 6 (1978): 27–62. The works by Robert P. Kraynak are "Hobbes's *Behemoth* and the Argument for Absolutism," *American Political Science Review* 76 (1982): 837–47; "Hobbes on Barbarism and Civilization," *Journal of Politics* 45 (1983): 86–109; and *History and Modernity in the Thought of Thomas Hobbes* (Ithaca, N.Y.: Cornell University Press, 1990). In addition to his introduction to the

So, there is, at last, a literature on *Behemoth,* although the novelty of the subject is betrayed in the mistakes that scholars make: Kraynak, for example, thinks *Behemoth* was published only after Hobbes's death, though there were, as we have seen, five (admittedly unauthorized) editions during his lifetime.[31] But this literature has been produced by scholars primarily interested in interpreting *Leviathan.* What they look for in *Behemoth* is something that either contrasts with, or corresponds to, what they believe is to be found in *Leviathan. Behemoth* is now read, simply and solely, as a Hobbesian text.

Let us, for the moment, put *Leviathan* to one side and instead consider *Behemoth* as a work of history: Until we can place the text within a tradition of historical writing, we are unlikely to be able to understand what Hobbes was trying to accomplish in writing it. Let us start with Hobbes's dedication, to Sir Henry Bennett:

> I present your Lordship with four short dialogues concerning the memorable civil war in his Majesty's dominions from 1640 to 1660. The first contains the seed of it, certain opinions in divinity and politics. The second hath the growth of it in declarations, remonstrances, and other writings between the King and Parliament published. The two last are a very short epitome of the war itself, drawn out of Mr. Heath's chronicle.[32]

This, it should at once be apparent, is not a conventional history book. Just how unconventional it is may be recognized by comparing it with Hobbes's preface to his translation of Thucydides.[33] There he praises Thucydides for confining himself to narrative, without discussing causes and consequences, and for rigidly sticking to chronology, advancing half year by half year from beginning to end. Thucydides's great achievement, Hobbes tells us, was to provide a description so lifelike that it was a valid substitute for experience: Reading Thucydides was as good as being

---

Chicago reprint of the Tönnies edition, see Stephen Holmes, "Political Psychology in Hobbes's *Behemoth,*" in *Thomas Hobbes and Political Theory,* ed. Dietz, 120–52. Also relevant are Mary G. Dietz, "Hobbes's Subject as Citizen," ibid., 91–119; and Deborah Baumgold, "Hobbes's Political Sensibility: The Menace of Political Ambition," ibid., 74–90. The essay by S. A. Lloyd is "Theory in Practice: *Leviathan* and *Behemoth,*" in *Ideals as Interests in Hobbes's Leviathan* (Cambridge: Cambridge University Press, 1992), 189–231. Literature on *Behemoth* also includes Noam Flinker, "The View from the "Devil's Mountain": Dramatic Tension in Hobbes's *Behemoth,*" *Hobbes Studies* 2 (1989): 10–22; and William R. Lund, "Hobbes on Opinion, Private Judgment and Civil War," *History of Political Thought* 13 (1992): 55–72.

[31] Tuck, *Philosophy and Government,* gets this right on p. 341 but wrong on p. 344.

[32] Tönnies prints this dedication before his own preface.

[33] Hobbes, "To the Readers," *English Works,* 8:vii–xi; see also "The Life and History of Thucydides," xxvi–xxxii.

there. In *Behemoth* we have, by contrast, not a narrative, but a dialogue; a very loose chronology (the "certain opinions in divinity and politics" turn out to include the views of Moses and Cicero); and the opposite of a lifelike story, a bald epitome.

For a twentieth-century reader of Hobbes, the sheer eccentricity of the form of *Behemoth* may not be immediately apparent. We are used to history books that are, as *Behemoth* is, about causes and consequences, about long-term factors and short-term triggers. Readers of Hobbes's day (even readers of the next century) were not. Why throw aside the long-established conventions of historical discourse, which were as alive for Francesco Guicciardini or Clarendon as they had been for Livy or Tacitus and which had changed little in the meantime? The answer, I suspect, is to be found yet again in Hobbes's preface to Thucydides. There he defends Thucydides against the charge that he is hard to understand. Of course, Hobbes replies, you will be unable to make sense of Thucydides if you do not understand how the world works. You have to bring to Thucydides a grasp of how and why things happen in order to make sense of him; if his history is a substitute for experience, it is not a substitute for interpretation.[34] *Behemoth* is the opposite of Thucydides, just as the anonymous "Discourse upon the Beginning of Tacitus" is the opposite of Tacitus himself. In *Behemoth* Hobbes offers, above all, interpretation, so that those who experienced the war but failed to learn from it can be taught the right conclusions. History as a substitute for experience must have seemed woefully insufficient at a moment when England, with the experience of civil war far from forgotten, seemed in the process of repeating old mistakes, endangering new stability. Instead Hobbes offers "the history, not so much of those actions that passed in the time of the late troubles, as of their causes, and of the counsels and artifice by which they were brought to pass."[35]

In order to write this new type of history, Hobbes has to abandon chronology. The founding of preaching orders and of universities in the thirteenth century is, he insists, relevant to his story. The preaching orders and universities contain the seeds of contemporary conflicts, even if they may have lain dormant for centuries. Then there is "the growth": the period beginning, at the latest, with the Petition of Right, when the issues around which the war would be fought were crystallizing. Finally there is

[34] Hobbes, "Life and History of Thucydides," xxix–xxx.   [35] *Behemoth*, 45.

the war itself. This tripartite division marks the emergence of a new way of thinking about history. It would be helpful, I think, if readers of *Behemoth* had in mind not *Leviathan* but a great history book from our own century, Fernand Braudel's *Mediterranean*. As part of the *Annales* school's revolt against mere narrative history, Braudel started by writing a history of things that do not change, or scarcely change, as the centuries go by (climate, geography, trade routes); he then discussed things that change in the medium term (economic cycles, demographic fluctuations); and only then did he describe a specific series of events, a war. This is Hobbes's method. In the first place he is interested in a culture that has, for over a thousand years, brought intellectuals and priests into conflict with the state. It is this culture that is the underlying cause of the civil war. Second, he is interested in a medium-term development, the growth of Presbyterianism and of what modern historians call the common law mind. And third, he wants to tell, against this larger backdrop, the story of the war. Hobbes is perhaps the first to see that these are the three basic temporal scales that need to be part of any historical explanation, and the first to struggle with the formal problem of combining these three scales within one story. If Hobbes began by defending Thucydides against the charge that he was shackled to chronology and reluctant to look beneath the surface of events, it would seem that he ended up persuaded that Thucydides was not the model to imitate. He would have to look elsewhere.

Strangely, no one has ever asked what Hobbes's models were in writing *Behemoth*. *Leviathan* is so obviously a book without parallel that Hobbes scholars are unaccustomed to thinking in terms of imitation. And, of course, Hobbes is no help to anyone who does ask such a question. He mentions four modern works in *Behemoth*: James Heath's chronicle; Richard Allestree's *The Whole Duty of a Christian Man* as an example of Anglican moral philosophy; Philippe Du Plessis Mornay's *Mystery of Iniquity*; and Thomas Morton's *Grand Imposture*. None of them is very helpful for understanding Hobbes. Leaving them aside, I think we can identify two authors who influenced *Behemoth*.

The subject of Hobbes's first dialogue is the long-term conflict between the clergy (including, of course, university teachers) and the state. For any English intellectual in the middle of the seventeenth century there was one author who would at once have sprung to mind as both the great authority on the relative rights of church and state and the great historian of the evolution of the church's claims. That author was Paolo Sarpi. He had

222   DAVID WOOTTON

written a series of tracts in defense of Venice when it had been placed under
interdict in 1606 for contesting the jurisdictional claims of the papacy; he
had written *History of Benefices*, in which he had argued that the evolution
of the church's doctrine and institutions over the centuries had been
shaped by its efforts to maximize the wealth under clerical, and ultimately
papal, control (as Hobbes puts it: "They are the questions of authority and
power over the Church, or of profit, or of honour to Churchmen, that for
the most part raise all controversies"[36]); and he had written *History of the
Council of Trent.* All English intellectuals of the mid-seventeenth century
were familiar with Sarpi's works, but Hobbes was probably particularly
familiar with them: He had perhaps met Sarpi, and he had certainly translated and annotated his correspondence.[37] When he set out to write about
the "seed" of church-state conflict, Sarpi was, I suspect, his model: What
he had to do was show how Sarpi's discussion of Catholicism could be
extended to include an account of the "magisterial" (to use a term
employed by modern historians) Reformation. In writing a rigorously
Erastian history, in stressing the threat orthodox Christianity posed for
political authority, Hobbes was treading in Sarpi's footsteps. He would
probably have been perfectly happy to admit as much.

Hobbes's interest in long-term causes is reminiscent of Sarpi. But it is,
of course, reminiscent of Machiavelli as well. Why, Machiavelli asked,
was Italy not united? Because of the power of the papacy. Why did
republics survive in the Holy Roman Empire? Because of the peculiar
balance of power within the imperial system.[38] In the pages of *The Prince*
and *The Discourses* such long-term causes jostle uncomfortably with the
analysis of individual moments, just as they do in *Behemoth.* Machiavelli
was the preeminent authority on causes, counsels, and artifices.

Hobbes, though, claimed that, unlike any of his predecessors, he had a
scientific conception of the nature of political authority, and one naturally turns to *Behemoth* to find a clear expression of Hobbes's political
philosophy. What one finds is in fact extremely confusing, for at different

---

36 Ibid., 63.
37 On Sarpi and Hobbes, see Vittorio Gabrieli, "Bacone, la Riforma e Roma nella versione
   Hobbesiana d'un carteggio di Fulgenzio Micanzio," *English Miscellany* 8 (1957): 195–
   250; David Wootton, *Paolo Sarpi: From Renaissance to Enlightenment* (Cambridge:
   Cambridge University Press, 1983), 117, 169; Richard Tuck, *Hobbes* (Oxford: Oxford
   University Press, 1989), 1–11; Tuck, *Philosophy and Government,* 281, 333; and Paul
   Rahe, *Republics Ancient and Modern,* 367, 970.
38 Niccolò Machiavelli, *Il principe,* ed. F. Chabod and L. Firpo (Turin: Einaudi, 1961),
   chaps. 10–11.

moments Hobbes provides a series of quite different accounts of political power. Here is a sample:

- Power lies in consent: "The sovereign power is essentially annexed to the representative of the people."[39]
- Power lies in public opinion: "The power of the mighty hath no foundation but in the opinion and belief of the people."[40]
- Power lies in obedience: "It is not the right of the sovereign, though granted to him by everyman's express consent, that can enable him to do his office; it is the obedience of the subject which must do that."[41]
- Power grows out of the barrel of a gun: "He that hath the power of levying and commanding the soldiers has all other rights of sovereignty which he shall please to claim."[42]
- Money is power: "If the king had money he might have had soldiers enough."[43]

The situation is even worse if we try to apply these five descriptions of power to England in 1640. "In the year 1640," says "A," who speaks for Hobbes, "the government in England was monarchical." Yet the people thought it was Parliament, not the King, who was their representative. Most people did not realize that they were under an obligation to obey the king, if, for example, he raised taxes without parliamentary consent. He was unable, in practice, to command obedience. He had no troops, and no money. It is not surprising that "B," A's student, should conclude: "In such a condition of people, methinks, the King is already ousted of his government."[44]

If the King was already ousted of his government in 1640, why should one have supported him during the civil war? The de factoist arguments that are often attributed to Hobbes would appear to justify the conclusion that in 1640 it was already Parliament that held power, and that it was the king, not Parliament, who was the rebel. Hobbes does not agree:

The greatest part of the Lords in Parliament, and of the gentry throughout England, were more affected to monarchy than to a popular government, but so as not to endure to hear of the King's absolute power; which made them in time of Parliament easily to condescend to abridge it, and bring the government to a mixed monarchy, as they called it; wherein the absolute sovereignty should be divided.[45]

---

[39] Hobbes, *Behemoth*, 180.
[40] Ibid., 16. Opinion is evidently shaped by rhetoric, on which see below, n. 96.
[41] Ibid., 144.
[42] Ibid., 80; see also 79, 102; and compare Hobbes, *Leviathan*, 235; and Cavendish, *Advice* (below, n. 78), cited in Condren, "Casuistry to Newcastle," 174.
[43] Hobbes, *Behemoth*, 2.   [44] Ibid., 1, 4.   [45] Ibid., 33.

Since in Hobbes's view the whole notion of mixed monarchy is incoherent, there was no satisfactory way of establishing, in 1640, where power lay: It was up for grabs. Strictly speaking there was no government in 1640, but a state of nature, for "if the essential rights of sovereignty be taken away, the commonwealth is thereby dissolved."[46] Between 1640 and 1648 no de factoist could be entirely sure which side to support: The party to which he owed his allegiance would be the one with the best capacity to concentrate power in its hands. Concentration of power might be achieved through elections, propaganda, taxation, or military victory – it might be possible to cash in any one of these, or any combination of these, to obtain practical obedience. Until such obedience had been won by an undivided sovereign there must remain some doubt as to who had the right and the power to deserve obedience. In the meantime both king and Parliament denied that they intended to concentrate all power in their own hands. Each sought to acquire the preconditions for absolute sovereignty, but both insisted that, though they willed the means, they did not will the end. In the end, naturally enough, power slipped from their hands.

The king's great mistake had been not to seek to conquer his kingdom afresh, as William the Conqueror had done, offering his troops the land of his subjects as booty; Hobbes, unlike the citizens of London, was not "amazed at the very thought of plundering."[47] The year 1642 was a Machiavellian moment, when the king should have ruthlessly sought victory on the battlefield, not wasted time on a futile paper war. The year 1660 was another, when George Monk, with a small body of troops, effectively conquered the nation without firing a shot ("the greatest stratagem that is extant in history"[48]) and handed it over to Charles II. Once again the king had an opportunity for radical innovation, an opportunity that he allowed to pass him by. On each occasion, Hobbes intends us to understand, the fault lay with a man he never mentions: Clarendon, the general of the paper war of 1642 and the architect of the settlement of 1660.[49] If the politics of *Behemoth* are a politics of conquest, the target of *Behemoth* is Clarendon, who, at the time Hobbes wrote, was teetering

---

[46] Hobbes, *Leviathan*, 376.   [47] Hobbes, *Behemoth*, 142.

[48] Ibid., 204. These are the book's final words.

[49] For Hobbes's long-running conflict with Clarendon, see Tuck, *Philosophy and Government*, 320–2, 326, 336. It is probably not a coincidence that two of Hobbes's closest associates, John Aubrey and Samuel Sorbière, also found themselves at odds with Clarendon. *The Correspondence of Thomas Hobbes*, ed. Noel Malcolm (Oxford: Clarendon Press, 1994), 2:781, 898.

or toppling – teetering, one suspects, given the fact that Hobbes never names him. The year 1667 was thus another Machiavellian moment: The king still had command of the militia, and, as Machiavelli had insisted, a ruler with his own militia could accomplish anything.

Behemoth is about the need to ruthlessly concentrate power in the hands of one man (or, at the worst, one committee). The politics of *Behemoth* are the politics of *The Prince,* and it seems improbable that Hobbes would not have been aware of that fact. Indeed, *Behemoth* echoes the uncertainties that lie at the heart of *The Prince.* Machiavelli is quite clear how a conqueror like Cesare Borgia should behave: Charles I had in 1642 the chance to follow his advice. But he is much less certain what a ruler should do if troops other than his own place him in charge of a city used to governing itself. That he should concentrate power in his own hands seems clear in *The Prince,* but in *The Discourses* he argues that "princes begin to lose their state the moment they begin to break the laws and to disregard the ancient traditions and customs under which men have long lived."[50] It was far from clear, then, what a Machiavellian response to the situation in 1660 or 1667 would be. It is this uncertainty that gives life to the dialogue form of *Behemoth;* and at the root of this uncertainty is the difficulty of knowing what power is, or what one need do to get it.

How to test the suggestion that *Behemoth* is a Machiavellian work? One looks, naturally, for a discussion of that notorious Machiavellian theme, the difference between *virtù* and virtue, and one promptly finds it, barely concealed as a discussion of wisdom:

A: *wise* as I define it, is he that knows how to bring his business to pass (without the assistance of knavery and ignoble shifts) by the sole strength of his good contrivance. A fool may win from a better gamester, by the advantage of false dice, and the packing of cards.

B: According to your definition, there be few wise men now-a-days. Such wisdom is a kind of gallantry, that few are brought up to, and most think folly. Fine clothes, great feathers, civility towards men that will not swallow injuries, and injury towards them that will, is the present gallantry.[51]

If such wisdom is folly, then all we can ask of a ruler is that he should be effective, which is what Machiavelli usually means by the term *virtu-*

---

[50] Machiavelli, *Discorsi,* bk. 3, chap. 5.
[51] Hobbes, *Behemoth,* 38. Hobbes had also admired, without recommending, such "Gallantnesse of courage" in *Leviathan* (207).

oso (virtuous). And this, or something close to it, is what Hobbes does say a few pages later:

B: It seems you make a difference between the ethics of subjects and the ethics of sovereigns.

A: So I do. The virtue of a subject is comprehended wholly in obedience to the laws of the commonwealth. . . . The virtues of sovereigns are such as tend to the maintenance of peace at home, and to the resistance of foreign enemies. Fortitude is a royal virtue. . . . Frugality (though perhaps you will think it strange) is also a royal virtue. . . . Liberality also is a royal virtue: For the commonwealth cannot be well served without extraordinary diligence and service of ministers, and great fidelity to their Sovereign; who ought therefore to be encouraged. . . . In sum all actions and habits are to be esteemed good or evil by their causes and usefulness in reference to the commonwealth, and not by their mediocrity, nor by their being commended. For several men praise several customs, and that which is virtue with one, is blamed by others; and contrarily what one calls vice another calls virtue.[52]

It is common knowledge that it was a characteristic of reason-of-state theorists to distinguish between the ethics of subjects and those of sovereigns, and what Hobbes is offering here is in part a mere summary of reason-of-state theory. The relativity of virtue was, similarly, a familiar skeptical trope. But this passage is, I think, slightly more than an appeal to such commonplace notions. For the question whether rulers should be forbidden to "cheat," or could be allowed to use knavery and ignoble shifts, was Machiavelli's question. The paradoxical defense of frugality combined with an insistence on the need for generosity (at least toward faithful councillors) is also Machiavelli's.[53] It was Machiavelli who had insisted that though one should seem to have those qualities people commended, one need not actually have them. Typically Machiavellian, too, is Hobbes's insistence that subjects should be religious, without any corresponding claim that rulers need to be.[54] My claim, in short, is that *Behemoth* contains not only the advertised epitome of Mr. Heath's chronicle, but also an unadvertised epitome of *The Prince*.

It is because Hobbes approaches politics in Machiavellian terms that he is prepared to advocate what is euphemistically called "preventive war" and is otherwise termed cold-blooded murder. "Had it not been much better that those seditious ministers [the Presbyterians], which were not perhaps 1000, had been all killed before they had preached? It had been (I confess) a great massacre; but the killing of 100,000 is a

[52] Hobbes, *Behemoth*, 44–5. [53] Machiavelli, *Principe*, chaps. 18, 16.
[54] Hobbes, *Behemoth*, 45.

greater."[55] Machiavelli was, of course, the great advocate of the assassination of political enemies, defending such actions, as Hobbes did, as a way of economizing on bloodshed. He particularly insisted on the need to eliminate opponents after seizing power, that is, to kill the sons of Brutus,[56] and Hobbes seems puzzled at the failure of the Parliament to conduct a massacre of royalists in 1649. A Machiavellian, reading him, would be quick to conclude that more bloodshed in 1649 would have prevented a Restoration in 1660; and that more bloodshed in 1660 might have given the monarchy a securer hold on power in 1667.

We find, then, in *Behemoth* both a bold statement of Machiavellian "principle" and an epitome of *The Prince* itself. Once alerted to these, we are bound to note a recurrence of lesser Machiavellian themes. Machiavelli, for example, believed that the military supremacy of the Romans derived in part from the way they drew up their troops on the battlefield, which allowed a retreating body of soldiers to fall back without disrupting those coming up behind them, and he claimed that modern armies often defeated themselves because they were unable to carry out this maneuver. Twice Hobbes describes an army defeating itself as its ranks clash: If the point catches his attention, it is, I suggest, because he has been studying Machiavelli.[57] Machiavelli insisted that mercenary and auxiliary troops were dangerous. Hobbes offers a pithy epitome of his arguments when he says that "they that keep an army, and cannot master it, must be subject to it as much as he that keeps a lion in his house."[58] Machiavelli liked to describe how power naturally moved in a cycle from democracy to monarchy and back; Hobbes too is concerned to analyze a "circular motion of the sovereign power."[59]

Yet if Machiavelli seems obviously present in the text, his name is nowhere to be found. It was commonplace when discussing the rise of Cromwell to describe him as Machiavellian, yet, where one would expect Hobbes to bring Machiavelli in, he fails to do so. Again, most people blamed Machiavelli for corrupting modern political theory: Hobbes blames only those Greeks and Romans who are read at the university.[60] Harrington seized on this point: It was Machiavelli, he insisted, to whom we owed our knowledge of "ancient Prudence," and his significance

---

[55] Ibid., 95.   [56] Machiavelli, *Discorsi,* bk. 3, chaps. 3, 4.
[57] Ibid., bk. 2, chap. 16; Hobbes, *Behemoth,* 150, 168.
[58] Machiavelli, *Principe,* chap. 12; Hobbes, *Behemoth,* 193.
[59] Machiavelli, *Discorsi,* bk. 1, chap. 2; Hobbes, *Behemoth,* 204.
[60] Hobbes, *Leviathan,* 369.

deserved to be acknowledged.[61] If the moderns are unjustly excluded, as
Harrington asserts, it is also true that some of the ancients are unfairly
treated: Hobbes had insisted in his preface to Thucydides that Thucydides should be regarded as a monarchist, so why not now recognize his
exceptional status? Hobbes's blanket condemnation of the ancients and
total silence regarding the moderns is truly peculiar, and needs explanation. I offer my explanation for what it is worth. The modern who
interests him is Machiavelli, and the republican Machiavelli is condemned as an honorary ancient; the Machiavelli of *The Prince* is implicitly approved as a proto-Hobbesian. So, too, the ancient who interests
him is Thucydides, but Thucydides is an "impartial" historian.[62] He
offers us both the Hobbesian arguments of the Athenian ambassadors,
and the example of the Melians, who were prepared to die for liberty (for
the Melians had proved the Athenians wrong and had not yielded to such
conditions as they could get).

It is because *Behemoth* never admits to being what it is, a study in
Machiavellian politics, that nobody has been sure how to read it. And yet
Hobbes invites us at the very beginning to wonder what he is up to:

If in time, as in place, there were degrees of high and low, I verily believe that the
highest of time would be that which passed between the years of 1640 and 1660.
For he that thence, as from the Devil's Mountain, should have looked upon the
world and observed the actions of men, especially in England, might have had a
prospect of all kinds of injustice, and of all kinds of folly, that the world could
afford.[63]

Remember, the devil took Christ up onto a mountain and showed him the
kingdoms of the world, offering them to him. Christ, of course, rejected
his offer. Hobbes surely expects his readers to be profoundly uncomfortable at the thought of Thomas Hobbes standing beside Jesus Christ on the
Devil's Mountain – so uncomfortable as to ask themselves what on earth
(or what in heaven's name) he is up to. Hobbes is certainly no Christ: He
wants to learn how to acquire power in this world. This, too, had been
Machiavelli's concern, and as a result the English had done nothing less

---

[61] James Harrington, *The Political Works,* ed. J. G. A. Pocock (Cambridge: Cambridge
University Press, 1977) 178; discussed in Raab, *English Face,* 194–5.

[62] In defending Thucydides' impartiality, Hobbes quotes Lucian: "a writer of history ought,
in his writings, to be a foreigner, without country, living under his own law only, subject
to no king, nor caring what any man will like or dislike, but laying out the matter as it
is." "Life and History of Thucydides," 8:xxvi. We must not expect such impartiality of
Hobbes himself.

[63] Hobbes, *Behemoth,* 1.

than name the devil after him: Old Nick, for Niccolò. Is this Devil's Mountain also Niccolò's Mountain? How otherwise to explain the gross misapplication of a biblical quotation? *The Prince,* too, begins with talk of mountains and valleys and degrees of high and low. Machiavelli says that from his low station he can best understand the doings of princes, just as Hobbes, from his mountaintop, seeks to understand the crimes of the common people.

If I am right that *Behemoth* is about the need for a Machiavellian politics, we need scarcely be surprised that Hobbes does not admit the fact. In 1667 there were already threats to try him for heresy;[64] it would have done his cause no good to associate his own ideas with those of Machiavelli. There are plenty of good reasons why *Behemoth* as it stands was unlikely to win the king's favor, for it is a direct attack on the Anglican Church (for claiming independent spiritual authority) and on those royal advisers, Clarendon above all, who had approved of "mixarchy." But there was no point in Hobbes's concealing his views on these questions: *Behemoth* was nothing less than an appeal to the king to reform the church, the universities, and the political principles of the nation by requiring that Hobbesian philosophy be taught throughout the land. What Hobbes could avoid doing was letting it be apparent how far his views were identical to Machiavelli's.

I must hasten at this point to stress something readers already know: Hobbes's political theory is not the same as Machiavelli's. Machiavelli approves of mixed constitutions, Hobbes does not. Machiavelli approves of conflict within states, Hobbes does not. Machiavelli often writes in praise of liberty, Hobbes does not. Machiavelli is not interested in natural jurisprudence, but Hobbes is. Hobbes is concerned to stress the difference between power and right (which is why a description of him as a de factoist is no more than a useful shorthand), insisting that right exists only where there has been consent,[65] whereas Machiavelli is not. I could extend my list. But there are important points at which Machiavelli's theory and Hobbes's straightforwardly overlap, and I think we should assume that Hobbes was fully conscious of these points. I have suggested that in 1667 Hobbes thought Charles I should have been a Cesare Borgia, and that he hoped that Charles II would prove to be something more than

---

[64] The danger Hobbes faced is reassessed in Philip Milton, "Hobbes, Heresy and Lord Arlington," *History of Political Thought* 14 (1993): 501–46.

[65] Hobbes, *Leviathan,* 193; see also A. P. Martinich, *The Two Gods of Leviathan* (Cambridge: Cambridge University Press, 1992), 357–8.

a mere Lorenzo de' Medici. These were not new opinions, for if we turn back to *Leviathan* we find Machiavellian themes also present there.

Revealing, for our immediate purposes, is Hobbes's chart of the different types of knowledge. Ethics, justice, rhetoric, and logic are all part of the study of the consequences of bodies natural; but politics is a quite separate branch of knowledge, based on the study of artificial bodies, and it is in politics that one studies the rights and duties of sovereigns and the duties and rights of subjects. The subject matter of conventional unscientific history – the actions, particularly the moral actions, of individuals and governments – is thus split apart into distinct sciences, with radically different foundations and principles.[66] The disjuncture between politics and ethics opens the way to a Machiavellian politics.

The most important respect in which this disjuncture manifests itself is in Hobbes's insistence that governments are in a state of nature with regard to each other. In two parallel passages Hobbes maintains that the state of nature was like the present state of international relations, and that relations between states are like relations in the state of nature. What he describes in the process is Machiavelli's account of the relations between states, even if he does not share Machiavelli's view of how the internal affairs of states should be conducted: "Kings and persons of Soveraigne authority . . . are in continuall jealousies, and in the state and posture of Gladiators; having their weapons pointing, and their eyes fixed on one another. . . ."[67] Sovereigns are therefore free to inflict evil on innocent men, provided they are not their own subjects, as long as the state benefits. Machiavelli would have been happy to accept that in the war of every state against every state "nothing can be Unjust. The notions of Right and Wrong, Justice and Injustice have there no place. Where there is no common Power there is no Law: where no Law, no Injustice. Force, and Fraud, are in warre the two Cardinall vertues."[68]

The word virtue here takes one aback, but Hobbes has prepared for it by a careful definition of "virtue" that is equally applicable to Machiavellian *virtù:* "Virtue generally, in all sorts of subjects, is somewhat that is valued for eminence, and consisteth in comparison."[69] Hobbes's point is Machiavelli's, "That it is a glorious thing to use fraud in the conduct of a war."[70] I conclude that we can substitute for Kraynak's claim that

[66] Hobbes, *Leviathan,* 149.
[67] Machiavelli, *Principe,* chap. 14; Hobbes *Leviathan,* 187; cf. 394.
[68] Hobbes, *Leviathan,* 188.   [69] Ibid., 134.   [70] Machiavelli, *Discorsi,* bk. 3, chap. 40.

Hobbes's theory of the state of nature derives from his study of history the more specific claim that it derives from a study of Machiavelli.

As we go on through *Leviathan* we discover that there are certain key issues on which Hobbes and Machiavelli agree. In the first place, they agree on the psychology of competition. Men who already have power continue to seek power as vigorously as those who have none, hence "a perpetual and restless desire of power after power." Compare with this Machiavelli's chapter discussing how "Men advance from ambition to ambition, and, having first striven against ill-treatment, inflict it next upon others"; and with his insistence that "human appetites are insatiable."[71]

Second, they agree that competition shapes historical understanding. As Hobbes puts it: "Competition of praise enclineth to a reverence of antiquity, for men contend with the living not with the dead; to those ascribing more than their due, that they may obscure the glory of the other." Machiavelli devoted a chapter to the reverence for antiquity, remarking "since it is either through fear or through envy that men come to hate things, in the case of the past the two most powerful incentives for hating it are lacking, since the past cannot hurt you nor give you cause for envy. Whereas it is otherwise with events in which you play a part."[72]

Third, they agree on the logic of decision making. Here is Hobbes on pusillanimity: it "disposeth men to Irresolution, and consequently to lose the occasions, and fittest opportunities of action. For after men have been in deliberation till the time of action approach, if it be not then manifest what is best to be done, 'tis a signe, the difference of Motives, the one way and the other, are not great: Therefore not to resolve then, is to lose the occasion by weighing of trifles; which is pusillanimity." Compare this with Machiavelli's chapter describing how "The decisions of weak states are always fraught with ambiguity, and the slowness with which they arrive at them is harmful."[73]

They not only agree on the need to reach prompt and bold decisions, but they are also in substantial agreement about how decisions should be taken. Both think a ruler should consult with a number of expert individuals, but both agree that he should never ask the opinion of a council or committee, for conciliar decisions are likely to be halfhearted compromises, unduly influenced by personal interests. Councils constrain a ruler's freedom of initiative and make it hard for him to concentrate

---

[71] Hobbes, *Leviathan*, 161; Machiavelli, *Discorsi*, bk. 1, chap. 46; bk. 2, preface.
[72] Hobbes, *Leviathan*, 161; Machiavelli, *Discorsi*, bk. 2, preface.
[73] Hobbes, *Leviathan*, 164; Machiavelli, *Discorsi*, bk. 1, chap. 38.

responsibility in his own hands. Rulers should ensure that their advisers act not in concert but in competition with each other.[74]

Fourth, they agree on the inexorable logic of aggression. It is impossible for individuals or states in a state of nature to decide "to be at ease within modest bounds," for "they would not be able, long time, by standing only on their defence, to subsist": Like Machiavelli, Hobbes believes that commonwealths must pursue expansionary foreign policies.[75] Each of these key areas of agreement concerns the logic of competition, or what is now called game theory.

I could cite other themes common to our two authors (e.g., a concern about the risks posed by popular military commanders, and approval for the dictators of ancient Rome), but I hope I have said enough to show that there are close points of contact between Machiavellian and Hobbesian politics. Because Hobbes thought that there had never been a commonwealth where his principles had been properly recognized, he was bound to hold that all men were still imperfectly escaped from the state of nature, and that, if Machiavellian principles applied perfectly to relations between states, they must also, until sovereignty was properly respected, apply in large measure to political dealings within states. Indeed he was prepared to accept that if the logic of power imposed Machiavellian strategies on rulers, it also imposed them on rebels.[76]

Hobbes thought that the progress of knowledge made a theoretical discussion of politics worthwhile, where Machiavelli had insisted it was only practice, not abstract theory, that mattered; but both could agree on the sort of objectives and techniques with which a ruler should concern himself. Hobbes's practical politics is a Machiavellian politics shorn of any sympathy with republicanism, all *Prince* and no *Discourses*. By adding to Machiavelli's analysis of fact an account of right, Hobbes may have thought that he had completed the revolution that Machiavelli had inaugurated and had boldly compared to the discovery of a new continent.[77]

If my argument is right, then one would expect to find some confusion among commentators as to whether certain arguments, encountered in a

[74] Hobbes, *Leviathan,* chap. 25; Machiavelli, *Principe,* chap. 22.
[75] Hobbes, *Leviathan,* 185; Machiavelli, *Discorsi,* bk. 1, chap. 6. Hobbes's logic applies more straightforwardly to commonwealths than individuals, for individuals can make use of only a finite number of objects, whereas commonwealths can absorb the whole world.
[76] Cf. Jean Hampton, *Hobbes and the Social Contract Tradition* (Cambridge: Cambridge University Press, 1986), 199.
[77] Machiavelli, *Discorsi,* bk. 1, preface.

new context, are to be labeled Machiavellian or Hobbesian. In one striking instance this is exactly what we do find. William Cavendish, earl of
Newcastle, cousin of the William Cavendish who wrote at least part of
the *Horae Subsecivae,* friend of Thomas Hobbes and governor of the
future Charles II, wrote a lengthy *Advice* for Charles in 1659.[78] Two
commentators have been in no doubt that the text is a Machiavellian
essay.[79] Thomas Slaughter, the first in this century to draw attention to it,
claimed it as Hobbesian.[80] The simple truth, it seems to me, is that it is
both. There are passages that contain clear echoes of Machiavelli, others
that present distinctly Hobbesian arguments.[81] The two coexist quite
comfortably, because their practical implications are virtually identical.[82]

Recognizing the similarities between Machiavelli and Hobbes, one is
also bound to recognize that Hobbes did not have as many excuses as
Machiavelli had. Italian states in Machiavelli's day really were at the
mercy of foreign powers, and they had little prospect of controlling the
dangerously volatile network of alliances within which they found themselves. Only the most cynical realpolitik could keep them afloat. England
in the mid-seventeenth century, by contrast, was relatively immune from
invasion except from a lesser power, Scotland; and she had had, until
1642, a long tradition of relatively stable political life. English political
theorists did not have Machiavellian principles imposed on them to the

---

[78] The importance of Hobbes's relationship with Newcastle is a recurring theme of Tuck,
Philosophy and Government. The *Advice* is reprinted in *Ideology and Politics on the Eve
of the Restoration: Newcastle's Advice to Charles II,* ed. Thomas P. Slaughter (Philadelphia: American Philosophical Society, 1984).

[79] Condren, "Casuistry to Newcastle," passim; and Gloria Anzilotti, *An English Prince:
Newcastle's Machiavellian Guide to Charles II* (Pisa: Giardini, 1988).

[80] *Ideology and Politics,* ed. Slaughter, xvii–xxiv.

[81] The Hobbesian passages are: "The Bible in English under Every weavers, & Chamber
maids Armes hath Done us much hurte" (19); the argument for censorship on the
grounds that "controversy is a Civill warr with the Pen, which pulls out the sorde soone
afterwards" (21); "For Disputts will never have an Ende, & make new And Great
Disorders, butt force quietts all things" (23); "that cannot Punish, & reward, In Juste
time, cannot Governe, for there Is no more to governe, this world, but by reward &
punishmente, & itt muste bee done in the very nicke of time, or Else Itt is to no
purpose, – wee know no more that God Almighty Hath but reward, & punishmente"
(58). Even Condren (who is otherwise preoccupied with the Machiavellian passages)
recognizes a moment when Cavendish seems more Hobbesian than Machiavellian.
"Casuistry to Newcastle," 179, 183–4.

[82] Those who think that Hobbes was advocating a more tolerant society might bear in mind
Newcastle's advice that not only the press but private correspondence be effectively
censored: "this will so Coole the nation & quiett state speritts, as your Majestie & your
subjects will finde greate Ease in itt, – so all our discourse will bee of Hunting &
Hawkeing, Boling, Cocking, & such things, & bee Ever ready To serve your Majestie."
Advice, 56. These are the freedoms of *Leviathan.*

extent that they were imposed upon Machiavelli himself. Above all, Hobbes, the first of those who fled, had never faced death on the battlefield or experienced torture. Machiavelli could at least claim to be prepared to accept the consequences of his own advice.

I have argued so far that *Behemoth* is a rather interesting piece of historical analysis (particularly interesting, I might add, at the moment, because its emphasis on long- and medium-term causes of the civil war is so sharply at odds with the argument of the revisionist school); that its fundamental presuppositions are Machiavellian, which is why it has been misunderstood; and that these Machiavellian presuppositions are also to be found in *Leviathan*. My argument implies a somewhat different context in which Hobbes should be read from that commonly proposed, and I want now to argue that it also implies a different understanding of what Hobbes is about in *Leviathan*.

A helpful starting point is Jean Hampton's admirable study of "the logic of *Leviathan*."[83] Hampton's argument can be summarized as follows: The logic of *Leviathan* is defective. Hobbes should have seen that his claims that government is founded on consent, that rulers are the representatives of the ruled, and, above all, that human beings have an inalienable right to self-preservation were incompatible with his argument for absolute monarchy. Had he recognized this, he would have been forced into a fallback position, of which traces are to be found in the text, a position much closer to John Locke's. Social contract theorists ought to accept that governments are answerable to the people. But Hobbes equivocated, and rather than accept the logic of his own argument, he imposed an absolutist ideology onto a contractualist logic.

In order to formulate this argument, Hampton has to engage in a certain amount of equivocation herself. In the first place, she has to argue that Hobbes was committed to the view that individuals seek to preserve their own lives before all else. They are, she says, "hard-wired" to do so. Consequently, whenever they feel that the state is a threat to their own interests, they will be bound to withdraw their support for it. *Leviathan* can therefore be shown to be a "rebel's catechism."[84]

But it is certainly not Hobbes's view that individuals will always act to

---

[83] Hampton, *Hobbes and the Social Contract Tradition*, passim. David Gauthier's critique of Hampton's argument should be read alongside Hampton's book. Gauthier, "Hobbes's Social Contract," in *Perspectives on Thomas Hobbes*, ed. Rogers and Ryan, 125–52. Hampton's criticisms of Hobbes may be compared with those of Leibniz: see Hobbes, *Correspondence*, 2:731–35.

[84] Hampton, *Hobbes and the Social Contract Tradition*, 211, 197–207.

protect what they take to be their worldly interests. In *Behemoth* Hobbes quotes at length from Diodorus Siculus, concluding with the following passage:

> But the strangest thing of all is, that which they [the AEthopians] do concerning the death of their Kings. For the priests that live in Meroe, and spend their time about the worship and honour of their Gods, and are in greatest authority; when they have a mind to it, send a messenger to the King to bid him die, for that the Gods have given such order, and that the commandments of the immortals are not by any means to be neglected by those that are, by nature, mortal; using also other speeches to him, which men of simple judgement, and that have not reason enough to dispute against those unnecessary commands, as being educated in an old and indelible custom, are content to admit of. Therefore in former times the Kings did obey the priests, not as mastered by force and arms, but as having their reason mastered by superstition. But in the time of Ptolemy II, Ergamenes, King of the AEthopians, having had his breeding in philosophy after the manner of the Greeks, being the first that durst despise their power, took heart as befitted a King; came with soldiers to a place called Abaton, where was then the golden temple of the AEthopians; killed all the priests, abolished the custom, and rectified the kingdom according to his will.[85]

If this example proves anything it is that human beings are not hardwired for self-preservation: One might rather claim that they are hardwired for superstition, and consequently for self-destruction. A clear determination to place this-worldly benefits above other-worldly ones requires philosophical education, software not hardware.

Hampton's claim is that Hobbesian men and women are psychologically incapable of the "conversion" that would enable them to identify their own interests with those of their government.[86] But in fact Hobbes believes that "true" religion is precisely capable of bringing this conversion about.[87] The point has been well made by Stephen Holmes, who argues that "Religion solves the problem of how to create political power. . . . Power is based on nothing more substantial than a 'reputation' for power. Fiction becomes reality. . . . Authority . . . depends ultimately on a sleight of hand. . . . By a primitive bootstrapping operation, political institutions can be created even though no one possesses, at the outset, visible political resources."[88] The sleight of hand involved is that of persuading subjects to accept that the state's interests are their own.

---

[85] Hobbes, *Behemoth*, 94.
[86] Hampton, *Hobbes and the Social Contract Tradition*, 208–20.
[87] It is an obvious defect of Hampton's book that she provides only the briefest of discussions of religion (94–6, 260), and ignores it entirely when discussing "conversion."
[88] Holmes, introduction to *Behemoth*, xlvi–xlvii.

Hampton also argues that Hobbes cannot retreat from his account of a commonwealth by institution (founded on a contract between equals) to his account of a commonwealth by acquisition (founded in military conquest) because this second account is also incoherent.[89] Hobbes believes commonwealths by acquisition are founded on a contract, extorted under threat, between ruler and ruled, but Hampton holds with Locke that no such contract can be valid. The agreement, she argues, is not in the interest of the vanquished in advance of the threat, and an agreement made under threat benefits only one party. When such an agreement is reached, all that has happened is that one party has found a way of exploiting the other. True consent must be uncoerced (although it may be induced) consent. Hampton's argument at first seems to turn on the claim that there is a significant difference between induced and coerced consent. However, she later recognizes that this difference is not a structural but a moral one. Yet she gives no grounds for thinking that the moral argument is one that Hobbes would have recognized. In the end she falls back on the claim that sovereigns are not really in the position to coerce consent in the first place, an argument that would scarcely persuade any conquered nation.[90]

The problem of coerced consent is a complex one. Locke, for example, does not rule out coerced consent – e.g., a starving man's being forced to pay an exorbitant price for food – provided the coercion is external to the contracting parties.[91] It is clear that if Hobbes were to adopt this Lockean premise he would be quickly forced to reach Lockean conclusions, but it is also clear that Hobbes is not without a response to Hampton's argu-

---

[89] Hampton, *Hobbes and the Social Contract Tradition,* 166–73.

[90] Hampton acknowledges that "negative selective incentives" can be used to win consent: see her discussion of "battle-of-the-sexes" problems (154), which have a similar structure to the negotiations in establishing commonwealths by acquisition. On p. 169 she accepts that "the acquisition scenario [in Robert Nozick's version] is a nice example of an 'invisible-hand incentive solution' to a battle-of-the-sexes problem." Yet where the negative selective incentives are crucial, she argues, there is "no exchange, or coordination" (170). Her argument at this point turns on her ability to distinguish between threats as "incentives" and threats as "primary incentives." But on p. 233 she recognizes that "There is no *structural difference* between . . . a coerced exchange and an agency agreement": this "would seem to vindicate those who take a 'normative' approach to defining coercion." But this is not the argument on which she relies: she claims rather that a regime cannot be legitimated by a coerced contract between sovereign and subject because the people are really more powerful than the ruler (233–4). This argument does not apply to the case where the Athenians are the sovereign and the Melians the people, or other similar cases of "acquisition" (as her own discussion of imperialism implicitly recognizes [254–5]).

[91] John Locke, "Venditio," in *Political Writings,* ed. D. Wootton (New York: Mentor, 1993), 442–6.

ment. The end product of a situation where one party defeats another, where there is no mutual exchange of benefits and no contract, is not servitude, Hobbes insists, but slavery.[92] A victor who announces the intention to treat the vanquished as a slave is engaging in the sort of "threat" envisaged by Hampton, in which there is no offer of an exchange of benefits. In such a case, both Hobbes and Locke agree, the state of war between the two in reality continues. As Hobbes puts it, slaves "have no obligation at all; but may . . . kill . . . their Master justly."[93]

Let us go back to the Melian dialogue.[94] The Melians rejected the argument of the Athenians that they should surrender their town; they fought on, and when they were defeated the men were killed, the women sold into slavery. This was the natural outcome of a refusal to enter into a contract when threatened with coercion. But what the Athenians had offered them was a quite different fate: They were to become subjects of the Athenian empire, forced to pay taxes but able to administer their collection themselves. They would have been left with their lives and the liberty of their bodies, and they would have been guaranteed both protection against external enemies and the benefits of the rule of law. Such an agreement may not have been in their interests before the outbreak of war, but arguably it was afterwards. It involved both an exchange of benefits and a coordination of the actions of both parties. It fell short of an outright win by the Athenians (which would have involved the destruction of both the city and its inhabitants), even if it was more beneficial to them than an outright win could be. Hobbes would thus argue that Hampton's objections to coerced contracts apply to enslavement, but that he never imagines there can be a contract for slavery. They do not apply to enserfment, or anything short of enslavement, for these are arrangements from which both parties can emerge as better off than they would otherwise have been. (Locke appears to hold the same view in the first but not in the second of his *Two Treatises of Government*.[95])

---

92 Hampton, unfortunately, uses "servant" and "slave" interchangeably, although she knows Hobbes does not. *Hobbes and the Social Contract Tradition*, 120–2 n.

93 Hobbes, *Leviathan*, 255.

94 Hampton, *Hobbes and the Social Contract Tradition*, does not discuss the Melian case, which is one reason why she misses the game-theoretic structure of at least some commonwealths by acquisition. Von Neumann, by contrast, was enamored of Thucydides and could quote the key passage from the Melian dialogue from memory. It seems reasonable that, if Hobbes's argument has a game-theoretic structure, he too should have paid attention to it. William Poundstone, *Prisoner's Dilemma* (Oxford: Oxford University Press, 1993), 143.

95 See D. Wootton, introduction to Locke, *Political Writings*, 76.

Hobbes would therefore argue that his concept of absolute government was much more stable than Hampton recognizes: Conversion is possible, and force can legitimately act as a social cement. Subjects, if pious or frightened, will never withdraw their consent, and governments that claim the support of the gods and monopolize force can properly claim to be legitimate. Machiavelli, too, thought that the best rulers were armed prophets. Hampton constructs a plausible Lockean fallback position that she thinks Hobbes ought to be prepared to adopt, but a reading of *Behemoth* should be enough to persuade one that Hobbes's preferred fallback position is not Lockean, but Machiavellian. If reason cannot triumph, force and fraud can. Indeed Hobbes wants to persuade us that the triumph of force and fraud is both rational and legitimate.

Hobbes lived in a world that was in one important respect different from Machiavelli's: It was a world of widespread literacy and cheap printing. And yet one of the things Hobbes is most concerned to do in *Behemoth* is play down the significance of the printing press.[96] The king was wrong to engage in the pamphlet war of 1642. He should have concentrated on preparing to fight. For the most part people are influenced not by books, but by the opinions of their social betters and prominent neighbors. Even those in danger of being corrupted by the reading of Greek and Roman histories can be cured if their reading is accompanied by appropriate teaching. The universities are, in Hobbes's view, of strategic importance because of the face-to-face teaching that goes on in them; once taught, university students go out into the nation to shape the thinking of their friends, neighbors, and tenants. If the universities are, in

---

[96] Hobbes, *Behemoth*, 109, 115–7. My argument implies that Hobbes is less concerned to stress the importance of rhetoric (at least as conveyed through the press) than is sometimes thought. Quentin Skinner finds in *Behemoth* an account of the "triumph of rhetoric over rationality." "*Scientia Civilis*," 93 n. This needs to be squared with Hobbes's impatience with paper wars. Evidently "the goddess of rhetoric" (*Behemoth*, 69) reigns in popular assemblies, not on the printed page. What concerns Hobbes when he is discussing sedition is preachers and orators, not authors. Cromwell's power depends, in the end, upon "a whisper" (ibid., 137). On the other hand, he had repeatedly stressed many years before that Thucydides had to be read, not heard. "Life and History of Thucydides," 8:xxvii, xxxi. He had evidently given some thought to the differences between oral and written communication. One might argue that Hobbes implies the following ranking: force; oral rhetoric; money; printed rhetoric. The ambiguities in Hobbes's ranking are reminiscent of those that emerge in Antonio Gramsci as he discusses wars of position and wars of maneuver. See the fine essay by Perry Anderson, "The Antinomies of Antonio Gramsci," *New Left Review* 100 (1976): 5–78. These ambiguities are in part a Machiavellian legacy. Both the difficulties and the possibility of such a ranking are implied by Hobbes's frequent comparison of politics to a game of cards.

Hobbes's phrase, a "Trojan horse" within the state,[97] it is because of the hand-to-hand fighting that those who issue from them engage in. In this world it is not the book that most matters, but oral persuasion; particularly dangerous are the clergy, for they are professional rhetoricians. Most dangerous is any decision making in an assembly, where "the goddess of rhetoric" is liable to carry the day.[98] Machiavelli, too, had worried that popular assemblies were liable to take rash decisions,[99] but he had been much less dismayed at the theatrical power of rhetoric to nourish false belief and illusion, much more confident that plain speaking could have its effect. In Hobbes's view, "the Common-peoples minds, unless they be tainted with dependence on the Potent, or scribbled over with opinions of their Doctors, are like clean paper, fit to receive whatsoever by Publique Authority shall be imprinted in them";[100] but it was not mass-produced books that were going to print uniform opinions in the minds of the masses, but orchestrated sermons and coordinated school curricula.[101]

Machiavelli had insisted, against the evidence, that gunpowder had made no fundamental difference to warfare; Hobbes was concerned to insist that the printing press had made no fundamental difference to politics. Hence it is entirely appropriate that *Behemoth* should have been given to the king, and only stolen for the press, for Hobbes was comfortable in the Machiavellian role of adviser to princes, and much less comfortable with the incipient democracy of the book trade.

It is only because Hobbes had this skeptical view of the power of the

---

97 Hobbes, *Behemoth*, 40.   98 Ibid., 69.   99 Machiavelli, *Discorsi*, bk. 1, chap. 53.

100 Hobbes, *Leviathan*, 379. See also Thomas Hobbes, *The Elements of Law*, ed. Ferdinand Tönnies, (London: Cass, 1969), 51, 183–4.

101 In *Behemoth* B holds that "people always have been, and always will be, ignorant of their duty to the public, as never meditating anything but their particular interest; in other things following their immediate leaders; which are either the preachers, or the most potent of the gentlemen that dwell amongst them: as common soldiers for the most part follow their immediate captains, if they like them"(39). A insists that the people can be taught their duty, but agrees with B's account of how opinion is passed from the elite to the masses: "it is impossible that the multitude should ever learn their duty, but from the pulpit and upon holidays" (39). Mary Dietz, "Hobbes's Subject as Citizen," 96–101, interprets this exchange (in the slightly different form in which it appears in *English Works*, 6:212) as implying that Hobbes is a theorist of civic virtue, but I do not see how virtue can be inculcated in people who are necessarily enslaved to their immediate leaders. There is no indication that Hobbes attributes to the unarmed multitude the relative independence he recognizes in common soldiers. See also *Leviathan*, 391: "the Universities are the Fountains of Civill and Morall Doctrine, from whence the Preachers and the Gentry, drawing such water as they find, use to sprinkle the same (both from the Pulpit and in their Conversation) upon the people." Such sprinkling produces healthy vegetables, not virtuous citizens.

press that he was able to reconcile himself to the Bible in English. Of course he could comfort himself with the claim that there was much in favor of authority in the Bible, but he also knew that there was much that could be used against it. He could puzzle over the government's failure to shape the authorized translation to its own purposes: A Hobbesian state would not have hesitated, we gather, to adjust the biblical text if need be. Above all, though, he was convinced that people found in the Bible what others told them to find there. Men and women whose views had been properly "imprinted" could be trusted with printed books, for they would interpret them as authority instructed them.[102]

Recent interpreters of Hobbes have, I think, painted an unduly kindly picture of him. Hampton invites us to find in him an incipient liberalism. Alan Ryan assures us that he was really tolerant of the views of others and sympathetic to religious freedom.[103] But the Hobbes of *Behemoth* wanted to impose a state religion on a country where there was a measure of toleration, and to impose a state ideology on universities in which a certain amount of intellectual diversity was permitted. Between 1642 and 1651 Hobbes had studied, and eventually moved to, a country where there was effective freedom of the press. This alone had made the publication of *Leviathan* possible. In 1667 what he wanted to see was more pervasive and effective censorship. He recognized that it was impossible to impose one's beliefs on others if they had prior commitments. Such men have minds already "scribbled over." But infants are true blank pages: "For what other cause can there bee assigned, why in Christian Common-wealths all men either beleeve, or at least professe the Scripture to bee the Word of God, and in other Common-wealths scarce any; but

---

[102] Hobbes, *Behemoth*, 21–2, 52–5.

[103] My own view is closer to that of Sheldon Wolin, "Hobbes and the Culture of Despotism," in *Thomas Hobbes and Political Theory*, ed. Dietz, 9–36. For Alan Ryan, see "Hobbes, Toleration and the Inner Life," in *The Nature of Political Theory*, ed. David Miller and L. A. Siedentop (Oxford: Clarendon Press, 1983), 197–218; "A More Tolerant Hobbes?" in *Essays on Toleration*, ed. Susan Mendus (Cambridge: Cambridge University Press, 1988), 37–59; and "Hobbes and Individualism." See also Richard Tuck, "Hobbes and Locke on Toleration," in *Thomas Hobbes and Political Theory*, ed. Dietz, 153–71; and Lund, "Hobbes on Opinion." The key passage in *Behemoth* in favor of a "tolerant" Hobbes is "A state can constrain obedience, but convince no error, nor alter the minds of them that believe they have the better reason. Suppression of doctrine does but unite and exasperate, that is, increase both the malice and power of them that have already believed them" (62). But this needs to be set beside Hobbes's conviction that it would have been sensible to massacre large numbers of Presbyterians. Perhaps the crucial distinction is between suppressing doctrines and suppressing people.

that in Christian common-wealths they are taught it from their infance; and in other places they are taught otherwise?"[104]

Hobbes believes that force, indoctrination, and coerced consent can produce a stable political order. But, though I think he could defend his arguments against Hampton's account of them, they are open to one fundamental objection. The argument I want to rely on was formulated clearly by the Athenians in the Melian dialogue. They protested that they were not allowed to address the multitude, "for fear lest when they hear our persuasive and unanswerable arguments all at once in a continued oration, they should chance to be seduced; (for we know that this is the scope of your bringing us to audience before *the few*)."[105] The Athenians, it should be remembered, were not only imperialists but also democrats; the Melians not only defenders of liberty but also oligarchs, determined to deny the multitude a chance to choose new masters. Hobbes, if he takes the Athenian view of force, takes the Melian view of open debate. It is this combination that creates a fundamental conflict between his natural-right jurisprudence and his Machiavellian politics.

The Prince, in the end, proved a handbook for citizens as well as rulers, for it taught the weak what to expect from the strong.[106] There are still those who think (mistakenly) that this was Machiavelli's true purpose. It certainly was not Hobbes's, but I like to think that some (perhaps all) of the five editions of *Behemoth* that appeared during the Exclusion Crisis were sponsored by Locke and his associates, people who thought that reading *Behemoth* would expose, not reinforce, the logic of absolutism. These "persuasive and unanswerable arguments" were more likely to put people on their guard than to seduce.

Steven Shapin and Simon Schaffer have taught us that Hobbes had some powerful arguments against the "liberal" (as we would now term them) notions of public debate, free discussion, and impartial evidence. Both as geometer and politician, Hobbes thought there was no point in putting his correct views on everything (to borrow a phrase from Leszek Kolakowski) to the vote.[107] The test of logic was not popular approval,

---

[104] Hobbes, *Leviathan*, 614.

[105] Hobbes, *History of the Grecian War*, 9:97–8.

[106] For example, Edward d'Acres, who published a translation of *The Prince* in 1640, claimed that the revelation of evil is medicinal. Condren, "Casuistry to Newcastle," 184 n.

[107] Steven Shapin and Simon Schaffer, *Leviathan and the Air-Pump* (Princeton: Princeton University Press, 1985), passim.

the test of legitimacy not popular elections. My purpose here is not to defend Robert Boyle's empiricism or Locke's natural-right theory against Hobbes. I merely want to point out that Machiavelli held both books and the common people in higher esteem than Hobbes did, and that Hobbes's willingness to approve censorship involves him in inconsistency. It is hard, I submit, to see how politics can be about self-interest if it is claimed that most people are incapable of processing information or making up their own minds; a politics of individual self-interest is incompatible with a politics of censorship and brainwashing.

10

The background of Hobbes's *Behemoth*

FRITZ LEVY

> It is a thing very dangerous for men to gouerne themselues by examples, if there
> be not a concurrence of the same reasons, not onely in generall, but euen in all
> particularities; and if things be not ruled with the same wisedome: and if lastly,
> ouer and besides all other foundations, the selfe same fortune haue not her part.
> – Francesco Guicciardini, *The Historie of Guicciardin*

Let me confess at the outset that this will be a very speculative essay, about a work that appears to sort oddly with the rest of the Hobbes canon. While it seems a little unkind to blame the subject of my inquiry for the difficulty of the endeavor, the fact remains that Thomas Hobbes controlled with great care what he wished posterity to remember, not merely by means of the various versions of his autobiography but even in his conversations with his garrulous friend, John Aubrey. Hobbes was reluctant, as a matter of principle, to name intellectual ancestors, either directly or by way of citation. Like Francis Bacon, he castigated the use of authority; unlike Bacon, he acted on what he preached. Central to Hobbes's conception of himself, even though it was not an entirely accurate description of his philosophy, was the Euclidean metaphor, the notion that an entire, coherent, and true system could be built on the basis of a few axioms. Like Athena springing fully armed from the head of Zeus, the world of *Leviathan* and its associated works was to appear as if it had sprung in its entirety solely from the brain of Hobbes. But there is no reason why we should accept Hobbes at his own valuation, least of all in reference to a work so implicated in the doings of the transitory world as *Behemoth*.

Hobbes moreover portrayed himself as philosophically consistent over the entirety of his life, and for many years the scholarship devoted to the philosopher took him at his word to an astonishing extent. Yet it appears highly unlikely that a thinker who outlived his ninetieth birthday, who (despite beginning late) had a writing career stretching over more than half a century, would be able successfully to avoid all false starts, all inconsistencies, all errors. There is no need to believe that the author of *Behemoth* held precisely the same views about history as the translator of Thucydides nearly forty years before, or to believe that these works were conceived in total disregard of the historical debates of the time.

Nor need we take altogether literally the report that Hobbes owned few books. Those most likely to be found on Hobbes's table, Aubrey said, were Homer and Vergil, sometimes Xenophon, or some history, along with a Greek New Testament. Then he added that Hobbes "was wont to say that if he had read as much as other men, he should have knowne no more then other men."[1] But this was Hobbes in his old age, and Aubrey shrewdly added that, considering his long life, Hobbes had read much. Nor need we lament the apparent emptiness of his room, for the substantial library of his Cavendish patrons was in his charge.[2] Furthermore, even in that part of his career before the publication of Thucydides, Hobbes was closely associated with Sir Francis Bacon, and with the circle around Ben Jonson; it was in these years that his reading consisted (we are told) largely of histories, romances, and plays.[3] Later, he shared his Parisian exile with the poet and playwright William Davenant. In short, despite Hobbes's best efforts, at least some of the materials for an intellectual biography of *Behemoth* exist.

I shall begin with a discussion of *Behemoth,* primarily to determine where it fits into the generic categories of the day. Because that investigation takes us to Francis Bacon, I shall continue by looking at the controverted question of the relationship between the two men. That in turn will take me to an examination of the intellectual history of the 1620s, of which Hobbes's translation of Thucydides was part. In doing so, I will concentrate on the arguments about the definition and utility of history, to which, it seems to me, *Behemoth* is reacting.

---

[1] John Aubrey, *'Brief Lives,' chiefly of Contemporaries . . .* , ed. Andrew Clark (Oxford: Clarendon Press, 1898), 1:349.

[2] James Jay Hamilton, "Hobbes's Study and the Hardwick Library," *Journal of the History of Philosophy* 16 (1978): 445–53.

[3] Aubrey, *Lives,* 1:332, 365; 1:361. See also "The Autobiography of Thomas Hobbes," trans. Benjamin Farrington, *The Rationalist Annual* (1958), 25.

I

Like so much of Hobbes's work, *Behemoth* (1679) attracted controversy and misunderstanding from the beginning. The work appeared originally in a pirated edition; though Hobbes seems to have made arrangements for its posthumous appearance, he was nevertheless displeased to see it published during his own lifetime.[4] Moreover, the "foolish title set to it" – with its obvious (if unclear) linkage to the notorious *Leviathan* – annoyed the author and has misled readers from that day to this.[5] Contrary to expectation, *Behemoth* is not a little *Leviathan,* nor does even a careful study of the book help us very much to come to grips with the complications of its author's political philosophy. Instead, *Behemoth* more closely resembles a book of history – but even here the generic fit is not very good. There is no narrative; the analysis, while often acute, appears erratic; and the whole is presented in the unusual form of a dialogue.

As Hobbes himself noted, underlying his dialogue was James Heath's *A Brief Chronicle of the Late Intestine War,* a work appearing first in 1662, with a second (and much enlarged) edition in 1663.[6] Unlike Hobbes, Heath was traditional and cautious, eager to avoid wounding the reputation of any man still living. Instead, Heath tells us that he labored to find authentic accounts of the events of the civil war, and to fill out his history larded his story with the texts of printed (but scarce) proclamations and speeches. His own royalist bias was clear enough, nor did he leave any doubt about his intention: to settle in their allegiance those born during the revolution, and thus too young to have any first-

---

[4] On the publication history of *Behemoth,* see Hugh Macdonald and Mary Hargreaves, *Thomas Hobbes. A Bibliography* (London: The Bibliographical Society, 1952), 64 ff. See also Aubrey, *Lives,* 1:342.

[5] Ferdinand Tönnies, preface to *Behemoth, or The Long Parliament,* by Thomas Hobbes, ed. Tönnies, 2d ed. (New York: Barnes and Noble, 1969), ix. (I cite this edition of *Behemoth* throughout.) Tönnies argued that Hobbes's annoyance was at the omission of the subtitle, a conjecture reinforced by Royce MacGillivray's observation that the word "Behemoth" is a plural form of the Hebrew word for "monster" or "beast." The failure of the members of the Long Parliament to coalesce into a working sovereign is part (but only a part) of Hobbes's complaint against them. See Royce MacGillivray, "Thomas Hobbes's History of the English Civil War: A Study of *Behemoth," Journal of the History of Ideas* [*JHI*] 31 (1970): 181–5, cited in Robert P. Kraynak, *History and Modernity in the Thought of Thomas Hobbes* (Ithaca, N.Y.: Cornell University Press, 1990), 35–6. See also MacGillivray's *Restoration Historians and the English Civil War* (The Hague: Martin Nijhoff, 1974), 68 ff.

[6] Hobbes, *Behemoth,* dedication to Sir Henry Bennet, Baron Arlington (printed by Tönnies from the MS at St. John's College, Oxford), v.

hand knowledge of its causes, so that they might be "more satisfied with their voluntary obedience." Heath himself blamed the revolution on "the popular cheats of Religion and Liberty."[7]

While Hobbes would not have disagreed with Heath's royalist purposes, his commentary on the history of this period made clear that a narrative of events was not the best way to achieve them. Indeed, as B, the more passive of the two participants in the dialogue, reminds his opposite number,

> I suppose, your purpose was, to acquaint me with the history, not so much of those actions that passed in the time of the late troubles, as of their causes, and of the councils and artifice by which they were brought to pass. There be divers men that have written the history, out of whom I might have learned what they did, and somewhat also of the contrivance; but I find little in them of what I would ask.[8]

What Hobbes asks – and what Heath conspicuously refuses to ask – is how, and by whom, the people of England were brought to revolt against their king. Hobbes believes firmly that the people were *seduced* from their allegiance by ministers of faiths normally antipathetic to each other's views. Presbyterians, Catholics, and (later) Independents had in common the belief that their ability, and right, to interpret Scripture exceeded that of the king and the Church of England. The clergy, however, were not solely culpable, for a "great number of men of the better sort," corrupted by their reading in some of the more tendentious classics of the Greek and Roman world, were ready at any moment to call the king a tyrant. Urban merchants, envious of Dutch prosperity and attributing it to the Netherlandish revolt against the Spanish monarchy, came to the (erroneous) conclusion that a similar change in England would produce a similar result. Bankrupts saw war as a way of restoring their fortunes. For their part, the people in general were ignorant of their duty and, instead of recognizing the office of king as unique, believed that "king" was no more than the highest title "which gentleman, knight, baron, earl, duke, were but steps to ascend to, with the help of riches."[9] In all this, the worst villains were the universities, not only neglectful of their duty to teach right doctrine but actively promoting wrong, and thus as dangerous to England "as the wooden horse was to the Trojans."[10] Ultimately, Hobbes believed (and never tired of repeating), blame for the civil war might be attributed to the arrogance of the intellectuals.

---

[7] H-I [James Heath], *A Brief Chronicle of the Late Intestine War,* 2d ed. (London: J. Best for William Lee, 1663), The Preface to the Reader (unpaginated).
[8] Hobbes, *Behemoth,* 45.   [9] Ibid., 3, 4.   [10] Ibid., 40.

If repetition be a reliable guide, Hobbes believed strongly that ideas bear the principal responsibility for stabilizing or destabilizing states, indeed that ideas shape events. The process by which ideas exerted this influence, however, was neither simple nor straightforward. Most men, he was convinced, were too concerned with their own affairs to have sufficient leisure to study seriously matters of government, even such essentials as knowledge of the duty they owed their rulers and of the right by which those rulers governed. So they turned for help to those they thought better qualified. As we have seen, "the chief leaders were ambitious ministers and ambitious gentlemen; the ministers envying the authority of bishops, whom they thought less learned; and the gentlemen envying the privy-council and principal courtiers, whom they thought less wise than themselves."[11] Of these, the latter group had been corrupted "with arguments for liberty out of the works of Aristotle, Plato, Cicero, Seneca, and out of the histories of Rome and Greece, for their disputation against the necessary power of their sovereigns"; then, themselves using arguments taken from books in such high esteem, they were able to draw in those who depended on their judgment.[12] Unfortunately, the interpretation of the great classical authors was not so simple, "for several men praise several customs, and that which is virtue with one, is blamed by others; and, contrarily, what one calls vice, another calls virtue, as their present affections lead them."[13]

Hobbes was here accusing the opponents of the king of having adopted the ancient view that history is to be subservient to rhetoric, that the role of history is to supply examples useful to the orator in making his case. In addition, however, Hobbes also believed that these men were themselves victims of the same faulty use of the historical record. Matters of right (including the right of the Parliament to act as it had in its efforts to seize control of the civil government) could never be decided on historical grounds: "for the records, seeing they are of things done only, sometimes justly, sometimes unjustly, you can never by them know what right

---

[11] Ibid., 23.   [12] Ibid., 56.

[13] Ibid., 45; on this, and on Hobbes and humanist rhetoric generally, see Quentin Skinner, "Thomas Hobbes: Rhetoric and the Construction of Morality," *Proceedings of the British Academy* 76 (1991): 1–61. Skinner has continued the discussion in " 'Scientia Civilis' in Classical Rhetoric and in the Early Hobbes," in *Political Discourse in Early Modern Britain,* ed. Nicholas Phillipson and Quentin Skinner (Cambridge: Cambridge University Press, 1993), 67–93. The latter essay makes the point – altogether omitted in David Johnston's otherwise highly interesting *The Rhetoric of Leviathan* (Princeton: Princeton University Press, 1986) – that Hobbes's humanist period did not end in the 1620s, and that *Behemoth* thus should be considered in discussions of Hobbes's humanism.

they had, but only what right they pretended."[14] Hobbes had already
recognized the problem in *Leviathan,* and he had attempted to solve it by
radically deemphasizing the use of historical examples, replacing them
with a political theory derived from first principles and thus inarguable.
In a historical book like *Behemoth,* however, that option plainly was not
open to him. Instead, he lumped the misuse of historical examples in with
the misdefinition of key words as part of a more general assault on
rhetorical abuses.

There is a certain irony in Hobbes's use of a work of history to condemn the misuses of history, not least because some of what he does is in
imitation of those he has just criticized. Like so many before him, Hobbes
turned to an analysis of the past to provide him with an example, in the
hope that such an example might get men to change their ways. He would
undoubtedly have preferred to convert them to his position by the force
of reasoning contained in *Leviathan,* but by the time he came to write
Behemoth such optimism had perhaps faded, in part because he now
knew that the greatest villains had cozened themselves as well as the
commoner sort. "The craftiest knaves of all the Rump . . . did believe that
the same things which they imposed upon the generality, were just and
reasonable."[15] Such men – along with their descendants – needed to be
convinced by the same weapons they used on others.

To understand what is happening here, we need to know what sort of
work of history *Behemoth* is. By referring his readers to Heath's chronicle, Hobbes made it clear that he was not writing a narrative of the usual
sort. Nor was it customary to use the dialogue form in discussing "the
Register of *Knowledge of Fact* [which] is called *History.*"[16] Instead,
Hobbes composed what Francis Bacon described as "discourse upon
histories or examples." Bacon noted that such discourses had been used
by Machiavelli to analyze the wisdom of government, but himself believed they were most valuable as a way of exploring that division of civil
knowledge called the wisdom of business or negotiation. By this he meant
the sort of advice once offered in a parable or fable, or – as he illustrated
at length – in The Wisdom of Solomon. Histories, examples, made another and even better source for such personal advice, "for knowledge
drawn freshly and in our view out of particulars, knoweth the way best to
particulars again." Moreover, knowledge expressed in this way – where

---

[14] Hobbes, *Behemoth,* 76.   [15] Ibid., 158.
[16] Thomas Hobbes, *Leviathan,* ed. Richard Tuck (Cambridge: Cambridge University Press,
1991), 60.

the discourse commented on the examples, rather than the examples following the discourse – was particularly effective in influencing practice, for the particulars, the circumstances, made it "a very pattern for action."[17]

In *The Advancement of Learning* (1605), Bacon considered these Machiavellian discourses on history as something quite distinct from history itself, for history writing in its various forms was associated with memory, while civil knowledge (including discourses) was part of philosophy and so linked with reason. Thus "ruminated history," defined as a form of writing about those scattered actions the author thought worth remembering, along with a political commentary, was cast out of the realm of history and defined as part of policy. Bacon's reason for evicting such a discourselike history was a belief that "it is the true office of history to represent the events themselves together with the counsels, and to leave the observations and conclusions thereupon to the liberty and faculty of every man's judgement."[18] In a later, expanded version of the text known as *De Augmentis*, ruminated history – now thought of as a mixed mode – was allowed to claim a place within the sphere of civil history, while the very similar Machiavellian discourses continued to help expound the civil knowledge of "negotiation."

This is not to say that Machiavelli's *Discorsi* and *Behemoth* are identical in form. Machiavelli's work is a discourse on a text, Hobbes's a discourse on examples (with Heath serving as little more than an *aide-mémoire* for an author who had lived through the events under discussion). Machiavelli ranged very widely: He used Livy as a springboard to discuss government everywhere in the ancient and modern world. Hobbes was much more narrowly focused, with relatively few references to Greek and Roman history, and fewer still to England before the accession of the Stuarts. Nevertheless, Hobbes – like Machiavelli – included occasional reflections on human nature drawn inductively from history. King Charles's advisors, said A, undermined their own cause by their readiness to compromise, thereby alienating those of their supporters who had hoped for booty; to which B responded, "they had reason: for a civil war never ends by treaty, without the sacrifice of those who were on both sides the sharpest. You know well enough how things passed at the

---

[17] Francis Bacon, *The Advancement of Learning,* in *The Works of Francis Bacon,* ed. James Spedding, Robert Leslie Ellis, and Douglas Denon Heath (London: Longmans, 1857–59), 3:453.

[18] Ibid., 339.

reconciliation of Augustus and Antonius in Rome." More broadly, and without citing specific examples, A remarked that "We cannot safely judge of men's intentions," but then continued by adding

I have observed often, that such as seek preferment, by their stubbornness have missed of their aim; and on the other side, that those princes that with preferment are forced to buy the obedience of their subjects, are already, or must be soon after, in a very weak condition. For in a market where honour and power is to be bought with stubbornness, there will be a great many as able to buy.[19]

This has a true Machiavellian ring. Curiously, however, Hobbes used the dialogue form in which he couched his treatise to allot such pronouncements to both of his interlocutors – not merely to the magisterial A – and so diffused the authority deriving from a unitary authorial voice; Machiavelli's similar statements have about them an air of coming ex cathedra. Nevertheless, despite the differences, *Behemoth* fits into the Baconian categories as principally a discourse on histories or examples, but with enough narrative surviving (especially in the third and fourth dialogues) to suggest that the mixed mode of ruminated history may have been lurking at the back of its author's mind.

II

All of this implies that *Behemoth* was something other than a rephrased *Leviathan*, and that Hobbes was aware of some of the debates about the place of history, and of poetry, that had been running throughout the sixteenth and early seventeenth centuries. It is possible that such an awareness came only from a reading of Bacon's *Advancement of Learning*; however, there is evidence that Hobbes was very much part of the intellectual circles of the 1620s and 1630s, and that his views may well have reflected that contact. Of such connections, that with Bacon was probably the earliest. Within a year after Hobbes and his patron, William Cavendish (future second earl of Devonshire), returned from their pilgrimage to Italy in 1615, Cavendish was passing on to Bacon messages from Fra Fulgenzio Micanzio, the Venetian friar who was the close friend of Paolo Sarpi. As Cavendish's secretary and general factotum, Hobbes translated the Italian letters. By 1617, the correspondence is full of references to a possible Italian translation of Bacon's *Essays*, though in the end that appeared under the aegis of Bacon's old friend, the Italophile

---

[19] Hobbes, *Behemoth*, 115, 72.

Catholic convert Tobie Mathew. But there was to be a Latin translation as well, and the irrepressible John Aubrey stated that Hobbes "was employed in translating part of the Essayes, viz. three of them, one whereof was that of the Greatnesse of Cities, the other two I have now forgott."[20] Aubrey noted as well an even closer relationship between the two men:

Mr. Thomas Hobbes (Malmesburiensis) was beloved by his lordship, who was wont to have him walke with him in his delicate groves where he did meditate: and when a notion darted into his mind, Mr. Hobbs was presently to write it downe, and his lordship was wont to say that he did it better then any one els about him; for that many times, when he read their notes he scarce understood what they writt, because they understood it not clearly themselves.[21]

This has sometimes been taken to mean that Hobbes temporarily left the employ of Cavendish and took up residence at Bacon's house at Gorhambury, though that seems to me unlikely. Thomas Bushell, Bacon's own servant, ordinarily attended his lordship, pen and inkhorn in hand, though indeed Hobbes was employed "often in this service whilest he was there."[22] The visits, one suspects, were those of the young Cavendish, with Hobbes in attendance; and it was Cavendish whom Bacon remembered in his will. What is omitted, however, is any mention of the date at which the visits occurred. They certainly continued past the time of Bacon's disgrace and may have lasted to the time of his death.[23] Nor is it possible to speak with certainty about the contents of their conversations, though for our purposes it is worth noting that these were the years when Bacon was writing his *History of the Reign of King Henry VII*, revising the *Essays* for the last time, and converting and enlarging the early *Advancement of Learning* (including, of course, the section on discourses) into a part of the grandiose scheme called *Instauratio Magna*.

During these same years, Hobbes was also in contact with Ben Jonson, and it is possible that his reading of plays and romances was a reflection of this relationship. Like Bacon, Jonson had come to question

[20] Aubrey, *Lives,* 1:83. Aubrey gives Hobbes as his source but, characteristically, has the title of the essay slightly wrong: he probably meant "Of the true Greatnesse of Kingdomes and Estates." On Hobbes's trip to Italy, and his relations to the Italians, see Noel Malcolm, *De Dominis* (London: Strickland and Scott Academic Publishers, 1984), 47–54; and Linda Levy Peck, "Hobbes on the Grand Tour: Paris, Venice, or London?" *JHI* 57 (1996): 177–83.

[21] Aubrey, *Lives,* 1:70. Again, Aubrey claimed Hobbes as his source.   [22] Ibid., 83.

[23] There is a comment about Bacon's use of an amanuensis in a letter of 1623 in the Micanzio correspondence. Vittorio Gabrieli, "Bacone, la Riforma e Roma nella versione hobbesiana di un carteggio di Fulgenzio Micanzio," *English Miscellany* 8 (1957): 215. Gabrieli's article is generally helpful on the Bacon–Hobbes relationship.

where the dividing line between history and its neighbors was to be drawn. The case of *Sejanus* is particularly suggestive. Jonson had already located his comical satire *Poetaster* in the world of imperial Rome, but the objects of his wrath on that occasion were two competing playwrights. *Poetaster* did set Augustus Caesar on stage, but in the role of a wise leader and patron of poets, an emperor prepared to accept Vergil as a revered adviser. In contrast to that optimistic vision of the relationship between ruler and ruled, *Sejanus* illustrated the depravity of imperial rule gone sour, in part by depicting the persecution of critics like the historian Cremutius Cordus. Though there is nothing like unanimity on the details, contemporaries and modern scholars have all accepted the idea that the play intended to criticize the court of Queen Elizabeth and warn that of the newly crowned James I.[24] Histories, and most especially histories drawn from the writings of Tacitus, were usually seen as in some way critical of monarchy with audiences and readers expected to draw parallels between their own world and the world set before them. But as Jonson discovered when called before the Privy Council, criticism of this sort could be dangerous, and the playwright had to find a defense.

In essence, what Jonson did was to accept the doctrine of historical parallels, but add some new conditions to it. In the preface to the printed *Sejanus,* Jonson expanded a commonplace, the idea that tragedy should be based on historical themes, by specifying his own version of the unities: "truth of argument, dignity of persons, gravity and height of elocution, fulness and frequency of sentence."[25] Of these, "truth of argument" was potentially the most contentious. That historians might be beholden to "old mouse-eaten records" was commonly accepted: that poets should be bound in the same way was not.[26] As John Marston pointed out in his attack on Jonson's pedanticism, "know that I have not laboured in this poem to tie myself to relate anything as an historian, but to enlarge everything as a poet. To transcribe authors, quote authorities, and trans-

[24] Ben Jonson, *Sejanus,* ed. Jonas A. Barish (New Haven: Yale University Press, 1965); Ben Jonson, *Sejanus His Fall,* ed. Philip J. Ayres (Manchester and New York: Manchester University Press, 1990). See as well Blair Worden, "Ben Jonson among the Historians," in *Culture and Politics in Early Stuart England,* ed. Kevin Sharpe and Peter Lake (Stanford: Stanford University Press, 1993), 67–89.

[25] Jonson, *Sejanus His Fall,* 51; see also J. A. Bryant Jr., "The Significance of Ben Jonson's First Requirement for Tragedy: Truth of Argument," *Studies in Philology* 49 (1952): 195–213.

[26] Sir Philip Sidney, *An Apology for Poetry,* ed. Geoffrey Shepherd (Manchester: Manchester University Press, 1973), 105.

late Latin prose orations into English blank verse, hath, in this subject, been the least aim of my studies."[27] In other words, whereas Jonson took pride in his ability to footnote every detail of his play, Marston argued that, in the interests of promoting morality, the poet had not only the right but the duty to "enlarge everything." In this, Marston was following Philip Sidney (and Aristotle) in maintaining that the mere historian could never be as good a teacher of moral lessons as the poet because the intractability of the historian's materials might well show the evil enjoying their ill-gotten success while the good suffered in vain, whereas the poet had the advantage of rewriting the story so that it would end appropriately. However, it was precisely these enlargements that could be misinterpreted, in ways that were dangerous to the health of the poet. Jonson's response was to recast the printed text of his play by surrounding it with "sidenote" references to Tacitus and Dio Cassius, intended (at least in part) to deflect further criticism, but also to underline his argument that historical drama required "integrity in the story."[28]

Jonson's solution inevitably raised further problems, not the least of which was that a historical drama so mired in fact was likely to lack interest on the stage. *Sejanus* has always been more popular with readers and critics than with audiences. In addition, the debate between Marston and Jonson had the important effect of reviving and extending issues under discussion since Sidney's two-pronged attack on the role of the historian. Sidney had not, after all, limited himself to the Aristotelian position that the poet was a better moralist than the historian, but had gone on to say that the good historian, if he were to do more than chronicle events, had perforce to adopt the role of the poet. Historical causation was a matter of inference, of poetical insight; and – to go beyond Sidney for a moment – it was thus no wonder that, in the ancient histories, causes were often explored by way of fictional speeches. Historical drama, like *Sejanus* and its later companion piece, *Catiline,* simply extended the metaphor by converting the entire history into a series of fictional speeches; and Jonson's sidenotes reminded his readers (if not his auditors) that his text was not nearly so far from straightforward history as they might at first have thought. Nor should Jonson's point be treated as of purely theoretical interest, for historians, in their search for ways of

---

[27] John Marston, *Sophonisba*, in *The Selected Plays of John Marston*, ed. Macdonald P. Jackson and Michael Neill (Cambridge: Cambridge University Press, 1986), 401.
[28] See John Jowett, "Fall before this Booke: The 1605 Quarto of *Sejanus*," *TEXT* 4 (1988): 279–95.

organizing their materials into a coherent whole, themselves had frequent recourse to the theatrical metaphor.

Jonson's whole line of argument serves as a reminder that the boundary between history and fiction had not yet been firmly drawn.[29] Indeed, the border struggle was to continue along very similar lines for some time. The publication of Thomas May's translation of Lucan's *Pharsalia* (1627) – with a dedication to Hobbes's patron, the earl of Devonshire, and with a commendatory poem by Ben Jonson – triggered another exchange on history's relation to poetry and truth, not least because May defended Lucan by claiming the poem as a "true *History*" despite being "adorned and heightened with *Poetical raptures,* which doe not adulterate, nor corrupt the truth but giue it a more sweet and pleasant relish."[30] Thus May followed Jonson's lead in declaring that it was "truth of argument" that made a work about the past into a history, regardless of the garb in which the work might be clothed; and May's reasons for doing so might well have been the same as Jonson's, for Lucan's reputation as an anti-imperial republican could easily have proven dangerous for his translator.[31] All this was to emerge once more, again with reference to Lucan, in the exchange between Sir William Davenant and Hobbes.

If truth, even more than moral utility, was to be the hallmark of history, then certain rhetorical adornments, such as the invented speeches characteristic of the Greek and Roman historians, were bound to come under attack. Jean Bodin, whose *Method for the Easy Understanding of History* was widely read in England, had raised some doubts about these speeches, and even Edmund Bolton (yet another friend of Jonson's), who defended them on rhetorical grounds, nevertheless admitted that "*Orations,* such as were neuer spoken, and yet put into the mouthes of actors by authors . . . fill bookes by leaue, and not by the law of historie."[32]

[29] See William Nelson, *Fact or Fiction* (Cambridge, Mass.: Harvard University Press, 1973); Judith H. Anderson, *Biographical Truth* (New Haven and London: Yale University Press, 1984); and my review of Anderson, *Huntington Library Quarterly* [*HLQ*] 47 (1984): 233–40.

[30] Thomas May, trans., *Lucan's Pharsalia* (London: Thomas Iones and Iohn Marriott, 1627), The Epistle, Dedicatory, sig. A2v; cited in Gerald M. MacLean, *Time's Witness* (Madison: University of Wisconsin Press, 1990), 34–5. MacLean gives a history of the argument over whether Lucan was a poet or a historian writing in verse.

[31] David Norbrook, "Lucan, Thomas May, and the Creation of a Republican Literary Culture," in *Culture and Politics in Early Stuart England*, ed. Sharpe and Lake, 45–66.

[32] Edmund Bolton, "An Historical Parallel . . . ," appended to *Nero Caesar, or Monarchie Depraued*, 2d ed. (London: A. Mathewes, 1627), 15–16 (appended section "An Historical Parallel . . . "). The issue is discussed in connection with Bodin in Julian Franklin, *Jean Bodin and the Sixteenth-Century Revolution in the Methodology of Law and History* (New York: Columbia University Press, 1963), 138–42.

Other scholars, including John Selden, a member of Jonson's circle, narrowed the boundaries still further by insisting on the inclusion of historical sources within the narrative, as well as on greater rigor in the use of historical evidence, matters he considered vastly more important than style. "To labour with the fancie of a fairer language," he said, "without the carefull searching of these kindes of helps [i.e., the manuscript records], is but to spend that time & cost in plastering onely, or painting of a weake or poore building, which should be imployed in prouision of timber and stone for the strengthening and inlarging it." He illustrated his meaning in *Titles of Honor,* one of the few books Hobbes cited approvingly in *Leviathan.*[33]

Under siege by the radical skepticism so prominent at the end of the sixteenth century, historians of Selden's stripe narrowed the scope of the discipline in order to defend the truth of what remained. If history were to be useful, conjecture, invented speeches – the poetic aspects of the historian's craft – had to be abandoned. This still left the question: useful for what? As we have seen, some continued to believe – despite Sidney's passionate argument that the poet was the best moralist – that the poet and the historian competed with the philosopher as to which was most able to inspire moral activity. Nor was this the only utilitarian battleground. Historians – of whom the best known was Francesco Guicciardini – also laid claim to teach the arts of politics. The *History of Italy* was certainly the most compendious of the political histories, yet it is noteworthy that its author, in the passage quoted in the epigraph to this essay, also issued the clearest warnings against the abuse of historical examples.[34] Guicciardini's lament was aimed at Piero de' Medici, de facto ruler of Florence at the time of the French invasions, and thus the man in a position actually to make a decision affecting the future of his city and – it turned out – his own place at the head of government. Clearly, Piero was both too lazy and too full of his own importance to benefit from the study of history. But it was also possible to ask whether any prince could benefit. Guicciardini had specified that an example was applicable to a given situation only if fortune played her selfsame part. How was a prince to recognize when this was so?

---

[33] John Selden, "To my singular good Friend, Mr. Augustine Vincent," in *A Discoverie of Errours,* by Augustine Vincent (London: W. Jaggard, 1622), sig. a2r. Hobbes mentions *Titles of Honor* in *Leviathan,* 69. See the discussion of Selden in Daniel R. Woolf, *The Idea of History in Early Stuart England: Erudition, Ideology, and the "Light of Truth" from the Accession of James I to the Civil War* (Toronto: University of Toronto Press, 1990), 200–42.

[34] Francesco Guicciardini, *The Historie of Guicciardin,* trans. Geffray Fenton, 3d ed. (London: R. Field, sold by A. Johnson, 1618), 40.

Perhaps the historian's well-ruminated hindsight might help a prince seize an onrushing fortune the next time around, but this would work only if all the details were included in the story. Guicciardini's response to this dilemma was to write a relation of quite staggering length, providing both the materials and some indication of how they might profitably be used. However, a prince faced with a work the size of Guicciardini's might well have questioned the utility of examples when their use required a knowledge of *all* particulars.

One response to this problem was to extract the meat from the details, a path pointed to by Guicciardini's own Maxims, by the thematic index to his *History of Italy* prepared by his English translator, Geoffrey Fenton, or by abbreviators like Remigio Nannini and Robert Dallington.[35] Such a reading might, in its own turn, be boiled down into a series of political maxims. The difficulties were manifest. Bacon noticed that maxims were more likely to foreclose thought than to stimulate it. Furthermore, as Guicciardini himself recognized, while bare maxims made good copy for commonplace books, they could be applied, in the brutal world of politics, only by those who already knew enough not to need them. Two other possibilities remained: to follow the lead of Machiavelli's *Prince* and use the past as a series of examples from which a science of politics might be constructed; or to imitate the mode of his *Discorsi* and write a commentary on a historical text, a kind of ruminated history. Although he approved highly of the second of these methods of writing, Bacon nonetheless pointed out that the works it produced consisted of pieces "separate and selected according to the pleasure of the author," and so more closely resembled a handbook of political manners.[36] This in turn led to his uncertainty, already noted, about the degree to which such a mixed mode was really historical. More important, however, was Bacon's realization that these discourses should be seen as part of the political education of individual citizens rather than that of their rulers.

Around the end of the sixteenth century, the author most frequently examined in this context was Tacitus. The political uses of Tacitus, most especially in terms of resistance to imperial tyranny, have been the subject of a good deal of recent writing;[37] and we have just seen what Ben Jonson

---

[35] See F. J. Levy, "Hayward, Daniel, and the Beginnings of Politic History in England," *HLQ* 50 (1987): 1–34.

[36] Francis Bacon, *De Augmentis*, in *Works*, 4:310.

[37] F. J. Levy, "Hayward"; Alan T. Bradford, "Stuart Absolutism and the 'Utility' of Tacitus," *HLQ* 46 (1983): 127–55; J. H. M. Salmon, "Stoicism and Roman Example: Seneca and Tacitus in Jacobean England," *JHI* 50 (1989): 199–225.

made of him in *Sejanus*. But it is wise to remember that, in this situation as in so many others, an author might be interpreted in diametrically opposite ways. Justus Lipsius's commentaries, for example, use Tacitus to recommend a kind of Stoic acceptance of the power of the new monarchies, and so implicitly condemn the sort of resistance celebrated in Jonson's staging.[38] Edmund Bolton went much further than this, arguing that even Nero Caesar, although unquestionably a "villain," still taught one great secret of government: *"No Prince is so bad as not to make monarckie seeme the best forme of gouernment."*[39] For his part, Bolton's dedicatee, King James I, who detested Tacitus as an enemy of kingship, naturally was delighted with this effort to co-opt the Roman to the side of the rulers – though not to the point of rewarding Bolton enough to save him from debtors' prison.

III

The extent of Hobbes's involvement in these historiographical discussions cannot easily be measured, in part because of his habit of concealing intellectual debts, but also because of the uncertainty surrounding the authorship of *Horae subsecivae,* a collection of a dozen essays and four discourses, published in 1620. That these essays originated within the circle of his patron, the future second earl of Devonshire, is inarguable. Disentangling Hobbes's part in their production is much more difficult.[40]

[38] Gerhard Oestreich, *Neostoicism and the Early Modern State* (Cambridge: Cambridge University Press, 1982); and Richard Tuck, *Philosophy and Government 1572–1651* (Cambridge: Cambridge University Press, 1993), esp. 282.

[39] Bolton, *Nero Caesar,* sig. A3v.

[40] Leo Strauss was the first to suggest that Hobbes might have written the book: *The Political Philosophy of Hobbes* (1936; reprint, Chicago: University of Chicago Press, 1952), xii n. The argument was pushed much further by F. O. Wolf, *Die neue Wissenschaft des Thomas Hobbes* (Stuttgart-Bad Cannstatt: Frohman-Holzboog, 1969), who published in its entirety a MS draft (at Chatsworth) containing some of the essays; Wolf's argument was disputed by (among others) Douglas Bush, "Hobbes, William Cavendish, and 'Essayes,'" *Notes and Queries,* n.s. 20 (May 1973): 162–4. Arlene W. Saxonhouse, "Hobbes & the *Horae subsecivae,*" *Polity* 13 (1981): 541–67, presented a much more balanced view; she also discussed the relationship between Bacon and Hobbes. More recently, Noel B. Reynolds and John L. Hilton, "Thomas Hobbes and the Authorship of the *Horae subsecivae,*" *History of Political Thought* 14 (1993): 361–80, have published a statistical analysis in an effort to divide the honors between Hobbes and Devonshire. Reynolds and Hilton have now converted Saxonhouse to their cause. In "Hobbes and the *Horae subsecivae*" in *Three Discourses. A Critical Modern Edition of Newly Identified Works of the Young Hobbes,* ed. Noel B. Reynolds and Arlene W. Saxonhouse (Chicago: University of Chicago Press, 1995), 3–19, the two editors argue that Hobbes was the sole author of the discourses on Tacitus, Rome, and laws, leaving that on flattery, together with the essays, to Lord Cavendish or to some other, still unconsidered, author. While the statistics are impressive, other

What we know about the relationship between Hobbes and his patron strongly suggests that, whichever of the two wrote them, there was a high degree of collaboration, by way of discussion before the essays were written, of correction after, or both.[41] In any event, the details of authorship seem to me less important than the possibility of our being able to use the essays as evidence for what both men were thinking about in the years immediately following their return from Italy.

Given Cavendish's and Hobbes's association with the lord chancellor, it is not surprising that the shadow of Bacon looms over all the essays, in style and choice of subject alike. *Horae subsecivae* may also be said to fall primarily into the category of "institute," of books teaching the arts of good behavior, personal or political. Five of the essays are devoted to attacking vices such as arrogance, ambition, affectation, self-will, and detraction; four involve consideration of the life of the aristocrat, exploring such necessary subjects as master and servant, expenses, visits, and country life. Essays on death and religion serve as frames. Nor is everything based only on theory, for the substantial discourse on Rome not only offers general advice to travelers, but does so on the basis of personal experience of the city, while the discourse on law uses as an example the author's knowledge of the Bermuda and Virginia colonies.[42]

The last of the dozen essays, "Of Reading History," is surely the most Baconian. The division of history into natural and civil, civil history into that of church and commonwealth, commonwealth history into that written by way of commentaries or more perfectly "by ioyning together both times, persons, places, councels, and euents" resembles that of *The Advancement*.[43] The argument for the utility of reading history is largely conventional, though there is a touch of Baconian asperity in the observation that historians provide better guides than moral philosophers because the latter would rather engage in disputation than "make a man

---

evidence suggests that the relations between Hobbes and Cavendish were extremely close, and I am thus reluctant to rule out altogether the hand of either from any single section of *Horae subsecivae.*

[41] The only possible exception to this statement is the "Discourse against Flattery," published anonymously in 1611, with a dedication to Lord Kinross, probably Cavendish's father-in-law but (as Linda Levy Peck has pointed out to me in conversation), possibly his brother-in-law. The circumstances surrounding the writing of this discourse in 1610 or 1611 are sufficiently different from the situation in 1620 to make me hesitate to lump it together with the rest of *Horae subsecivae.*

[42] Noel Malcolm, "Hobbes, Sandys, and the Virginia Company," *Historical Journal* 24 (1981): 297–321.

[43] *Horae subsecivae* [H.S.] (London: [Eliot's Court Press for] E. Blount, 1620), 195.

either wise or vertuous."[44] Similarly, historians who search out the causes of great events are to be preferred to poets who limit themselves to such facts as "how great a slaughter was made at such a battell, or who killed most with his owne hand," while taking away "the precedent councels, attributing them to the gods."[45] Invented orations raise a question: On the one hand, "where truth is wanting, the iudgement shall want a foundation . . . *Truth* being the forme and essence of History, without which it is but the worst kinde of *Poetry*"; on the other, though orations are often false, they are so instructive that they should remain.[46] Similarly, though aware that some historians have been censured for their digressions and judgments upon the actors in the historical drama, nevertheless the author avers "I am of this minde, that if it bee done by a wise *Historiographer,* and such as hath been exercised in great affaires . . . a man should esteeme himselfe obliged to him."[47]

A man in pursuit of virtue could do no better than to read histories, but this was not work for the lazy. However much help a wise author offered – and, as we have seen, much was permitted – nevertheless it was up to the studious reader to bring all he read to bear on his own situation. The technique suggested here is

to compare the ages, and places one reades of, with that he liues in, and when occasion is giuen to make in a mans minde application of things past to the present, and to consider whether, and why, they hold, or hold not, is a kind of imaginary practice, to confirme, and make a man the readier for reall action, though farre from the perfection, that vse it selfe, and imployment in great affaires would bring forth.[48]

This resembles Sir Henry Wotton's remark that a soldier, in reading history, should refight mentally the battles he reads about, while a politician "should find the characters of personages and apply them to some of the Court he lives in, which will likewise confirm his memory and give scope and matter for conjecture and invention."[49] Similarly, Fulke Greville instructed the readers of his closet tragedies by reminding them that if they wished to see these actions on their true stage, they should look on the stage where they themselves were actors.[50] Histories and

---

[44] Ibid., 197.   [45] Ibid., 213, 214.   [46] Ibid., 208, 211.   [47] Ibid., 210.
[48] Ibid., 219–20.
[49] *The Life and Letters of Sir Henry Wotton,* ed. Logan Pearsall Smith (Oxford: Clarendon Press, 1907), 2:494.
[50] *The Prose Works of Fulke Greville, Lord Brooke,* ed. John Gouws (Oxford: Clarendon Press, 1986), 135.

tragedies, it would appear, might well teach the same lessons, and by the same means: the *imaginative* comparison of past and present. And this also lay at the root of Jonson's practice.

The expression of such views makes clear that while the authors of *Horae subsecivae* were aware of the debates exercising contemporary historians, in this essay they took a traditional position. They drew the boundary around history broadly, with much of what some thought of as fictional within the borders. Yet the next section of the book was altogether more unusual. Of the four discourses included, that "Vpon the beginning of *Tacitus*" was the only one that might be fitted into the pattern established by the Machiavellian "discourse upon histories or examples."[51] The passages of Tacitus treated in the discourse dealt with the origins of Roman government, and with the ways by which one form of government was converted to another. In that context, the meaning of kingship had inevitably to arise, together with the question of when opposition to it was justified. What did Tacitus mean by saying that, after the deposition of Tarquin for his son's rape of Lucrece, Lucius Brutus instituted both liberty and the consulship? Was bondage inevitably linked to monarchy? No, for resistance occurred only when "Kings abuse their places, tyrannize ouer their Subjects, and wink at all outrages, and abuses, committed against them by any either of their children, or fauorites"; only in such circumstances does human nature rebel against reason and religion.[52] However, where Machiavelli might have given such a passage a contemporary application, the authors of *Horae subsecivae* make no direct reference outside Roman history. Yet the passage hints at their views, as does a remark on the deaths of Brutus and Cassius:

> Though *Cremutius*, that called *Brutus* and *Cassius* the last of the *Romans*, writing it in a time which would not permit a man so much as to looke backe at the former state of the Commonwealth, was perhaps worthily punished; yet this may be truely said of them, that they were the last Champions of the *Roman* libertie.[53]

Bringing in Cremutius Cordus's punishment at this point is rather arbitrary, for the story occurs much later in Tacitus, in a passage beyond the authors' annotations. But the unhappy fate of Cremutius Cordus is the

---

[51] Arlene W. Saxonhouse, "Hobbes and the Beginnings of Modern Political Thought," in *Three Discourses*, 124 n. 2, has an interesting discussion of the idea of "discourse" with reference to Machiavelli but not to Bacon.
[52] *H.S.*, 228–9. [53] Ibid., 249–50.

central episode in Jonson's *Sejanus,* a play devoted to exposing the wiles of tyranny, and this appears to be more than a glancing reference to it.

The technique of analysis employed in the discourse often resembles that of Machiavelli, whereby a particular historical situation is explained by reference either to universal human nature or to general political principles. Of Augustus's preparations for leaving his power to a successor, for example, we are told that the Romans engaged in much debate whether liberty, civil war, or a new monarch were likeliest. Though the restoration of liberty was almost a hopeless cause, yet that did not prevent men from speaking of it: "for men haue generally this infirmity, that when they would fall into consideration of their hopes; they mistake, and enter into a fruitlesse discourse of their wishes."[54] Similarly, on Augustus's taking the title of tribune in order to ally himself with the people, then the strongest part of the state, the authors of *Horae subsecivae* comment that "seeing it is impossible to please all men, it is therefore best for a new Prince to ioyne himselfe to, and obtaine the fauour of that part in his State, which is most able to make resistance against him."[55] Yet despite the Machiavellian overtones, *Horae subsecivae* remains different from Machiavelli in one fundamental way: the refusal to extend the argument to other times and places, particularly to England. The result is that the generalizations give the impression of having been imposed on the text, of having been brought in from the outside rather than of having arisen naturally, and inductively, from the materials of history.

While *Horae subsecivae* reveals considerable awareness of contemporary historiographical discussions, the positions taken by its authors tend on the whole to be slightly old-fashioned. By the time Hobbes came to publish his translation of Thucydides, almost a decade later, his views of history had undergone considerable alteration. The choice of author is itself some measure of the change. In Baconian terms, Thucydides's *History of the Grecian War* fitted into that segment of "perfect history" called the relation of an action, and was particularly valuable because the limitation of subject matter ensured a text "more purely and exactly true" than might be found in large-scale works.[56] This was so because the narrowness of subject meant the author of a relation could have knowledge of all of it and so avoid the use of conjecture, though there was a concomitant danger he might succumb to bias because he was often a participant in the events described. Bacon remarked that ordinarily such

[54] Ibid., 310–11.   [55] Ibid., 257.   [56] Bacon, *Advancement,* 3:335.

bias might be controlled by reading several accounts of the same events. Perhaps because there were no other contemporary accounts of the Peloponnesian War, Hobbes prefaced his book with a "Life and History of Thucydides," so helping the reader to form some judgment of the author's reliability. Indeed, Hobbes was sufficiently influenced by historical scholars like Selden to go to considerable lengths to ensure the accuracy of his translation. Unlike most previous translators, both English and French, he went back to the original Greek. Then, to make it easier for the reader to understand the narrative, he provided maps (one drawn by himself) based on the best authors, with an index giving his sources.

The work was dedicated to the young third earl of Devonshire, who had recently succeeded his father, Hobbes's first patron, in the title. Thucydides's writings, Hobbes notes, were especially useful "as having in them profitable instruction for noblemen, and such as may come to have the managing of great and weighty actions," though he goes on to argue that their greatest value was personal: "For the principal and proper work of history [is] to instruct and enable men, by the knowledge of actions past, to bear themselves prudently in the present and providently towards the future."[57] More particularly, and even more helpful for the individual, "in history, actions of *honour* and *dishonour* do appear plainly and distinctly, which are which; but in the present age they are so disguised, that few there be, and those very careful, that be not grossly mistaken in them."[58] Thucydides was able to accomplish this, Hobbes tells us, by providing for his "auditor" all the materials for a theater of the mind, of the sort familiar to us from Wotton and Greville, thus making his reader almost a spectator of the events, able to draw from them the knowledge of the purposes and motives of the actors. But Thucydides's greatest virtue was his refusal to play the philosopher or "politic" historian. In all too many modern works, Hobbes says, the author insists on inserting wise discourses on manners and policy – but, however well done, these can never be part of the texture of the narration. Thucydides does not do that. Nor is he one of those in whose works "there be subtle conjectures at the secret aims and inward cogitations of such as fall under their pen." The problem, Hobbes notes, is that "these conjectures cannot often be certain, unless withal so evident,

---

[57] Hobbes, "Of the Life and History of Thucydides," in Thucydides, *Eight Bookes of the Peloponnesian Warre*, tr. Thomas Hobbes (London: Henry Seile, 1629), republished as *Hobbes's Thucydides*, ed. Richard Schlatter (New Brunswick, N.J.: Rutgers University Press, 1975), 3, 6.

[58] Ibid., 4.

that the narration itself may be sufficient to suggest the same also to the reader."[59] Instead, Thucydides's narration is so perspicuous that such interpretations are unnecessary.

The individual reader, then, provided he was prepared to work hard enough, might learn from Thucydides how to conduct himself. What is less clear is the extent to which Hobbes intended the readers of his translation to draw any specifically political lessons, that is, how much he saw the text as promoting or defending any particular political system. Looking back on the translation from the other side of the civil war, Hobbes noted that he had particularly favored Thucydides because "He taught me how stupid democracy is and by how much one man is wiser than an assembly,"[60] a view that savors more of Bolton's version of Taciteanism than of that in the *Horae subsecivae*. At the actual time of writing, however, Hobbes had limited himself to pointing out that Thucydides was certainly opposed to democracy and in favor of a mixed government of aristocracy and monarchy.[61] More broadly, the change of thinking illustrated by Hobbes's distorted recollection of his earlier work is symptomatic of the way his view of history had altered. No longer was history the master of the individual's moral life, or even of his political. History now served only as the basis for grand generalizations, which could as easily have been deduced from first principles.

IV

The peculiarities of *Behemoth* come into focus, and are best explained, when seen as part of a general historiographical shift. Looked at in its broadest aspects, this shift began in Italy, near the end of the fifteenth century, when writers like Machiavelli and Guicciardini abandoned the use of history as a source of moral examples and instead found in the past a mine of material that could be worked by practitioners of a fledgling political science.[62] Francis Bacon recognized this a century later when he agreed "that we are much beholden to Machiavel and

---

[59] Ibid., 7.   [60] Farrington, "The Autobiography of Thomas Hobbes," 25.
[61] Thucydides, *Eight Bookes*, 13–4. Hobbes also takes Thucydides's praise of Peisistratus and Pericles, together with the historian's own regal descent, as evidence that he approved of regal government.
[62] On this point, see Felix Gilbert, *Machiavelli and Guicciardini* (Princeton: Princeton University Press, 1965), 203–70; and, more recently, Robert Black, "The New Laws of History," *Renaissance Studies* 1 (1987): 126–56.

others, that write what men do and not what they ought to do."[63] Sir
Philip Sidney made the same point by arguing that the poet's ability to
generalize and idealize made him a better teacher of morality than the
historian, enmeshed as he was in immoral outcomes. In addition, Sidney
noted that the historian, whatever his pretensions to some sort of objective truth, was indebted to poetry – conjecture – for his analysis of
causes.[64] The point was underlined by the increasingly common recognition that invented speeches, in which such "fictional" causes were customarily embedded, had no real place in a historical narrative. As the
historians withdrew behind their ramparts, the poets did likewise, gradually abandoning their traditional historical subject matter.[65]

Bacon's *Advancement of Learning*, categorizing as it does the varieties
of history and of poetry, reflected Sidney's analysis; as Bacon rewrote *The
Advancement* and composed his own account of Henry VII's reign, he
became more aware of the problems raised by discourses using historical
examples and, indeed, of the difficulties involved in any attempt to draw
lessons from history. Yet for all his knowledge of the methods of "politic"
history, Bacon paid no attention to a more important movement in studying the past, the antiquarianism of William Camden, John Selden, and
their associates, who insisted on the analysis, use, and even inclusion of
all kinds of historical source material. Responding to the pressures of a
pervasive philosophical skepticism, these men labored to squeeze the
fictionality from history. In doing so, however, they also much reduced
the utility of history; nor did their style allure readers. During the 1620s,
by way of his contacts with Bacon as well as the poets, Hobbes found
himself in the midst of this and reacted to it, first (perhaps) by way of
Horae subsecivae, then certainly in his translation of Thucydides.

As I have pointed out, most of the essays in *Horae subsecivae* were
conventional (in a Baconian sense), with the only novelty coming in
appending a discourse on Tacitus. However, as some of the Taciteanism
of the 1620s became increasingly critical of the monarchy (for example,

[63] *Advancement*, 3:430.
[64] Sidney, *Apology*, 110; the point is elaborated in a letter by Philip to his brother, Robert,
    18 October 1580, in *The Prose Works of Sir Philip Sidney*, ed. Albert Feuillerat (Cam-
    bridge: Cambridge University Press, 1912–26; reprint 1965–68), 3:131.
[65] Hobbes was very much aware of this move by poets; see his "The Answer of Mr. Hobbes
    to Sir Will. D'Avenent's Preface before Gondibert," in *Sir William Davenant's* Gondibert,
    ed. David F. Gladish (Oxford: Clarendon Press, 1971), 46: "The subject of a Poeme is the
    manners of men, not naturall causes; manners presented, not dictated; and manners
    feyned (as the name of Poesy importes) not found in men."

in Sir John Elyot's speech comparing the Duke of Buckingham to Sejanus[66]), and while at the same time Bolton's use of Tacitus in *Nero Caesar* promoted the virtues of kingship, Hobbes retreated to the safer haven of Thucydides, a historian as political as Tacitus, but without the immense burden of interpretation carried by the Roman. Hobbes's reading of the text limited the possibilities further. Here was no collection of examples to inculcate virtue. Instead, the reader might learn something about honor and dishonor, valuable no doubt, but largely concerned with reputation rather than good and evil. In other words, Hobbes treated Thucydides as a useful text for those eager to make their own fortunes, eager too to do so by their own hard work, for in this regard Thucydides gave the reader a little help. Perhaps, too, readers might learn from Thucydides something of the inanity of popular government, and of the corrosive rhetoric that allowed it to flourish. But this was little enough gain for much labor.

By the end of the 1620s, Hobbes had abandoned the writing of history, turning instead to the greater certainties of Euclid and to science. When, finally, he returned to the subject, long after completing *Leviathan* and the other philosophical treatises, he did so reluctantly, and anticipating only a limited result. By this time he had become convinced that men could be taught the wisdom necessary to act in their private causes, but "for the government of a commonwealth, neither wit, nor prudence, nor diligence, is enough, without infallible rules and the true science of equity and justice."[67] Selden had taught him that the most that could be derived from the records were examples of fact, not arguments of right. And of course he believed that even the facts, let alone their interpretations, were debatable. Nor should we expect otherwise. One of the conclusions of *Behemoth* was, after all, that the history of Greece and Rome, misused and misinterpreted in the universities, was a principal cause of the English rebellion. So Hobbes limited himself to an analysis of the causes, done by way of commentary on selected events – in short, to a discourse on history – as a way of explaining why people had acted so foolishly. Except insofar as *Behemoth* shows in great detail how people were misled, it offers scarcely any instruction. There is very little effort to widen the discussion, to bring in other histories by comparison. All that was really unnecessary: the book's political conclusion might as easily have been

[66] Harold Hulme, *The Life of Sir John Eliot* (London: George Allen and Unwin, 1957), 137, 139.

[67] Hobbes, *Behemoth,* 70.

derived from the arguments of *Leviathan*. Indeed, the only practical reform that a wise ruler (or legislature) might have elicited from Hobbes's
lugubrious catalogue was the urgent need for a reform of the universities
to make them teach obedience.[68]

By the time he came to write *Behemoth*, Hobbes had lost all faith that
a reasonable person might learn very much of value from history; moreover, he had also come to realize that history could be manipulated by the
unscrupulous to serve their own ends, or the ends of their party. Hobbes
did not respond to this by taking an absolute position. There is no suggestion that the reading of histories be suppressed. He knew that most
people still took the old view of history, seeking in the past instructions
for acting in the present. To persuade them to act rightly, Hobbes took
over the position of his opponents, recommending that the histories not
be publicly read without the correctives necessary to take away their
venom.[69] *Behemoth*, as a disillusioned discourse on history, provided a
way of finding the correctives.

[68] Ibid., 58.   [69] Hobbes, *Leviathan*, 226.

11

Leviathan, mythic history, and national
historiography

PATRICIA SPRINGBORG

I have attempted (with what Successe I submit to the Reader) to collect out of
Sundrie Authors the Philosophicall sense of these fables of Ouid, if I may call
them his, when most of them are more antient then any extant Author, or perhaps
then Letters themselves; before which, as they expressed their Conceptions in
Hieroglyphics, so did they their Philosophie and Diuinite under the Fables and
Parables: a way not un-trod by the sacred Pen-men; as by the prudent Law-giuers,
in their reducing of the old World to ciuilitie, leauing behind a deeper impression,
then can be made by the liuelesse precepts of Philosophie.
 – George Sandys, preface to the reader to *Ovid's Metamorphosis Englished,*
Mythologiz'd and Represented in Figures

HOBBES, SANDYS, DAVENANT, AND THE
VIRGINIA COMPANY

The Virginia Company of London records in its official minutes that in
1623 George Sandys, newly appointed treasurer of that company, while
crossing the Atlantic to take up his post, "amongst the rorering of the
seas, the rustling of the Shroude, and the clamour of the sailors," accomplished the translation of the first two books of Ovid's *Metamorphoses.*
Once in Virginia he translated eight more, taking the completed manuscript with him on his return to England, where it was published in 1626
and republished in 1632.[1] Believed to be the first work of poetry in the
English language written in the Americas, the first edition is no longer
extant, the Folger Shakespeare Library in Washington, D.C., holding the
only known copy of the second edition.[2] Why did this government offi-

---

[1] Richard B. Davis, *George Sandys, Poet Adventurer: A Study in Anglo-American Culture
in the Seventeenth Century* (New York: Columbia University Press, 1955), 140.
[2] George Sandys, *Ovid's Metamorphosis Englished, Mythologiz'd and Represented in Figures* (Oxford, 1632). I cite this edition.

267

cial, in transit to the New World under the most difficult of conditions, feel compelled to labor at such a work? Of the five or more English translations of Ovid completed between 1590 and 1632, which include those of playwrights such as Arthur Golding, Christopher Marlowe, and John Dryden, Sandys's outdoes all the others in the elaborateness of its textual apparatus, the commentary on some books exceeding even the length of Publius Ovidius Naso's original text.[3] Why were these pioneers of the English theater – and fabricators of the nation – engaged in the translation of Ovid at all?

Some clue may be gained from Sandys's preface to the reader. Explaining his title, *Ovid's Metamorphosis Englished, Mythologized and Represented in Figures,* Sandys observes that "since there is between Poetry and Picture so great a congruitte; the one called by *Simonides* a speaking Picture, and the other a silent Poesie," he has included pictures. For poetry and pictures

Both are Daughters of the Imagination, both busied in the imitation of Nature, or transcending it for the better with equall liberty: the one born in the beginning of the World; and the other soon after, as appears by the Hieroglyphical Figures on the Aegyptian Obelisques which were long before the invention of Letters: the one feasting the Eare, and the other the Eye, the noblest of the sences, by which the Vnderstanding is onely informed, and the mind sincerely delighted.

Sandys advises his readers to find his intentions in the "Minde of the Frontispece and Argument of this Worke . . . for in these ancient Fables lie the mysteries of all Philosophie."[4] His commentary focuses on foundation myths, the colonization of the Peloponnese by Danaus the Egyptian and of Boeotia by Cadmus the Phoenician, who brought with him the science of letters. Of all who recount the genealogies and exploits of the eponymous founder kings and heroes, Ovid – more than Homer, Hesiod, Pausanias, Pindar, Strabo, Diodorus Siculus, Apollodorus, Apuleius, Pliny, Propertius, Horace, and Lucian – most explicitly chronicles the colonization story. Was it for this reason that it attracted the new treasurer of the Virginia Company? How seriously are we to take his case for the primacy of myth over philosophy, the superiority of the ancient wisdom of the Egyptians over the received wisdom? And what does this have to do with *Leviathan?*

---

[3] Even Shakespeare, though no translator himself, draws heavily on the Golding Ovid. See Arthur Golding, trans., *Ovid's Metamorphoses* (1567). In 1599 the *Stationer's Register* records the Archbishop of Canterbury's calling in Marlowe's translation of Ovid's *Elegyes.*
[4] Sandys, epistle to the reader to *Ovid's Metamorphosis Englished,* x.

An excellent piece of detective work by Noel Malcolm, alerting us to the specific issues and contacts out of which Hobbes's apparently more abstract philosophical works were generated, has revealed Hobbes's membership in the Virginia Company as secretary to William Cavendish, earl of Devonshire, a shareholder.[5] In the some thirty-seven meetings of the company Hobbes is recorded as having attended with his patron, issues discussed ranged from fishing rights to justifications for settlement. Rationales canvassed included the natural-rights arguments of Sir Edwin Sandys, brother of George; the right of conquest, officially endorsed by James I; the conversion of Indians preached by John Donne, who, at a meeting attended by Hobbes and Cavendish in November 1622, showed he could turn a Grotian argument just as nicely as Hobbes.[6] Hobbes's friend John Selden, who had been hired separately by James I to write against Grotian law of the sea and who had published his *De Mare Clausum* in 1618 or 1619, may also have been actively involved in the Virginia Company at this time.[7]

Malcolm makes the inspired guess that participation in the Virginia Company was a political school for Hobbes, to which he may have been referring in the preface to his translation of Thucydides (dedicated to Cavendish) when he observes: "Look how much a man of understanding might have added to his experience, if he had then lived a beholder of their proceedings, and familiar with the men of business of the time."[8] In the forcing ground of the Virginia Company Hobbes encountered among its active members the scientists Sir Robert Killigrew and Nicholas Ferrar, friends of Chancellor Francis Bacon; Sir Edward Sackville, Sir Edwin Sandys, the playwright, and his brother George.

Hobbes's association with Bacon has been dated to 1621, Cavendish's to 1616, the year in which the chancellor entered into correspondence with Fra Fulgenzio Micanzio, the Venetian political commentator, through Cavendish's good offices.[9] Cavendish's own years of correspon-

[5] See Noel Malcolm's fine essay, "Hobbes, Sandys and the Virginia Company," *The Historical Journal* 24 (1981): 297–321.

[6] Ibid., 298, 303. [7] Ibid., 306.

[8] *The English Works of Thomas Hobbes,* ed. Sir William Molesworth, (London: John Bohn, 1839–45), 8:viii; cited in Malcolm, "Virginia Company," 315. (*English Works* cited hereafter as *E. W.*)

[9] Malcolm, "Virginia Company," 316. See also Karl Schuhmann, *Hobbes. Une Chronique* (Paris: Vrin, 1996) which professor Schuhmann kindly showed me in preparation. The correspondence between William Cavendish and Fra Furlgenzio Micanzio has been published along with Hobbes's translation as *Lettre a William Cavendish (1615–1628), nella versione inglese de Thomas Hobbes,* ed. Roberto Ferrini and Enrico de Mas (Rome: Instituto Storico D.S.M., 1987).

dence with Micanzio extended from 1615 to 1628, and Hobbes was his translator.

George Sandys, treasurer of the Virginia Company, had his equal in Sir William Davenant, also a company officer. A member of the English emigré community in Paris and renowned as the queen's poet, Davenant was dispatched by Henrietta Maria to Maryland to take care of matters for her there.[10] The newly appointed lieutenant-governor carried on the journey to his post the half-completed manuscript of his long and tedious historical poem, *Gondibert*. And there the parallel with Sandys ends, for en route Davenant was captured by a parliamentary ship and returned to England, where he was imprisoned. In 1650 specimens of *Gondibert*, together with a long preface to Hobbes and Hobbes's reply, were published in Paris, on the subject of which Davenant mused to his respondent, "Why should I trouble you with these thoughts for which I am pretty certain I shall be hanged next week?"[11] In the event, Davenant, largely through the intercession of John Milton, was granted a reprieve. In 1651 *Gondibert* was published in three books, followed in 1653 by Sir John Denham's *An Essay in Explanation of Mr. Hobbes . . . ;*[12] and in 1655, by Davenant's Gondibert *Vindicated*.

As we shall see, Sandys embraced a *pictura poesis* theory of representation famous from Horace's *De arte poetica* and much employed by Elizabethan and Jacobean theorists of poetics. Historiographers and rhetoricians from Lucian, Quintilian, and Cicero to Walter Raleigh, Edmund Spenser, Philip Sidney, and Davenant, keeping the power of the image in their sights, invoked it. The historian, Lucian, had argued in *How to Write History,*

---

[10] See Robert D. Hume's authoritative account of Davenant's role in *The Development of English Drama in the Late Seventeenth Century* (Oxford: Oxford University Press, 1976); and the recent biography by Mary Edmond, *Rare Sir William Davenant* (Manchester: University of Manchester Press, 1987). My account of the nexus between the Caroline court and the stage is greatly indebted to Nancy Klein Maguire's study of politicians as playwrights in *Regicide and Restoration: English Tragicomedy, 1660–1671* (Cambridge: Cambridge University Press, 1992); and to the comments made by Maguire on this essay. For Davenant's individual plays, see *The London Stage* (London, 1824–27), vol. 1 (calendar of plays, 1660–1700).

[11] Sir William Davenant, *A discourse upon Gondibert* (Paris: chez Matthiev Gvillemot, 1650).

[12] Denham's essay appeared in *Certain Verses written by Severall of the Authours Friends; to be Reprinted with the Second Edition of Gondibert* (London, 1653). Quite what relation these works bear to one another has been insufficiently investigated. A. H. Nethercot notes that Sir John Denham once listed himself, along with Davenant's rival stage producer Thomas Killigrew and Killigrew's brother-in-law William Crofts, as "dire foes" of Davenant's *Gondibert*. A. H. Nethercot, *Sir William D'Avenant, Poet Laureate and Playwright-Manager* (Chicago: University of Chicago Press, 1938), 244.

must adopt the stance of the impartial spectator, and the images he supplies must be "in no way displaced, dimmed or distorted."[13] This metaphor, adopted by Gerhard Voss in 1623 to define history as the mirror of humanity (*speculum vitae humanae*), found its echo in the discussions of Hobbes and Davenant prefacing *Gondibert.* I have elsewhere speculated that Gerhard Voss, a familiar figure of the London literary scene, was probably an unacknowledged source for Hobbes's own historical poem, the *Historia Ecclesiastica.*[14] Voss's massive history of the pagan religions, *De theologia gentili, et physiologia christiana,* addressed a topic of general interest to Hobbes and his associates, and was specifically cited by Hobbes's friend, the well-known early English deist Edward Herbert, in his *De religione gentilis errorumque apud eos causis,*[15] as well as by another friend of Hobbes, John Selden, author of *De diis syriis* (1617) and by Hobbes's biographer John Aubrey, author of the *Remaines of Gentilisme and Judaisme* (1666).[16]

Not only did histories as mirrors give rise to a specific genre, mirrors for princes (*speculum regum*), but they raised general questions about the relation of history to truth, the role of judgment in history, and history and memory, questions addressed by Cicero in his memorable phraseology: "History indeed is the witness of time, the light of truth, the life of the memory, the messenger of antiquity; with what voice other than that of the orator should it be recommended for immortality?"[17] In reflections on the writing of history, whether mythic or national, *pictura poesis* representation found a powerful role in explaining how the images conjured up by historians translated into behavioral stimuli for readers and how historical *exempla,* therefore, could produce a moral effect. It is small surprise that

[13] See Lucian, *Works,* ed. A. M. Harmon (London: Heinemann, Loeb Classical Library, 1959), 133. Note the important reflections of Reinhart Koselleck on this topos in "Perspective and Temporality: A Contribution to the Historiographical Exposure of the Historical Word," in *Futures Past: On the Semantics of Historical Time,* trans. Keith Tribe (Cambridge, Mass.: MIT Press, 1985), 130–55.

[14] Patricia Springborg, "Hobbes, Heresy and the *Historia Ecclesiastica,*" *Journal of the History of Ideas* 55 (1994): 553–71.

[15] Edward Herbert, *De religione gentilis, errorumque apud eos causis* (Amsterdam, 1663); published in English as *The Ancient Religion of the Gentiles and Causes of Errors Considered* (London, 1705), 141ff.

[16] John Aubrey, *Remaines of Gentilisme,* in *John Aubrey, Three Prose Works,* ed. John Buchanan-Brown (Fontwell, Sussex: Centaur Press, 1972).

[17] "Historia vero testis temporum, lux veritatis, vita memoriae, magistra vitae, nuntia vetustatis, qua voce alia nisi oratoris immortalitati commendatur?" Cicero *De oratore* 2.9.36; cited in the fine essay by Reinhart Koselleck, "*Historia Magistra Vitae:* The Dissolution of the Topos into the Perspective of a Modernized Historical Process," in *Futures Past,* 23.

Hobbes, a humanist reared on the classics who established his credentials as a courtier's client by imitating classical forms, should have demonstrated his acquaintance with a standard principle of historiography in the prefaces to his translations of Thucydides and Homer. Not only does Hobbes once again take his cue from a classical source, but in this case the source is the rhetorician Quintilian, who developed an influential theory of the image-making powers of the imagination:

There are certain experiences which the Greeks call *fantasia*, and the Romans *visions*, whereby things absent are presented to our imagination with such extreme vividness that they seem actually to be before our eyes. It is the man who is really sensitive to such impressions who will have the greatest power over the emotions. . . . From such impressions arises that *energeia* which Cicero calls *illumination* and *actuality*, which makes us seem not so much to narrate as to exhibit the actual scene, while our emotions will be no less actively stirred than if we were present at the actual occurrence.[18]

Hobbes, who imitated the encyclopedic philosophers by elaborating a physics, ethics, politics, rhetoric, and aesthetics, went further than any previous philosopher, except perhaps René Descartes, in refining *pictura poesis* theories of representation in a scientific psychology. Hobbes's psychology takes the production of images based on sense-data to be a mental reflex as mechanical as the creation of images on the retina in optics. It is a small step from seeing the creation of images as the work of the senses to seeing ideas as aggregated images and memory as the relics of decayed sense.[19]

Hobbes elaborated his sensationalist psychology in successive works, in each of which it takes pride of place as the starting point for the exposition of his system. Each of these works had a strategic purpose. *The Elements of Law*, dated 9 May 1640 in the prefatory dedication to the earl of Newcastle, but published in two pirated parts (*Humane Nature* and *De Corpore Politico*) only in 1650, nevertheless began its career

---

[18] Quintilian, *Institutio Oratoria*, trans. H. E. Butler (Cambridge, Mass.: Harvard University Press, 1953), 2:433–7; cited in David Johnston, *The Rhetoric of Leviathan* (Princeton: Princeton University Press, 1986), 19.

[19] Mirror theory, governed by the analogue of the retina in optics, had been raised to a neurological science in Hobbes's lifetime by Thomas Willis, author of two important works: *Cerebri anatome: cui accessit nervorumque descriptio et usus* (1664), illustrated by Sir Christopher Wren, and *De anima brutorum quae hominis vitalis ac sensitiva est* (1672). Willis, a medical doctor, foundation member of the Royal Society, and fellow of the Royal College of Physicians from 1666, argued that the corpus callosus of the brain acted like a retina, or perhaps a kaleidoscope, assembling images directed to it by the optic nerve. I would like to thank Renato Mazzolini, professor of the history of science at the University of Trento, for this information and more general advice.

early.[20] Written as "the Parliament sat, that began in April 1640 and was dissolved in May following," Hobbes tells us, "the little treatise . . . did set forth and demonstrate, that the said power and rights were inseparably annexed to the sovereignty" – that is to say, the power and rights being claimed by Parliament were property of the crowns. He added, "Of this treatise, though not printed, many gentlemen had copies."[21]

In *De Cive* of 1642, revised in 1647, and *Leviathan* of 1651 Hobbes's sensationalist psychology was subtly refined. His theory does not trace a direct path, however, and it is for this reason that the Hobbes–Davenant exchange is so important, presenting us with a snapshot of the theory at a point at which it has not yet been fully disclosed, even within his own circle. In its fully developed form in *Leviathan,* whose contents were clearly as yet unknown to Davenant at the time of the exchange, Hobbes's scientific psychology was both to synthesize his early studies in optics and provide the state with an instrument of crowd control. This was a program Davenant himself come to endorse and elaborate in the *Proposition for Advancement of Morality, By a new way of Entertainment of the People,* dated London, 1653/4.[22]

Pictura poesis theories of poetic representation elaborated by Sandys and Davenant; the relation between history and myth, among myth, collective memory, and the mob; the educative function of music, masques, and poetry – these were all issues that Hobbes directly addressed. Sandys's Ovid's *Metamorphosis* is listed among the books in the Cavendish library catalogued by Hobbes at shelf number v. 2.B, and given that Hobbes was acquainted with the man through the Virginia Company, his poetic theory may well have referred to Sandys's preface as well as to the more historically prominent Richard Puttenham, Sidney, and Spenser. Hobbes's participation in a tradition of humanist poetic history and classical historiography belies his reputation for materialist philosophy and the new science.

---

[20] Thomas Hobbes, *Human Nature: Or, the fundamental Elements of Policie* (London, 1650); *De Corpore Politico. Or, the Elements of Law, Moral & Politick* (London, 1650).

[21] Thomas Hobbes, *Considerations upon the Reputation of T. Hobbes,* in *E.W.,* 4:414; cited in Cornell Dowlin's useful *Sir William Davenant's Gondibert, Its Preface and Hobbes's Answer: A Study in Neoclassicism* (Philadelphia: n.p., 1934), 45.

[22] Sir William Davenant, *A Proposition for Advancement of Morality, By a new way of Entertainment of the People,* (London, 1653/4), Published as the appendix to James R. Jacob and Timothy Raylor, "Opera and Obedience: Thomas Hobbes and *A Proposition for Advancement of Morality* by Sir William Davenant," *The Seventeenth Century* 6 (1991): 241–9. For the sake of convenience, parenthetical references to this appendix will be given following citations of the 1653/4 anonymously published edition.

Nor can his early literary works, in particular *De Mirabilibus Pecci Carmen* and *De Motibus Solis,* be dismissed as juvenilia, for Hobbes returned to poetic history in the late *Historia ecclesiastica,* written over some years, and wrote proudly of his early Latin antipastoral poem, *De Mirabilibus Pecci Carmen,* in his *Vita.*[23] In these works, in his introduction to his translation of Homer and Thucydides, and in his response to Davenant's preface to *Gondibert,* we have a compendium of his views on rhetoric that to some extent runs counter to the received view of Hobbes. The list Hobbes gives in the *Vita* of his friends – including the antiquarian historians Herbert of Cherbury, John Selden, and John Aubrey and the two poet laureates, Ben Jonson and William Davenant – along with his allusion there to William Camden and the art of chorography alerts us to a man deeply involved in the humanist aesthetic and historiographical debates of his day as well as in the perennial philosophical issues that lay behind them.

HISTORY AND THE "THE KINGDOM OF LANGUAGE"

What is the content of the poem *Gondibert* that Hobbes should, as the author tells us, have given it "a daily examination as it was writing"[24] and have seen fit to respond in difficult circumstances to a dedicatory preface? Davenant's "Heroick Poem," as he calls it in his subtitle, is a frontal attack on the metamorphic mode, and specifically Spenser's *Faerie Queen,* which otherwise might seem to be its closest relative. For *Gondibert* is a Christian romance in the Arthurian tradition, a royalist poem written from an aristocratic perspective, hostile to the mob, proselytizing for Protestantism against Catholicism. Thus far there seems little ground between Spenser and Davenant. But *Gondibert* also campaigns for the new science and against Catholic metaphysics; for didactic history and against allegory, even though it is itself clothed in allegorical dress – for reasons of security, one supposes. There is a hidden agenda to *Gondibert,* which Hobbes approves. Begun as Charles I is beheaded, the poem, replete with references to *Eikon Basilike,* may be read as an

---

[23] "Tunc etiam prodiit elegans illud poema *De Mirabilibus Pecci,* quo nomine venit Derviensis agri pars occidentalio, regio montosa atque aspera,* (*Vide Camdeni Britanniam) sed nonnullis, quae rariora habentur, celeberrima." Hobbes, *Vitae Hobbinae Auctarium,* in *Thomae Hobbes . . . Opera Philosophica quae Latine scrisit omnia,* ed. Sir William Molesworth (London, 1939–45), 1:xxvii. *De Mirabilibus Pecci, Carmen* lacks a modern-edition or even a proper translation. See the forthcoming critical edition by Patricia Springborg and Patricia Harris-Staeblein, in the series edited by Cedric Brown (Reading, U.K.: Whiteknights Press, forthcoming).

[24] Sir William Davenant, preface to *Gondibert: an Heroick Poem* (London, 1651), 1.

exhortation to the future Charles II to extricate his kingdom from the Commonwealth.[25] Disguised in their medieval doublets, the cast of characters may be entirely contemporary. If Gondibert is the young Charles II, Astragon the scientist is Francis Bacon, on whom Book 2, cantos 5 and 6, focus; canto 5 gives an account of the court of Astragon, "little academe," modeled on Bacon's *New Atlantis;* and the whole poem constitutes a tribute to the new science and deism.[26] Oswald appears to be Oliver Cromwell and Princess Rhodalind, Henrietta Maria, who had commissioned Davenant to write *Love and Honour* (1634). Davenant, in what is clearly intented to be yet another mirror for princes, assumes the role of the poet as "unacknowledged legislator" – as he had in the early play *Madagascar,* which attempted to coax Prince Rupert into invading it.[27]

Davenant's preface begins with a straightforward indictment of the ancient "historicall poets" for their resort to fantastic fictions, gods, ghosts, and giants. Homer and Lucian come off badly, but Vergil and Statius are better because they situate their poems at home rather than in heaven or hell.[28] The proper business of the poet is the "History of Nature" and a "selected Diary of Fortune," and he ridicules those who resort to the "descending of Gods in gay Clouds" and believe it "more manly to be frighted with the rising of Ghosts in Smoke."[29]

Let us look more closely at Davenant's objections to the poets. Tasso, "his Councill assembled in Heaven, his Witches Expeditions through the Aire, and enchanted Woods inhabited with Ghosts," was the "first of the Moderns, but his errors deriv't from the Ancients"; he is to be condemned for the following reasons:

the elder Poets (which were then the sacred Priests) fed the world with supernaturall Tales, and so compounded the Religion of Pleasure and Mystery (two Ingredients which never fail'd to work upon the People). . . . Yet a Christian Poet, whose

[25] David F. Gladish, *Sir William Davenant's* Gondibert. (Oxford: Clarendon Press, 1971), xiv, xv.

[26] Ibid., xvii.   [27] Ibid., xv, 290.   [28] Davenant, preface to *Gondibert,* 3–6.

[29] Ibid., 5–6. It is my deep suspicion that this is a Cavendishian–Jonsonian joke, referring simultaneously to the ghost of Leicester, a character in Jonson's *The Masque of Owls,* at *Kenilworth,* delivered at the Leicester family seat in 1626; and Manly, protagonist of the duke of Newcastle's play *The Varietie,* and another latter-day Leicester look-alike in the Jonsonian mode. That Newcastle's plays contain abundant internal reference to those of Jonson, his protégé, and that Davenant belonged to the Newcastle–Cavendish circle, we are in no doubt. For the cross-referencing between Jonson and Newcastle, see the excellent essay by Anne Barton, "Harking Back to Elizabeth: Ben Jonson and Caroline Nostalgia," *ELH* 48 (1981): 706–31.

Religion little needs the aids of Invention, hath less occasion to imitate such Fables.[30]

Davenant turns immediately to Spenser, "the last of their short File of Heroick Poets," with power to "outlast even Makers of Laws and Founders of Empires," who is doubly indicted in this tale. Davenant claims "obsolete language" to be "the most vulgar accusation laid to his charge. Language (which is the onely Creature of Man's creation)," he muses, "hath like a Plant, seasons of flourishing and clearly . . . the unlucky choice of his *Stanza,* hath by repetition of Rime, brought him to the necessity of many exploded words."[31] One of Davenant's modern commentators notes that "exploded" words are "clapped out," or those that lead the author to be "clapped off the stage"[32] – we may guess for political reasons. Davenant seems here to be referring to the famous debate between Spenser and Gabriel Harvey over the relative merits of classical meter and "Gothick rime." It was a debate over the "kingdom of language" that seems to have been replayed between members of the Cavendish circle, to which Hobbes and Davenant belonged, Hobbes undertaking to persuade the martial and Machiavellian earl of Newcastle, who openly scoffed at bookishness and antiquarianism,[33] of the power of rhetoric in politics.

Davenant further convicts Spenser of failing to discharge his duty to his country and of resorting instead to "painted history," the dreamworld of his fever-crazed brain:

His allegoricall story [is] (methinks) a continuance of extraordinary Dreams: such as excellent Poets, and Painters, by being over-studious may have in the beginning of Feavers: And those moral Visions are just of so much use to human application, as painted History, when with the cousinage of lights it is represented in Scenes, by which we are much less inform'd then by actions on the Stage.[34]

Davenant, having clearly read Hobbes's *Elements,* appeals to Hobbesian psychological empiricism to make a case against "fayrieland" with which he expected the master to agree. But his expectations were dashed, in fact, for between the *Elements* and *Leviathan,* Hobbes had refined his theory to provide a role for outrageous fictions. So Hobbes approves

---

[30] Davenant, preface to *Gondibert,* 6–7.   [31] Ibid., 7–8.
[32] Gladish, *Davenant's Gondibert,* 289.
[33] Earl of Newcastle, *Letter of Instructions to Prince Charles for his Studies, Conduct and Behaviour,* from a copy preserved with the Royal Letters in the Harleian MS., 6988, Art. 62; reprinted as appendix 2 to Margaret, duchess of Newcastle, *Life of William Cavendish, Duke of Newcastle,* ed. C. H. Firth (London: Routledge, 1907), 186.
[34] Davenant, preface to *Gondibert,* 7–8.

Davenant's judgment of Spenser, and on the same grounds, but not necessarily his judgment of Homer and Vergil:

There are some that are not pleased with fiction unless it be bold; not only to exceed the *work*, but also the *possibility* of nature, they would have impenetrable Armors, Inchanted Castles, invulnerable bodies, Iron Men, flying Horses, and a thousand other such things, which are easily feigned by them that dare. Against such I defend you (without assenting to those that condemn either *Homer* or *Virgil*) by dissenting only from those that think the beauty of a Poem consisteth in the exorbitancy of the fiction. For as truth is the bound of Historical, so the Resemblance of truth is the limit of Poeticall Liberty.[35]

On formalistic grounds Hobbes rules out the claims to poetry of Empedocles, Lucretius, Phocylides Theognis, Pybrach, and Lucian, who qualify rather as "Historians, or Philosophers." He invokes Aristotle's distinction between historians and poets – historians as chroniclers and tellers of tales, and poets as priests – declaring: "But the subject of a Poem is the manners of men, not natural causes; manners presented, not dictated; and manners feigned (as the name of Poesy imports) not found in men."[36]

Hobbes's insistence that ideas are the reflex of sensations produced a theory of environmental conditioning that made memory, imagination, and history problematic. Since we cannot experience the past, how can we know it? His answer was, in fact, derived from works in aesthetics and poetics that theorized the imagination as constituted of bits of remembered sense-data. These included Sir Philip Sidney's *Apologie for Poetrie* (1595) and the earlier and influential *Arte of English Poesie,* attributed to George Puttenham but issued anonymously in 1589 by Richard Field with a dedication to Lord Burghley. Debates conducted between members of the self-styled Areopagus – including Sidney, Edmund Spenser, and Gabriel Harvey, who frequently met at Leicester House between the years 1578 and 1579 – turned on the uses of tradition and the comparative merits of imperial meter and Gothic rhyme, poetry and politics, truth and persuasion, nature and the kingdom of the imagination.

In a much-cited debate between Spenser and Harvey over language conducted between 1579 and 1580, Spenser, in service to the queen's favorite, Leicester, had posed to Harvey the famous rhetorical question, "Why in God's name, may not we, as else the Greeks, have a kingdom of our own language?"[37] Harvey, Spenser's mentor at Cambridge, who de-

---

[35] Thomas Hobbes, *Answer to Davenant's Preface to* Gondibert, 1651, 81.   [36] Ibid., 73.
[37] See Seth Werner, "Spenser's Study of English Syllables and Its Completion by Thomas Campion," *Spenser Studies* 3 (1982): 3. Richard Helgerson prefaces *Forms of Nation-*

fended classical Latin hexameters against native blank verse, certainly understood the game. Challenged by Spenser who claimed to "hate your late English hexameters so exceedingly well," Harvey used the time-honored discourse of rights of resistance to satirize Spenser's subservience to the Crown in tyrannizing over language, asking why:

you must needs . . . against all order of law and in despite of custom forcibly usurp and tyrannize upon a quiet company of words that so far beyond the memory of man have so peaceably enjoyed their several privileges and liberties without any disturbance or the least controlment?[38]

The debate had in fact begun much earlier with the queen's tutor, Roger Ascham, whose *Scholemaster* of 1570 was a mirror for Elizabeth and an early guide to rhetoric. Anticipating the debate between Spenser and Harvey that was to follow over the relative merits of the Gothic versus the imperial traditions, Ascham framed the question in favor of cosmopolitanism against localism. His analogue for nativism was the society of acorn-eating primitives Socrates had drawn in the preliminaries to *The Republic,* lampooned by Glaucon as a "society of pigs," and referred to famously by Lucretius in *De rerum natura:*

Now, when we know the difference and have examples both of the best and of the worst surely to follow rather the Goths in riming than the Greeks in true versifying were even to eat acorns with swine when we may freely eat wheat bread amongst men.[39]

At a deeper level what the Spenser–Harvey debate over the kingdom of language represented was a struggle between neoclassical imperial claims and the claims of those representing the ancient constitution and the rights of free born Englishmen. It was thus an anticipation of the

hood: The Elizabethan Writing of England (Chicago: University of Chicago Press, 1992), his fine study of the fabrication of English nationhood in early modern Europe, with this quotation (1). Helgerson notes the following references to the Spenser–Harvey debate: John Lyly's heroic poem, *Euphues* (1578), part 1 of which is Hellenizing, part 2 Anglicizing, aimed at Ascham, Spenser, Harvey; and William Webbe's *Discourse of English Poetry* (1586). Richard Stanyhurst quotes the Spenser–Harvey correspondence and Ascham's project in his 1582 hexameter translation of *Aeneid*, Books 1–4. Helgerson, *Forms of Nationhood,* 30–3. See also Gabriel Harvey, *A New letter of Notable Contents with a Strange Sonet Entituled Gorgon or the wonderfull yeare* (London: John Wolfe, 1593), a reply to Thomas Nashe's *Christ's Teares over Jerusalem;* see also J. Payne Collier's hand-written transcription (Folger Shakespeare Library, Y.d.7 54b).

[38] See *The Works of Edmund Spenser: A Variorum Edition,* ed. Edwin Greenlaw, C. G. Osgood, et al. (Baltimore: Johns Hopkins University Press) 10:16, 10:473–4. Cited in Helgerson, *Forms of Nationhood,* 25, 27–8.

[39] Roger Ascham, *The Scholemaster* (London: John Day, 1570), 145.

terms in which the English civil war of the seventeenth century was to be fought. Hobbes seems to have appreciated this, and perhaps Davenant did as well. Whereas Spenser believed that "reason (or judgement) supplies memory with selected sense impressions" of which it made "an ethical arrangement,"[40] Sidney maintained that poets can improve on nature, defending their free range over the supernatural terrain of gods and heroes:

> Onely the Poet, disdayning to be tied to any such subiection [truth to nature], lifted up with the vigor of his owne invention, dooth growe in effect another nature, in making things either better then Nature bringeth forth, or, quite a newe, formes such as never were in Nature, as the *Heroes, Demigods, Cyclops, Chimeras, Furies,* and such like: so as hee goeth hand in hand with Nature, not inclosed within the narrow warrant of her guifts, but freely ranging onely within the Zodiack of his owne wit.[41]

PICTURA POESIS REPRESENTATION AND THE MIRROR-THEORY OF IMAGINATION

The network of connections between members of the Newcastle–Cavendish circle and Jacobean poets included Davenant, once a page in the household of Fulke Greville, Lord Brooke, Sidney's political biographer. Davenant follows Sidney in recounting the differences between poetry and history, depicting the earliest poets as priests, recalling Alexander the Great's admiration of Homer, and generally making the claim for poetry as a weapon in the armory of the prince. Both see poetry as a "speaking picture," and both claim Plato's disparaging remarks about poets applied only to those who spread false religious beliefs.[42] Not only did Elizabethan and Jacobean theorists of poetics emphasize the political value of the poet above all else, but most of them had a personal reason for doing so. George Puttenham was married to Margery, sister of Sir Thomas Elyot, author of *The Governor*. His *Education or Bringinge up of Children*, dedicated to Margery, urged her to train his nephews on Plutarch. Puttenham, who accompanied Sir Thomas on his embassies to France, Spain, and Italy, wrote a handbook of poetics presented by his publisher

---

[40] D. C. Boughner, "The Psychology of Memory in Spenser's *Faerie Queene*," *PMLA* 47 (1932): 89; cited by Dowlin, *Preface, and Hobbe's Answer*, 57, n. 52. See *Faerie Queene* 2.9.

[41] Sir Philip Sidney, *An Apology for Poetry*, in *Elizabethan Critical Essays*, ed. G. G. Smith (Oxford: Oxford University Press, 1904), 1:156.

[42] See Dowlin, *Preface, and Hobbe's Answer*, 58–9.

as being specifically for Elizabeth's use. Demonstrating extensive knowledge of classical and Italian literature, and citing Quintilian to critique contemporary English poetry, Puttenham declared "historicall" poetry "of all others next the divine most honorable and worthy" because of its power to "perswade," and thereupon introduced his famous mirror theory of memory with clear didactic purposes: "behold as it were in a glasse the liuely image of our dear forefathers, their noble and vertuous maner of life, with other things autentike, which because we are not able otherwise to attaine to the knowledge of by any of our sences, we apprehend them by memory.[43] Puttenham was a likely source for Hobbes's sensationalist psychology, designed like Puttenham's to plumb the psyche of the masses:

And this phantasie may be resembled to a glasse, as hath been sayd, whereof there be many tempers and manners of makinges, as the *perspectives* doe acknowledge for some be false glasses and shew thinges otherwise than they be in deede, and others right as they be in deede, neither fairer nor fouler, nor greater nor smaller. There be againe of these glasses that shew thinges exceeding faire and comely; others that shew figures very monstruous & illfauored. Euen so is the phantasticall part of man (if it be not disordered) a representer of the best, most comely, and bewtifull images or apparances of thinges to the soule and according to their very truth. If otherwise, then doth it breed *Chimeres* & monsters in mans imaginations, & not onely in his imaginations, but also in all his ordinarie actions and life which ensues.[44]

The figure of the glass in which objects are rightly or wrongly arrayed as an image for the mind led Puttenham straight to the mirrorist:

Wherefore such persons as be illuminated with the brightest irradiations of knowledge and of the veritie and due proportion of things, they are called by the learned men not *phantastici* but *euphantasioti;* and of this sort of phantasie are all good Poets, notable Captaines stratagematique, all cunning artificers and enginers, all Legislators Polititiens, & Counsellours of estate, in whose exercises exercises the inuentive part is most employed, and is to the sound and true iugement of man most needful.[45]

There is a directness and transparency to Puttenham's purpose that is proto-Hobbesian. Note the parallels with the opening lines of Hobbes's *Leviathan,* with its emphasis on the artificiality of the state, a product of the artfulness of its engineers responsible for the almost clanking mecha-

---

[43] George Puttenham, *The Arte of English Poesie* (1589), in *Elizabethan Critical Essays,* ed. Smith, 2:41.
[44] Ibid., 2:20.   [45] Ibid.

nism of its constructed body: "For seeing life is but a motion of Limbs, the beginning of which is in some principall part within; why may we not say that all *Automata* (Engines that move themselves by springs and wheeles as doth a watch) have an artificiall life?" Not by chance, when Hobbes comes to characterize the state, he invokes the image of the Gallic Hercules, the mythical king of rhetoric recorded by Diodorus Siculus and of whom the Syrian rhetorician Lucian noted: "That old Hercules of theirs drags after him a great crowd of men who are all tethered by the ears" to his tongue; so Hobbes describes his "Artificiall Man, which we call a Common-wealth," tied by "Artificiall Chains, called *Civill Lawes*, which [citizens] themselves, by mutual covenants, have fastened at one end, to the lips of that Man, or Assembly, to whom they have given the Soveraigne Power; and at the other end to their own Ears."[46] Artful in the double sense of being constructed by art and using the art of rhetoric as his medium, the Gallic Hercules cues us to Hobbes's audiences: rhetoricians and Renaissance mirrorists among the cognoscenti; and beyond, the general reader whom they all hoped to target.

Davenant employs mirror theory in his prefatory reference to "any Heroick Poem that [may be] a perfect glass of Nature," an allusion perhaps to Puttenham, and certainly to Hobbes's theory of sensationalist psychology in *De Corpore Politico*, which he had clearly read. The mirror of the imagination is a metaphor to which Hobbes subscribes: "memory is the World (though not really, yet so as in a looking glass)."[47] He gives Davenant credit for having successfully created in his poem a display in which, as in a kaleidoscope, are mirrored the virtues of its author, distributed among its characters; a glass in which, Hobbes ironically notes, the author sees only the specter of himself:

I beleeve (Sir) you have seen a curious kinde of perspective, where, he that lookes through a short hollow pipe, upon a picture conteyning diverse figures, sees none of those that are there paynted, but some one person made up of their partes,

---

[46] Thomas Hobbes, *Leviathan*, ed. Richard Tuck (Cambridge: Cambridge University Press, 1991), 147. I owe my interest in the Gallic Hercules as a figure for *Leviathan* to the observation of Quentin Skinner in "Thomas Hobbes on the Proper Signification of Liberty," *Transactions of the Royal Historical Society* 40 (1990): 123. Hobbes's reference to the Gallic Hercules may have been very pointed. See Corrado Vivanti, "Henry IV, the Gallic Hercules," *Journal of the Warburg and Courtauld Institutes*, 30 (1967): 185; and Lawrence M. Bryant, "Politics, Ceremonies, and Embodiments of Majesty in Henry II's France," in *European Monarchy: Its Evolution and Practice from Roman Antiquity to Modern Times* (Stuttgart: Franz Steinen Verlag, 1992) 127–54.
[47] Davenant, preface to *Gondibert*, 9–10; Hobbes, *Answer to* Gondibert, line 155, Gladish edn, 49.

conveigned to the eye by the artificiall cutting of a glass. I find in my imagination an effect not unlike it from your Poeme. The vertues you distribute there amongst so many noble Persons, represent (in the reading) the image but of one mans vertue to my fancy, which is your owne.[48]

What may seem at first glance to be only a metaphor or poetic conceit turns out to be an observation that is philosophically serious. In Hobbes's materialist or empiricist theory the mind as a black box with sense-data inputs and cognitive responses lives in the present tense. It can reach into the past by virtue of memory, a retrieval system for items of sense-data from the past. History beyond the reach even of memory can be retrieved only if it can provide its own images to the imagination. Hobbes's historical hermeneutics, not surprisingly, comprises a theory of icons and emblems, images that the poetical historian devises to enliven the facts and put flesh and blood on bare bones. It is in this context that Hobbes remonstrates with Davenant, who follows Puttenham in believing the epic should treat the remote past but finds fault with the heroic poets, whose imaginations were not sufficiently governed by the facts. But imaging the past was, as Hobbes correctly saw, the only way in which its "facts" could be disclosed. Davenant's judgment of Homer was particularly harsh; he reduces his portents to witchcraft and thinks them demeaned by the addition of the witch's familiar, a furry animal with connotations of female sexuality:

he doth too frequently intermixe such Fables, as are objects lifted above the Eyes of Nature; and as he often interrogates his Muse, not as his rationall Spirit but as a *Familiar*, separated from his body, so her replyes bring him where he spends time in immortall conversation; whilst supernaturally he doth often advance his men to the quality of Gods, and depose his Gods to the condition of men.[49]

Clearly supernatural inversions and the power of the poet as priest worried Davenant most. But Hobbes leaped to the defense of the historians, and particularly Homer. It is *"fancy"* that is the source of "those grateful similies, metaphors and other tropes, by which both *poets* and *orators* have it in their power to make things please or displease, and show well or ill to others, as they like themselves." Fancy, Hobbes tells us, informed by true philosophy, is precisely what separates "the ciuility of Europe, from the Barbarity of the American savages,"[50] to whose com-

---

48 Ibid., lines 381–8, Gladish edn, 55.
49 Davenant, preface to *Gondibert,* lines 27–33, Gladish edn, 3–4.
50 Hobbes, *Answer to* Gondibert, lines 151–80, Gladish edn, 49. Bishop Richard Hurd, not necessarily sympathetic to Davenant and Hobbes, nevertheless, in his *Letters on Chivalry and Romance* (*Works,* vol. 4, no. 10, 324; cited in Dowlin, 126) percipiently commented:

pany Davenant would have been condemned, had it not been for the parliamentary ship that unceremoniously rescued him from his fate.

In this exchange we have, I believe, evidence that Davenant had read *De Corpore*, but that the contents of *Leviathan* were unknown to him. Hobbes may even have revised his theory in the latter work precisely to address the conclusions Davenant drew from his earlier work with which he disagreed. *Leviathan* launches an apparently encyclopedic philosophical system intended, Hobbes leaves us in no doubt, to replace the Aristotelian system prevalent in the universities of his day. It begins with a physics, elegantly dispatched in the first few pages. There Hobbes establishes the fundamental principle of atomic physics that matter at rest remains at rest unless acted upon, and its corollary, that matter in motion remains in motion unless impeded.[51] From this theorem he moves straight to a sensationalist psychology in which the mind is activated by the friction exerted on the senses by matter from the external world: "And as pressing, rubbing, or striking the Eye, makes us fancy a light; and pressing the Eare, produceth a dinne; so do the bodies also we see, or hear, produce the same by their strong, though unobserved action."[52]

Hobbes's highly tactile account of the phenomena of sensation, combined with an optically focused theory of cognition, represents some of his most elegant writing. Couched in the elemental, astral language of the Stoics, Epicureans, and Skeptics, Hobbes's theory of mind focuses on images and emblems as the materials with which cognition works. Optics supplies the imagery as well as a technical account of how perception allows the transfer of images, produced by the abrasions of the external

> To speak in the philosophic language of Mr. Hobbes, it [Italian magic] is something much *beyond the actual bounds, and only within the conceived possibility* of nature. But the source of bad criticism, as universally of bad philosophy, is the abuse of terms. . . . Whereas the poet has a world of his own, where experience has less to do than consistent imagination. He has, besides, a supernatural world to range in. . . . Thus in the poets world, all is marvellous and extraordinary, yet not unnatural in one sense, as it agrees to the conceptions that are readily entertained of their magical and wonder-making natures.

51 Hobbes, *Leviathan*, 15:

> That when a thing lies still, unlesse somewhat els stirre it, it will lye still for ever, is a truth that no man doubts of. But that when a thing is in motion, it will eternally be in motion, unlesse somewhat els stay it, though the reason be the same, (namely, that nothing can change it selfe), is not so easily assented to.

Note that Hobbes takes the opportunity to reject the principle of metamorphosis and to guard his own theory against the charge of false logic, as a syllogism with an undistributed middle, by supplying the suppressed middle term in the principle that "nothing can change it selfe."

52 Ibid., 14.

world, from the retina to the brain: "pressure, by the mediation of Nerves, and other strings, and membranes of the body, continued inwards to the Brain, and Heart."[53]

Hobbes accounts for ideas as images sorted by a mechanism that responds to the push and pull of pleasure and pain, reverting to physical atomism pioneered by the Hellenistic philosophers and revived in the Renaissance by the English humanist Sir Thomas Harriot and Hobbes's Dutch acquaintance of the 1640s and member of the Mersenne circle, Pierre Gassendi. The language of strings, sinews, and nerves, of physics and acoustics, in which his theory is expressed not only links Hobbes with his friends and associates, physicians like William Harvey, musicians and humanists like Sir Robert North, but prepares readers for the image of the Gallic Hercules with which Hobbes introduces the sovereign, a figure tied by his lips to the ears of his subjects. By such imagery Hobbes maintains an integral link between his physics and his principal subject matter, and shows his purpose unchanged from what it was in the *Elements:* "to set forth and demonstrate, that the said power and rights were inseparably annexed to the sovereignty."

Perhaps the most startling departure in *Leviathan* from earlier formulations of his psychological theory is the technical role Hobbes assigns imagination or fancy. Distinguishing casuistically between the Latin term "imagination" and the Greek term "phantasie," or "fancy," as he translates it, Hobbes attempts to redefine a concept too often understood to connote the realm of the passions or the irrational. Hobbes insists that the imagination is precisely that mental zone to which the images of sensation are transferred for sorting. While in dreams or half-waking it may sometimes approximate the fever-crazed brain of Davenant's depiction, in fact the imagination is a technical instrument of cognition that therefore describes a value-neutral field.

From the notion that ideas are constituted by images produced in the imagination, Hobbes moves to a theory of memory as a residue of images subject to the onslaught that each new wave of sensation brings to the surface of the mind. It is from this important notion of memory as bits of remembered sense-data that his theory of history is drawn. History writing must produce images and exempla, which are capable of revivifying the past for the purposes of the present. Nor does Hobbes consider the written word the only medium capable of producing this effect. In an age

---

[53] Ibid., 13.

in which a semiliterate audience was reached by emblem books (the comic books of early modernity), Hobbes, like Sandys, set about to provide his readers with "speaking pictures" as well as text. In the famous frontispiece to *Leviathan* and the line drawings illustrating *De Cive* (1642) and its pirated English translation, *Philosophical Rudiments* (1651), we have fine examples. Maurice Goldsmith has drawn our attention to plates in the latter works that copy the illustrations accompanying verses of Horace in an emblem book from Antwerp, *Quinti Horatii Flacii Emblemata* (1612).[54]

DAVENANT'S LESSON LEARNED WELL:
THE *PROPOSITION*

Davenant, it must be said in his defense, proved he had the power to learn: he turned from a rigorous condemnation of poetic devices to advocacy of the performing and dramatic arts in the service of the state. In his *Proposition for Advancement of Morality,* Davenant advocated the foundation of schools where, under government scrutiny, the public would be educated in civic virtue through discourse and the performing arts, masques for the elite and opera for the masses. His piece begins with reference to a Machiavellian text. Observing that "As 'tis the principal Art of Military Chiefs to make their Armies civil, so it is of Statesmen to civilize the people; by which Governours procure much ease to themselves, and benefit to those that are govern'd," Davenant goes on to qualify Machiavelli's statement in *The Prince* on the purgative effects of war on the softness (*mollizia*) of the people: "For the civilizing of a Nation makes them not effeminate, or too soft for such discipline of war as enables them to affront their Enemies, but takes off that rudeness by which they grow injurious to one another, and impudent towards Authority." Davenant sets forth an enlightened *mission civilitrice,* applying through education a schedule of rewards and punishments that will render "penall Statutes and Prisons" unnecessary.[55] Restating with these qualifications fundamental Machiavellian principles endorsed by Newcas-

---

[54] See Maurice Goldsmith, "Hobbes's Ambiguous Politics," *History of Political Thought* 11 (1990): 639–73, esp. plates 4–7.
[55] Davenant, *Proposition*, 1–2 (Jacob and Raylor, 242–3).

> subjects should receive good education from the State, as from vertuous Philosophers, who did anciently with excellent success correct the peoples manners, not by penall Statutes and Prisons, but by Morall Schooles and Heroick Representations at the publick charge; obliging them thus to the Supream Power for their mutual quiet.

tle in his minute on the education of Charles II, Davenant, like his master
Hobbes, promotes a program that substitutes rhetoric and the lessons of
history for religion and the lessons of war:

All Nations are sway'd by the Powers that rule in *Religion, Armes* and *Laws;*
but it is not amiss to observe how ill the generality of men digest these Three
ingredients of Government, by the operations of which the pulick health is
conserv'd. . . . *Armies,* whose Leaders are the Guardians of Empire (for Empire
should be still in Nonage, and ever growing) are improper to command belief
and conformity, because they do it by compulsion; for the mind (being of too
subtil a nature to be toucht with humane force) should be govern'd by the
insinuations of perswasion.[56]

Davenant begins like Hobbes from the premise that "the generality of
mankinde are solely instructed by their senses, and by immediate impressions of particular objects."[57] Cynically observing a general lack of reflec-
tiveness in the general public, easily caught by this or that tinsel image,
and "somuch the sooner gain'd, by how much the first representations
are either illustrious or charming; whether this be by the Eye or Eare,"
Davenant resolves to play to the people's weakness. Perhaps with
Hobbes's support, certainly on the basis of his psychology, he draws up a
political program of performing arts for propagandistic purposes: "For
as great *Buildings,* fair *Pictures, Statues,* and *Medals,* intice the *Virtuosi,*
so *Triumphs, Pageants, Cavalcades,* or any thing new brings the common
people about them."[58]

If Davenant ultimately took one path to pacification, that of dramatic
poetry and opera, and Hobbes another, that of philosophy and history,
their object was the same. Davenant shared Hobbes's suspicion of the
mob, voiced in the latter's prefatory dedication to his translation of Thucydides.[59] Davenant advises:

The people will ever be unquiet whilst they are ignorant of themselves, and
unacquainted with those Engins that scrue them up, which are their passions, in
true characters of the beauties and deformities of vertue and vice.[60]

This is a quite specific appeal to Hobbesian sensationalist psychology, the
push and pull of pleasure and pain, against which theological abstractions have no purchase – "For commonly *Divinity* speaks in abstractions
and high Theories above their understanding, and seldome descends to

---

[56] Ibid., 3–5 (Jacob and Raylor, 243).   [57] Ibid., 9–10 (Jacob and Raylor, 244).
[58] Ibid., 10–11 (Jacob and Raylor, 244).   [59] Hobbes, *E. W.* 8:vii.
[60] Davenant, *Proposition,* 11–12. (Jacob and Raylor, 244).

those usefull parts which are necessary to be learnt."[61] Davenant's is an oblique and prospective criticism of even the most minimal civic religion as incapable of pacifying the masses without the assistance of visual media. He expresses the prophetic view that masques and entertainments for the masses would have a power over popular opinion without parallel in other genres, a view consonant with Hobbes's own program.

By these ommissions the clouds of common mindes continue undisperst, and breed dispair of knowledg, which begets aversion, and aversion begets open defection; but if the peoples senses were charm'd and entertain'd with things familiar to them, they would easily follow the voices of their shepherds; especially if there were set up some Entertainment, which their Eyes might be subdu'ed with *Heroicall Pictures* and changes of *Scenes,* their Eares civiliz'd with Musick and wholsome discourses, by some *Academie* where may be presented in a Theater severall ingenious *Mechanicks,* as *Motion* and *Transposition of Lights,* to make a more naturall resemblance of the great and vertuous Actions of such as are eminent in Story; without any scandalous disguising of men in women's habits, as have bin us'd in Playes; the former would not only divert the people from disorder, but by degrees enamour them with consideration of the conveniences and protections of Government.[62]

This, Davenant concludes, "the wise *Athenians* knew; who dividing into three parts the Publick Revenew, expended one in Shows to divert the people from meeting to consult of their Rulers merit and the defects of Government." They were not the only imperialists to do so: "the *Romans* had not long continu'd their Empire, but for the same diversion at a vaster charge."[63]

Differences of opinion among members of the loosely defined New-castle–Cavendish circles on how to handle the masses were not necessarily as great as these randomly preserved texts might suggest. The earl of Newcastle, in his *Letter of Instructions to Prince Charles for his Studies, Conduct and Behaviour,* a work displaying both Machiavellian pragmatism and Hobbesian nominalism, counsels his prince to read history, "and the best chosen histories, that so you might compare the dead with the living; for the same humour is now as was then; there is no alteration but in names, and though you meet not with a Caesar for Emperor in the whole world, yet he may have the same passions." He proceeds to a discussion of pacification of the masses, which emphasizes social distance, court etiquette, and ways to instill it:

---

[61] Ibid., 12 (Jacob and Raylor, 244).
[62] Ibid., 13–15 (Jacob and Raylor, 244–5).   [63] Ibid., 15 (Jacob and Raylor, 245).

To lose your dignity and set by your state, I do not advise you to that, but the contrary: for what preserves you Kings more than ceremony. The cloth of estates, the distance people are with you, great officers, heralds, drums, trumpeters, rich coaches, rich furniture for horses, guards, marshals men making room, disorders to be laboured by their staff of office, and cry 'now the King comes'; I know these maskers the people sufficiently; aye, even the wisest though he knew it and not accustomed to it, shall shake off his wisdom and shake for fear of it, for this is the mist is cast before us and maskers the Commonwealth.[64]

Like Newcastle, Davenant was explicit both that sensationalist psychology was his rationale and crowd control his motive. The language, like that of Lucian's Gallic Hercules and Hobbes's *Leviathan,* is of eyes and ears and of the means to reach them by persuasion. Thinking undoubtedly of his own poem *Gondibert,* Davenant claims that poetry, worked "the channell of *Mortality,*" could be a "great commander of mindes, and like *Hercules* in the Embleme draw all by the Eares." Spectacle is thus a program of pacification in general:

since there hath not been found a perfect meanes to retaine the people in quiet (they being naturally passionate and turbulent, and yet reducible) and that Perswasion must be join'd to Force, it can be compass'd no other way then by surprisall of their Eyes and Ears.[65]

The shock value of *Leviathan* was greatly enhanced by the choice of a monster figure as its blazon. The frontispiece, produced by his printer Andrew Crooke under Hobbes's supervision, and perhaps executed by Hobbes's acquaintance and Charles I's former tutor in drawing, the engraver Wenceslaus Holler, shows a figure that might equally be the Gallic Hercules as the specter from the Book of Job, as I have elsewhere noted.[66] It represents Hobbes's own "hieroglyphics," perhaps influenced by Sandys. Davenant could not have anticipated such a retrospective rebuke to his attack on the classical use of monsters, ghosts, and ghouls.[67] It was

---

[64] Earl of Newcastle, *Letter of Instructions,* 186.

[65] Davenant, *Proposition,* 19, 11 (Jacob and Raylor, 245, 244).

[66] On the frontispiece to *Leviathan,* see Keith Brown, "The Artist of the *Leviathan* Title Page," *British Library Journal* 4 (1978): 24–36; Arnold A. Rogow, *Thomas Hobbes: Radical in the Service of Reaction* (New York: W. W. Norton, 1986), 156–60; A. P. Martinich, *The Two Gods of Leviathan* (Cambridge: Cambridge University Press, 1992), 362–5; Tracy Strong, "How to Write Scripture: Words, Authority, and Politics in Thomas Hobbes," *Critical Inquiry* 20 (1993): 128–59, esp. 128–30; and Patricia Springborg, "Hobbes's Biblical Beasts: Leviathan and Behemoth," *Political Theory* 23 (1995): 353–75.

[67] Davenant might have found the Gallic Hercules easier to accommodate than the figure from the Book of Job, and his reference to the Gallic Hercules in his *Proposition* might therefore also be read as an implied reference to *Leviathan.*

not easy for Hobbes to accommodate them in a materialist metaphysics, either. For instance, even angels he could account for only as being messengers or as having thin or aerial bodies, because "there is no text in that part of the Old Testament, which the church of England holdeth for Canonicall; from which we can conclude, there is, or hath been created, any permanent thing (understood by the name of *Spirit* or *Angel*,) that hath not quantity."[68] In strict philosophical terms Hobbes's account in *Leviathan* of apparently supernatural phenomena is consistent with his account in the *Answer* to Davenant in the following way. That is, one can give no ontological account of them at all, except as "Idols of the brain, which represent Bodies to us, where they are not, as in a Looking-glasse, in a Dream, or to a Distempered brain waking, they are (as the Apostle saith generally of all Idols) nothing; Nothing at all."[69]

If we look for reasons for the incendiary choice of *Leviathan* as his title – and indeed it came close to being a burning matter – we find several. Having settled, although not without difficulty, the provenance of literary hobgoblins, ghosts, and ghouls, Hobbes insisted on retaining them as useful rhetorical devices. He makes it clear that it is not their fantastic nature as such that is at fault, but the uses to which they are put. Homeric and Vergilian monsters, in fact, served a useful purpose, along with auguries and oracles, miracles and "fantastic shews," in harnessing the popular religions of antiquity to the state. The fault of the Christian religions was to be found less in the nature of their fantastic doctrines than in the uses to which they were put: the establishment of a church-based counterorganization to the state. The clinical judgment of the *Oxford English Dictionary* that Hobbes's *Leviathan* marks a departure from the primeval snake and monster figure the word connoted in Mesopotamian and Canaanite myth to become a technical term for the commonwealth is not beyond query. In the long and highly Vergilian chapter on the "Kingdom of Darkness," Hobbes makes it plain that he has no wish to dispense with devil figures as long as they are useful in the service of the state.

But the title had more than rhetorical uses. It is my suspicion that the old "beare,"[70] renowned for his pugnacity, chose the title of *Leviathan* to offend the Puritans. Hobbes's detestation of Puritanism, running deeper

---

[68] Hobbes, *Leviathan*, 277.   [69] Ibid., 270.
[70] Charles II said of Hobbes, "Here comes the beare to be bayted," as reported by John Aubrey in *"Brief Lives," chiefly of Contemporaries . . .* , ed. Andrew Clark (Oxford: Clarendon Press, 1898), 1:340.

even than his dislike of papists, caused him to object to textual fundamentalism as readily in the case of secular as religious texts. Puritans who read the Bible literally had closed the theaters and imposed a fundamentalist poetics with which Hobbes could never agree. Moreover, since like the ancient historians and epic poets Hobbes was at least as interested in rhetoric as a means of crowd control as he was in art for art's sake, he objected to the denaturalization of the poets' political powers. If Spenser was Puritan-leaning, Davenant's position was ambiguous. But *Leviathan* put Hobbes's work squarely in the Continental cosmopolitan tradition against the supporters of localism, nativism, parliamentarianism, as registered in the Spenser–Harvey debate in defense of imperial meter against the supporters of native rhyme.

The choice of the Satan figure Leviathan and Hobbes's long disquisition on the "Kingdom of Darkness" figured as a Vergilian underworld stamped his work as a burlesque in the French tradition worthy of François Rabelais and Paul Scarron, French *literateurs* of whose company Hobbes proves he is worthy in his scurrilous country-house poem, *De Mirabilibus Pecci Carmen.* Leviathan as an image owes as much to the author of *Gargantua* and *Pantagruel* as it does to the Book of Job; Hobbes's book is in spirit a true Rabelaisian work, irreverent and mocking, a burlesque in disguise of a treatise. At the same time, however, *Leviathan* produces a scientific theory of the imagination that synthesizes Hobbes's work on optics and the theories of poets and rhetoricians accounting for the power of the image. In this work of synthesis only Descartes preceded him. The Hobbes–Davenant exchange in fact anticipates in a different medium the long disquisition of John Locke on Descartes's notion of clear and distinct ideas in his letters to Edward Stillingfleet, Bishop of Worcester. For it was Hobbes's genius to see in a sense-data-based theory of the imagination a fulcrum for the levers of political power, an intuition gleaned from rhetoricians from antiquity whose works were similarly politically focused.

Hobbes's fantasizing did not stop with *Leviathan.* Behemoth is the name of another monster from the Book of Job, and one that Hobbes had suggested to John Bramhall, Bishop of Derby, his most percipient critic, as the fitting title of the bishop's rebuttal of *Leviathan* only to find it deployed as a title to his own history of the Long Parliament. Not only did these figures suggest Hobbes's penchant for the primeval expressions of the ancient antique religions, but they underlined his mental agility in accommodating images that did not conform to a strictly atomist physics or sensationalist psychology. Fancy created a zone of "appearance" in which images were generated as a reflex of sense experience, ready for reassembly in ways either constructive or destructive of the state, depending on the inducements it was capable of providing. If Hobbes produced a physics long attributed to Newton, he was equally responsible for a theory of sensationalist psychology long attributed to Locke. It is my belief that Hobbes's physics, metaphysics, psychology, and theory of history must be read back from his politics, not in a reductionist way, but to acknowledge that, like all great systematizers, he was prompted to clarify those gray areas with which most of us are content to live, in ways concomitant with, and even for promotion of, his cause.

HOBBES ON EPIC HISTORY, THUCYDIDES, AND HOMER

Hobbes's closing salute to Davenant's dedicatory preface is consistent with his project, pacification of the masses through poetry, to which he had made a contribution in the translation of Thucydides and later Homer. Hobbes invokes the "kingdom of language" metaphor, seeming to come down Harvey's side against Spenser, in favor of classical languages of empire as opposed to the vernacular tongue:

I never yet saw a Poeme, that had so much shape of Art, health of Morality, and vigour and bewty of Expression as this of yours. And but for the clamour of the multitude, that hide their Envy of the present, under a Reverence of Antiquity, I should say further, that it would last as long as either the *Aeneid,* or *Iliad,* but for one Disadvantage; and the Disadvantage is this: the languages of the *Greekes* and *Romanes* (by their Colonies and Conquests) have put off flesh and bloud, and are become immutable, which none of the moderne tongues are like to be.[71]

Hobbes was forthright about his own contribution to the instruction of rulers in the preface to his translation of Thucydides, which was dedicated to William Cavendish, earl of Devonshire. There he describes his work in the elaborate metaphor of an image maker among the idol-worshiping gentiles, punningly complimenting Cavendish as the mirror of his father:

And now, imitating in this *civil* worship the *religious* worship of the gentiles; who, when they dedicated any thing to their gods, brought and presented the same to their images: I bring and present this gift of mine, THE HISTORY OF THUCYDIDES, translated into English with much more diligence than elegance, to your Lordship; who are the image of your father, (for never was a man more

---

[71] Hobbes, *Answer to Gondibert,* 87.

exactly copied out than he in you), and who have in you the seeds of his virtues already springing up.

Giving Thucydides a spurious genealogy – "he had in his veins the blood of kings" – Hobbes chooses to commend his writings on different grounds, "as having in them profitable instruction for noblemen, and such as may come to have the managing of great and weighty actions."[72]

Hobbes's judgment of Thucydides is very precise. Among political historians, he has no peer:

It hath been noted by divers, that Homer in poesy, Aristotle in philosophy, Demosthenes in eloquence, and others of the ancients in other knowledge, do still maintain their primacy: none of the exceeded, some not approached, by any in these later ages. . . . But Thucydides is one, who, though he never digress to read a lecture, moral or political, upon his own text, nor enter into men's hearts further than the acts themselves evidently guide him: is yet accounted the most politic historiographer that ever writ.

The reasons are the following. Thucydides is no mere narrator, nor does he break into a narrative to insert a homily. And yet Thucydides has the power to instruct that marks political history:

For the principal and proper work of history being to instruct and enable men, by the knowledge of actions past, to bear themselves prudently in the present and providently towards the future: there is not extant any other (merely human) that doth more naturally and fully perform it, than this of my author.

How does he do it? Not by intrusive speculations or conjectures that distort the story line for no clear gain:

It is true, that there be many excellent and profitable histories written since: and in some of them there be inserted very wise discourses, both of manners and policy. But being discourses inserted, and not of the contexture of the narration, they indeed commend the knowledge of the writer, but not the history itself: the nature whereof is merely narrative. In others, there be subtle conjectures at the secret aims and inward cogitations of such as fall under their pen; which is also not of the least virtues in a history, where conjecture is thoroughly grounded, not forced to serve the purpose of the writer in adorning his style, or manifesting his subtlety in conjecturing. But these conjectures cannot often be certain, unless withal so evident, that the narration itself may be sufficient to suggest the same also to the reader.[73]

The historian's task, we must remember, is to revivify the past, to bring to the surface of the mind relics of sense-data. The historian, like the poet,

[72] Hobbes, *E.W.*, 8:v.   [73] Ibid., vii.

must paint images. With clear reference to Plutarch, Hobbes compares history to spectacle, noting Thucydides's unequaled power to recreate in his readers the passions of the past by

aim[ing] always at this; to make his auditor a spectator, and to cast his reader into the same passions that they were in that were beholders . . . these things, I say, are so described and so evidently before our eyes, that the mind of the reader is not less affected therewith than if he had been present in the actions.

Thucydides' superiority lies in the subtlety with which his lessons are imparted, but they are lessons for all that they are subtle:

Digressions for instruction's cause, and other such open conveyances of precepts, (which is the philosopher's part), he never useth; as having so clearly set before men's eyes the ways and events of good and evil counsels, that the narration itself doth secretly instruct the reader, and more effectually than can possibly be done by precept.[74]

Warning his patron to beware of the mob and its fickleness, Hobbes recommends him to use this private history as a weapon against public intransigence:

Though this translation have already past the censure of some, whose judgments I very much esteem: yet because there is something, I know not what, in the censure of a multitude, more terrible than any single judgment, how severe or exact soever, I have thought it discretion in all men, that have to do with so many, and to me, in my want of perfection, necessary, to bespeak my candour. Which that I may upon the better reason hope for, I am willing to acquaint you briefly, upon what grounds I undertook this work at first; and have since, by publishing it, put myself upon the hazard of your censure, with so small hope of glory as from a thing of this nature can be expected.[75]

The year 1628 had been a turning point for Hobbes. It was the year in which his translation of Thucydides was readied for publication; in which he presented *De Mirabilibus Pecci Carmen* to his patron, the second earl of Devonshire; and the year in which his patron died. Both works of that year touched themes of schism and scandal, dogma and heresy, and the tumult of false opinion that could end only in civil war. Discretion and secrecy were not necessarily incompatible with the obligation of the poet and historian to tell the truth, Hobbes maintained, but they were certainly an injunction on them not to broadcast it too widely. In Hobbes's later address "To the Reader" – a very restricted readership as he makes clear –

---

[74] Ibid., xxii.   [75] Ibid., vii.

prefacing his translation of *The Iliads and Odysseys of Homer* (1673), he notes that "the first indiscretion is, the use of such words as to the readers of poesy (which are commonly persons of the best quality) are not sufficiently known." This caution notwithstanding, Hobbes emphasizes that "justice and impartiality . . . belongeth as well to history as to poetry. For both the poet and the historian writeth only, or should do, matters of fact. And as far as the truth of fact can defame a man, so far they are allowed to blemish the reputation of persons."[76] Impartiality and truth mark the divide between poetry and history on the one hand, and rhetoric on the other. By this criterion, Lucan, who "shows himself openly in the Pompeian faction, inveighing against Caesar throughout his poem, like Cicero against Cataline or Marc Antony . . . is therefore justly reckoned by Quintilian as a rhetorician rather than a poet"; whereas "Homer and Virgil, especially Homer, do everywhere what they can to preserve the reputation of their heroes."[77]

Hobbes's notions of historical description and poetic representation converge in a representational theory of truth that is peculiarly emblematic. If in his taxonomy of the virtues of heroic poetry, "and indeed in all writings published," the first, comprehending all others, can be summed up "in this one word – discretion," or judgment, the sixth "consists in the perfection and curiosity of descriptions, which the ancient writers of eloquence call *icones,* that is *images.*"[78] Hobbes compares at length the methods of Vergil and Homer, to the advantage of the latter:

And in an image is always a part, or rather a ground of the poetical comparison. So, for example, when Virgil would set before our eyes the fall of Troy, he describes perhaps the whole labour of many men together in the felling of some great tree, and with how much ado it fell. This is the image. To which if you but add these words, "So fell Troy." you have the comparison entire; the grace whereof lieth in the lightsomeness, and is but the description of all, even the minutest, parts of the thing described; that not only they that stand far off, but also they that stand near, and look upon it with the oldest spectacles of a critic, may approve it.[79]

---

[76] Ibid., 10:iv, vi. [77] Ibid., viii. [78] Ibid., iv, vi.

[79] Ibid., vi. See also Hobbes's long discussion, in the preface to the reader to *The Iliads and Odyssys of Homer* (1673), of whether Vergil adds anything to the images of Homer, of which the following is an epitome:

> If we compare Homer and Virgil by the sixth virtue, which is the clearness of images, or descriptions, it is manifest that Homer ought to be preferred, though Virgil himself were to be the judge. For there are very few images in Virgil besides those which he hath translated out of Homer; so that Virgil's images are Homer's praises. . . . If it then be lawful for Julius Scaliger to say, that if Jupiter would have

It is curious that Hobbes, the rigorous empiricist and materialist who officially spurns allegory, should set such store by metaphor in the representation of history.

MYTHIC HISTORY AND NATIONAL HISTORIOGRAPHY

The writing of history was never politically uncomplicated. In the period 1500 to 1800 it faced several peculiar challenges. The first was a long tradition of history as allegory. History as a fund of exempla was a rich and syncretic field that allowed innovation under the cover of sameness. It had a serious philosophical undergirding in the Ovid *moralisé* tradition, in explorations of the problem of mutability, and in humanist notions of the will as that which imposed shape on the flux of fortune – within certain irreducible limits – and could stay the ineluctable turn of her wheel. To this humanist tradition the early Hobbes belonged, translator of Thucydides and author of *De Mirabilibus Pecci Carmen*. The phraseology of Hobbes's dedication to his translation of Thucydides was, as I indicated earlier, replete with mirror images, and contained as well a pregnant reference to "gentilism" in which he compares this, his offering to his patron, with the offerings the pagans made to their gods.

But surprisingly perhaps, to those for whom Hobbes was the harbinger of the new science, they were humanist tasks to which he returned late in life as the translator of Homer, and at its close as author of *Historia Ecclesiastica*. Had it not been for the impact of Descartes, Robert Boyle, and the mathematician John Wallis, whose works recaptured for Hobbes the power of Euclid, and for experiments in optics that turned geometry into a demonstrable science, he might never have forsaken classical history and rhetoric for philosophy. But in his philosophy, his science, and even his theology, he was still a mirrorist.

Protestant canons of biblical criticism ushered in by the Reformation had put pressure on allegorical tradition associated with the myth and mysteries of Catholicism and the power of priests. These considerations probably motivated the rigorism of Davenant, whom Hobbes had cause to reprove, but it was Hobbes who was later credited as being among those who eventually forced allegory to depart the field. The allegorical titles of his greatest works, *Leviathan* and *Behemoth*, are witness that this

described the fall of a tree, he could not have mended this of Virgil; it will be lawful for me to repeat an old epigram of Antipater, to the like purpose, in favour of Homer. (*E.W.* 10: viii–x).

was not a project that he unequivocally endorsed, however, and that he retained a role for allegory, like rhetoric, in the service of the state.

The emergence of modern historiography was further thwarted by the prevalence of censorship and active persecution of dissidents by the Tudor and Stuart state, so that political commentators, even those who were theoretically disinclined to accept its premises, hid their teachings under the veil of myth. Some did so because their advice was politically unpalatable, others because they supported the state's right to protect its secrets in the Machiavellian *arcana imperii* tradition.[80] Under a miasma of state secrets and intrigue the modern apparatus of the state grew up, sheltered from the public eye. It is arguable that a right of public access to history was not established until John Locke pioneered the principles of common-language philosophy. The democratization of history was a consequence. Thomas Hobbes, John Selden, Gerhard Voss, and Cluverius, among those who had established a limited field for critical history, cleared the path by removing obstacles the old allegorical tradition posed for the modern state. They declared open season on priestcraft, superstition, and localism but mounted no defense of history as a critical field of inquiry open to all comers.

It may even be the case, as Quentin Skinner's recent papers suggest, that as Hobbes's philosophy matured the scope for rhetoric expanded and the field of history narrowed.[81] "Experience concludeth nothing universally" was a programmatic statement that revisited the principles of Aristotle on history, poetry, and rhetoric, seeming to abandon history in

[80] See Annabel Patterson, *Censorship and Interpretation: The Conditions of Writing and Reading in Early Modern England* (Madison: University of Wisconsin Press, 1984); and Lois Potten, *Secret Rites and Secret Writing: Royalist Literature 1641–1660* (Cambridge: Cambridge University Press, 1989). Even in the early days of a free press, late in the seventeenth century, with the lapse of the printing legislation in force from 1672 to 1679, the Crown put constant and successful pressure on the courts to intervene to protect *arcana* and to force authors of politically sensitive works to have them licensed or face prosecution for "seditious libel." See Philip Hamburger, "The Development of the Law of Seditious Libel and the Control of the Press," *Stanford Law Review* 37 (1985): 662–765.

[81] Quentin Skinner, "Thomas Hobbes on the Proper Signification of Liberty," *Translations of the Royal Historical Society* 40 (1990): 121–51; "Thomas Hobbes: Rhetoric and the Construction of Morality," *Proceedings of the British Academy* 76 (1991): 1–61; "*Scientia civilis* in Clamial Rhetoric and in the Early Hobbes," in *Political Discourse in Early Modern Britain,* ed. Nicholas Phillipson and Quentin Skinner (Cambridge: Cambridge University Press, 1996), 67–93. Quentin Skinner's magisterial *Reason and Rhetoric in the Philosophy of Thomas Hobbes* (Cambridge: Cambridge University Press, 1996), was not available to me when this essay was written, but see my forthcoming review "View from the Devil's Mountain: Quentin Skinner's *Reason and Rhetoric in the Philosophy of Thomas Hobbes,*" *History of Political Thought.*

favor of philosophy and the deduction of propositions from theorems. At the same time it expressed the epistemic difficulties history posed to theorists of sensationalist psychology. For the eternal present of sense perception problematized history. What residues might a retrieval system bring to the surface?

It fell to Hobbes to draw the implications of optics and mathematics for poetics and history. Add to optics – the study of transference of images to the retina – geometry, which made the truths of mathematics transparent to visual perception by spatialization, and you had a potent theory of the power of the images. Hobbes could not dispense with the mirror of memory, as that which presents the past to cognition. And he made a virtue of necessity. Imaginative retrieval practiced by skilled historians with control over their material offered an unparalleled opportunity to focus for political purposes the lens through which the past is viewed. How this was to be done was the subject of debate between the old master and Davenant, his student. Among the few early humanist works of Hobbes published with his consent, the Hobbes–Davenant exchange prefacing *Gondibert* alerts us to the policy perspective of a courtier's client whose works have for too long been viewed as manifestations of the new science *tout court*. Not only did Hobbes mobilize the image-focused poetics of his Elizabethan and Jacobean contemporaries to produce a sensationalist psychology that drove his politics. But he called into play the ancient rhetoricians and heroic poets as bit-players in the participation of the masses as well.

12

Protesting fiction, constructing history

J. PAUL HUNTER

Just over three hundred years ago, a typical 1690s pamphlet called *The Second Spira* appeared in a London bookshop in the Poultry, looking a lot like scores of other publications of the time. It reported a recent news item, recounting in detail the tormented death and last words of an unnamed religious apostate; its story was concisely and quite movingly told, the message explicit, the bead on the reader steady, and the tone predictably didactic. The death had occurred a month earlier in Westminster, and here was a circumstantial, last-hours account of someone who had literally suffered the agony of the damned – emotionally and physically – before giving up the ghost on 8 December 1692. When it appeared at John Dunton's shop on 9 January, the pamphlet was said to have been prepared from the notes of one J. S., a minister of the Church of England who had witnessed the death and recorded the agonized confession.

It is a vivid and rather well-written account, and in a decade enamored of the then-new journalism, with the last words of prisoners hanged on Tyburn's fatal tree, with the propagation of the gospel and the reformation of manners, and with the rising tides of confession and celebratory subjectivity that Jonathan Swift mocked in *A Tale of a Tub,* such a pamphlet on such a topic might have been expected to sell fairly well, several hundred copies perhaps. But no one (certainly not the author or bookseller) would have predicted the sensation it made. A jealous rival six months later guessed that it had sold eighteen thousand copies,[1] and the bookseller himself, who later repudiated the pamphlet and in his autobiography listed it as one of seven books he wished he had never published,

---

[1] The guess was made by E. S. (usually taken to be Elkanah Settle) in *The New Athenian Comedy* (London, 1693), a play that was probably never performed.

said that it actually sold thirty thousand copies in its first six weeks,[2] very likely making it the runaway best-seller of the decade – and quite possibly of the century – in so short a time.

The tercentenary of *The Second Spira* is not likely to seem in need of commemoration, especially since there are not many modern readers who know, care about, or have even heard of the first Spira, a sixteenth-century Italian named Francis or Francesco Spira who had converted to Protestantism but repudiated his conversion and died, according to Protestant versions, an apostate in wretched torment. His story was known in England in the late seventeenth century largely because John Bunyan had retold it in *Grace Abounding* (1666), though there were several other accounts as well. Why a sequel – involving a contemporary Englishman who was also a backslider from his faith and who had died in similar agonies of mind and spirit – made such a splash is a bit of a puzzle. London readers of the 1690s were notoriously hungry for news and novelty,[3] and stories of surprising events – murders, fires, robberies, unusual births, or other "news" – often got attention for a day or two; it was not at all odd for such an event to have a pamphlet to itself. Sometimes coffeehouse talk or London urban buzz meant that a second edition was produced, but this happened seldom, especially when there was no development to the story or subsequent event to report, and for a pamphlet to go through six editions – editions of exceptionally large printings – as *The Second Spira* did is very unusual indeed. As journalistic reporting, as a narrated story, and as a pointed didactic tract aimed at the young, the pamphlet is competently enough done, but it is hard to account for the widely shared desire to own a copy at a price that was not trivial (6d.), especially since the full story would have been readily available orally and the written account itself easily findable in public gathering places. Besides, the event and account were quickly rumored to be fakes, and no original for the dead apostate was ever found, in spite of the pamphlet's claims that a specific clergyman had been present at the deathbed, recorded the substance of the dying words, and turned

---

[2] See *The Life and Errors of John Dunton* (London, 1705), p. 157. Stephen Parks is certainly right in implying that Dunton was at least ambivalent about the pamphlet's success; see *John Dunton and the English Book Trade* (New York: Garland Publishing, 1976), 57–9.

[3] Foreign visitors to London in the late seventeenth and early eighteenth centuries often comment on this "modern" English habit. For an account, see my "'News and new Things': Contemporaneity and the Early English Novel," *Critical Inquiry* 14 (1988): 500–4; incorporated in somewhat different form in *Before Novels: The Cultural Contexts of Eighteenth-Century English Fiction* (New York: W. W. Norton, 1990), 172 ff.

over his full notes to a "methodizer" who ordered the materials for the
press – and also in spite of the bookseller's offer to provide proof of authenticity to anyone who inquired at his shop. How to explain the popularity,
the public fuss, the economic bonanza for the bookseller?[4]

I have briefly brought up the popularity of this pamphlet before, suggesting that the astonishing public response testified to a cultural revelation there someplace, but attributing the success of *The Second Spira*
largely to its vividness, suspense, and other so-called literary qualities.[5] I
am a traditional enough student of texts still to feel unabashed in thinking that quality of writing counts for something even in journalistic accounts and everyday didactic tracts, but I now think that quality alone is
not a sufficient explanation for such unusual popularity, and I think that
the pamphlet touched a sensitive cultural nerve. I want here to revisit the
question of cultural significance in the context of larger issues about fact
and fiction in England at the end of the seventeenth century, and to argue
that the uncertainty about authenticity actually aided sales and was a
major factor in raising the pamphlet to public notoriety.

I

The question of exactly why novelistic fiction emerged when it did as a
major cultural phenomenon in England is still a vexing one even after the
brilliant contributions to intellectual history of Michael McKeon, the
insights into gendered social history of Nancy Armstrong, the canny
Foucauldian addresses of John Bender, and my own attempts to place
novels and novellike narratives and discourses contextually within developing print genres, the loss of oral tradition, and the complex in-
terworkings of expanding urban popular culture.[6] Why does a deeply
Protestant culture slowly edging its way into secularity rather suddenly

---

[4] Contemporary booksellers tried for several years to cash in on the pamphlet's popularity
by offering other sequels, each claiming to be more genuine than the last. See, for example,
Spira Respirans (London, 1695), *A True Second Spira* (London, 1697), and *The Third
Spira* (London, 1724).

[5] *Before Novels*, 182–5.

[6] See Michael McKeon, *The Origins of the English Novel, 1600–1740* (Baltimore: Johns
Hopkins University Press, 1987); Nancy Armstrong, *Desire and Domestic Fiction: A
Political History of the Novel* (New York and Oxford: Oxford University Press, 1987);
John Bender, *Imagining the Penitentiary: Fiction and the Architecture of Mind in
Eighteenth-Century England* (Chicago: University of Chicago Press, 1987); and my *Be-
fore Novels*.

begin to tolerate – even celebrate – fictions that it seems to profoundly disapprove in principle, and why are so many of its major contributors – early English novelists like Penelope Aubin, Daniel Defoe, and Samuel Richardson – those from the specific segment of society most rigidly opposed on religious grounds to works of imagination in virtually any form? The high correlation between Puritanism and the new fiction (like that between Puritanism and the new science) has, of course, long been noted and its contradictions pondered in the light of adamant condemnations of the use of fictionality or feigning in any form, even for didactic, edifying, or devotional purposes – by critics and historians from Romantics to postmodernists.[7] But the pondering has never added up to much beyond puzzlement, and accounts tend to cluster under headings like paradox and irony rather than any kind of historical or cultural explanation.[8] More specifically, the basic cultural questions seem to involve how Puritan writers and audiences resolved their fear of fiction and factitiousness more generally into a taste for – even a fascination with – constructing and consuming stories that either had no basis in fact or, more frequently, were based on actual occurrences but were considerably embellished by writers more interested in telling a good story, entertaining their audiences, or providing a cogent rhetorical discourse than in faithfully recounting verifiable events. It is long since a cliché that the early novel based itself in a kind of verisimilitude or realism that prized apparent truthfulness and made fictions from plausible structures of ordinary human experience – making probability and familiarity of situation, pattern, and character its norms and thereby distancing itself from older fictions, which allowed considerable freedom for exoticism, fantasy, or even magic. But even so, the appearance of truth did not provide then a

---

[7] A different emphasis has recently been provided by Catherine Gallagher, who notes the dominant conservative, Tory perspective of many early women writers. See *Nobody's Story* (Berkeley and Los Angeles: University of California Press, 1996), especially chap. 11. The Puritan background of many early novelists and the Tory politics of struggling commercial women writers are not necessarily contradictory, however. In any event, when I speak here of the "Puritan" background of many early novelists, I refer to their having been reared in restrictive social environments where "entertainments" of any kind were largely suspect – not necessarily to their formal religious affiliation. Richardson, for example, was a faithful Anglican, though he continued to believe in most of the narrow, prescriptive rules of conduct from his youth. And Richard Baxter, who perhaps speaks most consistently and adamantly for the antifiction position, had meant to stay in the Anglican priesthood, though he of course ultimately found that impossible.

[8] The most sustained discussion of this seeming contradiction is in Leopold Damrosch Jr., *God's Plot and Man's Stories* (Chicago: University of Chicago Press, 1985).

satisfactory defense against the traditional prohibitions of fiction, nor does the similarity of method employed by fictions and historical narratives offer now a plausible theoretical account of why such philosophical slippage was allowed to take place, especially among groups known for literal-mindedness, unbending principle, and respect for the integrity of the printed word. It is ultimately to address this large theoretical and historical issue that I wish to examine the text and reception of *The Second Spira*, a work that contains in little all the elements we associate with the popular fiction that emerges as the dominant cultural expression a few decades later:

- circumstantial narrative about an ordinary, contemporary person who experiences dire conflict in everyday human events and choices;
- clear, forceful writing in unstilted and "unliterary" language that thematizes its story along lines that interpret the outcomes of human desire as they play themselves out in the experience of an ordinary individual;
- recognition and appreciation of individual subjectivity so that considerable emphasis falls on the interest of seeing the unique perspective that a single human life provides on larger patterns of human experience;
- a strong didactic impulse that professes its concern about audience response and tries to fudge any doubt about authenticity, first by claiming historical truth, then by offering "proof" from outside the work, and finally by repeating endlessly the good intentions of the writer and asserting the potential edification of readers; and
- a voracious reception among readers, especially urban readers, readers (both men and women) of lower- and middle-station backgrounds, and readers in solitary circumstances who apparently found that it somehow spoke to their personal interests and desires in spite of its dubious claims to historical truth.

I will return shortly to the textual specifics of *The Second Spira*, but first I want to recall in some detail how deep the cultural distrust of fiction could be, how strong the sanctions were against writing or reading it, and how the broad fear of fiction became narrowed into a focus on the specific dangers of reading "feigned Histories" and other printed materials created for individual readers in solitary, as distinguished from communal, circumstances. And in order to do so I want to drop back briefly to a cultural moment a generation before the appearance of *The Second Spira*, a moment thirty-three years earlier, when the restoration of the monarchy was about to occur and when a kind of preview enactment of the Enlightenment took place.

II

The moment I want to reimagine is the moment in the spring of 1660 when the eighteen-year darkness of the London theaters ended and the first lights at the Red Bull in Islington began to flicker on. No such *exact* moment in historical time probably existed, of course; like other crucial cultural moments it exists as a construct, no less real in the cultural life of England because a single candle did not at some specific point dispel the deep accumulated darkness. We now know that the lights may never have gone off completely, that performances may have been sometimes allowed to continue surreptitiously during parts of the Interregnum, and that more regular productions may have begun to take place before even the ambiguous theatrical production of Sir William Davenant's *Siege of Rhodes*. But the artificial light that illuminated the first theater allowed to reopen systematically and officially in anticipation of Charles's return symbolically signals the relaxation of a formal prohibition of public performances of stageplays that the Puritans had made a crucial part of their cultural agenda. From that moment forward, even if the moment was in fact diffused over some period of time and possibly several venues, the public, official enforcement of the ban against staging works of the imagination – "feigned Histories" – was over, the attempt to legislate in the public sphere the fear of fiction gone. No longer could English culture claim the unique experiment of trying to physically prevent falsity – of doctrine, church government, representation, or storytelling – from embodying itself in a public place. The official effort absolutely to expunge feigning was now over. Truth would now have to compete with falseness and fight for supremacy in open battle, just as some leading strict thinkers – John Milton, for instance – had always insisted it should and could.

The grounds for the banning of stage plays – and for the fear behind it – were quite complicated, and the several objections were often allowed to usefully intersect, intertwine, and shade into one another. Several objections had specifically to do with performance or communal response in public places: The objections to acting, for example, included worries about the representation of immoral, inappropriate, or incendiary acts and about the falseness to self or integrity involved in an actor's pretending to be someone else; and objections to the public viewing of theater included both fears of sheeplike collective thinking and moblike collective action. Both these objections had a philosophical/psychological dimension and a pragmatic/political one, and which objections were the more persuasive ultimately in the culture may be impossible to say because of the creative entangling of reasons and the rush to judgment once the Puritans had the power to act. In individual discourses one can find particular arguments privileged, but in the cultural discussion that brought and justified the ban of theatrical performances, reasons were allowed to accumulate and overlap (as often happens in the real world) because the desired result – darkening the theaters – was the same for a variety of people with a variety of motives. But quite beyond the performance and communal aspects of plays lay another, deeper problem: Plays were acts of imagination representing actions or saying words that were not literally true, and this feature was part of the entangled reasoning as well. Even when plays recreated actual, certifiable historical events in a responsible way or retold stories of religious, moral, or exemplary significance – even, in fact, when they portrayed the lives of Protestant saints or dramatized biblical stories – a kind of feigning, embroidering, or outright fabrication was still going on, and that fact bothered many theologians, theorists, and cultural watchdogs as well, not just those in the chapels of dissent, but the larger group in narrow-church Anglicanism. The objection to the literal untruth of plays was often phrased in the same terms as objections to any other kind of "false" story, whether fairy tales, sagas, romances, mythologies, politicized accounts of history, Roman Catholic hagiographies, or perjuries at law. Like performance in a public place, this falseness carried a double implication: Its *conceptual* feigning involved philosophical untruth, and its results might mean that responders or readers learned the wrong kind of lessons. The role of the individual imagination thus became isolated and enlarged in either kind of objection, and individual interpretation, so heavily privileged theoretically in relation to sacred texts, was denied its ability to operate – or at least suspected of inadequacy – in the practical, secular sphere. Only the literal truths of "history" – God's truths as worked out in providential events – could be trusted to produce proper responses and effects, whereas human variants were altogether suspect.

The reopening of the theater as a major cultural institution narrowed and focused the traditional objections in particular ways. The distrust of – and prurient interest in – performance did not, of course, go away; even though drama came back to London with a vengeance, enjoying enormous popularity in court and elite literary circles, strong suspicion remained in the minds of many about the entire theatrical experience, both as a vehicle for acting and as communal response. The fact that

Restoration theater played to a limited, coterie audience may have muted a good deal of felt anger, for the people who now frequented plays could be regarded as degenerate and probably hopeless in any case. At the end of the century, during and just after the Williamite reformation movements that tackled such "manners" evils as swearing, public drunkenness, and Sabbath breaking, there were again two waves of objections, first under the impetus of the Rev. Jeremy Collier in 1698, and second (in a less focused way) in the wake of the theater's responses to the great storm of 1703, when timely performances of *MacBeth* and *The Tempest* were widely regarded as blasphemous.[9]

But the reopening of the theaters did tend to refocus the objections to stage plays as criticisms of fiction and feigning more generally and then to concentrate the fear onto worries about printed materials intended for reading in solitary circumstances. Criticism of the stage as an institution did not disappear once playhouses were officially open and sanctioned again, and there were of course many vivid and exaggerated accounts of the cultural immorality brought about by the theater as an institution, as well as by the lasciviousness of individual plays and productions and the immoral conduct both on and off the stage of actors and, especially, actresses. Plays, for many, stood for the immorality of the court and the nation more generally, and pamphlet readers were constantly reminded that a marked lowering of cultural standards was taking place under the restored monarchy. But, perhaps because plays had lost their general popularity and become an upper-class phenomenon, or perhaps because there was widespread national despair about the possibility of any deep cultural revolution, worry shifted noticeably to concern about readers and reading. Even when plays were discussed in the ubiquitous conduct manuals, it was usually their form as playbooks – reading material rather than performance scores – that drew the attention of moral commentators and would-be reformers.

III

Worries about private reading did have specific "performance" implications, of course: The conduct manuals often stressed the evil actions –

---

[9] On the Collier controversy, there is an especially trenchant analysis of the issues in Aubrey L. Williams, *An Approach to Congreve* (New Haven: Yale University Press, 1979), 58–9. On the controversy in the wake of the storm, see Arthur Bedford, *Serious Reflections on the Scandalous Abuse and Effects of the Stage* (Bristol, 1705); and William Smithies Jr., *The Coffee-House Preachers* (London, 1706).

hasty marriages, work left undone, or sexual misconduct – that might result from reading bad books. But the basic worry was about what the reading of fictions could do to the imagination of readers, something with far more lasting and resonant impact. Wasn't the lost judgment about reality that was involved for writers in the imagining of fictions somehow contagious to the imagination of readers? The danger was most often represented as overheating of the passions or as restlessness about one's social place or station. The incendiary desires that might result from reading love stories were mentioned over and over, so often that in *Gulliver's Travels* Swift could parody them without literally mentioning heated desire at all: It is a servant maid reading a romance who starts the fire in the Lilliputian palace. The efficient cause a reader might be inclined to blame could, of course, be a literal candle, but every reader who knew the oft-repeated truisms about romances knew that the fire here came from the inflammatory nature of such stories and the overheating of the imagination. The most abstract worries about social and personal expectation were often voiced as a threat to the social order, for readers were commonly thought to become dissatisfied with their station when they read about others who had more exciting lives. Samuel Johnson's famous *Rambler* 4 essay is very provocative on why the new novelistic fiction, unlike the old romances, poses just this danger.

Replacing the attacks on stage plays as such after 1660 were vigorous, and often repeated, attacks on written forms of feigning. The attacks – in conduct books, sermons, memoirs, and accounts of public manners – almost always listed several kinds of works of imagination and yoked them together to insist on their common danger, using terms such as "playbooks, romances, and false histories" or "novels, romances, and plays" to encompass the kinds of books that endangered all readers but especially young and female ones. Usually, for some reason, the combination involved three terms, but sometimes there were more, as if the intention were to conflate works of the imagination and put them all on the danger list at once. Richard Baxter, for example, made constant attacks on dangerous books, calling them in three separate sections of his *Christian Directory* "vain Romances, Play-books, and false Stories"; "*Play-books, Romances and feigned Histories*"; and "Play-books, and Romances or Love-books, and false bewitching stories" – in each case insisting on feigning or falsehood as the common element.[10] Whatever the terms, the constant aim was

---

[10] Richard Baxter, *A Christian Directory* (London, 1673), 60, 292, 580.

to distinguish lying from truth, fiction from fact, feigning from reality; and works of imagination were always associated with refusal to tell the truth or inability to distinguish reality from fantasy: either delusion was involved or seduction into irrational thoughts and hopes. Those who insisted that *their* narratives were true found themselves buying into the same terminology and value system, distinguishing what they wrote from the dangerous feigning of others: "a Story, a *Whimwham*, or a *what d'ye call 'em*," was what one 1691 fiction that claimed to be autobiography called the books it wanted to distinguish itself from,[11] and Defoe a full generation later used similar terms to say what *Moll Flanders* and *Robinson Crusoe* were not: *Moll* is, he says in the preface, "a private History" in danger of being confused "with Novels and Romances," and in the preface to Crusoe's *Farther Adventures,* he claims that "All the Endeavours of envious People to reproach [*Robinson Crusoe*] with being a Romance . . . have proved abortive, and as impotent as malicious." Though by Defoe's time, one can sense the slippage (especially in the prefaces to *Serious Reflections* and *Moll Flanders*), Defoe still goes so far as to insist that every single detail is factually true, seeming to leave no room for compromise between fact and fiction and apparently accepting the premise that the distinction between imagination and reality was absolute.[12]

This absoluteness – whatever its practical results, a matter I shall come to – seems to derive from an anxiety similar to, yet significantly different from, that which sponsored the prohibition of public performance, the anxiety about corrupting an audience that would find taint irresistible because of the immediacy and easy contagion of theater. The difference now was that the dangers came to the solitary self; individuals would now be corrupted in their own private closets, the victims not of the example of others and the temptation of communal experience but of their own willful choice, something they could not readily pass off as accident or public infection. Those who read in their own closets books they had been warned about not only corrupted their private places of prayer and private meditation, but submitted themselves willingly to the verbal power of texts that could be too much for their own

---

[11] John Dunton, *A Voyage Round the World,* 3 vols. (1691), 1:7.
[12] Daniel Defoe, *Moll Flanders* (London, 1722), iii; *Farther Adventures of Robinson Crusoe,* (London, 1720), folio A2v. Some works of fiction, some of Eliza Haywood's novels, for example, made little pretense to be true, but they also cast themselves as light entertainment. Much more common was a bold statement (*Oroonoko* is said on its title page to be "A True History") or an elaborate circumstantial account of how the true account came to be obtained.

integrity and strength, an altogether more frightening and dangerous phenomenon because it resided within themselves. In one sense, the view of danger had simply moved from a rural, communal setting to an urban, dislocated one, so that means and audience were merely accidents of time and social change, but the difference was profound from a theological point of view: Given the presumed power of the word and the exaltation of the written text, the alteration in both textual vehicle and the responsibility of the receptor meant that the fabled power of the individual to read and interpret by his or her own lights was called radically into doubt. The theory of texts, by keeping the distinction between truth and falsehood rigid, could claim that only false texts – that is, those infected with lies or injections of human imagination – were truly dangerous and that "truth" texts (those controlled, like the Bible, by a strict adherence to actual historical fact) were safe. But how were readers to know the true text from the false unless their spiritual guides and counselors kept feigning and fiction out of the marketplace altogether?

There is a deep dilemma and a contradiction at the heart of this anxiety about fiction, and of course the human desire to skate on the edge of disaster – something Calvinism and English dissent had always admitted or at least refused to deny – meant that in practice testing the truth of texts by reading ones of uncertain authenticity had a fascination that, in one sense, was even approved or commended. What in fact were readers to do in the face of a text recommending religion and virtue when there might have been an imaginary thrust or fictive event somewhere in the construction of the "history"? Were they corrupted by implication, automatically, irretrievably – subtly destroyed by the insidious introduction of a falsehood not suspected or noticed in time? Or could good intentions and effective rhetoric of well-meaning writers overcome the inherent evils of falsehood and mistake, and could lies be turned to the public good? The answer was not altogether clear in spite of the rigid rejections of feigning. Conduct manuals preached abstinence and refused to waver or give grains. But, meanwhile, writers (sometimes even those whose piety could not be challenged) were not always sure.

John Bunyan had, in a way, faced the dilemma almost a generation before readers of *The Second Spira* confronted it in 1693. What was he to do when, desiring to teach but deprived of a congregation, he found in 1678 that the most convenient and persuasive way of writing was via metaphor, allegory, and parable? He painfully worried it out in an eight-page verse apology, after quoting a justification from scripture on his title page: "I have used Similitudes" (Hosea 12.10).

May I not write in such a stile as this?
In such a method too, and yet not miss
Mine end, thy good? why may it not be done?

He tries his product out on others and asks their advice about his imaginings:

And some said, let them live; some, let them die,
Some said, John, print it; other said, Not so;
Some said, It might do good; others said, No.

But ultimately he rehearses the basic objections and rationalizes a solution:

Why, what's the matter! it is dark, what tho?
But it is feigned. What of that I tro?
Some men by feigning words as dark as mine,
Make truth to spangle, and its rayes to shine.

Still not satisfied even with his agonized rationalizations, he constructs his narrative into a dream sequence, thus in effect making God the creator of the story instead of attributing it to his own imagination. No conscious human intention and no human failings could thus be charged, if readers accepted the premise and believed it to be a dream. "I dreamed a dream . . . ," he says at the start of the narrative account of his pilgrim; "I dreamed, and behold I saw . . . ," the narrative says again and again.[13]

The Second Spira's imagined events could have been justified in much the same way, had the author thought of it, because its aims were just as edificatory, and its events, like those of *The Pilgrim's Progress*, were not fabricated but simply translated from one set of individual human circumstances to another. Richard Sault, who apparently wrote the pamphlet, had himself suffered most of the pangs attributed to his "hero,"[14] just as Bunyan's story about an Everyman named Christian might easily have happened in slightly more particular terms to Bunyan himself, to some other historical individual in the 1670s, or to an aggregated group. What

[13] John Bunyan, *The Pilgrim's Progress,* ed. James Blanton Wharey; revised by Roger Sharrock, 2d ed. (Oxford: Clarenden Press, 1960), 2, 3–4, 8.

[14] Dunton apparently came to believe that Sault had written the narrative and palmed it off as authentic, though whether Dunton had put Sault up to it remains in some doubt. Dunton later claimed that he heard Sault himself wail, "I am Damn'd! I am Damn'd!" – thereby enacting the situation of the second Spira. See "Double Hell," in the "30th" edition of *The Second Spira* published by Dunton in 1719.

Richard Sault apparently did was to vent his own feelings in the guise of letting a dying man express them; he did not exactly imagine the feelings or even the story, but he described his own feelings of depression and attributed them to a character he had made up. Was this fiction or fact, autobiography, projection, or an act of imagination?[15] It would have been hard for Sault himself to say, and *The Second Spira* was his way of not saying it: the pamphlet becomes the kind of allegory of himself that Defoe later claimed *he* had written in portraying Robinson Crusoe's long solitude as a kind of dissenter-in-exile during the twenty-eight-year repressive reign between the Restoration and the Glorious Revolution.[16] And Dunton – midwife to the pamphlet and quite possibly himself mystified by its origins and history – found it hard to sort out the fiction and fact as well. For months he defended the pamphlet's (and event's) authenticity, probably himself believing at first in the version he printed; and the uncertainty of readers about the historicity of what they read may well have been replicated by all those involved in the perpetration of the pamphlet, however much a hoax or fake it actually was.

Readers of *The Second Spira* in 1693 were, in fact, allowed – even encouraged – to have it both ways. The official word was that the account was true, yet there were widespread doubts constantly talked about and even alluded to in the advertisements. The "methodizer" and bookseller gave their honorable word, surely enough to salve any queasy conscience, yet the titillation of something that might be feigned was still available. However unconscious the author and bookseller may have been of their strategies, the message they sent to readers was the kind of mix that amounted to a safe come-on: Here is a story that is efficacious in its teachings and we certify it to be true, though some say it is a fake. Dunton in fact played the game extremely well in this instance, whatever his own belief about authorship and authenticity; he could be extremely shrewd in diagnosing the reading public and his culture more generally, and sometimes (as with the question-and-answer strategy of *The Athenian Mercury* or the proto-Shandean modernism of *A Voyage Round the World*) he saw the directions of the culture far more cannily than any of his contemporaries. But his actions usually mixed bad judgment and an

---

[15] Was Sault a convert to Protestantism, possibly from the same background as Spira? (Sault's name is from western Provence, what is now the Vaucluse region.)

[16] Daniel Defoe, preface to *Serious Reflections*, vol. 3 of *Robinson Crusoe* (London, 1720), fols. A2–A7. See Michael Seidel, *Exile and the Narrative Imagination* (New Haven and London: Yale University Press, 1986), 19–43.

unstable mind with his canniness and flair, so that he seldom followed one success with another, or even got any one success exactly right. In the case of *The Second Spira,* the chances are that his sincerity and shrewdness for a moment found a useful partnership: His repeated announcements about *The Second Spira* in *The Athenian Mercury* stressed *both* authenticity and the challenges made by others, so that the controversy remained alive and readers were almost daily reminded of it. In effect the ads projected uncertainty, a suspension between truth and falsity, inviting potential buyers and readers to invest in the ambiguity. Even Dunton's own doubts about whether Sault had put one over on him – and he did break with Sault shortly after the episode, apparently because he felt he had been misled – served to further and extend the controversy and allow readers some liminal space for histories that just might be fictions, one couldn't be sure.[17] I swear this is true, I dare you to doubt it.

This was the space novels came to occupy until their widespread acceptance by the general public allowed the pretense of literal truth – history – to disappear.[18] It took a long time for that to happen; in the short run, novels insisted they were copied from newly discovered manuscripts, collections of letters found by passersby or collected by arbiters who wanted to set family history straight, memoranda left behind to instruct later generations, secret memoirs surreptitiously made public – stories found, pieced together, made public in spite of attempts to suppress them, or specially revealed, but never made up. By the middle of the eighteenth century, however, that pretense was no longer seen to be needed, and many novels and novelists – not just the boisterous Henry Fielding – celebrated their fiction, their imagination, their conscious art. In the 1750s, a wide variety of novelists (or writers of "histories," as they styled themselves) – Charlotte Lennox, Eliza Haywood, Tobias Smollett, Samuel Richardson, Sarah Fielding – no longer had to hide behind a

---

[17] Booksellers of the time frequently manufactured controversies (though more often about political or theological issues than about events per se) and got their hacks to write on both sides, thereby garnering sales however the reactions went, as long as the debate stayed alive. Whether Dunton consciously had such a strategy in mind with *The Second Spira* is doubtful, though he did issue (besides the five new editions of the pamphlet itself in 1693 and another many years later, in 1719) at least one spin-off work designed to capitalize on the controversy, *A Conference Betwixt a Modern Atheist, and his Friend. By the Methodizer of the Second Spira* (London, 1693).

[18] I am using the term "history" here to mean what those making distinctions between "fiction" and "history" in the seventeenth century were trying to make it mean: factual history; and I have not except by analogy and implication engaged more recent theoretical accounts of the historicity of history.

claim of truth beyond the invoking of history as a label. One indication of the change in fiction's status and acceptability is the way the term "history" had by then come to be used regularly to mean either a true account or an imaginary one.[19] It is not just that in titles "history" was a generic indicator that meant new fiction, what we have come to call the novel, as in *The History of Tom Jones, a Foundling* (1749) and *Clarissa: or The History of a Young Lady* (1747–8). If the species had taken its name from common usage then it would have been "history" and not "novel." But by the 1750s, the term history had changed and broadened to mean simply "story," true or not, so that the terms "history" and "narrative" were now interchangeable. In *The Stage-Coach: Containing the Character of Mr. Manly, and the History of his Fellow-Travellers* (1753), for example, not only is "history" used typically in the title, but the contents of Book 1 is summarized this way: "Conveys the passengers from Scarborough to Ware, and opens the history of a young coquet." Even more clear about the meaning of terms is the summary of Book 2: "Chap. I. Mr. Manly prepares to relate an history. . . . Chap. II. Contains the beginning of an history. . . . Chap. III. Mr. Manley [sic] continues his narrative."[20]

IV

Readers in the 1690s may not, then, have been all wrong when they believed they were reading fact – or when in reading a pamphlet they suspected to be fiction they suspended disbelief and shelled out their shilling in any case. Their act symbolized what vulnerable readers had to do when faced with apparently absolute choices that, sadly, in reality considerably overlapped. Such a circumstance in fact created the liminal space in which fiction – prohibited in principle and edict and even banned for all practical purposes by the very purists who made it happen when they fudged on their beliefs – was culturally allowed to exist. Had there not been stories *pretending* to tell actual tales – and following distinctions that assumed an absolute difference between fact and fiction – there could not have been the novel as we have come to know it. And had audiences not bought into – literally – publications that honored the dis-

---

[19] It remains the case, however, that novels were never really acceptable to many moralists and many readers until well into the nineteenth century. See, e.g., Kathleen Tillotson, *Novels of the Eighteen-Forties* (Oxford: Clarendon Press, 1954), 13–16.

[20] *The Stage-Coach: Containing the Character of Mr. Manly, and the History of his Fellow-Travellers* (London, 1753), iii, iv.

tinction but bridged it anyway, there could not have been cultural space for something between fiction and fact. Works like *The Second Spira* (and there are many of them, mostly "autobiographical" or "eyewitness" accounts of contemporary episodes) are a kind of missing link between the species sharply distinguished and insisted on in seventeenth-century literary and moral theory.[21] Without them there would have been no movement between species, no leap between kinds, no historical motion within accepted traditions. In effect, the psychological space created by uncertainty, desire, and hope allowed something new to develop in the interstices between set and approved genres.

V

When the next wave of literary history is written – one that both confronts the stories of popular culture and admits the uncertainties behind literary-model theory – texts that show how taste becomes unsettled and modified will have to be acknowledged, whether or not they themselves make any significant theoretical moves or lay out patterns for other texts to follow. *The Second Spira* is not a great, brilliant, or paradigm-breaking work; it clumps along in history, obeying the principle of textual natural selection: it follows the guidelines laid out by the past and is not responsible for the future it helps clumsily to open up. Richard Sault is not the father of the novel or the theorist of the early modern consciousness any more than is the tuned-in – but often confused – bookseller whom Sault probably outwitted but helped to survive for at least another fiscal year. Sault told a story that was, as hagiographers say, "ethically" true – a phrase and concept the Puritans could not have tolerated for even a minute in their literal-minded way – but literally feigned: It occupied that liminal space between fact and fiction that the novel had at first to depend on, a space that gave the appearance of fact and actuality (what clunky critics later came to call realism in an imperfect effort to grasp the subtleties of cultural ambiguity) to things that the imagination gave readers as psychological insight or cultural whole cloth. The novel was neither precisely fact nor fiction, but the work of the imagination operating along lines that imitated fact and its historical sequences accurately enough to be sometimes mistaken by close readers for the real thing – that at first

---

[21] Two quite well-known works that resemble *The Second Spira* are *The Apparition of Mrs. Veal* (London, 1705) and *An Account of Some Remarkable Passages in the Life of a Private Gentleman*, 2d ed. (London, 1711).

depended on uncertainty and suspended dependence on historical truth. When writers could simulate – or fake (and they did both) – didactic intentions accurately enough to persuade practiced readers that they were getting historical truth turned to educational ends, they got a readership of serious students of history who allowed themselves the indulgence of following stories of everyday and stories that never were in everyday. Such stories were difficult to tell apart and finally impossible to separate in a world of pamphlets, plots, and politics that depended on calculated uncertainty veneered as fact. Events like the appearance of *The Second Spira* are not making or enabling events, but they are illustrative ones, suggesting that a cultural shift in perception was in the process of occurring. The much-overworked (and probably wrongheaded) term episteme is far too strong to label this shift, but the tidal stillness of the moment when *The Second Spira* appeared helps us to see more clearly the conflicting directions.

VI

But why did an event like *The Second Spira* occur in the 1690s, and what do Williamite habits have to do with creating a cultural space for fiction a generation later? I think the tone of the '90s and the historical myth that came to surround the reign of William and Mary were crucial to the cast of mind that ultimately admitted, against its avowed principles, a space for feigned stories that had a moral and socially useful purpose. I will shortly review the versions of history and the mythologizing of monarchs that were deemed culturally necessary in the climate of political upheaval in the late seventeenth century and especially after 1688. But first I want to recall, in very broad outline, what had and had not been happening in the history of fiction during the seventeenth century in England and on the Continent.

The broad outline shows a clear and plain pattern: among the language systems of the then-powerful modern European national cultures, only two, Spain and France, developed important, internationally influential traditions of prose fiction during the seventeenth century. The Spanish development, represented most brilliantly by Cervantes, was first and perhaps more impressive but relatively brief, as Spanish power, influence, and confidence began to lag. The French tradition developed steadily and cumulatively, so that by the second half of the century there was already something like the modern novel – less subjective, less realistic, and less devoted to ordinariness and contemporaneity than the novel that came out of the eighteenth century once the English got into the creative act, but still recognizable as what we now call the novel. Meanwhile, in England, on the Protestant side nothing much was happening before 1688: There were, as Paul Salzman reminds us, a few individual works of some imagination and accomplishment (Francis Kirkman's *The Unlucky Citizen* [1673], for example, or Aphra Behn's *Love Letters* [1683, 1685, and 1687] and *Oroonoko* [1688] – a very thin tradition.[22] There wasn't much devotion to the reading of fiction there or any deep taste for it. A fair number of French and Italian works, mostly of a romantic, socially backward-looking sort, were translated; some few old-fashioned stories, mostly of a picaresque kind, were newly created; and there were a fair number of love stories old and new available – highly romanticized and fantasized, of novella length and usually called "novels." But nothing in England re-motely resembled the developments across the Channel. In traditional imaginative poetic genres, England had already, by the late sixteenth century, begun to hold its own, but comparatively its most significant cultural accomplishment, symbolized by Shakespeare, was in plays that were then under strong attack from the Puritans – a hint, perhaps, of what would happen a century later in prose fiction.

The Protestant holding back of fiction – a kind of damming up of the imaginative impulse – may have helped develop England's own unique contribution, producing ultimately a version of fictional narrative that was more directly influenced by contemporary historical events and new cultural developments, as well as by Puritan habits of self-scrutiny and attitudes toward work, solitude, subjectivity, community, social ethics, and zealous didacticism, than the Continental version. The English novel, once established on its own distinct course, pushed the Continental novel in new directions and seriously changed the future of the form. But that development would have seemed highly unlikely, not to say dangerous, to the protesters against fiction in the late Restoration, and their "contribu-tion" to it was hardly conscious, voluntary, or cheerful.

Let me now return to the question of how the politics of history may have provided slippage, in the Williamite era, within habitual distinctions between fact and fiction. The old cliché that history is constructed by

---

22 See Paul Salzman, *English Prose Fiction 1558–1700: A Critical History* (Oxford: Claren-don Press, 1985). Catherine Gallagher's recent *Nobody's Story* suggests ways that late Restoration fiction relates to the unstable mix I've been describing, but however one accounts for the fictions of Behn and other Tory writers, the major rage for the new contemporary and probable fiction was still years away.

winners is, of course, only partly true, especially in the Restoration, when nearly everyone constructed history and many wrote it, and when a vast variety of perspectives was available in churches and chapels, court and country, London and villages – and in the many pamphlets and more formal histories that poured from the press. Still, some versions were clearly more accepted and powerful than others, and the rhetorical adjustments around major moments of change – 1660 and 1688, for example – made it clear that versions of history were very much under reconstruction all the time.

For oppositionists who observed and endured the royalist reconstructions between 1660 and 1688, the need to construct William as a viable king was plain, and the public press did a fundamentally good job of it, painting him as strong, brave, pious, and practical – and animating fears of foreign, Catholic control even as they domesticized William of Orange. The poetic exchange between John Tutchin (*The Foreigners,* 1700) and Defoe (*The True-Born Englishman,* 1701) over William's right to be considered English makes explicit not only the way the constructions took form but the way they had to. Those who defended the tight morality and rigid (and literal-minded) distinctions of Williamite reform depended for their authority on a mythologized William – just as early Restoration programs had depended on the open mythologizing of Charles II. It was not that many admitted publicly to constructionism, of course, but after twenty-eight years of watching Stuart royalists prop up their cause with careful image-building and sometimes skillful public relations, supporters of the new king saw plainly what had to be done to make the Glorious Revolution work. There seems to have been little talk, at least publicly, about practical royal politics, but the Williamite era sponsored a quite definable atmosphere of leadership and expediency.

Under Charles II and James II, royalist fictions were generally expected and accepted as theatrical conventions; no one, least of all Puritans, had to believe the myths that allowed them to rule, develop cultural norms and laws, or create dominant discourses. But the Williamite era was different. Here was a monarch – and, more important, an ethos – that validated standards that had been out of fashion for more than a generation, that empowered reformation of manners, and that seemed again to admit the possibility of history as destiny. Here was a reign – and an era – that promised that accuracy, truth, and literalness could again become a standard of historical evaluation and of all narratives that claimed validity. The only difficulty was that William himself – the champion, sponsor, and validator of this program – was there because of metaphor, sleight of hand, historical happenstance turned to advantage. Absolutes might obtain in the integrity of an isolated argument, but they were sponsored by a history that itself depended on utter fiction. William was there only because of a fiction that a broad range of people had agreed on; he had been constructed by those with laudable aims but no better sense of history or accuracy – arguably even a worse one – than those who had prevailed in the Restoration a generation earlier. The relativity of fact was, if not obvious, impossible to be denied. The Protestants who protested fiction in the 1690s were themselves authors of a history that could be demonstrated to be new and, although efficacious, based on a manifest fiction. Some of the readers of *The True-Born Englishman* and *The Second Spira* must have known that in their bones, whether or not they admitted the implications. In any case, observers three hundred years later cannot deny it, and perhaps we can find comfort in the productive literary developments that followed from such a creative misunderstanding of what separated fiction from fact.

My hypothesis is that a tolerance for quiet acceptance of the practical need for convenient fictions slipped unnoticed into cultural habits of mind in the Williamite years and soon became deeply embedded in the responses and behavior, if not the theory and theology, of wide varieties of Englishmen and Englishwomen, and that the practical distances between die-hard Puritans and cultural moderates were lessened just as were the social distances between Dissenters and Anglicans. Learning to tolerate ambiguity was not high on the list of Puritan priorities then or now, but if I am right both about attraction to danger and about subtle shifts in allowing uncertainty in matters of deep principle, readers in the 1690s were allowed, in the right circumstances – circumstances that depended on authoritative assurance in the light of broader cultural doubt – access to the forbidden. *The Second Spira* begins to suggest what feigned histories got to do two or three decades later, though the same pretense – perhaps even pretense often built on sincerity – was still necessary for a few decades more. The rest is, as they say, history.

13

Adam Smith and the history of private life:
Social and sentimental narratives in
eighteenth-century historiography

MARK SALBER PHILLIPS

The assumption that history should be written as a linear narrative of public life is an enduring legacy of the classical tradition in historiography. The link between linearity and public life was deeply held and far from trivial. Politics provided history with a coherent and dignified subject, while in turn the clarity of historical narrative made it a worthy and effective instrument of public instruction. In eighteenth-century Britain this understanding of historical writing retained enormous prestige, but characteristic tensions emerged between its ideal conception of narrative and a multiform practice responsive to a wider range of questions. This was an age, in short, that paid the highest tribute to the literary artistry of ancient historians while undermining some of the central assumptions on which classical politics and historiography were founded. Thus the same half century in which Britain eagerly welcomed David Hume, William Robertson, and Edward Gibbon as its triumvirate of classic historians also saw a busy experimentation with new historiographical genres that were only loosely connected with classical history-of-events, with its traditional focus on politics and statecraft.[1]

I wish to record my debt to a mentor who was one of our foremost students of the historical imagination, the late Felix Gilbert. I greatly regret that he saw only the beginning stages of this work. I am also deeply grateful to John Burrow, Stefan Collini, and Donald Winch, who have helped to guide my passage from fifteenth-century Italy to eighteenth-century Britain.
[1] On the expansion of the range of historical writing in the late eighteenth century, see Peter Burke, "Reflections on the Origins of Cultural History," in *Interpretation and Cultural History*, ed. J. Pittock and A. Wear (London: St. Martin's Press, 1991). An important earlier discussion is Arnaldo Momigliano, "The Eighteenth-Century Prelude to Mr. Gibbon," in *Sesto Contributo alla storia degli studi classici* (Rome: Edizioni di storia e letteratura, 1980), 249–63. Basic studies on the historiography of early modern Britain include Joseph Levine, *The Battle of the Books: History and Literature in the Augustan Age* (Ithaca, N.Y.: Cornell University Press, 1991), and D. R. Woolf, *The Idea of History in Early Stuart England: Erudition, Ideology and "Light of Truth" from the Accession of James I to the*

The classical tradition in historiography was founded on the assumption of the primacy of public life. Not only the literary form of historiography but its scope, value, and dignity were predicated on the view that history is a record of the public actions of public men. In the eighteenth century, however, the usefulness of this definition came into question as its limitations became increasingly evident. Without abandoning their respect for the ancients, writers in many areas of literature and philosophy explored conceptions of the self and society that undermined the presumption that politics could still be treated as an autonomous realm, either of action or understanding. At the same time and on a more pragmatic level, the same conclusion was brought home to a wider class of readers by the practical concerns of a commercial society. Historical writing, it was evident, would have to find ways to accommodate this audience and its recognition of the importance of private life, considered in both its social and its inward dimensions: the everyday world of work and custom as well as the inner one of the sentiments. The alternative (though really there was none) might have been for history to suffer the fate of epic and become a genre without application to modern life.[2]

I will begin with Adam Smith, who was both a dedicated "ancient" on matters of narrative and a seminal analyst of private life in both its social and sentimental dimensions. His *Lectures on Rhetoric and Belles Lettres* – a reconstruction of his lectures from student notes – contains a substantial discussion of historical writing, including a remarkable analysis of subjective effects in narrative that reflects his deep interest in issues of sympathy and spectatorship.[3] Smith's lectures – in the approaches to narrative that he opposes as well as in those he encourages – provide an introduction to

Civil War (Toronto: University of Toronto Press, 1990). For the period under discussion here, Thomas Peardon, *The Transition in English Historical Writing* (N.Y.: Columbia University Press, 1933) remains a broad and valuable survey, as does R. J. Smith, *Gothic Bequest* (Cambridge: Cambridge University Press, 1987). I have presented a critique of Momigliano's widely influential division of historical writing into history and antiquities and offered a wider generic model in "Reconsiderations on History and Antiquarianism: Arnaldo Momigliano and the Historiography of Early Modern Britain," *Journal of the History of Ideas* 20 (1996): 297–316.

[2] The sharp distinction in the classical world between private and public spheres is analyzed by Hannah Arendt, *The Human Condition* (Chicago: University of Chicago Press, 1958), 22–49. On the political language of eighteenth-century Britain, see especially J. G. A. Pocock, *Virtue, Commerce, and History* (Cambridge: Cambridge University Press, 1985).

[3] Adam Smith, *Lectures on Rhetoric and Belles Lettres*, ed. J. C. Bryce (Oxford: Oxford University Press, 1983); henceforth cited as *LRBL*. Smith lectured on rhetoric from 1748 to 1763. For a discussion of his teaching of rhetoric and of the manuscript sources for this text, see, in addition to Bryce's valuable introduction, Ian Simpson Ross, *The Life of Adam Smith* (Oxford: Clarendon Press, 1995), 87–96, 128–31.

the problems that challenged historical writing in his day. Moving from theory to practice, the remainder of my essay presents readings of a small but diverse group of texts to indicate a range of contemporary approaches to the problem of narrating the history of private life. Some of these histories lie beyond the usual canon, but I include them because it is essential to enlarge our view of the historical genres if we want to recover a wider understanding of the aims and resources of historiographical narrative in eighteenth-century Britain.

ADAM SMITH

It is something of a surprise that the most remarkable analysis of the contemporary tension in historiographical narrative comes from Adam Smith, a writer who is rarely thought of in relation to historiography. Moreover, Smith's views on historical composition, expressed in his *Lectures on Rhetoric and Belles Lettres,* can appear narrowly classical and rigidly conservative. As Dugald Stewart later noted in discussing the achievements of William Robertson, Smith was hostile to any device that compromised the continuity of narrative. He "carried to such a length his partiality to the ancient forms of classical composition," wrote Stewart, "that he considered every species of note as a blemish or imperfection; indicating either an idle accumulation of superfluous particulars, or a want of skill and comprehension in the general design."[4]

Smith's hostility to innovations in historical narrative put him at odds with the most innovative developments in contemporary practice, including the work of his good friend David Hume. Yet it was precisely because Smith would not abandon history's commitment to classically prescribed forms of narrative that he produced a fertile reexamination of the way in which a narrative of private life might be constructed. His desire to reconcile his spectatorial analysis of historical writing with the stringent formal demands of linear narrative produces the creative tension animating his discussion of historiography – and it adds a further dimension to the story that he believed that the greatest of the classical historians, anticipating his own theory of narrative, had already shaped their narratives along sentimental lines.

The four lectures at the center of Smith's description of history show

---

[4] Dugald Stewart, *Account of the Life and Writings of William Robertson,* 2d ed. (London, 1802), 141–2.

his classical tastes most clearly, including his uncompromising condemnation of philosophical digressions. Despite the incorporation of the doctrine of sympathy, which would become so central to his work as a moral philosopher, the reader's first impression is certainly that Smith's review of historiography proceeds along lines completely familiar in the classical tradition.[5] Likewise, in the discussion of the history of historiography that follows, where his judgments strongly favor the ancients over the moderns, there seems little reason to dissent from Dugald Stewart's picture of Smith's rigid classicism.

A more balanced and also a more interesting picture emerges, however, if we frame this discussion in wider terms. Smith joined Lord Kames and other proponents of the "new rhetoric" in attempting to put the study of literature on a more philosophical footing. This meant redirecting attention from the rules of composition to the effects of art on the mind of the viewer. But Smith adds to Kames's concerns a parallel interest growing out of his exploration of the moral importance of sympathy. Not only does literature trigger emotional response, it also is called upon to represent emotional states. Yet the emotions belong to the world of inward feeling; how then, Smith in effect asks, can narrative represent such interior, invisible events?

This question, which I find so revealing and so fertile, grows out of the way in which Smith divides his material. Every discourse, he writes, aims either to relate some fact or to prove some proposition. In the latter case we have either didactic or rhetorical discourse; in the former we have narrative, or "the historical style."[6] Smith's unwillingness to mix these two fundamental types of writing is, in formal terms, the basis for his antipathy to the philosophical historian's incorporation of didactic discourse into a historical text. Having characterized narrative in this strict way, Smith then adds a second fundamental division according to whether the events to be narrated are external or internal. The "Design of History," he adds, is "compounded" of both of these. Thus history, which had always been taken to be an account of observable events, is

---

[5] Smith, *LRBL*, 102.

[6] See *LRBL*, 89, where Smith refers to the "rules for narration in generall, that is for the historical Stile." History, then, for Smith is both a fundamental literary mode (i.e., narrative) and a literary genre. It is notable that history in the latter sense – that is, histories – provides him with a very large portion of his literary examples. Fictional narratives, in verse or prose, are much less prominent. This focus on works of history was noted in a contemporary account written by one of his auditors, James Woodrow. See Smith, *LRBL*, 11.

also in some measure the narrative of things unseen – "to wit the thoughts sentiments or designs of men, which pass in their mind." Smith emphasizes the difficulty of narrating these "dispositions of mind," a difficulty that is compounded by the fact that the causes of internal events may themselves be either internal or external.[7]

Smith's next step is to divide narrative technique along similar lines, that is, into direct and indirect methods. The symmetry between objects and techniques, however, is not complete. Internal events, such as the passions and affections, can be described only by the indirect method, that is, "by the Effects they produce either on the Body or the mind." Often, however, the same indirect technique is also the best resource for evoking external objects.[8] Here Smith cites Joseph Addison as an example: By describing the effect of St. Peter's on the beholder, he succeeded far better in conveying a notion of the size and proportions of the church than if he had provided exact dimensions of all its parts.[9]

Clearly Smith's "narratology" – like his moral philosophy – is spectatorial in character and is animated by the same conviction that currents of sympathy flow through and unify all parts of human life, including our reading of literature.[10] Like other sentimentalists, too, Smith stresses that narratives describing misfortune are the most affecting of all. For this reason, an impartial historian wanting to describe the effects of battle

---

[7] Smith, *LRBL,* 68, "The internall are such dispositions of mind as fit one for that certain passion or affection of mind; and the external are such objects as produce these effects on a mind so disposed." *LRBL,* 68. He adds: "But whatever difficulty there is in expressing the externall objects that are the objects of our senses; there must be far greater in describing the internal ones, which pass within the mind itself and are the object of none of our senses. . . . The easiest way of describing an object is by its parts, how then describe those which have no parts."

[8] Smith, *LRBL,* 67, "That way of expressing any quality of an object which does it by describing the severall parts that constitute the quality we want to express, may be called the direct method. When, again, we do it by describing the effects this quality produces on those who behold it may be called the indirect method. This latter in most cases is by far the best."

[9] Smith, *LRBL,* 74.

[10] "As it is mankind we are chiefly connected with it must be their actions which chiefly interest our attention. . . . 'Tis therefore the actions of men and of them such as are of the greatest importance and are most apt to draw our attention and make a deep impression on the heart, that form the ground of this species of description." Smith, *LRBL,* 85. Smith's explanation here of history's concern with important men hints at the fuller discussion elsewhere in these lectures – as well as in *A Theory of Moral Sentiments* – of the sympathetic basis for deference and the way in which natural deference to our superiors underpins the classical rules for tragedy. See *LRBL,* 124. For a helpful discussion of the spectatorial elements in Smith and in Scottish literary culture more generally, see John Dwyer, *Virtuous Discourse: Sensibility and Community in Late Eighteenth-Century Scotland* (Edinburgh: John Donald, 1987).

would be more likely to dwell on the "lamentations" of the defeated than the "exultations" of the victors. But even in respect to the most affecting events, direct description produces a "very languid and uninterresting [*sic*]" impression; "when we mean to affect the reader deeply we must have recourse to the indirect method of description, relating the effects the transaction produced both on the actors and Spectators."[11]

This is the heart of Smith's revaluation of the problem of narrative in the light of his idea of sympathy. The fertility of his discovery may not be fully evident, however, until we reach those lectures – in some ways the most conservative – where Smith reviews the history of historical writing and extols the virtues of the ancients against the inadequacies of the moderns. His judgments on the ancient historians consistently apply sentimentalist readings built on the divisions of narrative outlined earlier. Both Thucydides and Livy are analyzed in this way.[12] Smith's most extensive comments, however, are reserved for Tacitus, whom he credits, in effect, with anticipating his own understanding of narrative.[13] This remarkable reinterpretation is worth quoting at length:

> He had observed that those passages of the historians were most interesting which unfolded the effects the events related produced on the minds of the actors or spectators of those; He imagined therefore that if one could write a history consisting entirely of such events as were capable of interesting the minds of the Readers by accounts of the effects they produced or were themselves capable of producing this effect on the reader [*sic*].[14]

Smith connects the qualities of Tacitus's narrative to the peace and orderliness of his age. In the absence of pressing public affairs, Tacitus realizes that the incidents of private life, though less important than public ones, "would affect us more deeply and interest us more than those of a Publick nature." In calamities of a private nature, Smith adds, "our passions are fixt on one," rather than dispersed over the wider set of figures involved in common misfortunes. Accordingly Tacitus largely dis-

---

11 Smith, *LRBL,* 86–7.
12 Thucydides, for example, writes a "crowded" narrative, "accounting for every event by the externall causes that produced it. . . . He renders his narration at the same time interesting by the internall effects the events producd [*sic*] as in that before mention'd of the Battle in the night." Smith, *LRBL,* 106. So too Livy, the best of the Roman historians, "renders his descriptions extremely interesting by the great number of affecting circumstances he has thrown together." Smith, *LRBL,* 108–9.
13 I have examined Smith's revaluation of Tacitus (as well as the similar interpretation presented by Arthur Murphy's translation) in another context in "Reconsiderations on History." Cited in n.1.
14 Smith, *LRBL,* 111–12.

regards the question of the importance of events, considering instead their affective power. In doing so, he follows the techniques of indirect narration, describing events "by the internall effects" and accounting for them "in the same manner."[15]

Using these techniques more fully than any other historian, Tacitus created a kind of narrative that Smith clearly finds both disturbing and intriguing. Though the events of his history may often be considered secondary, "the method [by which] he describes these is so interesting, he leads us far into the sentiments and mind of the actors that they are some of the most striking and interesting passages to be met with in any history." And when Tacitus does concern himself with more important (that is, public) events, he disregards external causes in favor of the internal ones. The consequence is that his account may not instruct us in the causes of events; "yet it will be more interesting and lead us into a science no less usefull, to wit, the knowledge of the motives by which men act; a science too that could not be learned from [lacuna in text]."[16]

It is impossible to know how this intriguing sentence was completed when Smith spoke this lecture. But the "science no less useful" taught by Tacitus's history of private life clearly has some affinities to the one explored in these lectures and perfected in *The Theory of Moral Sentiments*. The comparison Smith wants to draw, however, is to the literature of contemporary France, where he finds the same luxury and refinement that marked the Roman Empire in the age of Trajan:

Sentiment must bee what will chiefly interest such a people. . . . Such a people, I say, having nothing to engage them in the hurry of life would naturally turn their attention to the motions of the human mind, and those events that were accounted for by the different internall affections that influenced the persons concerned, would be what most suited their taste.

It is for this reason, Smith concludes, that Tacitus so much resembles Pierre Marivaux and Crebillion – "as much as we can well imagine in works of so conterary [*sic*] a nature."[17]

As Smith well knew, this is an extraordinary comparison to make; after all, Tacitus's name had long been a byword for a ruthless, *un*sentimental acceptance of political reality, while in Britain more recently Tacitus had figured as the scourge of tyrants and the champion of lost republican virtue. Smith obviously felt the novelty of what he was doing, and he closes the lecture with an uncharacteristic flourish: "Such is the true Character of

[15] Smith, *LRBL,* 113.   [16] Ibid.   [17] Ibid., 112.

Tacitus," he proclaims, "which has been misrepresented by all his commentators from Boccalini down to Gordon."[18]

What, then, had Adam Smith discovered about Tacitus? He had discovered a sentimentalist, where others had seen a terse, tough, realistic politician. He had found an analyst of private life, where others had seen a critic of politics. He had turned traditional readings of Tacitus inside out. But he had also found something else – the possibility of a history registered in the eyes of spectators, a sentimental history concerned less with outward acts and public occasions than with the private passions and experiences of individuals. And all this without for a moment relinquishing his decided preference for linear narrative.

It must be concluded, in fact, that this conservative element in Smith's literary taste is in large measure responsible for his inventive reexamination of problems in historical narrative. After all, his concern for the operations of sympathy and his stress on the affective powers of literature – including history – were shared by men like Lord Kames, Adam Ferguson, and Joseph Priestley.[19] Smith's discussion is distinguished by his careful attention to the analysis of historical narrative and his conviction that, whatever tasks still challenged eighteenth-century historians, their first models and best mentors would continue to be the great historians of Greece and Rome.

SOCIAL NARRATIVES

Smith's analysis of narrative provides an opening to examine the ways in which eighteenth-century historians responded to the practical challenges implicit in narrating the history of private life. In the remainder of this essay, I would like to sketch two lines of discussion. First, since in practice most historians did not share Smith's purism, it is useful to explore some of the ways historians found to mediate the narrative tensions they encountered. These are histories that violate Smith's prohibition on mixed genres in order to incorporate social experiences lying beyond the framework of political narrative – experiences involving manners, commerce, law, or customs, which had been brought into prominence by the philosophical historians. Second, Smith's analysis of indirect narrative suggests

---

[18] Ibid., 114.
[19] On Lord Kames and the broader question of sentimental reading style in history, see my essay, "'If Mrs. Mure Be Not Sorry For Poor King Charles': History, Novel, and The Sentimental Reader," *History Workshop Journal* 43 (1997): 110–31.

the value of a broader look at techniques of spectatorial narrative as they operate in texts of a predominantly sentimental cast. Taken together, the two sorts of narrative – one, broadly speaking, concerned with manners, the other with the sentiments – contribute to an investigation of two distinct but allied dimensions of private life, the social and the inward. The challenge of narrating both of these dimensions was, I believe, a crucial part of the Enlightenment's widening exploration of human nature and experience.

In practice, few historians kept to the strict narrativist model that Smith upheld, or were prepared to sacrifice the advantages offered by the modern technique of incorporating discursive devices into a general narrative framework. A revealing exception is the fragmentary *History of the Early Part of the Reign of James the Second* [1808], written in retirement by the great Whig politician Charles James Fox and published posthumously by his nephew, Vassall Holland. In his apologetic introduction, Holland explains that one of the reasons for the slow progress of the work was the rigor of his uncle's classicism, which led him to oppose the "modern practice of notes" and to insist that "all which an historian wished to say, should be introduced as part of a continued narration."[20] Holland illustrates his uncle's strict standards by recounting a conversation about the literature of the period of James II in which Fox had lamented his inability to devise a method of "interweaving" any account of several authors. When Holland suggested the example of Hume and Voltaire, who had treated such topics either in a separate chapter or at the end of a reign, Fox firmly rejected the precedent: "such a contrivance might be a good mode of writing critical essays, but . . . it was, in his opinion, incompatible with the nature of his undertaking, which, if it ceased to be a narrative, ceased to be history."[21]

What is most interesting here is not so much Fox's views as Holland's tone. As his uncle's executor and editor, Holland does not intend to express any opinion of his own, but simply to present the fragment in its

[20] *A History of the Early Part of the Reign of James the Second*, by Charles James Fox (London, 1808), Vassall Holland, introduction to xxxvi. The passage reads:

> he formed his plan so exclusively on the model of ancient writers, that he not only felt some repugnance to the modern practice of notes, but he thought that all which an historian wished to say, should be introduced as part of a continued narration, and never assume the appearance of a digression, much less of a dissertation annexed to it. . . . [He] defined this duty as an author, to consist in recounting the facts as they arose, or in his simple forcible language, *in telling the story of those times.*

[21] Holland, introduction to *History of James,* xxxvii.

best light. Yet he feared that the work might be misjudged unless readers understood Fox's conception of the historian's "duties"; otherwise "some passages, which according to modern taste must be called peculiarities, might . . . pass for defects which he had overlooked, or imperfections which he intended to correct."[22] Evidently, Holland had difficulty believing that Fox's strict classicism was still tenable, or even fully recognizable: Despite Fox's well-known admiration for classical letters, he feared readers might simply mistake the character of his uncle's style. Even in Smith's day this sort of purism had been a conservative stance, but apparently by 1808 it had become merely eccentric.

Unsympathetic as each is to the mixed narrative form, neither Smith nor Holland says much about the reasons for its utility in modern compositions – though Fox's frustrated desire to incorporate a discussion of English literature into his history of the Glorious Revolution speaks for itself. Henry Steuart of Allanton, author of an extensive commentary on Sallust, takes up a middling position. Reviewing the progress of historical composition in Britain, Steuart praises the "wide, and philosophic views" open to the modern historian. But he is also troubled by the consequences:

Amidst these improvements, however, some doubts may be entertained, whether the Philosophy of History . . . have not been cultivated to the prejudice of Narrative. History, whatever other means it may adopt for instruction, should never depart from its essential and primary character, as a *relation of facts*.

The danger is that instead of "naturally giving rise to the reflections," narrative will seem to be nothing more than a platform for metaphysical speculation. In Steuart's view, the philosophic spirit, like "the hand of art," works best in concealment.[23]

As I have already noted, Dugald Stewart was alive to the same tensions, but he approached the problem in the spirit of the "moderns." In his brief life of William Robertson, Stewart gives particular praise to Robertson's skill in balancing the contradictory demands of narrative history and philosophical enquiry. The modern historian's task has become more difficult, Stewart remarks acutely, because of the new fashion

---

[22] Holland, introduction to *History of James*, xxxvi.
[23] Henry Steuart, *The Works of Sallust; to which are prefixed two essays; with notes by H. S.* (1806), 273. The problem for Steuart is a matter of narrative and genre: too overt a philosophic emphasis will mean "that the series of events, instead of naturally giving rise to the reflections, will seem only detailed on purpose to exhibit them; and history, departing from her proper sphere, will thus degenerate into a moral discourse, a mere tissue of metaphysical and political speculation" (273).

for combining political histories with a philosophic view of manners and conditions. "In consequence of this innovation, while the province of the historian has been enlarged and dignified, the difficulty of his task has increased in the same proportion, reduced, as he must frequently be to the alternative, either of interrupting unseasonably the chain of events, or by interweaving disquisition and narrative together, of sacrificing clearness to brevity."[24]

In Stewart's view, a good part of Robertson's success in retrieving the traditional excellence of narrative in the face of this challenge was owing in large part to his plan of "throwing" into notes and illustrations whatever discussions appeared "to interfere with the peculiar province of history." By this device, and by the "felicity" of his transitions, Robertson was able to sustain an uninterrupted narrative, giving his works "that unceasing interest which constitutes one of the principal charms in tales of fiction; an interest easy to support in relating a series of imaginary adventures, but which in historical composition, evinces, more than anything else, the hand of a master."[25]

Stewart recognizes Smith's opposition to Robertson's way of saving the continuity of narrative, but his own view is firmly in favor of it. In fact, he thinks the absence of notes considerably diminishes the value of the ancient historians, and he adds that readers of *The Wealth of Nations* had reasons to regret Smith's reluctance to use notes and appendixes. Gibbon, on the other hand, goes too far: "The curious research and the epigrammatic wit so often displayed in Mr. Gibbon's Notes, and which sometimes render them more amusing than even the eloquent narrative which they are meant to illustrate, serve only to add to the embarrassment occasioned by this unfortunate distribution of his materials."[26]

Robertson's *History of Charles V* (1769) is, indeed, a case study of the conflicting demands on historical composition in the eighteenth century.

---

[24] Stewart, *Robertson*, 139. Stewart writes: "In the art of narration too, which next to correctness in the statement of facts, is the most essential qualification of an historian, Dr. Robertson's skill is pre-eminent" (138).

[25] Stewart, *Robertson*, 141.

[26] Stewart, *Robertson*, 143–4. The passage on Smith appears on pp. 148–9: "Considered as sources of authentic and of accurate information, the value of the classics is infinitely diminished by this circumstance [i.e. lack of notes and appendixes]; and few, I believe, have studied Mr. Smith's works, (particularly his *Inquiry into the Nature and Causes of the Wealth of Nations*) without regretting, on some occasions, the omission of his authorities; and, on others, the digressions into which he has been led, by conforming so scrupulously to the example of antiquity." Stewart's strictures on the lack of authenticating notes in the classical historians echo Robertson's criticism of Voltaire, whom Robertson judged a great historian, but not a useful one.

But, unlike his biographer, Robertson chooses not to call attention to the problems he had to overcome. Rather, he points to divisions in his subject and in his audience to explain his procedures. In the modern period, Robertson writes, which begins with the reign of Charles, Europe's history stands as an interconnected whole, regulated by such principles as the balance of power. The long epoch between the fall of Rome and the emergence of the modern balance of power, on the other hand, lacked this unity, and its detailed history could be of interest only to separate nationalities. Yet taken as a whole, this history had enormous importance as the foundation for everything to come. Accordingly Robertson wrote the long prefatory essay that is now the best-known portion of his work: "A View of the Progress of Society in Europe." For this early period a true history would not be possible, since a political narrative would be too particular and a "view" sufficiently general could not be narrative. Thus the solution was reached that the history proper would be framed by a philosophical history, quite different in its structure, scope, and lessons.

It is evident that Robertson (and his readers) take for granted the primacy of narrative, with its traditional dignity, unity, and didactic force. The early history of Europe could not support such a narrative not only because it lacked unity, but also because the obscurity of the evidence would involve the historian in reasoning too complex or technical to interest the general reader. By its very nature, the "general view" stood half way to antiquarianism – "the province of the lawyer or antiquary" – and introduced considerations better kept separate from the text, even in this introductory book. Hence the need for the "Proofs and Illustrations" attached to the "View."

In a longer discussion it would be rewarding to examine the range and variety of problems and sources that Robertson felt he needed to handle in this manner. Here it is sufficient to say that the forty-three brief essays that make up this appendix can be read as a kind of index of excluded questions. "Many of my readers will, probably, give little attention to such researches," Robertson writes. "To some they may, perhaps, appear the most curious and interesting part of the work."[27] Thus Robertson sees the problem of structure as a matter of mediating between two audiences. The general literary public was the traditional audience for the instruction and entertainment provided by history, and it still carried the highest prestige.

---

[27] William Robertson, *History of Charles V* (London, 1769), xii.

Yet, as Robertson states several times in his works, he is not satisfied with
the level of evidence or argument customarily addressed to such readers.
He expects his history also to interest a more limited, expert audience,
whose antiquarian tests of evidence as well as philosophical sense of causation must also be addressed. Even so, the wider audience remains para-
mount, and – having completed his philosophical prelude with its antiquarian addenda – Robertson is free to commence the history proper with
the birth of the great emperor.

As a contrast to Robertson's deft balancing of audiences and structures, it is useful to recall Adam Anderson's *Historical and Chronological
Deduction of the Origin of Commerce* (1764), a wholly unartful attempt
to create an elementary narrative of the nonpolitical. In this pioneering
work of commercial history, twice reedited and supplemented, Anderson
could find no better narrative vehicle than a crude annual chronicle –
though he, too, supplements the core of his work with antiquarian discourses and enormously elaborated indexes.

The formal crudity of Anderson's chronicle of commerce sets off the
achievement of yet another Scot, Robert Henry, who staked his claim as
a historian to his remarkable experiment in simultaneous narrative.
Henry's *History of Great Britain* (1771–93) advertises the work as being
"Written on a new Plan." This may have been somewhat overstated,[28]
but no one was more determined than Henry in putting the case for a
reform of historiography through restructuring of narrative, and the idea
of a consistent multipartite narrative became identified with him. The
history, now all but forgotten, eventually gained considerable success,
and was often cited as an authority on the history of manners and
customs.

Henry's "plan" is to divide his history first by chronological epoch and
then again by theme. In this way, every period in British history is discussed under seven uniform headings: 1. civil and military; 2. religious
and ecclesiastical; 3. the history of the constitution, governments, laws,
and courts; 4. the history of learning, of learned men, and of the chief
seminaries of learning; 5. the history of arts, useful and ornamental; 6.
the history of commerce and of prices and commodities; 7. manners,
virtues, vices, remarkable customs, language, dress, diet, and diver-

---

[28] One possible prototype is Antoine-Yves Goguet's ancient history; an English translation
(attributed to Henry) was published in Edinburgh in 1761 as *The Origin of Laws, Arts,
and Sciences, and their Progress Among the Most Ancient Nations, translated from the
French of the President de Goguet.*

sions.[29] Henry insists on being as systematic as possible. Each of the ten books of the history is to be complete in itself, and at the same time "a perfect pattern and model of all the other books." To ensure the consistency of his plan, he proposes to keep the chapter numberings uniform throughout the work and even to treat the materials within the chapters, as far as possible, in the identical order.[30]

Robert Henry was obviously a man with a glint in his eye. But he had a serious critique of conventional practice, and he could make a very good case for the advantages offered to both reader and author by strict adherence to his plan. He stresses that his method requires the historian to give every part of his subject "a constant anxious attention." At the same time, he invites his readers, if they choose, to select the subjects closest to their tastes or "most suitable to their respective ways of life."[31]

Robertson rejected the exclusivity of classical narrative advocated by Smith and replaced it with a new narrative order incorporating a hierarchy of narrative and nonnarrative elements based in part on the needs of distinct audiences. Henry's experiment in simultaneous narrative carries these changes considerably further. He offers his own disciplined, systematic procedure as a new model of historiographical order, but it is evident that his simultaneity possesses less unifying power than Robertson had achieved through hierarchy. In Henry's account, the traditional narrative of politics still comes first, but public life has priority only in a literal sense, while histories of religion, learning, arts, commerce, and manners occupy a larger horizon. Perhaps the most radical sign of the displacement of politics, however, is Henry's suggestion that the reader might want to take advantage of the systematic arrangement of his chapters to

---

[29] Robert Henry, *The History of Great Britain from the Invasion of it by the Romans under Julius Caesar. Written on a new Plan,* 4th ed. (London, 1805–6), xi. Henry explains: "Each book begins and ends at some remarkable revolutions, and contains the history and delineation of the first of these revolutions and of the intervening period. Every one of these books is uniformly divided into seven chapters, which do not carry on the thread of the history one after another, as in other works of this kind; but all the seven chapters of the same book begin at the same point of time, run parallel to one another, and end together" (xi).

[30] Henry, *History,* "For example: the arts, which are the subject of the fifth chapter of every book, are disposed one after another in the same order of succession, in all the fifth chapters through the whole work. . . . By this means, as every book is a perfect model of all the other books of this work, so every chapter is also a perfect model of all the other chapters of the same number" (xii-xiii).

[31] Henry, *History,* (xvii, xix). His plan offers readers "an opportunity of indulging their peculiar tastes, and of studying, with the greatest attention, those particular subjects in the history of their country, which seem to them most useful and agreeable in themselves, or most suitable to their respective ways of life."

construct his own path through the history. This invitation offers a striking new possibility – a history whose comprehensiveness does not so
much enlarge the scope of history's traditional public concerns as open
the way for specialist readers to reconstruct the narrative according to
their own private needs. This readerly narrative would be not only a
history of private life, but also one open to being read for private purposes. And beyond Henry's valiant attempt to retain the unity of social
description lie any number of dispersed and particular histories, each
contributing to the wide array of historiographical genres that characterize the historical reading of this time.[32]

INWARD NARRATIVES

Adam Smith would surely have disapproved of Henry's experiment as
massively violating the necessary unity of narrative. Yet Smith's idea of
indirect narrative could be taken as licensing some equally radical alternatives. Nor was indirect narrative the only solution to the problem of
representing private and subjective experience. Historians, like novelists,
could also employ the parallel technique that Samuel Richardson, in the
preface to *Clarissa,* calls the "dramatic way."[33] In this case the reader
himself, rather than a textual surrogate, is made the immediate spectator
of events and experiences.

The works that I am about to discuss have a frankly sentimental
character, so much so that some may wish to set them aside as peripheral
to the main body of eighteenth-century historiography. But by marking
the interests of eighteenth-century audiences, histories of this sort can
enrich our reading of more canonical texts and establish the range of
questions and methods that characterize the wider spectrum of historiographical genres in this period.

On a small scale, sentimental effects are widespread in eighteenth-
century historiography – Hume's *History of England* is a famous example – but one of the fullest uses of spectatorial narrative I know of is Helen
Maria Williams's epistolary history of the French Revolution, *Letters writ-*

---

32 Biography, for example, was often recommended on the basis of a similar argument to
   Henry's. Biographers claimed that their work would be more interesting to men of
   private station because readers of this kind might find in individual lives a reflection of
   their own concerns.
33 Samuel Richardson, preface to *Clarissa, or the History of a Young Lady,* ed. Angus Ross
   (Harmondsworth: Penguin, 1985).

ten in France in the summer of 1790.[34] Williams is less interested in establishing a coherent outline of events than in conveying their atmosphere and emotional impact. This is accomplished through a set of formal devices – epistolary presentation, eyewitness reportage, a female narrator, and even an embedded memoir – that engage the reader's sympathies with witnesses standing closer to the scene. Most prominent, of course, is the narrator herself. As a woman, a foreigner, and a letter writer, she is perfectly placed to occupy the mediator's role: Neither an active participant in events nor a detached narrator as conventionally required, she is an ideal spectator, universal rather than impartial in her sympathies.[35]

By a further mediation that exemplifies Smith's insight into the power of indirect narration, the narrator can give expression to emotions that are by nature interior and, through ordinary means, indescribable:

I promised to send you a description of the federation: but it is not to be described! One must have been present, to form any judgment of a scene, the sublimity of which depended much less on its external magnificence than on the effect it produced on the minds of the spectators.[36]

Places, too, stand as mute witnesses to the great scenes of the Revolution, and Williams has a prescient sense of the evocative power of these historic sites. In a key passage she imagines herself as simply the first of many pilgrims, to be followed by others in years to come: "I see them eagerly searching for the place where they have heard it recorded, that the

---

[34] The edition I cite is Helen Maria Williams, *Letters Written in France in the Summer of 1790* (Dublin, 1791). The work was continued as *Letters from France* in eight volumes published serially between 1790 and 1796. The first two volumes, in particular, were very widely read. On Williams, see Mary Favret, *Romantic Correspondence: Women, Politics and the Fiction of Letters* (Cambridge: Cambridge University Press, 1993), 53–95. On the popularity of the work, see Robert Mayo, *The English Novel in the Magazines, 1740–1815* (Evanston, Ill.: Northwestern University Press, 1962), 259–61.

[35] Favret makes the point that Williams avoids overt partisanship and rarely refers to her meetings with influential Girondins and Jacobins. "In order to raise the letters 'beyond dispute,' all feeling and desire must be general and universal ('you will rejoice with me'). . . . This identification with the 'people,' reinforces Williams' democratic aspirations for France, and for England." Favret, *Correspondence,* 65.

[36] Williams, *Letters,* 5. In the same vein, she adds: "I may tell you of pavilions, of triumphal arches, of altars on which incense was burnt, of two hundred thousand men walking in procession; but how am I to give you an adequate idea of the behaviour of the spectators? How am I to paint the impetuous feelings of that immense, that exulting multitude? Half a million of people assembled at a spectacle, which furnished every image that can elevate the mind of man; which connected the enthusiasm of moral sentiment with the solemn pomp of religious ceremonies; which addressed itself at once to the imagination, the understanding, and the heart!"

National Assembly were seated! I think of these things, and then repeat to myself with transport, "I, was a spectator of the Federation."[37]

Williams also makes use of a second narrative form that contrasts with the predominant epistolary structure: an embedded biographical memoir, recounted by the author herself, concerning the unfortunate friends whom she had traveled to France to meet. The lengthy history of Mons. du F., persecuted by his aristocratic father because of his marriage to a woman of the middle class, stands as a sort of sentimental tale set into the larger narrative. It is presented as a microcosm of the system of tyranny, domestic as well as public, from which France had been liberated by the Revolution, and in telling it, Williams is at pains to point out the ways in which the old baron's cruelties to his son – involving *lettres de cachet* and so forth – required official support and aristocratic complicity. But the memoir is more than a metonymic representation of the evils of the old regime; it also represents a kind of personal knowledge that Williams – as a female spectator – could hold with entire confidence in her own judgment. The reasonings of philosophers might confuse her, she acknowledges, but when a proposition is addressed to her heart she has no doubts; "nor could I be more convinced of the truth of any demonstration in Euclid, than I am, that, that system of politics must be the best, by which those I love are made happy."[38]

The memoir of Mons. du F. recreates the conditions of the *ancien régime* against which the events of the summer of 1790 must be understood. In this way it extends the temporal and geographical range of Williams's *Letters,* overcoming some of the most obvious restrictions of the epistolary form. But on a more fundamental level the two parts of Williams's history unite in their assertion of the importance of direct experience and personal knowledge, even in the face of enormous public events. In short, like so many others on both sides of the Revolution debate, Williams embraced the view that the deepest meaning of the Revolution would be felt in private life, a perception difficult to express within the humanist tradition of linear narrative.

The epistolary form lent itself easily to a variety of didactic purposes,

---

[37] Williams, *Letters,* 107. I have discussed the evocation of place and its connection to associationalist psychology in eighteenth-century historiography in "William Godwin and the Idea of Historical Commemoration: History as Public Memory and Private Sentiment," in *Shifting the Boundaries: Transformations of the Languages of Public and Private in the Eighteenth Century,* ed. D. Castiglione and L. Sharpe (Exeter: Exeter University Press, 1995), 196–219.

[38] Williams, *Letters,* 196.

but expressive uses of this device such as we find in Williams remain a rare experiment, one more often encountered on the boundary of history writing, where travel or ethnography combines with the history of manners.[39] Among traditional historiographical genres, biography was certainly the prime vehicle for historians wanting to evoke the inward dimensions of the past. Well-recognized reciprocities between social customs and the individual mind encouraged the idea that biography could provide an entry into the history of common life. At the same time, historical biographers realized that by focusing on one person's experience of the social world they might overcome the centrifugal tendencies of other social narratives, the problem made so clear in Henry's multipartite work.[40]

But the eighteenth century's desire for a more inward understanding of personality also posed a problem of sources and ultimately of epistemology. To put it simply, a sentimental narrative – one focused on the subjective reflections of experience – would require sources giving authentic access to inward feeling. This is one of the reasons for the popularity of literary biography: An age attracted to the subjective and quotidian world of private life often found the words of poets more expressive than the actions of politicians. Historical biographers working in this vein sought out the impressions of witnesses less as evidence for the narrative of events than as documents of feeling. Similarly, seemingly naive narratives, such as medieval chronicles, were prized for their assumed sincerity. But best of all, perhaps, were letters and memoirs, whose first-person vantage seems to promise unmediated access to the past.

Two histories by the little-known Catholic medievalist Joseph Bering-

---

[39] An example of the epistolary form used in a plainly didactic manner is William Russell's popular *History of Modern Europe . . . in a series of letters from a nobleman to his son,* new ed. (London, 1788). An earlier example of the sentimental use of the form (combined with a journal) is Samuel Ancell, *A Circumstantial Journal of the Long and Tedious Blockade and Siege of Gibraltar . . . By an Officer* (Manchester, 1783). The work seems to have been popular, given that the British Library Catalogue lists five editions. Ancell, an Irish military writer, was the editor of *Ancell's Monthly Military Companion.* In such a work it is very difficult indeed to know how much fictional license Ancell allowed himself.

[40] This advantage is made particularly explicit by William Godwin in the preface to his *Life of Geoffrey Chaucer . . . with sketches of the manners, opinions, events, and literature of England in the 14th century,* 2 vols. (London, 1803). Priestley comments on the same point in his *Lectures on History and General Policy* (Dublin, 1788), lecture 32: "A method of making history particularly interesting and useful, is to make the object of it some particular person of distinguished eminence, whose history has a connexion with almost every thing of importance in the age in which he lives; and in writing his history to omit no transaction of any moment. Such a work is the *Memoirs of Petrarch* in three volumes quarto, which I have read several times with singular satisfaction" (202). He also singles out Joseph Berington's *Abeillard and Heloisa,* which I discuss below.

ton illustrate the attractions of this sort of biographical work, including
the kinds of documentation entailed. Berington's *History of the Lives of
Abeillard and Heloisa* (1787) makes use of the rich autobiographical
writings of the two central figures not so much to trace the outward
dramas of their lives as to create an intimate narrative of experience that
stands at the core of a wider history. As so often in the eighteenth century,
the emotional resonances of gender play a large role in explorations of
inwardness. What engages Berington most in this history is his desire to
understand Heloise's situation as she registered it with her own eyes and
feelings. As a sentimental heroine, she is at once the central figure and the
key spectator of the story. Accordingly, Berington skims close to his
sources, making a narrative out of expressive passages of quotation that
alternate with looser paraphrases and interpolated emotional responses
attributed indifferently to the historian and his reader.[41] Often, of course,
the evidence is thin or simply absent, but Berington is skillful in reading
silences. He strains every resource to recreate the tenor of the lovers'
relationship, often by exploring the omissions in Abelard's *Historia
calamitatum* in counterpoint to Heloise's more revealing letters, match-
ing the theologian's public account of his "calamities" against his lover's
devoted questionings, her combination of independent mind and female
submission.

In the techniques as well as the tone of this work, we see a historian
working in the environment of sentimental fiction. This is signaled in the
preface, where Berington warns us not to expect the entertainment of a
novel. But Berington's stress on the authentic documents that differenti-
ate his work of true history from Alexander Pope's poetic fable is not in
any real tension with the novelistic sentimentalism that infuses his portrait of Heloise. On the contrary, Berington is most novelistic when he is
closest to his documents. In this sense the translated letters of Abelard
and Heloise, which make up a substantial appendix to the work, represent a fusing of the methods of antiquarian scholarship with those of the
epistolary novel.

Berington's *History of the Reign of Henry the Second* (1790) contin-

---

[41] "The reader, whom Heloisa's romantic epistle had left animated and greatly interested in
her cause, will, I know, be sadly disappointed by this cold reply. To me it is all I looked
for and it stamps indelibly the character I had given to the man." Joseph Berington, *The
History of the Lives of Abeillard and Heloisa* (Birmingham, 1787), 224–5. In a similar
vein, he writes: "More reflections on this beautiful epistle will not be necessary. The
reader must have made many as he came along; and he must have admired, have pitied,
and have praised the lovely writer" (234).

ues the earlier history, changing the focus from the sufferings of a female heroine to the dramatic clash of masculine temperaments that culminated in the murder of Thomas à Becket. Here once again Berington pursues a story that could be evoked through expressive contemporary sources. The chronicles, memoirs, and letters thrown up by the Becket controversy permit Berington to reconstitute the conflict over ecclesiastical power in ways that bring to life the shape of individual experience in an age often left to the wide generalizations of philosophical historians.

To present this conflict Berington adopts what he calls the "*dramatic style*" – that is, the fiction of direct address – and in a series of well-staged scenes shows Becket and Henry speaking directly to each other and to us.[42] In justifying this device, he avoids the obvious fictional precedents, citing instead the Greek poets and historians, whose way of allowing their characters to speak for themselves "insensibly transports the reader into the company of their heroes and sages, obliterating, by a momentary magic, the distance of years, and the consciousness of present existence."[43]

Lord Kames called this obliteration of space and time "ideal presence," and in it he thought he had discovered the key to the moral and aesthetic workings of all the arts, including historiography.[44] But in practice Berington could not allow presence to prevail so entirely over distance; the reader must also be reminded of the unknowable darkness of history, which differentiates it from the simpler attractions of fictions. The book opens with a moody invocation of history as a quest for a remote, almost unreachable past:

Awful is the impression which now falls on my mind, when, with the annals of times long passed open before me, I sit down to contemplate the manners of men and the events of their days, and to trace, through the maze of its progress, the meandring [*sic*], and often evanescent, line of truth. *History* is the narration of *facts;* but we receive them on the testimony of men like ourselves, whom want of evidence sometimes misled, or incaution, or credulity, or views of party, or inability of discernment, exposed to error.[45]

---

[42] Joseph Berington, *The History of the Reign of Henry the Second* (Birmingham, 1790) xxvi–xvii: "I must notice the *dramatic* stile, which I have sedulously adopted, whenever the original writer had himself used it, and at other times, when the narration, from its circumstantial detail authorized the licence. Thus when the old writer related that such things were said in conversation or at interviews, I sometimes took the liberty to make the persons speak for themselves, as, on the occasion itself, they certainly had done."

[43] Berington, *Henry*, xxvii.

[44] On the Kamesian idea of "ideal presence" in historiography, see my essay "If Mrs. Mure." Cited in n.19.

[45] Berington, *Henry*, 1–2. Passages quoted in the next paragraph also occur on these pages.

Berington wants us to understand, too, that the student of the Middle Ages encounters particular difficulties and special charms. Accordingly he emphasizes the temporal and intellectual remoteness of his sources – men "whom the cowl covered, whom, in a dark age, genius did not illumine." Yet, by a sentimental logic that ranks inarticulate communication highest of all, the plainspoken heroes and their "unadorned" testimonies possess a simple directness capable of shattering the barriers separating a polished age from a primitive past.

Controlling the poetics of presence and distance is one of Berington's central concerns as a narrator. The price of failure would be to surrender either to flat factuality or sentimental fictionalization, while success, as Berington emphasizes, means an active sympathy with what is best in the past – a kind of nonphilosophical historicism. "The age, I own, was dark," he writes near the end of his book,

but it was a darkness arising form the obvious state of things. . . . Besides, the mind that divests itself of modern habits and modern prejudices, and goes back with some good temper into the times, I have described, will discover virtue that it may imitate. . . . The man is unequitable, who, possessing but one standard, measures by it all the characters and events of other days.[46]

READING LUCY HUTCHINSON

Berington's historical biographies, like Helen Maria Williams's epistolary history, provide examples of contemporary practice that fill out Adam Smith's discussion of the subjective possibilities inherent in indirect narration. But if we reconsider Smith's remarkable reinterpretation of Tacitus for the rereading it accomplishes rather than for what it explicitly teaches, another sort of inquiry suggests itself: one that looks beyond the intentions of writers to examine the transformative power of reading. Though reading practices are notoriously hard to recapture, there is good evidence that eighteenth-century readers turned to memoirs and other primary documents in order to pursue an interest in the history of private life in earlier times. This was especially the case for texts involving a female author, a female subject, or a female readership, any of which might offer occasion for a sentimental narrative – or to a sentimental rereading of an existing text.[47] An effective way to evoke inward experi-

---

[46] Berington, *Henry,* 645–6.
[47] I discuss at greater length the issues of gender and genre involved in understanding the reading style of the later eighteenth century in my essay "If Mrs. Mure."

ence, it appears, was to leap over the problem of narrative altogether and present the historical document unadorned. In a sense, this was to take the "dramatic way" to its limit: The historian retreats from author to editor in order to give the document the full range of its own expressive voice.

I will review one final narrative that strikingly illustrates this possibility, Lucy Hutchinson's *Memoirs of the Life of Colonel Hutchinson.* Students of English history who read this text in later, more scholarly editions will miss what earlier readers encountered in the first edition, a finely printed quarto, edited by the Rev. Julius Hutchinson in a spirit of family piety and modest antiquarianism.

Julius Hutchinson's first concern is to protect the political respectability of his ancestors, the republicans and regicides of an earlier revolution. This accomplished to his satisfaction, he devotes the remainder of the preface (as well as a number of exclamatory footnotes accompanying the body of the text) to guiding the reader to an appreciation of the *Life* – an appreciation, not surprisingly, that diminishes its political content in favor of its social and domestic elements. Julius Hutchinson begins by recommending the book as "a faithful, natural, and lively picture, of the public mind and manners," but he proceeds to emphasize more than anything else its evocative power. The greatest appeal will be to "lovers of biography," he thinks, since they will, "in fancy, have lived in times, and witnessed scenes the most interesting that can be imagined to the human mind, especially the mind of an Englishman."[48]

To this point, the gender of the author has not been particularly stressed and the reader remains conventionally male. But the preface moves toward an increasingly sentimental appreciation of the *Life* that inevitably concludes by linking its female author to a female readership

---

[48] Rev. Julius Hutchinson, preface to *Memoirs of the Life of Colonel Hutchinson Governor of Nottingham Castele and Town . . . with Original Anecdotes of Many of the Most Distinguished of his Contemporaries* [by his widow, Lucy Hutchinson], ed. Rev. Julius Hutchinson (London, 1806), xi, xii. Hutchinson writes:

> Perhaps the prevalence of this predilection may be traced to the circumstances of the reader's thus feeling himself to be, as it were, a party in the transactions which are recounted. A person of this taste will, it is hoped, here have his wishes completely gratified; for he will, in fancy, have lived in times, and witnessed scenes the most interesting that can be imagined to the human mind, especially the mind of an Englishman; he will have conversed with persons the most celebrated and extraordinary, whom one party represents as heroes and demigods, the other as demons. . . . He will have accompanied the Hero of the Tale, not only through all the ages of life, but through almost every situation in society. (xii)

and a presumptively female genre. Pointing to Lucy Hutchinson's talent for portraiture – "the delicate touch of the pencil of a female" – he ends with a direct appeal to an audience of women:

The ladies will feel that it carries with it all the interest of a novel strengthened with the authenticity of real history: they will no doubt feel an additional satisfaction in learning, that though the author added to the erudition of the scholar, the research of the philosopher, the politician, and even the divine, the zeal and magnanimity of a patriot; yet she descended from all these elevations to perform in the most exemplary manner, the functions of a wife, mother, and mistress of a family.[49]

This completes the intended depoliticization of the text. Instead, readers are invited to respond to those elements that allow the *Life* to be seen above all as a document of social customs and private feeling – a virtuously female memoir offered in devotion to the memory of a brave husband.[50]

Reviewing Hutchinson's *Life* in the *Edinburgh Review*, Francis Jeffrey takes pleasure in mocking Julius Hutchinson's politics, and – though he values its information on the condition of women – he generally resists the temptation to relegate it to the subordinate category of female memoir.[51] Rather, Jeffrey, who had been influenced by both Dugald Stewart and John Millar, takes a "philosophic" view of the work, which he prizes as a social rather than a sentimental narrative. For Jeffrey, Hutchinson's firsthand account is chiefly valuable as a portrait of the rural gentry, who were the predominant class of seventeenth-century England, the class from whom "the nation at large derived its habits, prejudices, and opinions."[52] In light of this early nineteenth-century fascination with the idea of "opinion," the *Life* held enormous interest for him, as indeed did the whole genre of memoir literature, with its promise of deeper insight into the private life of other times.[53]

---

[49] Hutchinson, preface to *Memoirs* (xiv).

[50] The title of "memoir" given to works of this kind is, of course, a first signal to the reader to expect something distinct from the conventional public framework of history.

[51] Jeffrey's review originally appeared in 1808; it is reprinted in his collected essays, *Contributions to the Edinburgh Review*, 2d ed. (London, 1846), 1:435–63. On the condition of women, Jeffrey remarks that, despite its clear importance, this is a subject on which "all histories of public events are almost necessarily defective" (439).

[52] Jeffrey, *Contributions*, 1:436.

[53] The contrast between public history and private memoir – a contrast evident in the remarks on the condition of women quoted above, n. 51 – is a mainstay of Jeffrey's critical response to histories. See particularly the opening remarks of his review of Samuel Pepys concerning "the gross defects of regular history," in *Contributions*, 1: 476–9.

Jeffrey's rereading of Julius Hutchinson's editing serves as a reminder of the instability of literary-historical categories, especially when the activity of readers is taken into account. At the same time, his transformation of this seventeenth-century document from sentimental to social narrative is a sign of crucial reciprocities linking these two dimensions of private life. Both forms of narrative, it is clear, reflected a common resistance to traditional restrictions that would limit history to an account of the public actions of public men.

"By far the most important part of history," Jeffrey writes, ". . . is that which makes us acquainted with the character, dispositions, and opinions" of the governing class. This conception of history's purpose implicitly calls not for a political history in classical or humanist style, but for a broadly conceived history of the class whose manners exercised hegemony in the social nation. Thomas Carlyle and Thomas Babington Macaulay – both of them Jeffrey's pupils – attempted in very different ways to fashion narratives of this kind, but the task was probably beyond the reach of anyone of Jeffrey's own generation. Certainly Jeffrey himself had no such ambition. Like Adam Smith, however, he proved himself to be a prescient reader of the narrative of private life.

Let me return briefly to my point of departure. It seems clear that writers working across a spectrum of eighteenth-century genres, including national historiography itself, were engaged in exploring dimensions of life excluded by the classical restriction of historical narrative to public action. It is also clear that the public narrative retained considerable authority. This authority is crucial to the constitution of all these genres, but the tensions it produced are perhaps most visible in the theory and practice of historiography, where ties to classical literary traditions were so strong.

The themes I have reviewed here in terms of historiographical responses to the problem of narrating common life and inward feeling have, of course, been discussed at length in other contexts. Historians of literature have explored the ways in which fictional narrative was shaped by the culture of sensibility, just as historians of political economy have traced the social narratives projected in conjectural histories. It is not easy to bring these various types of narrative under a single view. In the context of historical writing, however, such an alignment seems possible, even necessary, since history was a kind of middle term against which a whole range of genres positioned themselves. Reciprocally, this positioning meant that for eighteenth-century historians the challenge of new tasks was likely to be registered as a problem of genre. Faced with interests beyond the classical horizon, historians would increasingly show their awareness of the competition posed by less encumbered neighbors, while – as Adam Smith indicates – desiring to maintain history's ancient decorum.

14

Contemplative heroes and Gibbon's historical imagination

PATRICIA CRADDOCK

For his valedictory address as Regius Professor of History in 1980, H. R. Trevor-Roper chose as his topic "History and Imagination." He concluded that "it is the imagination of the historian, not his scholarship or his method (necessary though these are), which will discern the hidden forces of change." "Of the great 'philosophical' historians," in his judgment, "only Gibbon survives, and that not because he had a consistent philosophy, but because . . . his imagination never slept."[1] That imagination was formed, Edward Gibbon believed, by youthful immersion in ancient epic and history. In seminal statements now approximately half a century old, first Christopher Dawson and then Arnaldo Momigliano independently endorsed the view that ancient historiography was one of the formative influences on Gibbon's work.[2]

Gibbon came to see this influence on himself and on the unbroken line of readers of the ancient texts as a mixed blessing. Only half playfully, he complains in an unpublished revision of the first chapter of *The Decline*

---

[1] H. R. Trevor-Roper, "History and Imagination," in *History and Imagination: Essays in Honor of H. R. Trevor-Roper,* ed. Hugh Lloyd-Jones et al. (New York: Holmes and Meier, 1982), 367–8.

[2] According to Dawson, "Gibbon's treatment [of the classical world] still had a vital relation to its subject," though he was very much of his own age and also "the last of the Humanists." Christopher Dawson, *Proceedings of the British Academy* 20 (1934): 180, 163. More explicitly, in a 1952 speech in London, Momigliano analyzed Gibbon's contribution to historical method as combining the merits of the two competitive traditions, the philosophic and the erudite, with "the most endearing quality" of classical historiography, fascinating narrative. Arnaldo Momigliano, "Gibbon's Contribution to Historical Method," in *Studies in Historiography* (London: Weidenfeld and Nicolson, 1966), 40–55. The great literary scholar E. M. W. Tillyard devotes a chapter to *The Decline and Fall* as the last manifestation of the English epic tradition in *The English Epic and Its Background* (Oxford: Oxford University Press, 1954), 510–27, and E. Badian sneers at Gibbon's "Livyan" history in "Gibbon at War," in *Gibbon et Rome à la lumière de l'historiographie moderne,* ed. Pierre Ducrey (Geneva: Droz, 1977), 103–33.

and Fall that "Late generations, and far distant climates may impute their calamities to the immortal author of the Iliad. The spirit of Alexander was inflamed by the praises of Achilles: and succeeding Heroes have been ambitious to tread in the footsteps of Alexander."[3] One of the tasks facing historians like himself, he came to believe, was to transform or at least to enlarge humanity's conception of heroism, so that history would not share with poetry the guilt of encouraging humankind to overvalue military adventurers. But the very formation of his own historical imagination made the achievement of this aim problematic for him. While he never endorses a naive great-man theory of history, he knew from experience as well as history that whatever other lessons readers derive from historical reading, they are bound to learn what human activies are valued and survive in the collective memory and in the accounts of individual writers. Gibbon himself had learned the lessons of Achilles and Alexander, almost too well.

We all remember that "the dynasties of Assyria and Egypt were [young Edward's] top and cricket-ball."[4] But even earlier, when Edward Gibbon was a small, sickly boy, his beloved Aunt Kitty, his nurse and teacher, read and discussed with him many marvelous and heroic tales: "the Heroes of the Trojan war soon became my intimate acquaintance, and I often disputed with my aunt on the characters of Hector and Achilles," he tells us.[5] As he grew older, his idea of what was heroic and who had exemplified heroism of course developed. He came to admire not just Hector and Achilles, but heroes of civil life.

As a historian, however, he recognized, with Samuel Johnson, that history is often devoted to the exploits of figures who "left the name at which the world grew pale / To point a moral or adorn a tale" (*Vanity of Human Wishes,* ll. 221–2). Historical writing, which is popularly supposed to redress the unjust verdicts of contemporaries, in fact has a

---

[3] Edward Gibbon, "Materials for a Seventh Volume," in *The English Essays of Edward Gibbon,* ed. P. B. Craddock (Oxford: Clarendon Press, 1972), 339. The passage quoted was intended to replace the second sentence of the eighth paragraph of chap. 1, "The praises of Alexander, transmitted by a succession of poets and historians, had kindled a dangerous emulation in the mind of Trajan." Edward Gibbon, *The History of the Decline and Fall of the Roman Empire,* ed. J. B. Bury (London: Methuen, 1909–14; reprint, New York: AMS, 1974), 1:6. Bury's edition has a complicated publishing history; therefore, page numbers in different editions may differ.

[4] Edward Gibbon, *Memoirs of My Life,* ed. G. A. Bonnard (London: Thomas Nelson and Sons, 1966), 43.

[5] This sentence occurs in draft B of his memoirs, published in *The Autobiographies of Edward Gibbon,* ed. John Murray (London: Murray, 1896), 119.

tendency to belong not only to the victors, but to the generals, Gibbon suggests: Posterity is more likely to know even the losing prince or defeated war leader than the poet or historian who makes his name survive, and such a writer in turn has far more hope of an "immortal" reputation than other figures who may rationally deserve our admiration – inventors of better plows, builders of better roads, peaceful and industrious craftsmen, honest and adventurous merchants, or even (though Gibbon does not mention these) wise and loving parents. These figures, as individuals, are – or were – usually forgotten altogether by history, or at least by the epic poets and by historians of politics or even of *mœurs*.

In the ancient division between the active and contemplative ways of life those who choose the active typically preempt the attention of posterity; and they typically do so, Gibbon believes, as war leaders: "As long as mankind shall continue to bestow more liberal applause on their destroyers than on their benefactors, the thirst of military glory will ever be the vice of the most exalted characters."[6]

In *The Decline and Fall,* irony, sometimes almost tragic in tone, provides a method for recognizing this inherent injustice in history while at the same time allowing the conscientious observer to continue to practice the historian's craft. But irony solves only the problem of exposing false or limited ideas of heroism. It does not enable the historian to do justice to heroes of a quieter kind. In a passage separate from the drafts, but apparently intended for his memoirs, Gibbon makes clear his desire to portray and appropriately praise heroes of the contemplative life, such as Confucius, Edmund Spenser, and Henry Fielding:

The descendant of a King [should be considered] less truly noble than the offspring of a man of Genius, whose writings will instruct or delight the latest posterity. The family of Confucius is, in my opinion, the most illustrious in the World. . . . The nobility of the Spencers has been illustrated and enriched by the trophies of Marlborough; but I exhort them to consider the Faery Queen as the most precious jewel of their coronet. . . . Our immortal Fielding was of a younger branch of the Earls of Denbigh, who draw their origin from the Counts of Habsburgh. . . . [The English Habsburghs,] the Knights and Sheriffs of Leicestershire, have slowly risen to the dignity of a peerage; the [German Habsburghs,] the Emperors of Germany and Kings of Spain, have threatened the liberty of the old and invaded the treasures of the new World. The successors of Charles the fifth may disdain their humble brethren of England, but the Romance of Tom

---

[6] Gibbon, *The History of the Decline and Fall of the Roman Empire*, 1:6.

Jones, that exquisite picture of human manners, will outlive the palace of the Escurial and the Imperial Eagle of the house of Austria.[7]

This last happens to have been Gibbon's only unequivocally correct prediction of the future, but more fundamentally, it expresses clearly the ideas of relative merit that he intends to support in his mature writings.

Yet he succeeds in supporting this idea of what is truly admirable in human endeavor only in part. He undercuts the notions of mere military and political heroism, both obvious and subtle, with great skill. He also portrays one subset of the contemplative heroes with persuasive energy and sympathy, but that group is those who also shine in the active life: he never succeeds in portraying a hero of the mind as ultimately important in the narrative of history. Even when the history was that of his own life, and the proposed hero was Edward Gibbon, historian of the Roman Empire, he failed: his memoirs, notoriously, were never completed.

He could dismiss some conventions of active heroism easily enough, e.g., the "heroism" of Richard the Lionhearted: "if heroism be confined to brutal and ferocious valour, Richard Plantagenet will stand high among the heroes of the age." Gibbon introduces Richard's story with the evocation – and debunking – of the legendary significance of his name in both England and the Islamic world: "The memory . . . of the lion-hearted prince was long dear and glorious to his English subjects; . . . his tremendous name was employed by the Syrian mothers to silence their infants, and, if an horse suddenly started from the way, his rider was wont to exclaim, 'Dost thou think King Richard is in that bush?'" (6:365). After that introduction Gibbon can recount some truly extraordinary exploits within Richard's limited set of virtues without fear that the reader will lionize the king. For example, with only 317 companions Richard was surrounded by 60,000 Turks and Saracens: "we learn from the evidence of his enemies, that the king of England, grasping his lance, rode furiously along their front, from the right to the left wing, without meeting an adversary who dared to encounter his career. Am I writing the history of Orlando or Amadis?" (6:367). Thus Gibbon effortlessly dispells any reader's false esteem for mere action, or even mere valor and strength, even as he reports such heroics.

The historian of *The Decline and Fall* likewise had occasion to portray many eminent persons, less obviously than Richard mere brutes and

---

[7] Gibbon, *Memoirs*, 4–5.

bogeys, whose apparent achievements were soon reduced to ruins or whose greatness had marked history only destructively. Devastating parallel narratives of the Byzantine emperors and the Great Kings of Persia illustrate this pattern, recurrent especially in the last volumes of the history: Both Byzantium and Persia are laid waste, thousands are killed or maimed, arts and sciences come to a standstill, and the result is that neither country makes any territorial gains whatever. Dynastic wars are even more obviously futile. But historians and poets – and their readers – have shared with the militant heroes the responsibility for exaggerating the value and influence of military glory. Thus Gibbon knows that he must exhort the Spensers to value their great poet ancestor, the successors of Charles V to defer to the author of *Tom Jones,* the reader to admire heroes who create rather than destroy.

Looking back over his history two or three years after publishing its final volumes – some twenty years after writing its opening chapter – Gibbon revised somewhat his gloomy opinion that mankind would accord fame more readily to destroyers than to benefactors. In the margin of his own copy of the history, he wrote, "The first place in the temple of fame is due and is assigned to the successful heroes who . . . after signalizing their valour in the deliverance of their country have displayed their wisdom and virtue in foundation or government of a flourishing state. Such men as Moses, Cyrus Alfred Gustavus Vasa Henry iv of France &c."[8] But this reconsideration continues to deny the highest places in the temple to the scholar, the poet, the merchant, the scientist, or the inventor, to anyone whose effect on others (apart from his immediate companions) derived exclusively from the products of his mind, and not from his actions in a public arena.

Men of science and letters, it was true, were not "destroyers of mankind," except occasionally by proxy. But neither were they effectually its benefactors, until the products of their contemplation reached other hands. It is surprising how little power Gibbon seems to attribute to the written word, or at least to the written word as a product of genius. His readers sometimes credited skillful users of language, including Gibbon, with enormous practical power. Some of them indeed thought Gibbon aspired and expected to destroy the influence of Christianity by the power of his own literary genius, and those who both believed this and valued Christianity were duly outraged, especially those who thought he might well succeed.[9] Gibbon, however, professed to be surprised by the fervor of their attachment to the "name" of Christianity and repeatedly makes it clear in his history that he does not expect his own philosophical views to be accepted except by those who are already enlightened.[10]

In short, for Gibbon the written word, including his own, and even the ideas, events, persons, and objects written about, certainly manifest and may encourage actual change in human society, but they have power only over and through the actions they encourage in individual readers, except in two cases: explicit laws, and deceptive names. True names effect no change, but false ones occasionally acquire truth. To name a government a republic changes nothing if it is a republic, but may have a powerful effect if it is not a republic, Gibbon argues, most notably in Chapter 3: "Augustus was sensible that mankind is governed by names; nor was he deceived in his expectation that the senate and people would submit to slavery, provided they were respectfully assured that they still enjoyed their ancient freedom" (1:78).

Of course literary works, including belletristic works, can aspire to change many individual opinions. It is not, however, among the writers of polemical works, such as his own *Vindication of Some Passages in the Fifteenth and Sixteenth Chapters of the History of the Decline and Fall*, that Gibbon hoped to find his scholar-writer heroes. (A polemical work is one that seeks victory, even for the truth, rather than truth itself.) He wished rather to show the immortality of the authors of nonpolemical works – *The Iliad, Tom Jones, The Consolation of Philosophy, The Faerie Queene*, the *Scriptores rerum Italiarum*, and *The History of the Decline and Fall of the Roman Empire*. Of course many of these nonpolemical works have powerful views to propose and propagate, but the works are not directed toward victory at any cost. Rather, they are essentially interested in science, in the broad sense of that word, that is, in knowledge and wisdom – and in its preservation, development, dissemination through letters. The writers of such works as these are obviously

---

[9] See Shelby T. McCloy, *Gibbon's Antagonism to Christianity* (Chapel Hill: University of North Carolina Press, 1933; reprint, Burt Franklin Research and Source Work Series, no. 144). Many of the original tracts attacking Gibbon are reprinted in the seventeen-volume Garland reprint collection, *Gibboniana* (New York: Garland, 1974).

[10] While I do not endorse all the interpretations of Lionel Gossman in *The Empire Unpossess'd* (Cambridge: Cambridge University Press, 1981), he makes a strong case for Gibbon's expectation of and allowance for two sets of readers, whom we may metonymically represent by David Hume and Catherine Porten, respectively. See especially pages 51–5.

mankind's benefactors, if mankind will pay attention to the works. But the man of letters, as such, neither justifies himself nor renders himself culpable on the basis of the direct effect of his writings on society. Rather, his role is expository; he preserves, analyzes, dramatizes, makes recognizable or overt what his readers already in some sense know about the human condition, by providing a reliable and enriching context, real or imaginary, for that knowledge. The authority of even an author like Fielding (or a philosopher like David Hume) does not extend to real changes in mankind or manners, much less external nature, social institutions, or the past. His language does not have performative power. Its authority does, however, extend to the reader's understanding of events, persons, ideas, and institutions in the world of experience.

In his youthful *Essai sur l'étude de la littérature,* Gibbon proposes a justification or rather a glorification of the life of letters. There he notes that it is "more glorious to develop or perfect mankind than to extend the limits of the universe" (chap. 26) and argues that the philosophic spirit itself, though it cannot be acquired by any means whatever, can best be developed and exercised by the study of "literature," "this habit of becoming in turn Greek or Roman, disciple of Zeno or of Epicurus" (chap. 47).[11] Though by "literature" Gibbon meant at the time ancient texts both belletristic and nonbelletristic, the structure of the argument extends to all humanistic and scholarly pursuits – anything that expands the individual's perception of human and natural possibility beyond what he himself has experienced. These notions from his youthful work could have been used by Gibbon to add a positive virtue to the negative virtue of harmlessness in his representation of the life of letters. In fact, however, Gibbon's portrayals of men of letters, including himself, always seem to have a hint of dissatisfaction, or of patronizing praise.

Men of letters who produce writings without artistry are of course regarded as limited by the great literary historian, who would certainly have consented to Johnson's ironic definition of the lexicographer as a "harmless drudge" and who himself patronizingly praised his great erudite predecessor Sébastien Le Nain de Tillemont as a "sure-footed mule of the Alps." All writing could and should both delight and instruct. If it only instructed, even its instructiveness would be lost for want of readers.

[11] Edward Gibbon, *Essai sur l'étude de la littérature,* unpublished English translation of Patricia Craddock and Nelly K. Murstein. The French original may be found in Gibbon's *Miscellaneous Works,* ed. John, Lord Sheffield (London: John Murray, 1814), 4:1–94.

Thus the author of such a work could not expect to be a competitor for a place in the "temple of fame." Writing that was purely playful was acceptable in its place – no one admired Ariosto, for example, more than Gibbon did. Perhaps he would have accepted the implication of Johnson's famous epitaph for David Garrick, whose death "eclipsed the gaiety of nations" – that is, that to contribute to joyful hours was no small benefit to one's fellow man.[12] Still, it is not surprising that he does not claim as a hero someone who contributed to human experience nothing more than harmless recreation.

The real problem is Gibbon's attitude toward those who fulfill the ideal of the man of letters, whose works may be expected to instruct and delight uncountable generations of readers. Gibbon always gives credit to literary talent, even when it is imperfect or inconvenient, as can be seen in his treatment of the fourth-century poet and panegyrist Claudian.[13] Indeed, an age or country that does not produce great writers in some imaginative genre is automatically judged sterile and inferior by him – one reason Gibbon is capable of seeing a thousand years of Byzantine history as a constant decline is that he does not appreciate Byzantine art in any genre, and he especially believes that the Eastern empire produced no writers of permanent international merit. But great writers do not cause or even preserve civilization; they are only a sign and product of it.

His desires and problems as a literary biographer may be exemplified by two characters from *The Decline and Fall,* Boethius and Petrarch. Boethius was the minister of Theodoric, a Gothic king of Italy who was one of Gibbon's candidates for "first place in the temple of Fame," since he delivered his own countrymen and governed well the country he had conquered. But "at the close of a glorious life, the king of Italy discovered that he had excited the hatred of a people whose happiness he had so assiduously laboured to promote. . . . By the bigotry of his subjects and enemies, the most tolerant of princes was driven to the brink of persecution; and the life of Theodoric was too long, since he lived to condemn the virtue of Boethius and Symmachus" (4:210–11).

Boethius, who is thus preferred to Theodoric, is called "the last of the Romans whom Cato or Tully could have acknowledged for their country-

---

[12] "Sure-Footed Mule" in n. 126 (original numbering n. 121) to chap. 25 (3:50–1); Johnson on Garrick in Johnson's "Edmund Smith," *Lives of the Poets (Cowley to Prior)* (Garden City, N.Y.: Doubleday Dolphin, n.d.), 360.

[13] See James D. Garrison, "Gibbon and the 'Treacherous Language of Panegyrics,'" *Eighteenth-Century Studies* 11 (Fall 1977): 40–62.

man" (4:211). He had spent the early part of his life in study, perhaps in Athens. Then,

after his return to Rome and his marriage with the daughter of his friend, the patrician Symmachus, Boethius still continued, in a palace of ivory and marble, to prosecute the same studies. The church was edified by his profound defence of the orthodox creed. . . . The geometry of Euclid, the music of Pythagoras, the arithmetic of Nicomachus, the mechanics of Archimedes, the astronomy of Ptolemy, the theology of Plato, and the logic of Aristotle, with the commentary of Porphyry, were translated and illustrated by the indefatigable pen of the Roman senator. (4:212).

Boethius clearly qualifies as a worthy subject of literary biography, not only in his exercise of literary skills, but in not purchasing those skills at the price of other merits: "From . . . abstruse speculations, Boethius stooped, or, to speak more truly, he rose to the social duties of public and private life: the indigent were relieved by his liberality; and his elo-quence . . . was uniformly exerted in the cause of innocence and human-ity. Such conspicuous merit was felt and rewarded by a discerning prince, . . . and [Boethius's] talents were usefully employed in the impor-tant station of master of the offices" (4:213). He was also happy in his wife and children.

Gibbon then prepares for Boethius's fate by consideration of Boethius's complaints that he undertook public office only reluctantly. "A philosopher, liberal of his wealth and parsimonious of his time, might be insensible to the common allurements of ambition, the thirst of gold and employment. And some credit may be due to the asseveration of Boethius, that he had reluctantly obeyed the divine Plato, who enjoins every virtuous citizen to rescue the state from the usurpation of vice and ignorance" (4:213). But Gibbon clearly thinks that Boethius has suc-cumbed to a kind of innocent pride of accomplishment that contributes to his downfall, though without lessening the guilt of his opponents. Furthermore, while Boethius has never rescued his country by opposing foreign enemies, he has risked his own life to protect his fellow citizens: "Boethius alone had courage to oppose the tyranny of the Barbarians, elated by conquest, excited by avarice, and, as he complains, encouraged by impunity" (4:214). Perhaps, Gibbon speculates, Boethius became somewhat fanatical; his "rash confession," that "had he known of a conspiracy, the tyrant never should," might have given some color to a charge of treason. But in general "the favour and fidelity of Boethius declined in just proportion with the public happiness"; "his innocence must be presumed, since he was deprived by Theodoric of the means of justification" (4:214–15). Thus Boethius fully qualifies for the position of hero, and of tragic hero.

But there is more: Boethius is not only a great scholar, but the author of "a golden volume not unworthy of the leisure of Plato or Tully, but which claims incomparable merit from the barbarism of the times and the situation of the author," who wrote it while, "oppressed with fetters, [he] expected each moment the sentence or the stroke of death" (4:215). It is interesting that the first subject for historical writing Gibbon proposed to himself, Sir Walter Raleigh, similarly had the merit of producing great writing under threat of death. Under such circumstances, literary creation is as meritorious for courage and magnanimity as any possible action; in fact, it is the only form of action open to the actor. Gibbon is always eloquent on such topics. He does not believe that the actual content of *The Consolation* in fact eased Boethius's trials: "Such topics of consolation, so obvious, so vague, or so abstruse, are ineffectual to subdue the feelings of human nature. Yet the sense of misfortune may be diverted by the labour of thought; and the sage . . . must already have possessed the intrepid calmness which he affected to seek" (4:216). The merit of the work was independent of and different from the merit of the man. Here, perhaps, is part of Gibbon's uneasiness with literary heroes. Their greatness and that of their works are different, and the latter cannot be valorous. Boethius, for example, was eventually beaten to death. That fact is irrelevant to the meaning of his life, which lies in this: "his genius survived to diffuse a ray of knowledge over the darkest ages of the Latin world" (4:216). The sentence structure pretends that there is a close connection between the author's fate and the work's fate, a pretense not warranted by the data. Even a work threatened with unjust destruction can neither fear nor resist fear, and its survival may not be dependent on any qualities of the character of its author.

Boethius is accorded almost five pages of *The Decline and Fall* – more than most emperors. But he does not have the honor of ending the chapter, which has been devoted to the career of Theodoric. This chapter, the first in the concluding three volumes of Gibbon's history, portrays the career of the great Gothic king of Italy as a sort of miniature decline and fall, in which the early part of Theodoric's career parallels the reigns of the five great third-century emperors, but he at last becomes his own Commodus: "he lived to condemn the virtue of Boethius and Symmachus." At the end of this chapter, as if the life and death of even the greatest man of letters were not a sufficient climax, Gibbon places not just the death but the afterlife of Theodoric. The manner in which Gibbon does this is instructive. First he tells us that "humanity will be disposed to encourage any report which testifies the jurisdiction of conscience and the remorse of kings" (4:217). Humanity, moreover, is supported in this pious act by philosophy, which reports that physical and mental illnesses are conducive to hallucinations. Therefore Gibbon tells us a story about Theodoric's seeing a vision of his scholarly victims and repenting of their murder. In the footnote, Gibbon warns us that this vision is not at all well attested, but there it is, in the text.

Like the vision, the story of the vision has a practical function as a warning: The hallucination truly warns the king, and the fiction of the hallucination truly warns the reader. Perhaps in thus utilizing the powers of language Gibbon in fact provides a clue to the genuinely heroic effects of the life of the mind, but he does not seem aware of that possibility. At the conclusion of the chapter, after a brief summary of Theodoric's heirs and description of his monument, Gibbon comments ironically on another vision: "His spirit, after some previous expiation, might have been permitted to mingle with the benefactors of mankind" – that is, we might make that judgment of it – "if an Italian hermit had not been witness in a vision to [Theodoric's] . . . soul [being] plunged . . . into the vulcano of Lipari, one of the flaming mouths of the infernal world" (4:218). The philosophic reader, of course, rejects this vision and therefore rehabilitates Theodoric. But when we do so, what happens to the sense that Boethius is the true hero? Inevitably, I think, it is at the very least diminished, perhaps wholly lost.

But Boethius, we may say, wrote his greatest work only as he was preparing to die; perhaps the contemplative man whose life and works develop simultaneously is the true heroic figure. Petrarch is an apparent example. A great writer in the view of remote ages and countries, Petrarch also enjoyed great success in his own era, access to persons of power, and enormous talent and energy. Here, surely, was an excellent opportunity for the portrayal of a significant life of letters.

The first extensive references to Petrarch in *The Decline and Fall* occur in Chapter 66, a chapter devoted principally to the relationships between the Greek and Latin churches and to Western Europe's knowledge of Greek language and learning in the fourteenth and fifteenth centuries. "In the resurrection of science, Italy was the first that cast away her shroud; and the eloquent Petrarch, by his lessons and his example, may justly be applauded as the first harbinger of day" (7:122), says Gibbon approvingly but hardly ecstatically. He notes that Petrarch befriended Barlaam, "the first who revived beyond the Alps the memory or at least the writings of Homer" (7:123). But the point is Petrarch's failure to learn Greek. "The manifold avocations of Petrarch, love and friendship, his various correspondence and frequent journeys, the Roman laurel, and his elaborate compositions in prose and verse, in Latin and Italian, diverted him from a foreign idiom; and, as he advanced in life, the attainment of the Greek language was the object of his wishes rather than of his hopes" (7:124–5).

In this discussion the climax is a long quotation from Petrarch's grateful yet regretful letter to a friend who had given him a copy of Homer. Here is Gibbon's version of Petrarch:

> But alas! Homer is dumb, or I am deaf; nor is it in my power to enjoy the beauty which I possess. I have seated him by the side of Plato, the prince of poets near the prince of philosophers; and I glory in the sight of my illustrious guests. (7:125)

Petrarch's intentions were good but impotent, and Gibbon abandons him for the time being, going on to other men of letters, such as Boccaccio and Leontius Pilatus. Each brief glimpse of a life of contemplative achievement is subordinated to the general theme, the establishment of Greek learning in Italy. The summary paragraph about Petrarch is in fact the longest passage devoted to an individual in Gibbon's account of the beginnings of the renaissance in learning – yet Gibbon includes no consideration of Petrarch's accomplishments as a writer.

When Gibbon returns to Petrarch in Chapter 70, he begins by taking firm but delicate exception to the adulation of Petrarch's poetry: "I may hope or presume that the Italians do not compare the tedious uniformity of sonnets and elegies with the sublime compositions of their epic muse, the original wildness of Dante, the regular beauties of Tasso, and the boundless variety of the incomparable Ariosto" (7:265). Gibbon admits that as a foreigner he is not as well equipped as the Italians to appreciate Petrarch's poetical merits, and he claims that he is "still less qualified to appreciate" Petrarch's merits as a lover, while at the same time describing Petrarch's "metaphysical" passion and Laura's numerous progeny so as virtually to compel the reader to join him in depreciating those merits.

Nevertheless, in Gibbon's view, Petrarch matters: "Our gratitude must applaud the man who by precept and example revived the spirit and study of the Augustan age" (7:266). He matters, it here appears, not just as a contributer to the revival of ancient learning, but as a professional literary man: The sentence leads quickly to Petrarch's aspiration to, and achievement of, coronation as poet laureate. Gibbon devotes a considerable passage to this event:

In the thirty-sixth year of his age [Petrarch] was solicited to accept the object of his wishes; and on the same day . . . received a similar and solemn invitation from the senate of Rome and the university of Paris. The learning of a theological school, and the ignorance of a lawless city, were alike unqualified to bestow the ideal, though immortal, wreath which genius may obtain from the free applause of the public and of posterity; but the candidate dismissed this troublesome reflection, and, after some moments of complacency and suspense, preferred the summons of the metropolis of the world. (7:267)

After such a paragraph, only Gibbon would dare to continue, but he continues without difficulty, describing at length the ceremony in which the laurel was bestowed, and concluding by bestowing his own laurel:

The grant was ratified by the authority of the senate and the people; and the character of citizen was the recompense of his affection for the Roman name. They did him honour, but they did him justice. In the familiar society of Cicero and Livy, he had imbibed the ideas of an ancient patriot, and his ardent fancy kindled every idea to a sentiment and every sentiment to a passion. The aspect of the seven hills and their majestic ruins confirmed these lively impressions; and he loved a country by whose liberal spirit he had been crowned and adopted. (7:268)

Not only Petrarch himself, but Cicero and Livy, seem briefly to have the supreme power of the republic, the power of citizenship; and if the honor is only "ideal," it is just: Language kindles sentiments, sentiments kindle passions, passions confer characters confirmed by names – the Roman name, the name of citizen. Moreover, if the citizens of eighteenth-century Rome had been as "liberal" as their ancestors of the fourteenth century, Gibbon himself might have been the hero of this experience as he has recorded it, for he, too, had imbibed from the "familiar society of Cicero and Livy" the ideas of an ancient patriot and had felt his sentiments confirmed by "the aspect of the seven hills and their majestic ruins."

Gibbon enables us to share this sense of identification with Petrarch by moving into a narrative mode in which the narrator of *The Decline and Fall*, usually a strongly felt presence, is absent. We are in the dramatic present; we hear Petrarch address his newly adopted fellow citizens, albeit in indirect discourse: "Rome was still the lawful mistress of the world. . . . If she could resume her virtue, the republic might again vindicate her liberty and dominion." So far Gibbon has treated a major event of an important life of letters as if it were indeed a major historical event, like a synod of bishops or a parley of generals. But in the very next sentence, the limitation of a purely literary event, the way that letters can record, interpret, validate, but not, after all, change history, is exposed: "Amidst the indulgence of enthusiasm and eloquence," says the abruptly returned narrator, "Petrarch, Italy, and Europe were astonished by a revolution which realised, for a moment, his most splendid visions. The rise and fall of the tribune, Rienzi, will occupy the following pages" (7:269).

And if that did not sufficiently remove the reader from the dramatic illusion to a sense of the text before him, the next sentence and its notes would certainly do so. Gibbon becomes his own commentator and remarks, "the subject is interesting, the materials are rich, and the glance of a patriot-bard [Petrarch] will sometimes vivify the copious but simple narrative of the Florentine [here a reference], and more especially of the Roman [here a note] historian" (7:269). In this material Gibbon deals a devastating blow to his own and to our expectations of some kind of correlation between literary power and documentary power. A fragmentary history of Rome, though naive in every sense, becomes (thanks to Lodovico Muratori, its editor, and to Gibbon himself, who transmits its contents to a wide audience) of incomparably greater value to our understanding of these events than anything produced by an incomparably greater writer, Petrarch. While it is genius that makes the man of letters significant to his peers and to posterity, the influence of texts on public events and even on their image in history is surprisingly independent of their genius.

Genius may have one significant power over history that is denied to records without genius, however – power over its events, as well as its image. Great works have a better chance of molding the characters of those who do make history. Rienzi himself was an instance of this power, as were the heroes who read Homer. "The gift of a liberal education . . . was the cause of [Rienzi's] glory and untimely end. The study of history and eloquence, the writings of Cicero, Seneca, Livy, Caesar, and Valerius Maximus, elevated above his equals and contemporaries the genius of the young plebeian" (7:270). This (traditional) power of great writers is no small thing.

Yet Gibbon chooses this very moment to pause to give the reader (in a footnote) a "specimen of the original idiom" of a naive biography of Rienzi, which includes the passage, "Oh come spesso diceva, 'dove suono quelli buoni Romani? dove ene lore somma justitia? poteramme trovare in tempo che quessi fiuriano!' " – literally, something like, "Oh how often he said, 'where are those virtuous Romans? where such high justice as theirs? Could I but find myself in times like those!' " Gibbon had rendered this passage (in the main text) as follows: "he was often provoked to exclaim, 'where are now these Romans? their virtue, their justice, their power? why was I not born in those happy times?' " (7:270). Is Gibbon uneasy with even his own appropriation of raw historical material into literary history, enough so that he wishes to give the reader the chance to observe that it is he who makes Rienzi long for the "power" of the ancient Romans? Gibbon's own claim to a place in history rests on the power of his work, which in turn rests on its industry in discovering, its judgment in evaluating, its good faith in preserving the materials of the past; more particularly, the power of his work rests on its wisdom in connecting, selecting, emphasizing, and interpreting those materials and its ability to make both the materials and the wisdom affect the minds and imaginations of readers. Such a relationship between an earlier biographer and himself as this text and note represent is complex, and Gibbon may be seen either as confessing or as boasting about his transformation of the anonymous contemporary witness and even of the reported words of Rienzi himself.

Gibbon obviously believes that a historian may aspire to "benefit mankind" without portraying the events of his own time. He also makes it clear that the life of a private person does not derive its importance from the public figures with whom he or she was acquainted. But a private figure nevertheless fails to retain its hold on his imagination. I think the reason is that Gibbon sees one type of hero as superior not only to the man of letters, but even to the exalted characters who both rescue and govern well their countries. That character is the great man of action who is at the same time a man of letters – a Julian or a Marcus Aurelius. Cicero, not Horace, is Gibbon's model, though he can relinquish, without "a sigh," the role of Caesar, both on moral and on aesthetic grounds (he finds Caesar's writings disappointing).

The "exalted characters" who write great books both fulfill and transcend the model of the contemplative hero. Although the living of a life of letters was so important to Gibbon that at every crucial point of choice – love, travel, profession, dwelling place – he made the decision that supported his passion for scholarship, I do not think he ever quite gave up hoping that he might play another role with equal success; he could never quite see as heroic a career that *only* influenced the minds of generations of readers.

In the one completed account of his own life, draft E of his memoirs, he represents himself exclusively as the "historian of the Roman Empire." All the events of his youth and manhood are represented either as leading to the history, or as fruitless, false steps and blind alleys. At the end of this draft, he reflects very directly on his choice of the contemplative life and its significance both for his own happiness and for the historical meaning, if any, of that life:

I am disgusted with the affectation of men of letters, who complain that they have renounced a substance for a shadow, and that their fame (which sometimes is no insupportable weight) affords a poor compensation for envy, censure, and persecution. My own experience has taught me a very different lesson: twenty happy years have been animated by the labour of my history; and its success has given me a name, a rank, a character in the World, to which I should not otherwise have been entitled. . . . [An author's] social sympathy may be gratified by the idea that, now in the present hour, he is imparting some degree of amusement or knowledge to his friends in a distant land; that one day his mind will be familiar to the grandchildren of those who are yet unborn.

Yet he immediately qualifies this satisfactory picture: "two causes, the abbreviation of time and the failure of hope, will always tinge with a browner shade the evening of life," and the last sentence of the draft is a joke about the immunity of authors to this mortal failing: "In old age, the consolation of hope is reserved for the tenderness of parents . . . the faith of enthusiasts . . . and the vanity of authors, who presume the immortality of their name and writings."[14]

The whole draft, moreover, which so satisfactorily portrays the history of the historian that Barrett Mandel was outraged at Gibbon's abandoning it and Patricia Spacks awed by his courage in seeking to go beyond it, was rejected by Gibbon.[15] In the final but uncompleted draft, Gibbon portrays himself as a man who was definitely something more, if not something better, than "the historian of the Roman empire." Perhaps it was in part his dissatisfaction with a merely literary hero that forced him to begin anew; almost certainly some of the difficulties he experienced in completing his own biography on its expanded scheme arose from his

[14] Gibbon, *Memoirs*, 187–9.
[15] Barrett John Mandel, "The Problem of Narration in Edward Gibbon's *Autobiography*," *Studies in Philology* 67 (1970): 550–64. Patricia M. Spacks, "The Defenses of Form: Edward Gibbon," in *Imagining a Self* (Cambridge, Mass.: Harvard University Press, 1976), 92–126.

inability to consider himself a truly worthy hero, a hero both active and contemplative, a Julian or Marcus Aurelius. In spite of himself, Gibbon seems to have felt some of the prejudices of mankind in general; it was not quite enough to be "a man of Genius, whose writings will instruct or delight the latest posterity."

He was happy in the life of letters he created for himself – both in the living of it and in the portrayal of it. He was happy, but he was not content. He had begun his first book with the expression of a credo he never abandoned: "The history of empires is that of the misery of men. The history of knowledge – the sciences – is that of their greatness and happiness. If a thousand considerations inevitably make the latter study precious to philosophers, this is the one that should make it dear to every lover of humanity" (*Essai*, chap. 1). His version of the history of empires was greatly enriched and complicated by his knowing and valuing this other history. But like Alexander, he never quite escaped the influence of Homer: "he was never able to bring himself to treat as heroic the story of human knowledge and happiness. His mastery of the first species of history surely entitled him to a high place in the second kind, but, ironically, perhaps that same mastery prevented him from fully crediting the quiet heroism possible in a life devoted to the disinterested pursuit of knowledge – including his own.

Contributors

REBECCA BUSHNELL, Professor of English at the University of Pennsylvania, is the author of *Prophesying Tragedy, Tragedies of Tyrants,* and *The Culture of Teaching.*

PATRICK COLLINSON, Regius Professor of Modern History (Emeritus) at Trinity College, Cambridge University, is the author of *The Elizabethan Puritan Movement, The Religion of Protestants: The Church in British Society, 1559–1625, Godly People, The Birthpangs of Protestant England, Elizabethan Essays,* and *From Tyndale to Sancroft* (forthcoming).

PATRICIA CRADDOCK, Professor of English at the University of Florida at Gainesville, is the author of *Young Edward Gibbon: Gentleman of Letters* and *Edward Gibbon: Luminous Historian.*

RICHARD HELGERSON, Professor of English at the University of California, Santa Barbara, is the author of *Elizabethan Prodigals, Self-Crowned Laureates,* and *Forms of Nationhood.*

J. PAUL HUNTER, Chester D. Tripp Professor of English at the University of Chicago, is the author of *The Reluctant Pilgrim, Occasional Form,* and *Before Novels.*

DONALD R. KELLEY, executive editor of the *Journal of the History of Ideas* and James Westfall Thompson Professor of History at Rutgers University, is the author of seven books, among them *Foundations of Modern Historical Scholarship, The Beginning of Ideology: Consciousness and Society in the French Reformation, The Human Measure: Western Social Thought and the Legal Tradition,* and *The Faces of History* (forthcoming).

JOSEPH M. LEVINE, Distinguished Professor and Chair of the Department of History at Syracuse University, is the author of *Dr. Woodward's Shield,*

361

Humanism and History, The Battle of the Books, and *Between the Ancients and the Moderns* (forthcoming).

FRITZ LEVY, Professor of History at the University of Washington, is the author of *Tudor Historical Thought,* editor of Bacon's *Henry VII,* and a forthcoming book on print culture in early modern England.

ANNABEL PATTERSON, Karl Young Professor of English at Yale University, is the author of *Censorship and Interpretation, Pastoral and Ideology: Virgil to Valery, Shakespeare and the Popular Voice, Royal Parsons, Fables of Power, Reading Holinshed's Chronicles,* and *Early Modern Liberalism* (forthcoming).

MARK SALBER PHILLIPS, Professor of History at the University of British Columbia, is the author of *Francesco Guicciardini, The Memoir of Marco Parenti,* and a forthcoming study of the relations between historical narrative and the social analysis of the Scottish Enlightenment.

DAVID HARRIS SACKS, Professor of History and Humanities at Reed College, is the author of *Trade, Society, and Politics in Bristol, 1500–1640, The Widening Gate: Bristol and the Atlantic Economy, 1450–1700,* and *The Sweet Name of Liberty: Monopoly and Freedom in Early Modern England, 1558–1650* (forthcoming), and an edition of More's *Utopia* (forthcoming).

J. H. M. SALMON, Professor of History (Emeritus) at Bryn Mawr College, is the author of *The French Wars of Religion in English Political Thought, Cardinal de Retz, Society in Crisis,* and *Renaissance and Revolt.*

PATRICIA SPRINGBORG, Professor of Political Theory at the University of Sydney, is the author of *The Problem of Needs and the Critique of Civilisation, Royal Persons,* and *Western Republicanism and the Oriental Prince.*

D. R. WOOLF, Professor of History at Dalhousie University in Halifax, is the author of *The Idea of History in Early Stuart England* and *Origins of Modern Historical Culture* (forthcoming) and editor of *A Global Encyclopedia of Historical Writing.*

DAVID WOOTTON, Professor of History and Dean of the Faculty of Arts at Brunel University, is the author of *Paolo Sarpi between Renaissance and Enlightenment,* translator of Machiavelli's *Prince,* and editor of John Locke's *Political Writings* and other editions and anthologies of early modern political thought.

Index

Other books in the series

(continued from page ii)

Deborah S. Davis, Richard Kraus, Barry Naughton, and Elizabeth J. Perry, editors, *Urban Spaces in Contemporary China: The Potential for Autonomy and Community in Post-Mao China*

William M. Shea and Peter A. Huff, editors, *Knowledge and Belief in America: Enlightenment Traditions and Modern Religious Thought*

W. Elliot Brownlee, editor, *Funding the Modern American State, 1941–1995: The Rise and Fall of the Era of Easy Finance*

W. Elliot Brownlee, *Federal Taxation in America: A Short History*

R. H. Taylor, editor, *The Politics of Elections in Southeast Asia*